Postcard History Series

Historic Lodgings of Ocean City

The Fisher Collection

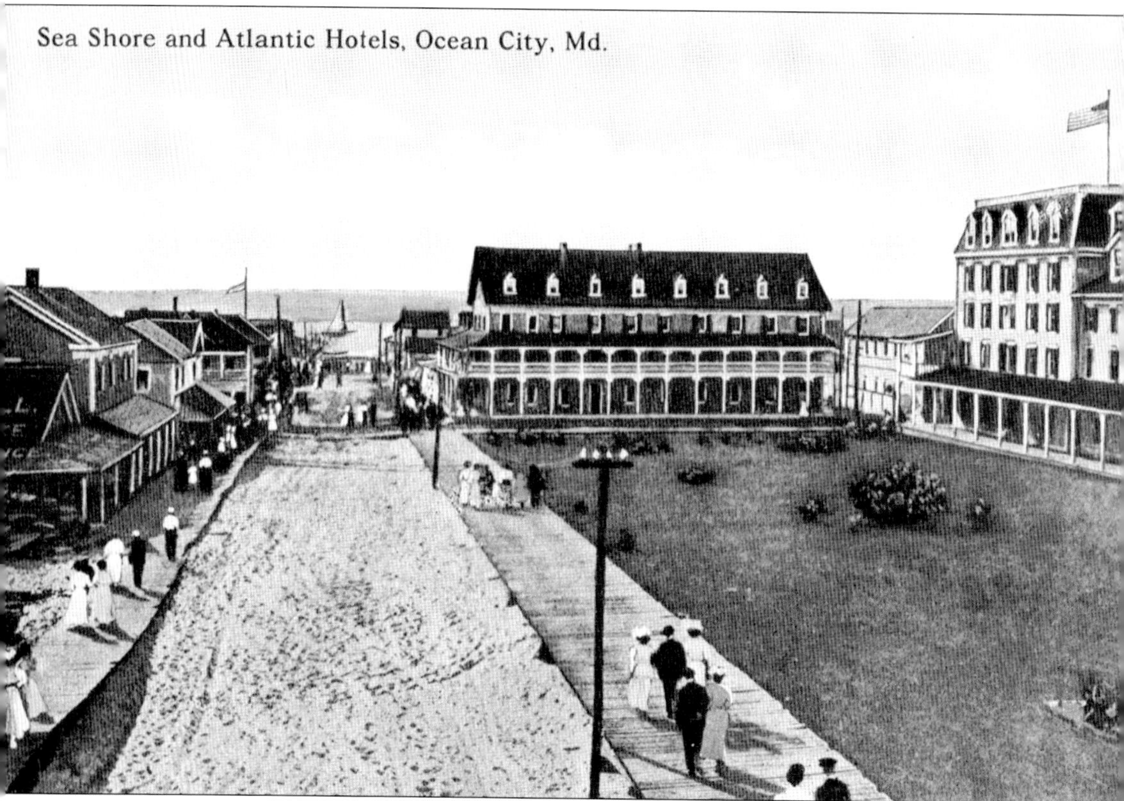

The Seaside Hotel (mislabeled as "Sea Shore") on Baltimore Avenue, which was enlarged in 1876–1877 from James Massey's 1872 boardinghouse, was one of the earliest hostelries built on the tract of land known as the Ladies Resort to the Ocean—later renamed Ocean City. The opening of the 1875 mansard-roofed Atlantic Hotel (visible at right) marks the establishment of Ocean City. The sand street is Wicomico Street, and the sidewalks are boardwalks. (Courtesy Bob and Kathy Fisher, The Fisher Collection.)

On the Front Cover: The historic Plimhimmon Hotel began as a turreted Victorian cottage and expanded early to include a larger block of rooms and an extended south verandah leading to a dance casino/pavilion. Following a 1962 fire, the rebuilt hotel remains today in a form barely approximating the rambling footprint and picturesque composition that originally provided the perfect setting for the fashionable ladies and gentlemen of the late 19th century. (Courtesy Bob and Kathy Fisher, The Fisher Collection.)

On the Back Cover: This postcard view of Baltimore Avenue, postmarked 1944, shows the streetscape from mid-block above North Division Street looking north to First Street and beyond. The two-story raised cottages with gables, dormers, and porches located only one block from the Boardwalk and beach provided tourist accommodations at less cost than oceanfront hotels. Many of these houses have been razed for parking lots, new motels, or hotel expansions. (Courtesy Bob and Kathy Fisher, The Fisher Collection.)

POSTCARD HISTORY SERIES

Historic Lodgings of Ocean City

The Fisher Collection

Robert M. Craig

ARCADIA
PUBLISHING

ISBN 978-1-4671-0926-0

Published by Arcadia Publishing
Charleston, South Carolina

Printed in the United States of America

Library of Congress Control Number: 2022947086

For all general information contact Arcadia Publishing at:
Telephone 843-853-2070
Fax 843-853-0044
E-mail sales@arcadiapublishing.com
For customer service and orders:
Toll-Free 1-888-313-2665

Visit us on the Internet at www.arcadiapublishing.com

To Bob and Kathy Fisher, whose postcard collection substantially illustrates this book, and whose dedication to the history of Worcester County, Maryland, and its landmark sites has been a lifetime contribution to local history.

Contents

Acknowledgments

The author first contacted Earl Pierce in the mid-1970s prior to writing a proposed, but eventually aborted, architectural history of Ocean City. The author learned that Earl and his wife, Imogene, had a postcard collection containing images of the town's buildings and streetscapes—a collection that was continued and substantially expanded by Pierce's daughter Kathy and her husband, Bob Fisher. In the 2010s, the Fishers generously provided the author the opportunity to copy much of the collection and granted permission for the use of the postcards in future books. Recognizing the uniqueness and completeness of the collection, the author envisioned developing this book around the collection both as a tribute to the Fishers and their preservation of postal images and ephemera but also to acknowledge their other contributions to historic preservation—at Furnace Town Historic Site (Nassawango Iron Furnace), for instance—as well as their leadership roles in the Worcester County Historical Society. This book is dedicated to the Fishers and could not have been written without their support.

I would also like to acknowledge the primary role of the Lake County Discovery Museum in preserving millions of postcards, most notably the Curt Teich Postcard Archives Collection. The German immigrant Curt Teich founded a Chicago-based postcard company that operated for 80 years (from 1898 to 1978) and, at its height, printed several million postcards per day. Agents traveled throughout the country, including to Ocean City, to photograph city views, streetscapes, and individual buildings, with many images then hand-colored in order to create an atmospheric and "artistic" line of postcards. Curt Teich & Company maintained an extensive archive preserving all of its postcards and photographs—a collection that the family donated in 1982 to the Lake County Discovery Museum, which was then located in Wauconda, Illinois (northwest of Chicago). Curators catalogued and digitized the collection, and scholars soon recognized it as a highly significant visual resource of architectural and urban history. Considered to be the largest public collection of postcards in the world, the Curt Teich Postcard Archives Collection was transferred to the Newberry Library (located in Chicago) in 2016. This book—along with many of the titles in Arcadia Publishing's Postcard History Series—is indebted to Teich.

Unless otherwise noted, all images appear courtesy of Bob and Kathy Fisher, The Fisher Collection. Where postcards do not exist, photographs were provided by Robert M. Craig and are marked "RMC."

Introduction

The history and development of lodgings in Ocean City followed a similar evolutionary path as places and buildings of accommodation across the United States. In Ocean City's early years, inns and hotels served patrons who arrived by railroad, and proprietors of private cottages (initially the wives of local fishermen) rented bedrooms to weekend travelers. Tourist homes offered less expensive alternatives to large hotels, which had more extensive amenities and also required troublesome tipping and surcharges. As mobility was enhanced by Model Ts and Model As, automobile-oriented accommodations lined highways leading into town and at the edge of Ocean City's expanding city limits; lodgings of the automobile age developed from tourist camps and cabins to motor courts and motels. The latter were often dressed in romantic architectural styles, given enchanting names (such as Shangri-La or the French Quarter), and overlaid with historic imagery to attract travelers from the road. Other motels (such as the Eden Roc) were distinctly modern, with contemporary styling to suggest up-to-date amenities, stylistic currency, and distinctly less stodgy character than older hotels.

A similar development characterized the habits and attire of clientele. Oceanfront hotels offered sweeping verandahs with rocking chairs overlooking the Boardwalk and beach. Large dining rooms offered Eastern Shore cuisine and the American plan (meals included), and dress codes required long dresses for women and stiff collars and white fedora hats for men; attire helped shape the imagery of the historic Ocean City lodging and sojourner.

On the beach, full-bodied black bathing costumes prevailed—these one-piece, short-legged tank suits were popular throughout the United States in places where both genders bathed in the same areas, as they did on Ocean City beaches. More daring separates included knee-length breeches and a short-sleeved or sleeveless shirt. Swimwear was fabricated of jersey, a wool knit that was heavy enough when wet to drag a person under, according to Robert S. Craig, an early captain of the Ocean City Beach Patrol (lifeguards). During the hotel era, men (as well as women) on the beach habitually covered their upper bodies, and by law, shirts were required when off the beach on or west of the Boardwalk.

By the mid-20th century, all of this had dramatically changed. In 1946, Louis Réard introduced the modern bikini in France (the garment was named for the Bikini Atoll, where atomic bomb tests took place, and this is perhaps the source of the expression "bombshell," which could be applied to a bikini's wearer). The image of the "beach girl" became iconic by 1959, when Gidget (Sandra Dee) arrived on the beach—although still in a one-piece swimsuit—surrounded by bare-chested hunks (Moondoggie and the Big Kahuna). The pop-singing group the Beach Boys formed in California in 1961, and both male and female surfers became icons of the endless summer. In 1962, Ursula Andress walked out of the ocean in a scene in the James Bond thriller *Dr. No* wearing an iconic white bikini, and the once scandalous two-piece suit began its journey to widespread acceptance.

A parallel minimalism marked developments in vacationers' accommodations. The American plan became increasingly rare as dining room space began to be perceived to be more lucrative as off-the-Boardwalk rental space. A five-course Eastern Shore feast devolved into a small box of french fries cooked in peanut oil or a carryout from a fast-food greasy spoon selling pizza by the slice. The dining room of the 1924 Lankford Hotel was converted into a knit shop, and other hotel dining rooms displaced oysters on the half shell with souvenir shops selling just the empty shells.

The most egregious transformation was the displacement of elegant hotel lobbies with oceanfront Boardwalk tourist shops selling innuendo T-shirts where shop facades are bestrewn with cheap beach attire with stenciled messages that would make a sailor blush and where string bikinis are displayed on anorexic mannequins. In the race for crossing the line, thongs displaced bikinis as the dress code for the liberated vacationing woman, and the term "smart casual" was expunged from the lexicon.

After World War II, resort motel lodgings displaced the Boardwalk hotel altogether for a while. In Ocean City, Harrison Hall (1951) and the Beach Plaza Hotel (1953) were the last Boardwalk hotels in a continuous history that began with the Atlantic Hotel in 1875 and continued for 78 years. Indeed, the Boardwalk ended at Fifteenth Street, in front of Harrison Hall, and beyond that, along the dunes northward, the first motels emerged, beginning with the Sea Scape Motel (1954), the Ocean Park Motel (1954), and the Santa Maria Motel (1956), all three of which have since been razed. The Boardwalk was extended to Twenty-Sixth Street, and in 1965, the city limits, temporarily cincturing the town limit at Forty-First Street, extended to the Delaware state line at 146th Street.

During this postwar period, motels dotted the landscape north of Ocean City both on the beachfront and along the Coastal Highway. One such establishment, the Dunes Motel, located on the Twenty-Seventh Street oceanfront at the end of the extended Boardwalk, was purchased by Milton and Thelma Connor in 1965. The Connors were old-family Ocean City; Milton's family business was the Hastings Hotel, where Thelma first worked in the hospitality industry following their marriage in 1940. Three decades later, during an era when motels had displaced hotels and multistoried condos were already rising north of town, Thelma built the Dunes Manor Hotel (see page 149), seeking to revive the Victorian hotel tradition. She opened the Dunes Manor Hotel on April Fools' Day in 1987, joking that only a fool would build a new hotel at the age of 74. By the time of Thelma's death in 1999, most other historic hotels in town had been razed, and most had been replaced by concrete condo blocks or chain hotels/motels. The Dunes Motel was now retro, and the Dunes Manor continues to maintain Thelma's dream of a traditional historic hotel, where she served afternoon tea to guests and the hotel regularly hosted evening sing-alongs with Shirley Toms at the lobby piano.

By the mid-1970s, when the Connors were still dreaming of reviving Ocean City's historic hotel tradition, north Ocean City's natural "dunescapes" and surfers' beach began to be replaced by condos. The Carousel Motel opened in 1962 on 117th Street—so far out of town that people thought its owner, Bobby Baker, was crazy. The motel attracted politicians from Washington, DC, and other big-city celebrities, but Baker's development plans "were cut short when he was charged with tax evasion and fraud leading to imprisonment" (carouselhotel.com/our-history). The motel was sold, and in the mid-1970s, a Carousel condo block was built with additional motel units and an atrium containing an ice-skating rink, an indoor pool, and a convention center. The Carousel was one of Ocean City's first concrete megastructures, and the stretch of once-empty dunes became Condo Row. This was the last phase of the development of the lodgings of Ocean City. Ironically, due to the "50-year rule" of the National Register of Historic Places, these early condo towers are now considered historic. Every plot of ground from Ocean City's inlet—where the Windsor Hotel once stood—to the Maryland/Delaware state line is now infilled with mostly commercial development and lodgings that range from hotels to motels to condos, and fewer and fewer traditional beach cottages with white picket fences remain.

One

Hotels

As early as 1524, Giovanni da Verrazzano (1485–1528) explored the bays and barrier island of the future Maryland coastline and called the area Arcadia "owing to the beauty of the trees." Although the Route 611 bridge (built in 1964) over Sinepuxent Bay to Assateague Island bears Verrazzano's name (spelled with one "Z"), historians are not in agreement that Arcadia and Assateague Island/Ocean City are the same. The eminent historian Samuel Eliot Morrison, for instance, wrote in *The European Discovery of America: The Northern Voyages*: "After flying along the entire [Atlantic] coast from Cape Fear River [North Carolina] to Barnegar, New Jersey, in search of a hilly section with big trees, I have no hesitation in locating Verrazzano's Arcadia at Kitty Hawk, North Carolina."

Whether Verrazzano ever stepped foot on the shores of Ocean City may never be known, but in the 250 years after his initial explorations, few individuals visited the barrier island, and no permanent settlement took place. As historian Bunk Mann observed, Assateague Island, stretching from Virginia to Delaware, consisted of "just marsh, mosquitos, and sand." In the mid-18th century, Capt. William Worthington obtained a land patent from Lord Baltimore for 1,000 acres in the Green Run area, and by 1771, he had patented nearly all the land from the Virginia line to the future site of Ocean City. Worthington subdivided the land into parcels ranging from 110 to 500 acres, intended for grazing and subsistence farming, but the effort came to naught, although some Worcester County farmers transported their livestock (horses and cows) by flat-topped scows for open grazing until winter set in. When the Green Run Life-Saving Station was commissioned on Assateague Island in 1875, a few families associated with the station moved to the island, and by 1887, a village of about 10 families existed there. In 1869, a farmer and waterman named Capt. James Scott built a seasonal hotel, Scott's Ocean House, which was sited bayside and large enough to accommodate 40 guests.

Scott's Ocean House, which was in operation from 1869 to 1894, attracted clientele from Pittsburgh, Philadelphia, Wilmington, Baltimore, and Washington, DC, but getting there was not easy. There was no bridge across the Chesapeake Bay near Annapolis, and visitors crossed the bay by boat and then traveled by stagecoach. An 1850s railroad (New York, Philadelphia & Norfolk) extended south down the Delmarva peninsula and was followed by spur lines of the Wicomico & Pocomoke Railroad that were constructed from Salisbury to Berlin in 1868; four years later, the Worcester Railroad line reached Snow Hill, the seat of Worcester County. From there, travelers hired liverymen to travel seven miles to Public Landing (then called Spence Landing), where a two-masted sloop, the *Fairfield*, sailed across Chincoteague Bay to Green Run and Scott's Ocean House.

In 1868, the year before Scott erected his Ocean House, a New Yorker named Stephen Taber (sometimes spelled Tabor) and his partner, hotelier Hepburn Benson, acquired two farms on the mainland and three land grants on the barrier island north of Scott's Ocean House. Taber's 1868 island tract extended about a mile north and south of today's North Division Street in Ocean City, comprising the full acreage within these limits between the Atlantic Ocean and Sinepuxent Bay. When Benson died, Taber bought out his partner's share from his widow. Although Taber initially intended to use the land to serve sportsmen (both hunters and fishermen), plans were soon underway to develop the Ladies Resort to the Ocean. By 1873, Taber owned eight and a quarter miles of beach on Assateague Island.

There was some precedent for considering the Taber tract's potential as a resort. As early as 1863, Isaac Coffin, a farmer and hunting guide, was operating an eating house and tavern on his mainland farm, an establishment that evolved into Coffin's Hotel by 1865. Coffin and his brother Joel ferried guests across the bay to the ocean beaches on the barrier island. References have also been made to a second inn on Coffin's Beach (thought to be just north of the future inlet at South Second Street in Ocean City). Equally elusive is the local lore regarding Coffin's Rhode Island Inn—that property (if it existed at all) was more likely built on Assateague Island closer to Coffin's mainland property than at the future site of Ocean City.

In 1872, S. James Massey of Berlin built a boardinghouse on the barrier island then known as Sinepuxent Beach. Enlarged in 1877 and renamed the Seaside Hotel, the much smaller and not oceanfront establishment was located on the northwest corner of Baltimore Avenue and Wicomico Street; it was soon overwhelmed by the Atlantic Hotel. Published accounts reference a small hotel in Ocean City named Ocean House, built in 1877 on South First Street and operated by Isaac Coffin's son Cornelius ("Neil") and son-in-law Levin D. Lynch. William B.R. Selby, a retired businessman from Philadelphia, bought the hotel in 1880; the following year, he added a large dining room extension and renamed the 110-room establishment Congress Hall. The Seaside Hotel, Atlantic Hotel, and Congress Hall all burned in the downtown fire of 1925, although the Atlantic was immediately rebuilt.

The July 4, 1875, opening of the Atlantic Hotel marks the establishment of Ocean City. In 1868, Col. Lemuel Showell and a group of associates incorporated the Atlantic Hotel Company and began planning to build a resort hotel and extend the railroad to Sinepuxent Bay. The Worcester & Pocomoke spur reached the bay in 1874, and a wooden trestle railroad bridge crossed the bay the following fall. In the meantime, Capt. Albert J.H. Ayres had built a small oceanfront cottage, and James Massey's boardinghouse was in operation. Meanwhile, from 1870 to 1873, Stephen Taber had consolidated his barrier island landholdings. Showell and his partners approached Taber with the proposition of building a large resort hotel. Taber agreed to give the group of investors an amount of land adequate for the hotel (10 acres) if they would finance the hotel's construction, knowing that if a resort hotel were erected, Taber's extensive landholdings elsewhere on the island (some 1,000 acres) would substantially increase in value. Once the hotel was built, additional acreage was provided for a town—50 acres in all, the Ladies Resort to the Ocean tract.

When the Atlantic Hotel opened in 1875, the rest of the Ladies Resort to the Ocean acreage was surveyed and subdivided into 205 building lots, with 104 investors agreeing to buy initial lots. North–south avenues were named for prominent cities (Baltimore, Philadelphia, and St. Louis), and east–west streets bore the names of Eastern Shore counties: Worcester, Wicomico, Somerset, Dorchester, Talbot, and Caroline, with South Division Street at the south end and North Division Street eventually at the north end. Streets north and south of Division Street were numbered, assuming the town would grow in both directions. In 1886, town boundaries extended a half mile north and south of Taber's original land deed, from North Seventh Street to South Seventh Street. The inlet that cut through in 1933 covered South Third Street and higher numbered streets projected southward, a low area with only a few fishing shanties erected by the early 1930s. North numbered streets were eventually laid out from North First Street to 146th Street at the Delaware line.

For the next 75 years, Ocean City was filled with the construction of shingle-clad hotels; by the 1920s, many of them were sporting grand porticos and, due to their oceanfront aspects, featuring verandahs and extensive porches furnished with rocking chairs. These may have been considered typical for their day but with two notable peculiarities: first, foundations consisted of pile-driven poles the size and length of telephone poles, hammered deep in the sand; second, builders, proprietors, and managers were often women. Rosalie Tilghman Shreve built the Plimhimmon Hotel in 1893–1894; Margaret Campbell Buell built the Mount Pleasant in 1900 (and it was bought in 1918 by Susan Mason, who rebuilt it in 1923 following a fire, doubling its size); Ella Phillips Dennis built the Dennis Hotel; in 1908, Minnie Moore built the Virginia Hotel and Minnie E. Newton built the Linmar; Harriett Dashiell built Wetipquin Hall in 1909; Josephine Hastings built the New Avelon (1903), Hastings (1916), Shoreham (1923), and Mayflower Hotels (1926); Ethel Kelly built the Royalton in 1926–1927; Mary B. Quillen built the Lankford in 1923–1924; and, as noted in the book's introduction, Thelma Connor built the Dunes Manor Hotel in 1987. Local historians cite a 1926 advertising brochure listing 32 hotels in Ocean City,

30 of which were owned and managed by women. The town's first real estate broker is said to have been Virginia Dale Ayres of Ayres Realty, established in 1932, which had offices in Ayresbilt next to The Lankford. Ayres was frequently seen toting a large key ring with keys to every rental apartment in town.

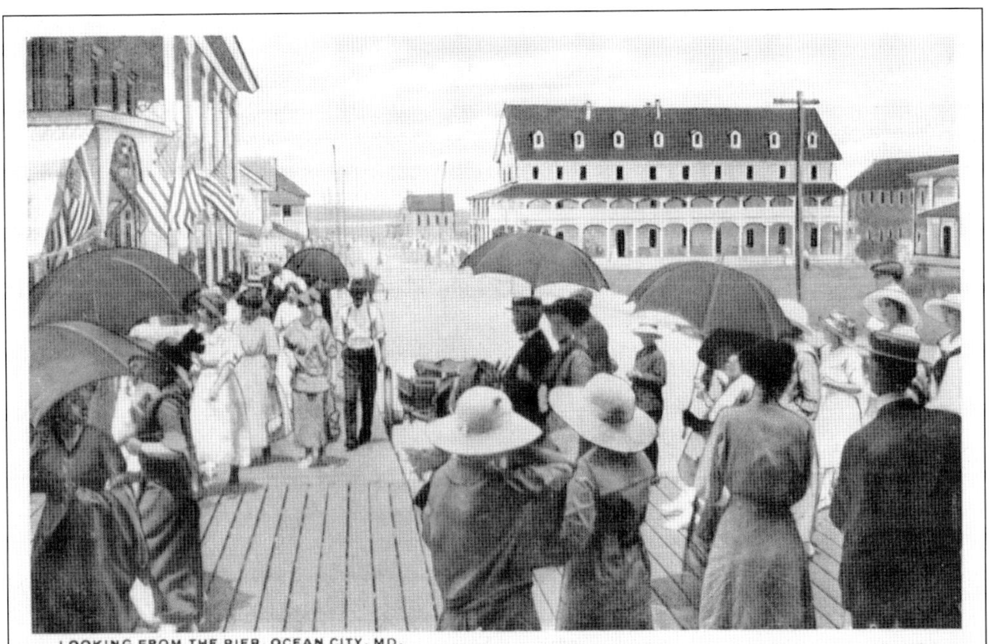

Ocean City's earliest hotels coordinated offerings with weekend railroad excursion rates during the town's first historic tourist boom. Although no longer extant, Seaside Hotel (pictured) and Congress Hall were early rivals to the Atlantic Hotel, the area's first major hotel. This postcard's umbrellas and profile silhouettes of Victorians enjoying leisure time are reminiscent of Georges Seurat's painting *A Sunday Afternoon on the Island of La Grande Jatte.*

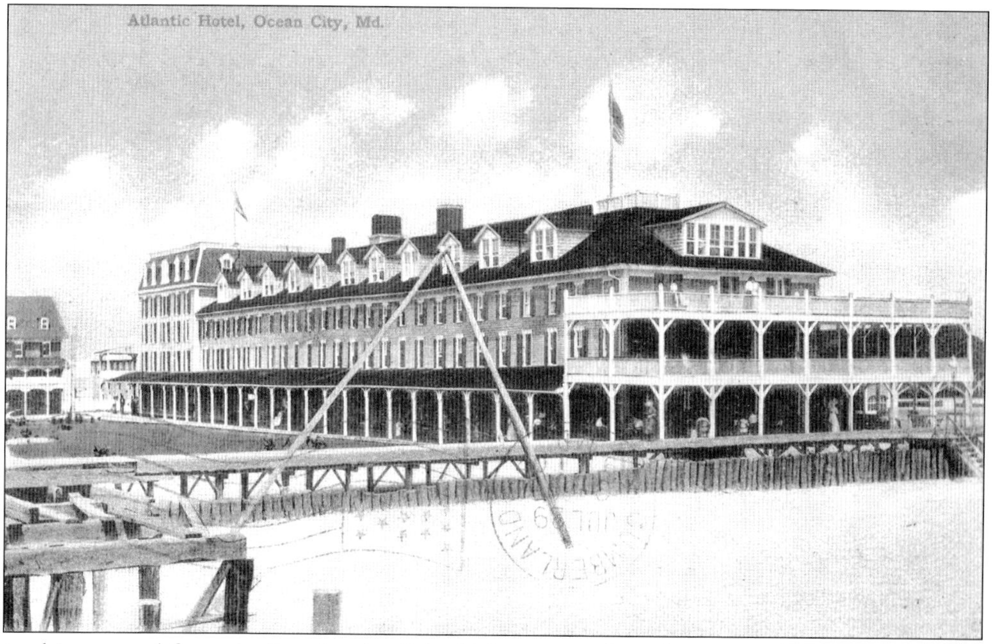

In this postcard from the first decade of the 20th century, the Atlantic Hotel is shown extending a full city block from beachfront pilings and a raised Boardwalk back to Baltimore Avenue, where the open tract of land to the south of the hotel, which later served as a car park, is overshadowed by the Seaside Hotel (visible at the left edge of the image).

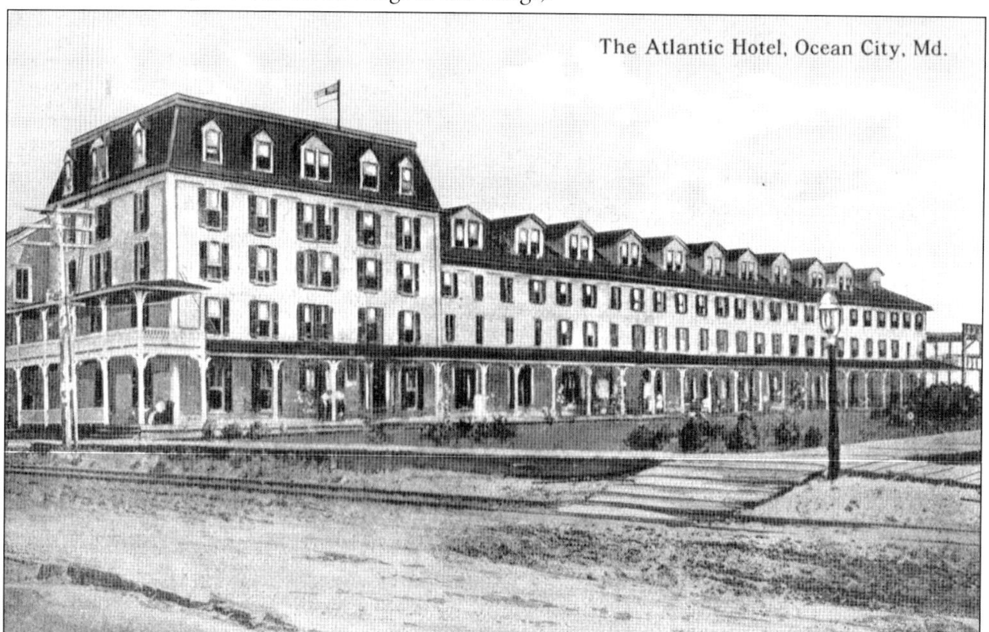

This Louis Kaufman postcard of the Atlantic Hotel as viewed from Baltimore Avenue shows the railroad tracks that brought the Worcester & Pocomoke spur line into Ocean City, delivering sojourners to a small depot opposite the hotel. Hawking hotel porters with wagons for luggage greeted the train and competed for customers. Sheltered verandahs extended across the west, south, and east fronts of the Atlantic Hotel—a welcomed feature during summer months.

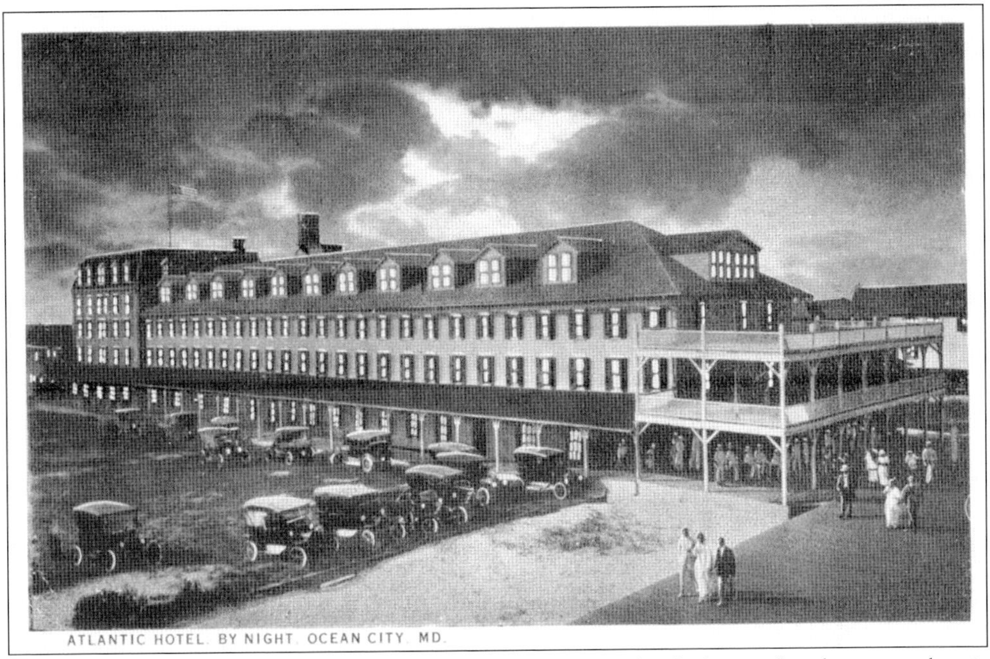

A nighttime view of the Atlantic Hotel, moonlit through partly cloudy skies and with interior electric lights ablaze, creates a romantic image of the resort. Fashionably dressed ladies and gentlemen promenade along the Boardwalk, while others gather on the broad verandah overlooking the beach and ocean. The hotel had a dance hall, a billiard room, and 210 rooms with full board. This atmospheric card was published by Louis Kaufman.

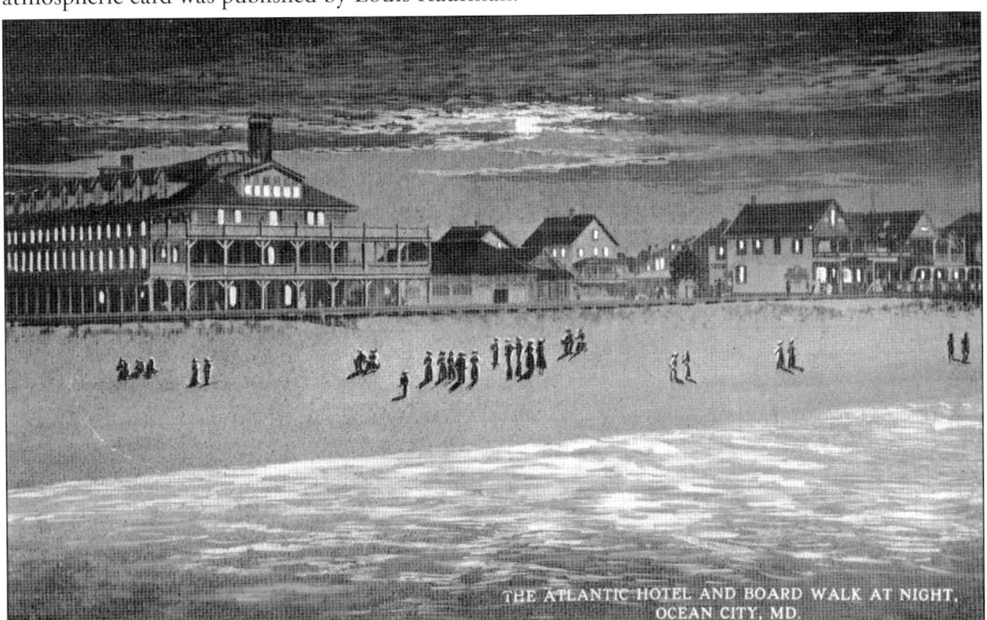

Another nighttime view shows the Atlantic Hotel overlooking a narrow beach, small dune line, and a Boardwalk. The Boardwalk extended north to cottages that began to populate lots along the oceanfront and Baltimore Avenue. Cottages and private homes, in turn, offered rooms for rent and were often enlarged to serve as boardinghouses, inns, and hotels.

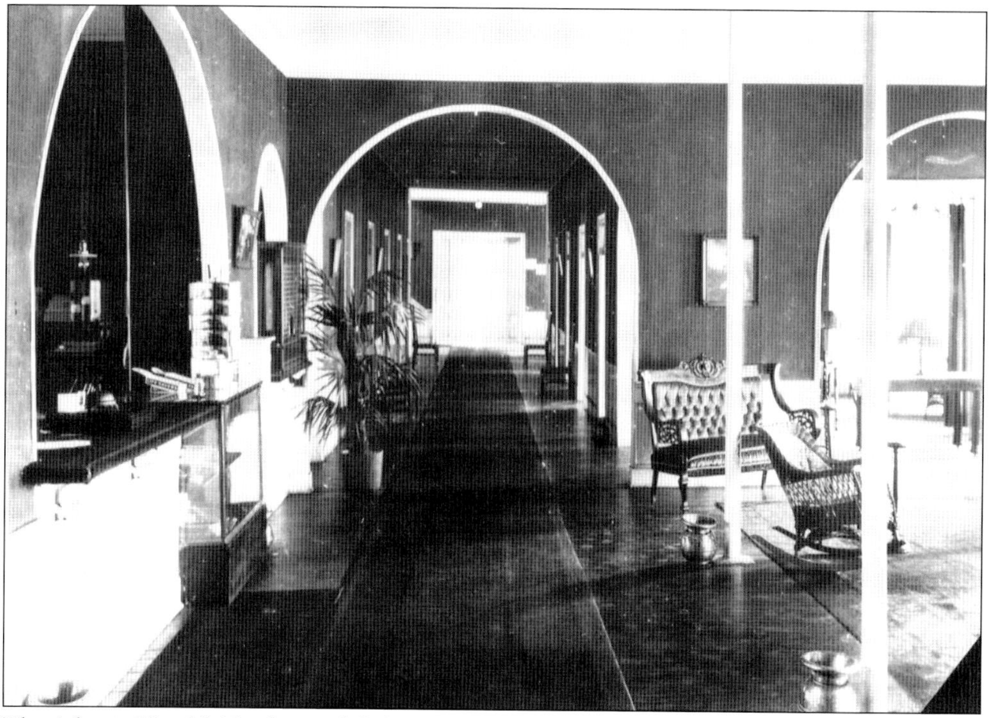

The Atlantic Hotel lobby featured fashionable late Victorian/Edwardian furnishings and popular wicker armchairs and rockers. Architectural features included arched openings and elongated cast-iron columns. Spittoons and ashtrays were scattered throughout the public space, and the glass case at registration appears to display cigar boxes and a postcard stand on the countertop. Before air-conditioning, hotel doors featured transoms for ventilation.

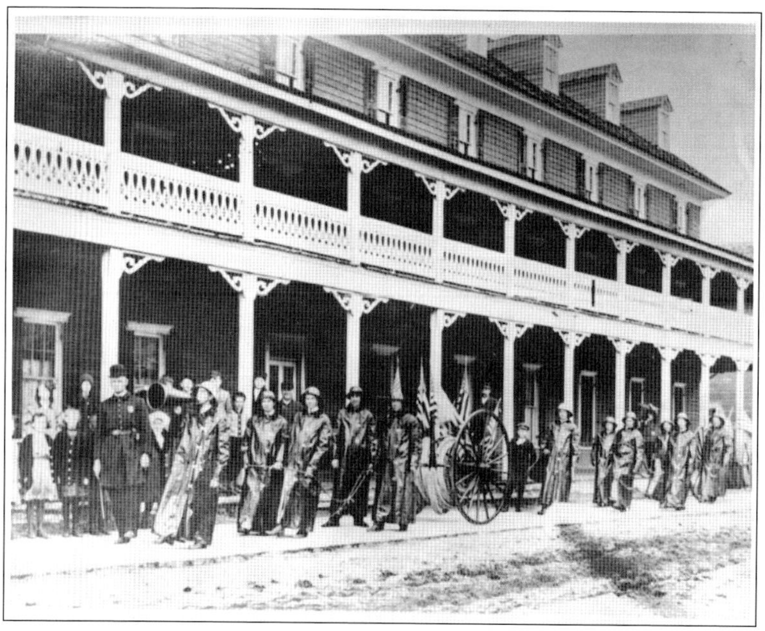

This image carries a certain irony with its group of volunteer firemen hauling hose along the boardwalk/sidewalk in front of the Seaside Hotel, as the hotel was destroyed by fire in 1925 and never rebuilt. The town established a volunteer fire company in 1905 and built its first firehouse in 1920.

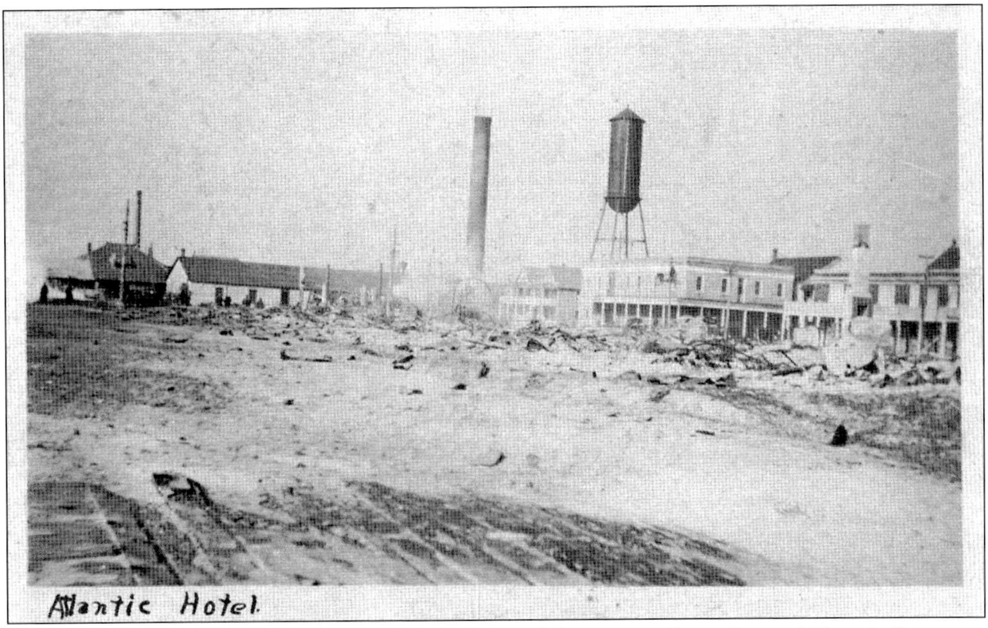

In December 1925, a major fire broke out at the plant of the Eastern Shore Gas and Electric Company and spread across three city blocks of downtown Ocean City, destroying the Seaside Hotel, the Atlantic Hotel, and the ocean pier. Along the Boardwalk, it destroyed the Casino Theater, a group of amusement buildings, the C.W. Purnell Cottage, and New York confectioner Rudolph Dolle's Candyland, including the Dolle family's residence over the store. Due to the frigid December temperatures, efforts to extinguish the fire were sorely hampered—fire hydrants froze, the fire engine broke down, and volunteers had to pump water from the bay. The pier, Dolle's, and the Atlantic Hotel were later rebuilt.

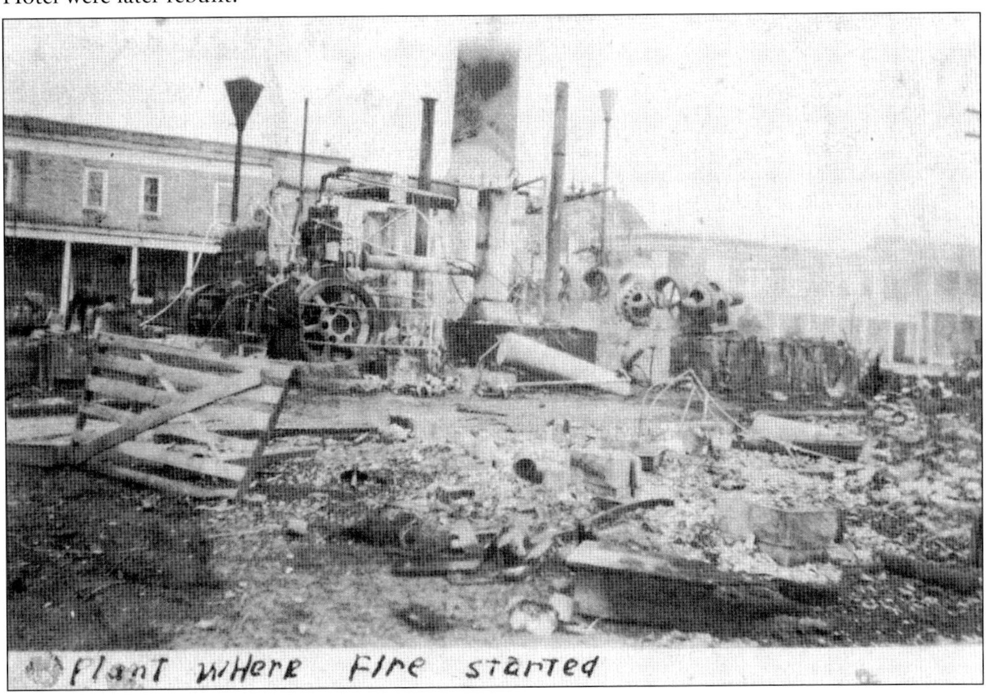

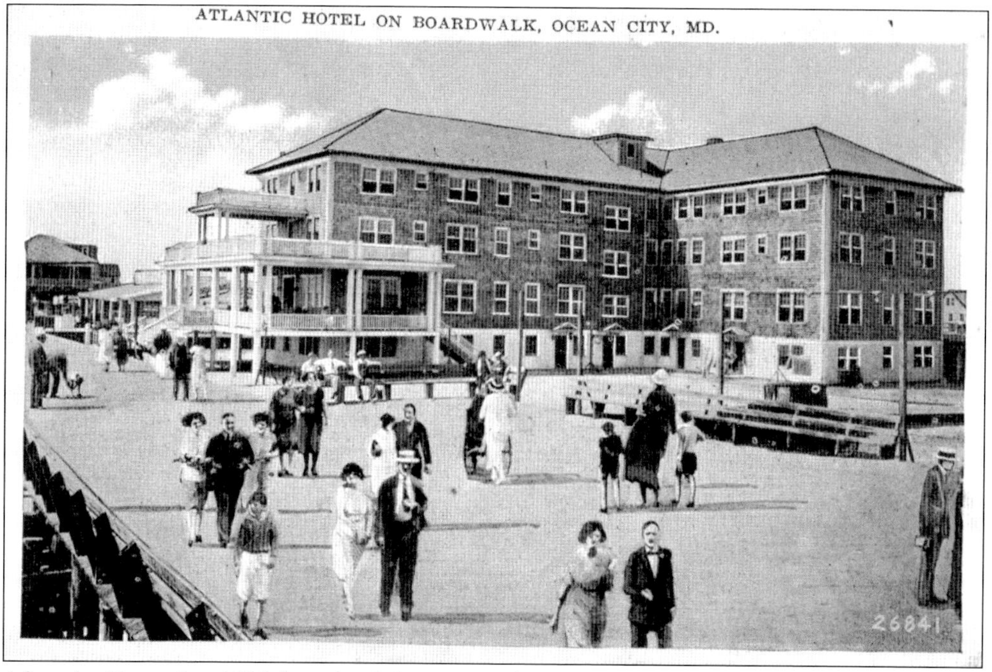

After the December 1925 fire, the Atlantic Hotel was immediately rebuilt, beginning with its south wing and hyphen only (as shown above), and opened as the New Atlantic Hotel in time for the 1926 summer season. Subsequently, a north wing was built with its east front matching the verandah and upper porches of the 1926 south wing (below). An undated (1950) visitor's guide to the town listed the hotel's capacity at 350. As with most of the early Ocean City hotels, the forms were simple shingle-clad blocks under hipped roofs (without roof dormers in the rebuilt hotel) and with white-trimmed windows (here, six-over-one), with some paired. Boardwalk frontage marked the hotel's most distinctive architectural elaboration—a set of wide stairs leading up to the principal floor (raised to avoid flooding during storm surges) and with open verandahs, here with simple piers and restrained balusters.

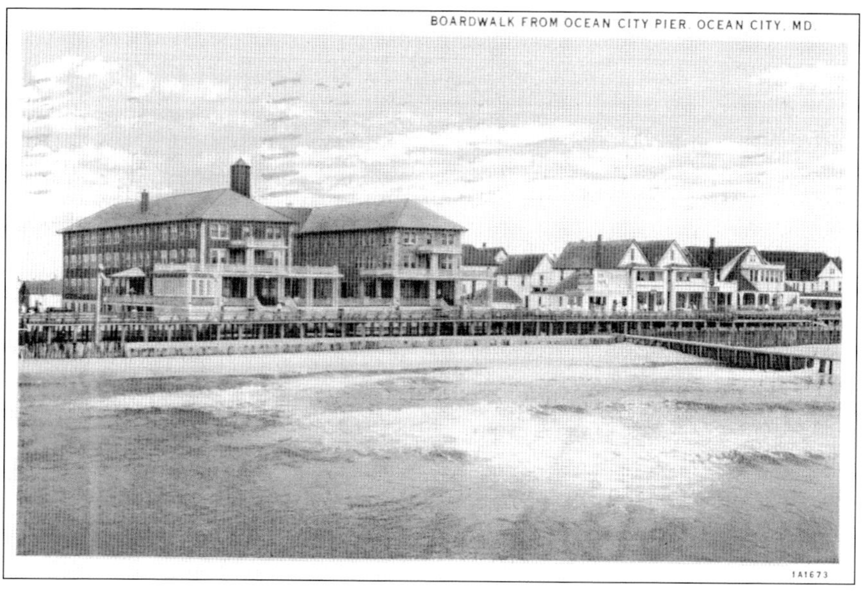

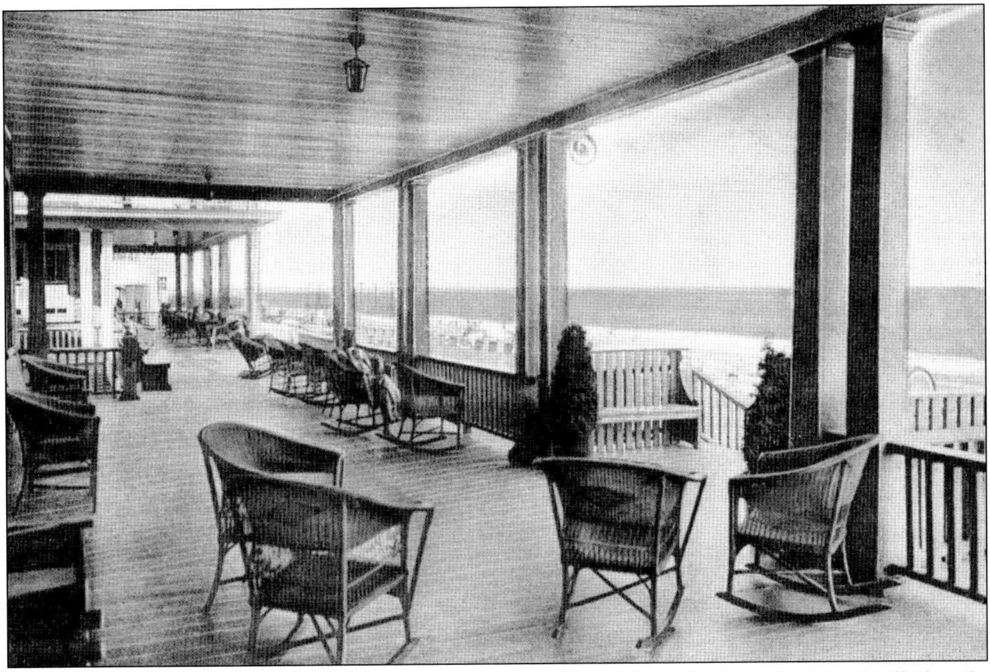

A visit to a fine Ocean City hotel was a social event, and the porch overlooking the Boardwalk, beach, and ocean became a setting for conversation and the delightful recreational activity of observing the grand Boardwalk promenade. Wicker rockers and armchairs, later supplanted by wooden rockers, were in high demand, and the open vista and narrow beach gave the impression of being on the open deck of an ocean liner. Postcards included views of the ocean from the hotel porch, suggesting that experiencing that view was among the highlights of a traveler's resort experience. The collective gathering on a communal porch has been replaced by today's oceanfront establishments with honeycombs of individual towel-draped balconies projecting from look-alike concrete cells.

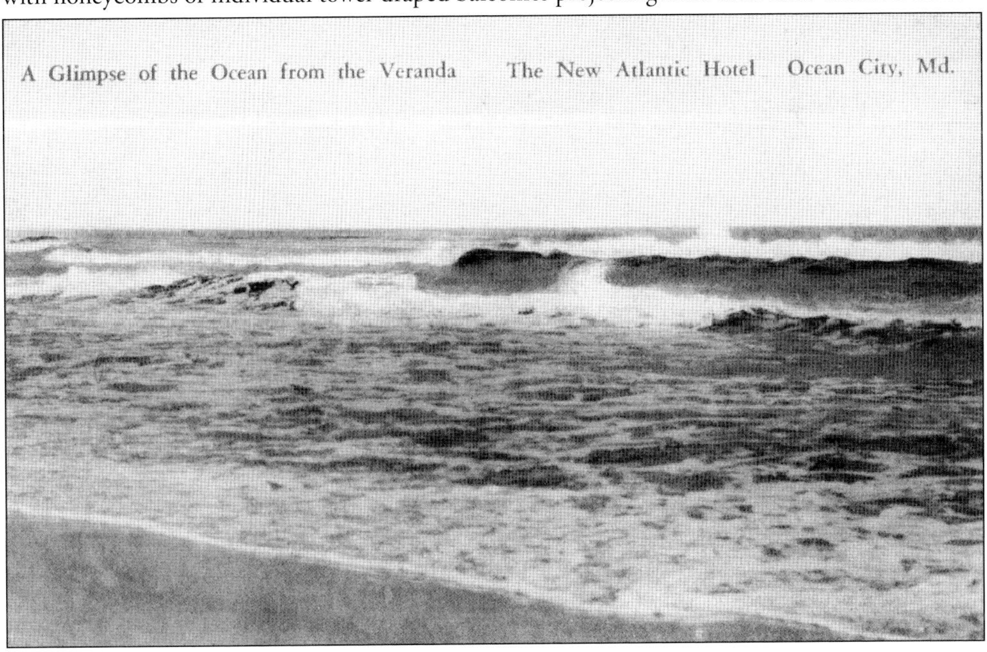

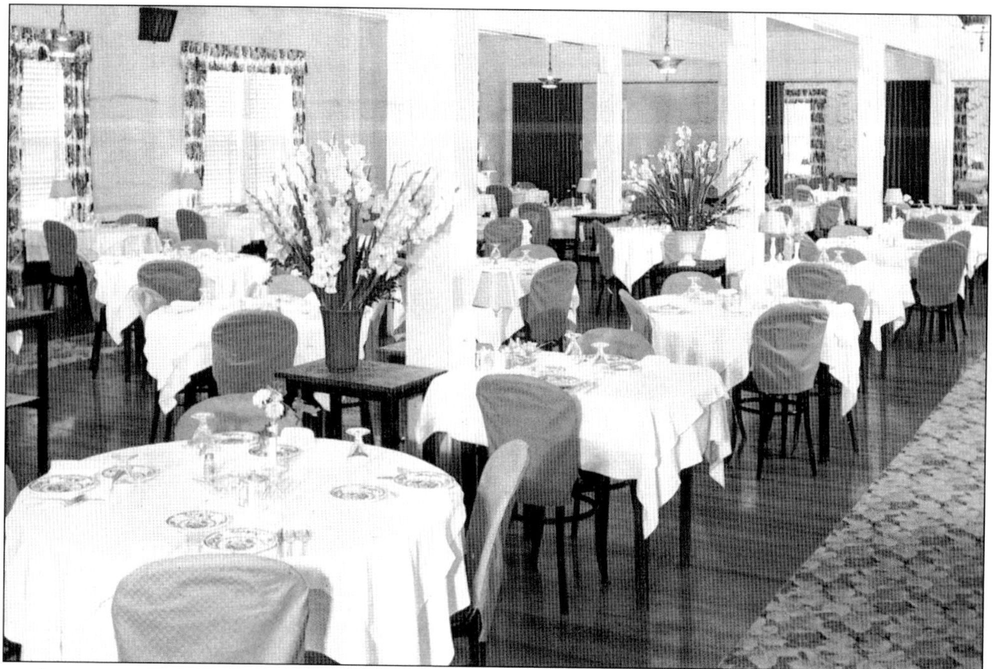

Early Ocean City hotels offered the American plan, whereby the room rate included three meals per day prepared in the on-premises kitchen and typically served in an elegant dining room by black-tie African American waiters. An undated rate schedule for the Atlantic Hotel provides per-person rates for room and board by the week or daily during the 1920s–1930s golden age of the historic resort hotels. Eastern Shore fare made many hotel dining rooms famous for their local cuisine, and those in high demand opened to the general public. All too soon, however, fashions change—tastes for fast food, consumed by yobs and louts in sleeveless tees accompanied by flouting females in skimpy bikinis, encouraged the rapid demise of the elegant Boardwalk hotel dining room.

THE ATLANTIC HOTEL

One of the finest hotels with the best service and location in Ocean City, Maryland

New Low American Plan Rates

Three or four in room with running water
$20.00 weekly, $4.00 daily.

Two in room with running water
$22.50 weekly, $4.25 daily.

One in room with hot and cold running water
$25.00 weekly, $5.00 daily.

Three or four in room with bath
$27.50 weekly, $5.00 daily.

Two in room with bath
$28.00 weekly, $5.50 daily.

One in room with bath
$40.00 weekly, $6.50 daily.

We have 100 rooms at the above rates. Rooms only, half the above rates. Rates quoted are for each person.

These are all nicely furnished rooms with outside exposure. Write, wire or phone Dr. C. W. Purnell, Phone 128, Ocean City, Maryland.

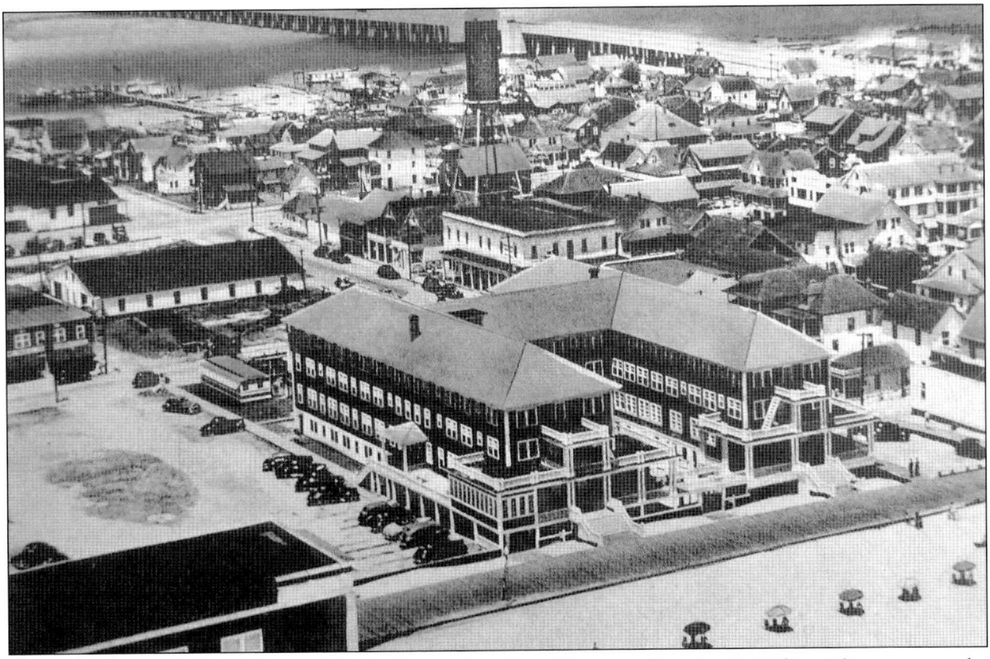

The New Atlantic Hotel changed little during the 50 to 60 years after the 1925 fire. These postcards, postmarked 1951 (above) and 1965 (below), show a proud grande dame, balanced and noble as it commands its Boardwalk site and overlooks a neat row of beach umbrellas and beach chairs set out each morning by local beach boys, usually in line with the lifeguard stands of the Ocean City Beach Patrol. As the town expanded northward, this pattern was repeated in front of the Plimhimmon, Mount Pleasant, Hastings, Breakers, Shoreham, Majestic, Lankford, Mayflower, Stephen Decatur, Beach Plaza, and Commander Hotels until Harrison Hall, built in 1951, marked the northern boundary of the town's historic hotel district. By the late 20th century, the Atlantic Hotel's location began to be associated with the "honky-tonk" end of town, prompting a new Boardwalk face-lift.

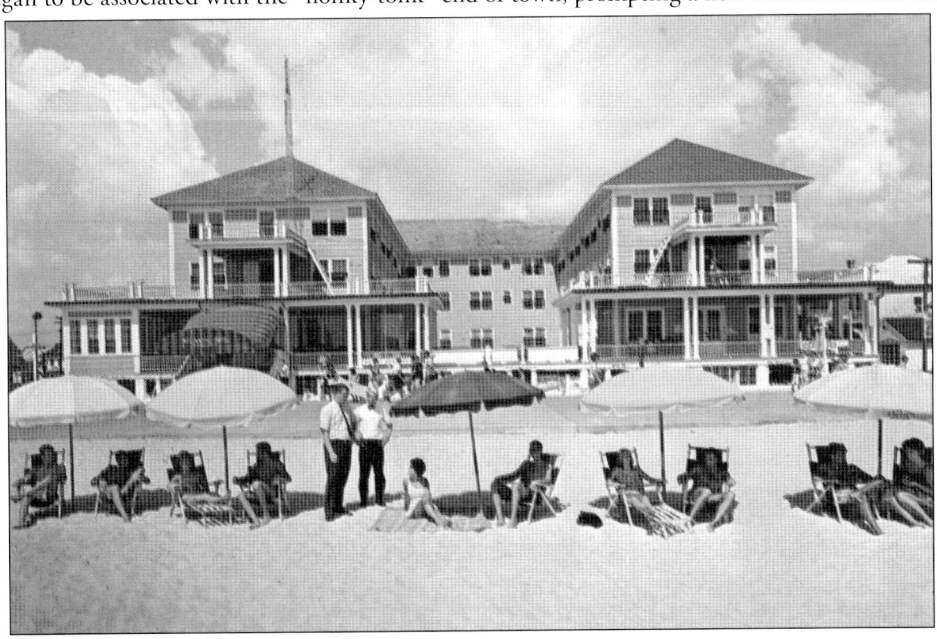

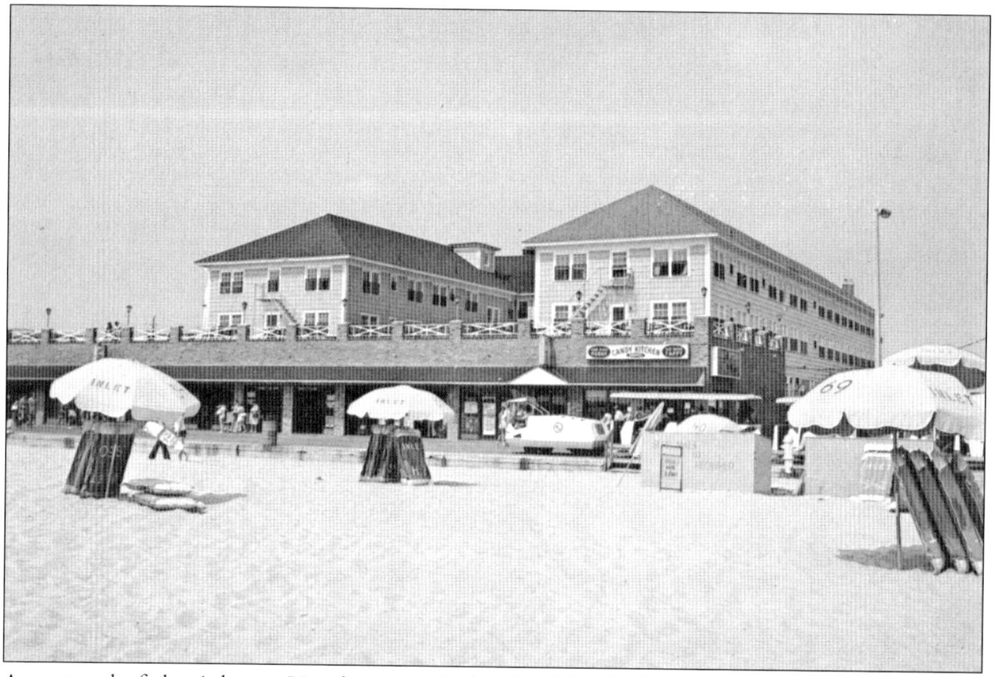

A postcard of the Atlantic Hotel postmarked 1992 (above) shows the new row of brick-faced commercial shops that closed off the open, welcoming verandahs and porches of the town's first grand hotel. The Atlantic built 10 shops along the hotel's Boardwalk frontage and five more along the side and rear; in 1993, these generated more profit than the hotel. The retail stores stretched from a "T-shirt factory" to a Candy Kitchen shop—both staples of the Boardwalk's increasing commercialism. Recreational porch-sitting now took place on the roof of what appeared to be a suburban commercial strip mall. As the local newspaper *OC Today* remarked about Boardwalk taste in 1993, "You couldn't sell the *Mona Lisa* for twenty bucks, but you can sell a T-shirt that says 'Kiss me, I'm Polish' for $11.99." (Below, RMC.)

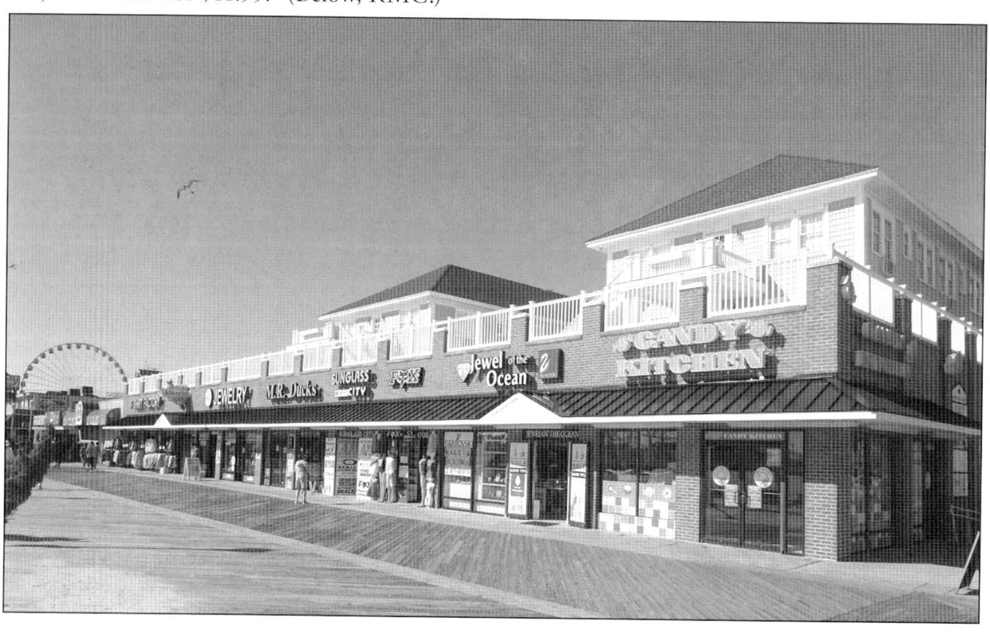

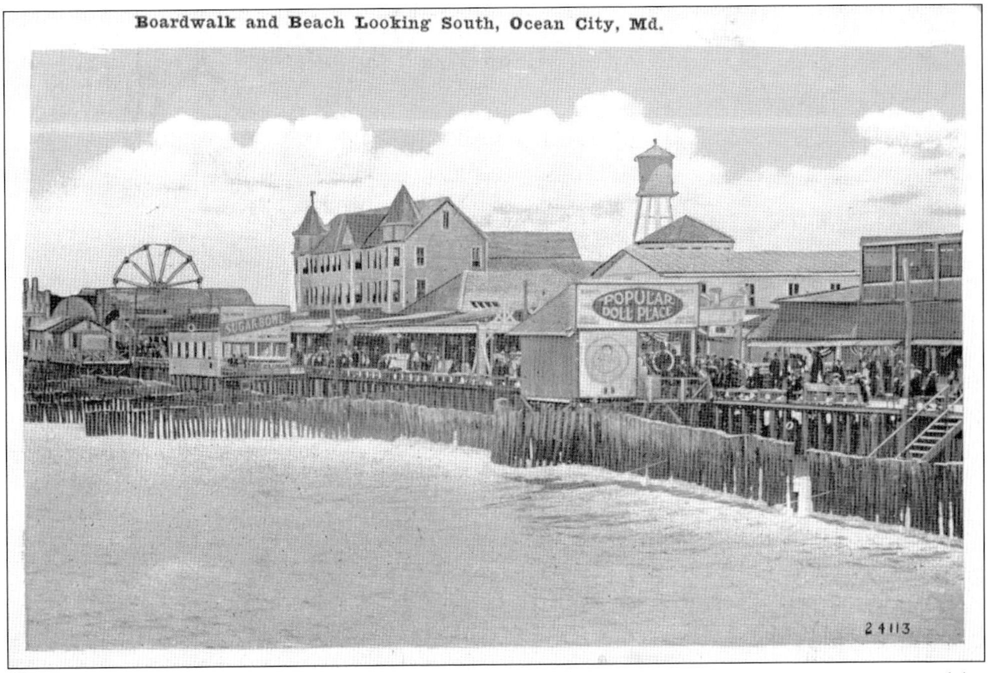

Several oceanfront hotels were built south of the Atlantic Hotel in the area now occupied by amusement arcades and Trimper's Rides (also known as Windsor Resort). Most prominent was the Windsor Hotel, shown here with its two turrets. Just below the water tower is the polygonal roof atop the merry-go-round building that still houses the hand-carved menagerie carousel Daniel Trimper purchased in 1912 from the Herschell-Spillman Company of North Tonawanda, New York. The Trimpers arrived in Ocean City in 1890 and soon owned property between South Division and South First Streets, including the Eastern Shore and Seabright Hotels. They rebuilt the latter after damage from a 1900 storm and named it the Windsor Hotel. In the next block south, Congress Hall and the smaller Cambridge Hotel had been erected by 1897 in the area later developed by the Trimpers as Luna Park amusements.

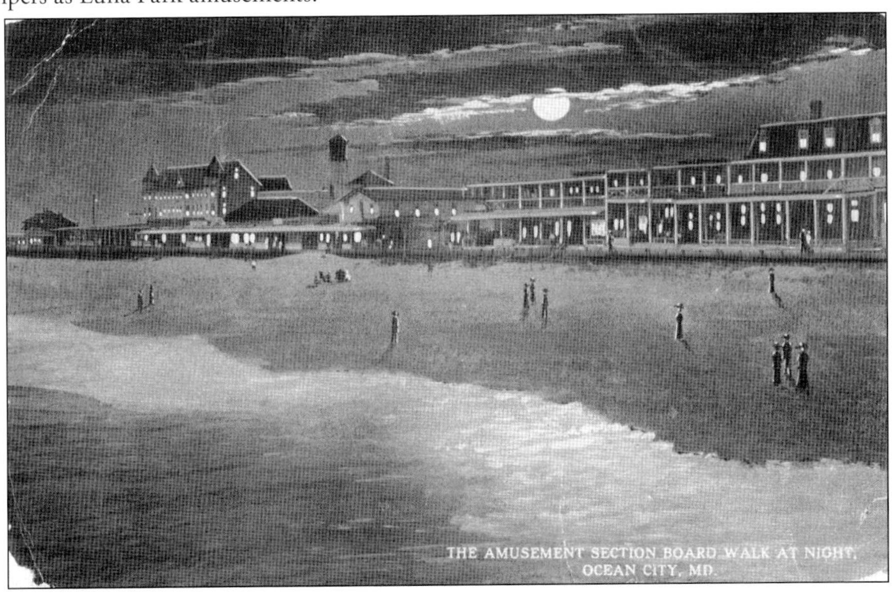

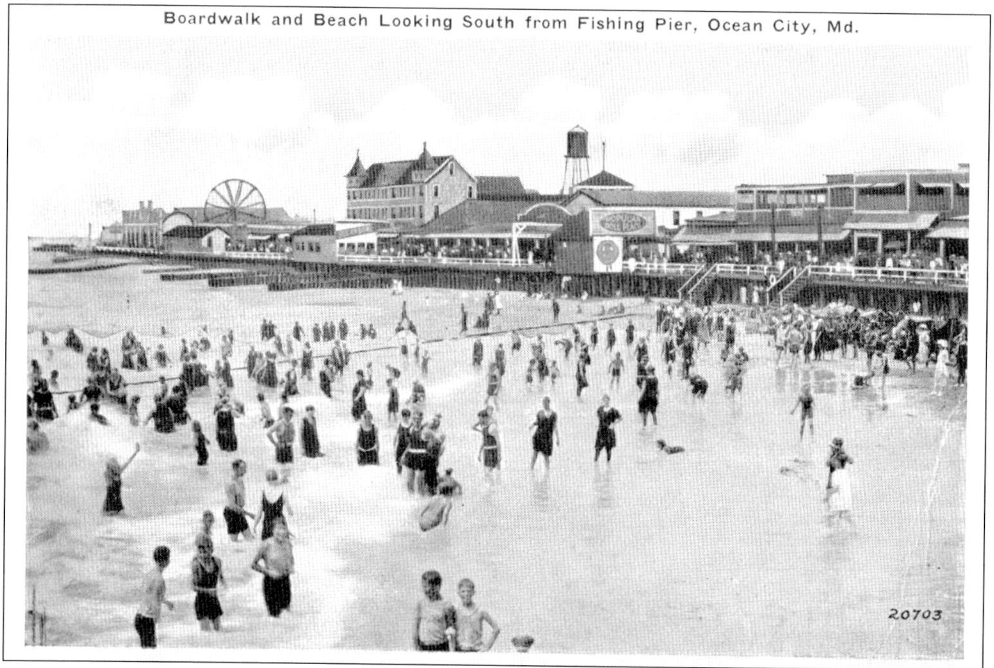

Around the time of these similar postcards (the one below, by George B. Connor, is postmarked 1906), the south end of Atlantic Avenue (now the Boardwalk) was crowded with resort buildings. In the far distance are, from left to right, Congress Hall (by 1904, the small Cambridge Hotel was no longer extant), the Windsor Hotel (formerly Seabright Hotel), E. Hobbs Bath House & Eastern Shore Hotel, and two verandah-fronted hotels—the Hotel de Cropper (with flags) and the Raynes Hotel (on the site of the former Hotel Belvidere). Beyond the edge of the postcard were the Casino Theater (pre-1897) and pier (both burned in the 1925 fire), then the Atlantic Hotel. Both postcard views were photographed from the pier. Note the Boardwalk, raised on pilings six feet above the beach level, and the fanny-dippers' safety rope.

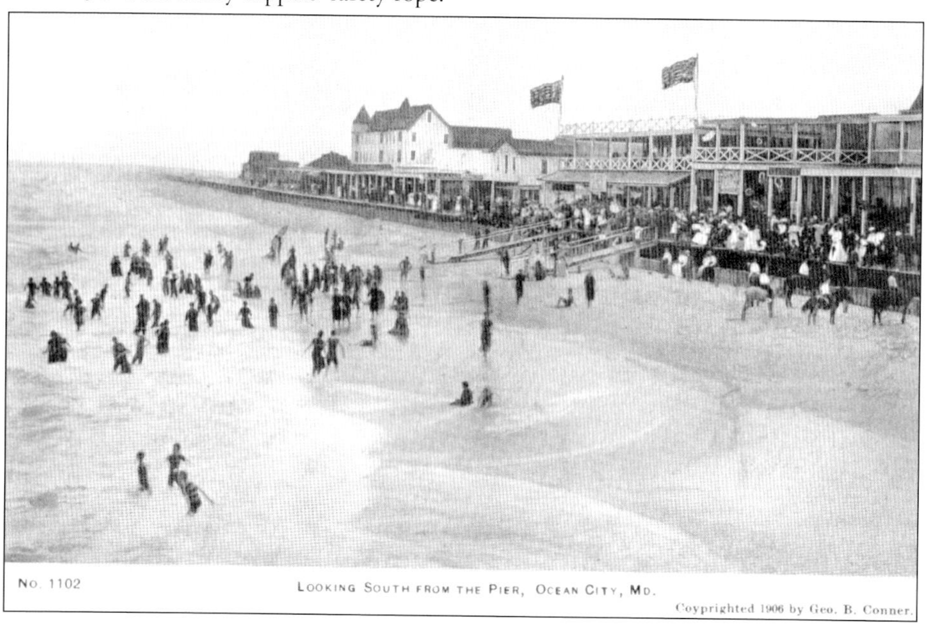

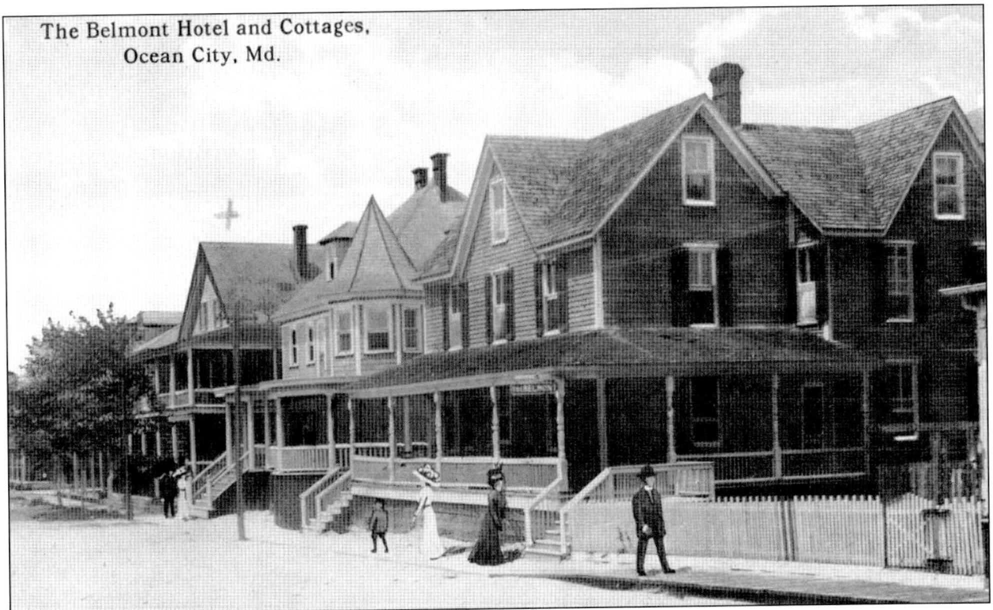

Several late-19th-century downtown hotels were built as residences and transformed into boardinghouses or small hotels. Some began as Queen Anne–styled cottages with bays, turrets, and porches; others had mansard roofs. Most had wide porches and sometimes wraparound verandahs. Aligned along Dorchester Street was a collection of three such structures that were eventually combined to become the Belmont Hotel/Belmont Cottage/the Hearne complex. In 1897, Lambert Ayres built a cottage; it was purchased in 1902 by Lizzie Hearne, who renovated the building and renamed it the Belmont Hotel. In 1910, a residence was added next door, and a sister hotel, the Hearne, later became part of the complex, with the three establishments managed by Lizzie and her descendants for over 100 years. In 2004, the picturesque Belmont-Hearne complex was razed and replaced by the Belmont Towers condominium block.

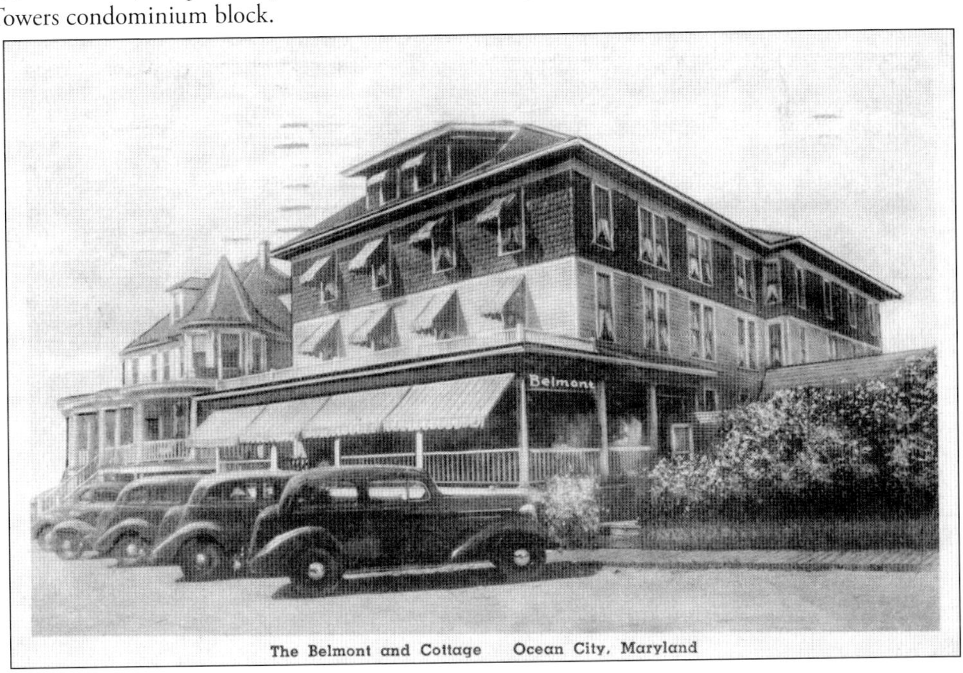

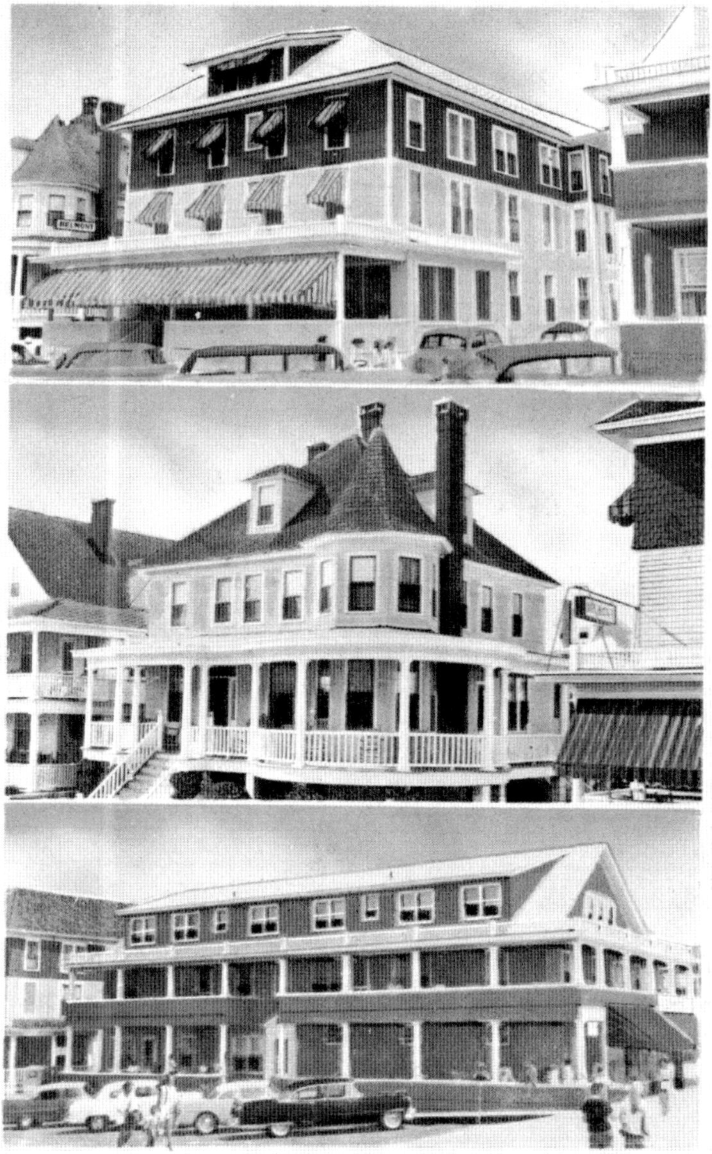

THE BELMONT, BELMONT COTTAGE AND THE HEARNE

Located just off the Boardwalk, and thus offering only oblique ocean view rooms, the three units of the Belmont-Hearne complex were sited on the north side of Dorchester Street, where southern exposure was maximized. At the west end was the Belmont Cottage (center) with its wraparound verandah offering shade and a southeast tower providing a panoramic view. To the east, the Belmont Hotel (top) is shown enlarged from its original cottage form and featuring a distinctive yellow and green exterior, a broad south-facing porch, and beachy striped awnings. Closest to the Boardwalk and ocean was the Hearne (bottom), a pre-1897 building with broad porches on two levels on its south and east sides and a continuous shed dormer providing additional third-floor rooms with southern exposure. Room rates were graduated to reflect these amenities as well as the varied plumbing offerings of running water in an in-room wash basin/lavatory versus a private bath.

EUROPEAN PLAN

Dining Room Service Available in Belmont Dining Room

DAILY RATES PER ROOM

Running Water		Private Bath
$ 6.00	Single Bed	$ 8.00-$ 9.00
$12.00-$14.00	Twin Beds	$14.00-$16.00
$11.00	Double Bed	$13.00-$15.00
$14.25-$17.25	Three in Room	$17.25-$20.25
$17.00-$21.00	Four in Room	$21.00-$25.00

APARTMENTS
4 to 6 Persons
BELMONT COTTAGE

	Per Week
Ground Floor - Two Bedrooms	$115.00
First Floor - Two Bedrooms	$135.00
Third Floor - One Bedroom	$95.00

THE HEARNE

First Floor - One Bedroom (Southern Exposure)	$100.00
Second Floor - Two Bedrooms (North-west Exposure)	$120.00
Second Floor - Two Bedrooms (North-east Exposure)	$140.00
Second Floor - Two Bedrooms (South-east Exposure)	$150.00
Second Floor - Two Bedrooms (Southern Exposure)	$150.00

Reduced Rates Are Available
Before June 15 and after Labor Day

RATE SCHEDULE

THE BELMONT
THE HEARNE
THE BELMONT COTTAGE

Boardwalk and Dorchester Street
OCEAN CITY, MARYLAND

Telephone ATlantic 9-7138

MRS. MINNIE HEARNE JONES
Owner-Manager

Convenient to
Churches - Stores - Amusements

Two undated rate schedules identify room costs on the "European Plan" (no meals) and the "modified American Plan," which included breakfast and dinner. The American plan would provide three meals daily. Long after other Ocean City hotels abandoned the American plan, the Belmont Hotel continued to offer rooms with meals, although its dining room never rivaled the elegance of those at the Atlantic, Commander, or other larger oceanfront hotels that provided the American plan. However, customers returned to the Belmont each season for decades, perhaps attracted by a nostalgia for older times and characteristically welcomed back like family by the colorful proprietor, Kate Bunting (1937?–1997), who worked for the family business as a teen (1950s–1960s), coinherited around 1969, bought out her siblings in 1977, and was proprietor of the Belmont until 1995.

All reservations subject to cancellation at the sole discretion of Management

Rates Per Person Modified American Plan

(Breakfast and Dinner included - Serving in Belmont Dining Room)

Rooms With Private Bath

Daily Each Person		Weekly Each Person
$10.00-$11.00	Single	$60.00-$66.00
$ 9.50-$10.50	Twin	$57.00-$63.00
$ 9.00-$10.00	Double	$54.00-$60.00
Three Adults in Room		
$ 8.50-$ 9.50		$51.00-$57.00
Four Adults in Room		
$ 8.00-$ 9.00		$48.00-$54.00

Rooms with Running Water

Daily Each Person		Weekly Each Person
$ 8.50	Single	$51.00
$ 8.50-$ 9.50	Twin	$51.00-$57.00
$ 8.00	Double	$48.00
Three Adults in Room		
$ 7.50-$ 8.50		$45.00-$51.00
Four Adults in Room		
$ 7.00-$ 8.00		$42.00-$48.00

(Week-end Reservations for two nights only)

(One Night Accommodations additional charge of $1.00 per person)

Two Rooms with Connecting Bath

Daily Each Person		Weekly Each Person
$ 9.00-$10.00	Twin	$54.00-$60.00
$ 8.50-$ 9.50	Double	$51.00-$57.00
$ 8.00-$ 9.00	Three in Room	$48.00-$54.00
$ 7.50-$ 8.50	Four in Room	$45.00-$51.00

Children occupying rooms with two or more adults.

	Daily	Weekly
to 3 yrs.	$3.25-$3.75	$19.50-$22.50
3 to 7 yrs.	$4.25-$4.75	$25.50-$28.50
7 to 11 yrs.	$5.50-$6.00	$33.00-$36.00

(Reduced rates are available in June and after Labor Day)

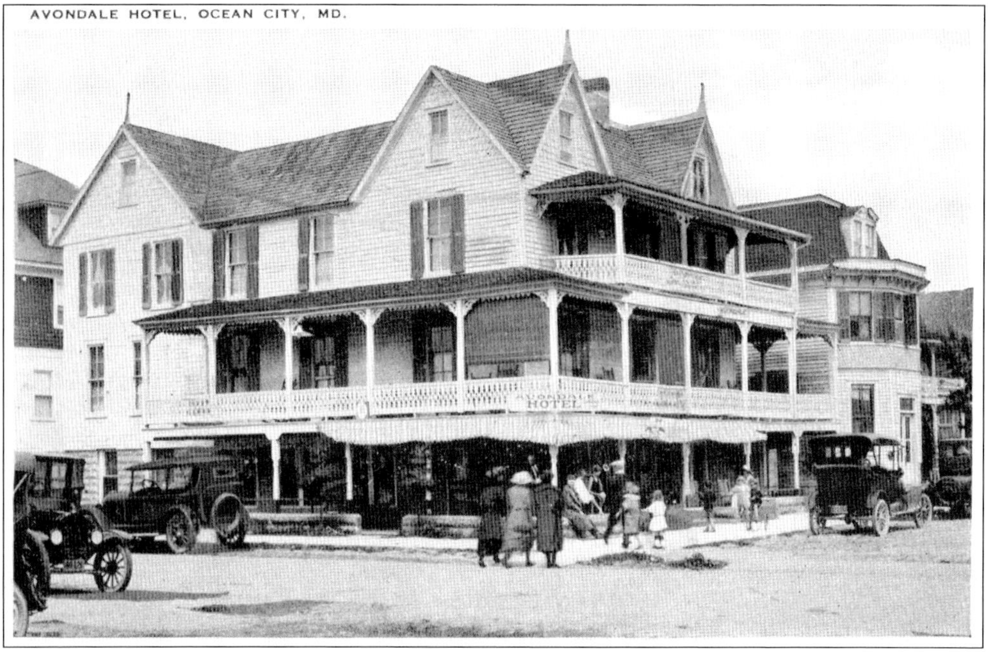

This late-19th-century hotel streetscape included the Avondale Hotel on the northeast corner of Talbot Street and Baltimore Avenue next door to the mansard-roofed Isle of Wight Hotel, both recorded on the 1897 Sanborn map. The below postcard is postmarked 1909, by which time the Isle of Wight had been renamed the Mount Vernon Hotel. An early hotel proprietor of note among the town's pioneer women hoteliers was Susie Amanda Rounds, who moved to Ocean City in 1904 and rented rooms in her house; 10 years later, she traded her house for the Avondale. In 1925, moving north with the times, Rounds and her husband, George, bought the New Avelon Hotel and renamed it as the Del-Mar-Va Hotel (located at Baltimore Avenue and First Street). She later purchased the Liberty Farms Hotel on Seventh Street and the Boardwalk (it was later renamed the Majestic Hotel).

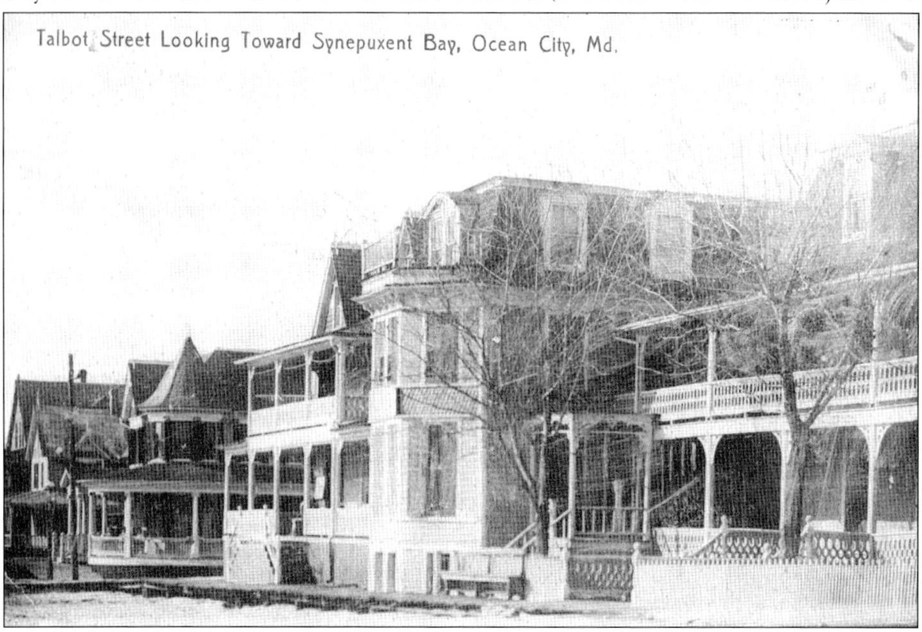

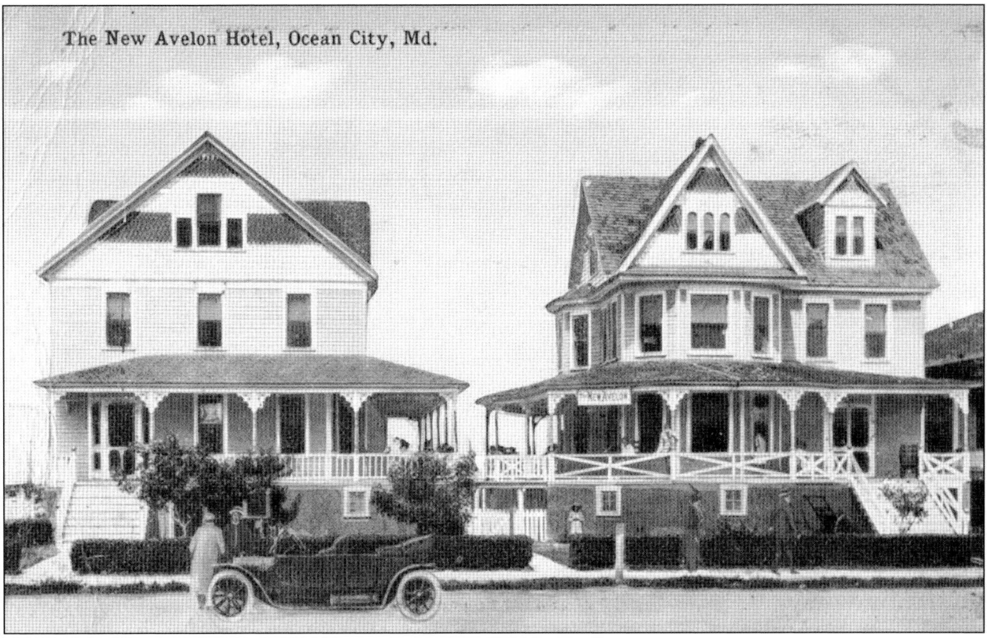

In 1902, a cottage was built on the west side of Baltimore Avenue on the second lot south of North First Street and began operating as the Avelon. Before 1911, a cottage was built to its south, and the two wraparound verandahs were joined by an open porch. The conjoined cottages began operating as the New Avelon Hotel. As noted on page 26, the hotel was purchased by Susie and George Rounds and renamed the Del-Mar-Va in 1925. A 1928 expansion added a lobby between the two buildings and rooms on the second floor. A third floor was added in 1935. The corner cottage, remaining detached, became part of the property, and during its later years, the hotel was renamed again as the Avelon Inn. All of these buildings were razed in 2008, and the site is now occupied by the Gateway Hotel.

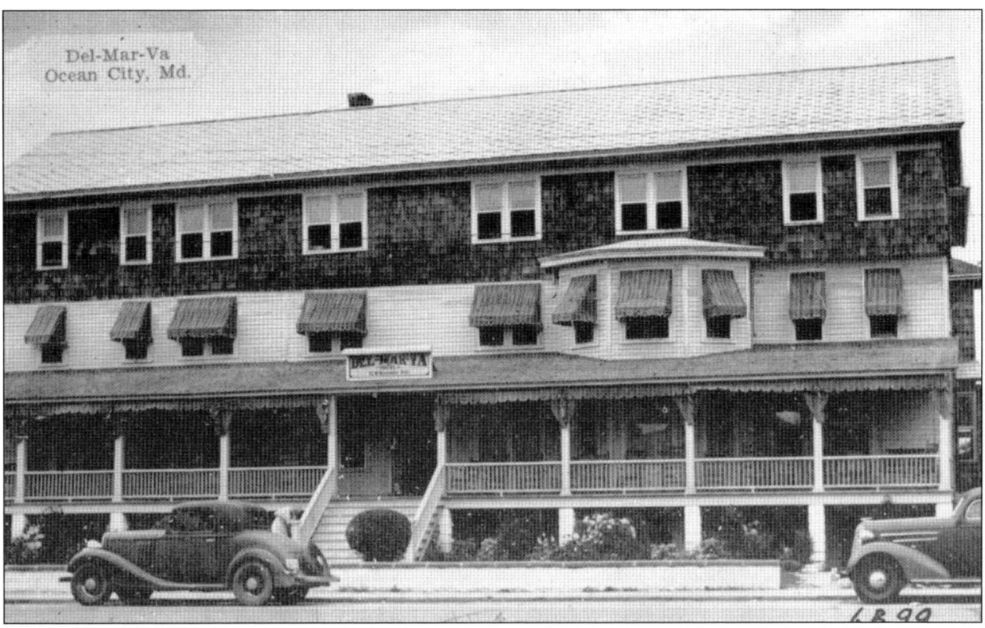

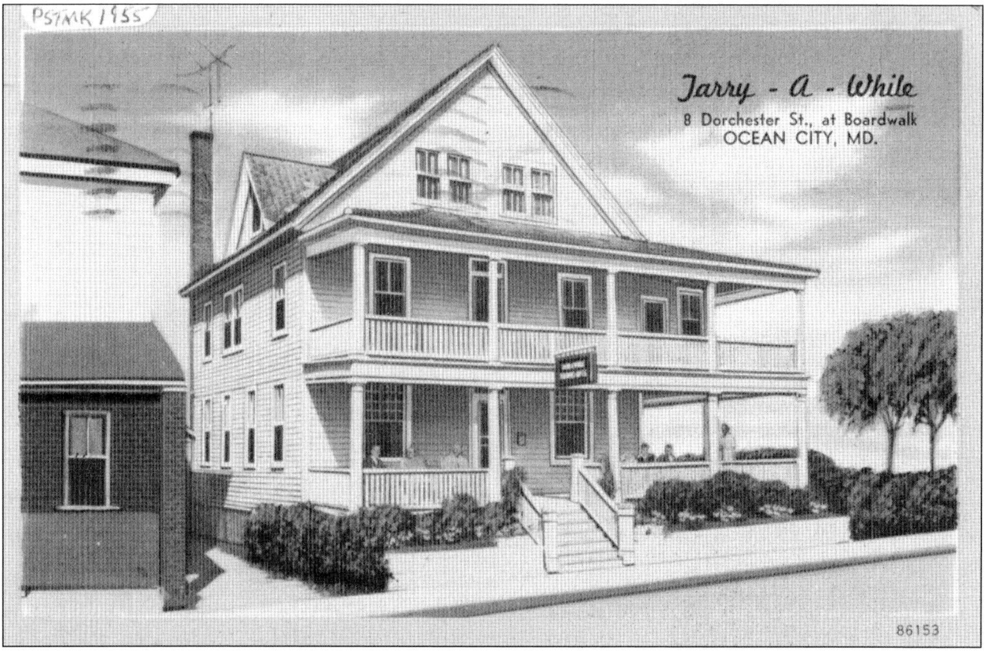

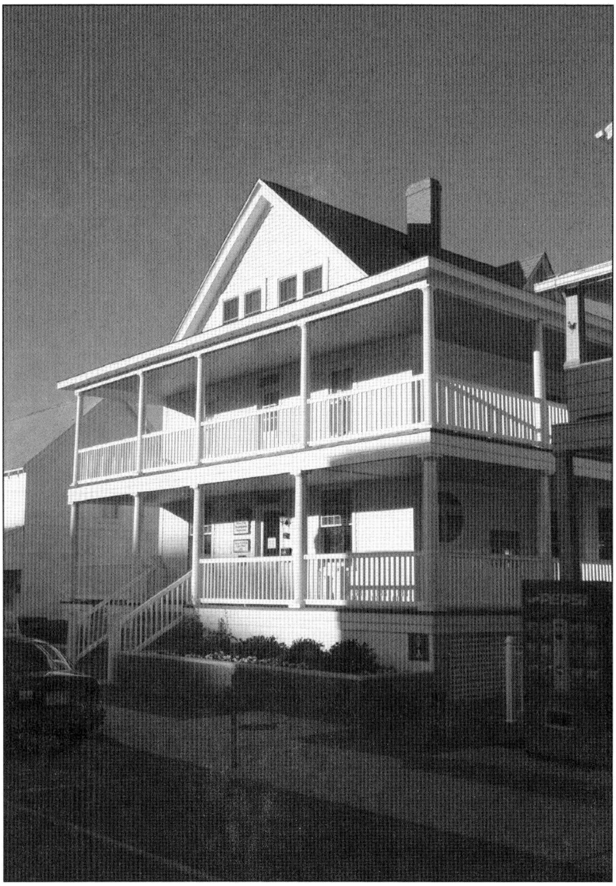

After her 1899 purchase of "Lot No. 39" on Dorchester Street (as designated on the original plan of Ocean City), Margaret Vandegrift of Pittsburgh, Pennsylvania, immediately improved the property by building a gabled frame residence following her receipt of a mortgage in January. However, due to a default in mortgage payment, the property, with its house already called Tarry-A-While, was sold to Thomas J. Cropper, father of Ocean City's future mayor Clifford Cropper (who held that office during World War II). Tarry-A-While was one of the town's earliest guesthouses to advertise the amenity of running water in each room. In 2007, Tarry-A-While was moved one block west from 8 to 108 Dorchester Street. Today, it serves as headquarters for the Ocean City Development Corporation and continues to provide guest rooms on the upper floors for seasonal town employees. (Left, RMC.)

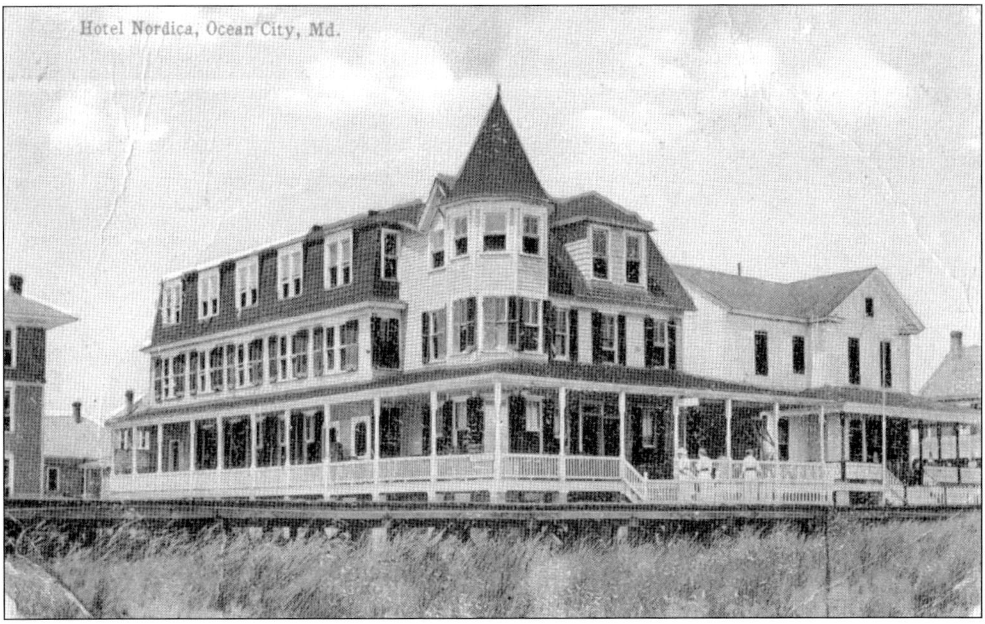

Built around 1903 (definitely sometime between 1897 and 1904), the Nordica Hotel displayed a narrow building width and domestic cottage scale at its Boardwalk frontage featuring an east and south porch, striped awning (which was added later), east-facing roof dormer, and Queen Anne–styled corner turret, with the whole serving as frontispiece to a French Second Empire, mansard-roofed rear wing of rooms. The image was part large Victorian cottage and part small hotel. Like numerous other hotels before and after its time, the Nordica later built architecturally insensitive retail store frontage along its Boardwalk face, obliterating the hotel's open porch in favor of a variegated Permastone facade. Although Permastone was popular in the 1950s (see pages 84 and 95), this was possibly (and thankfully) the only use of this fake masonry material on the Boardwalk. The Nordica was destroyed by arson in January 1973.

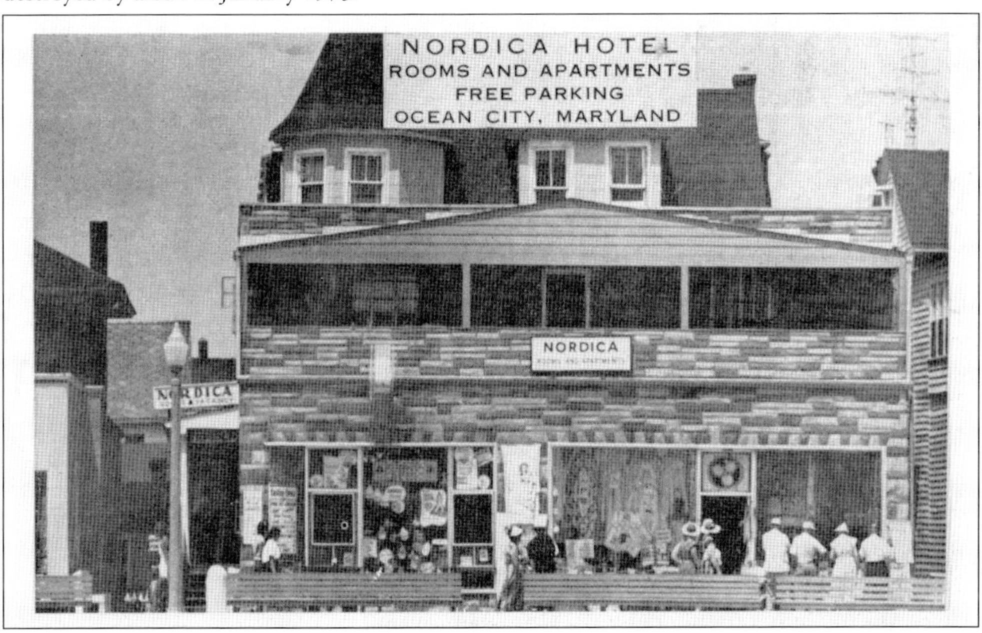

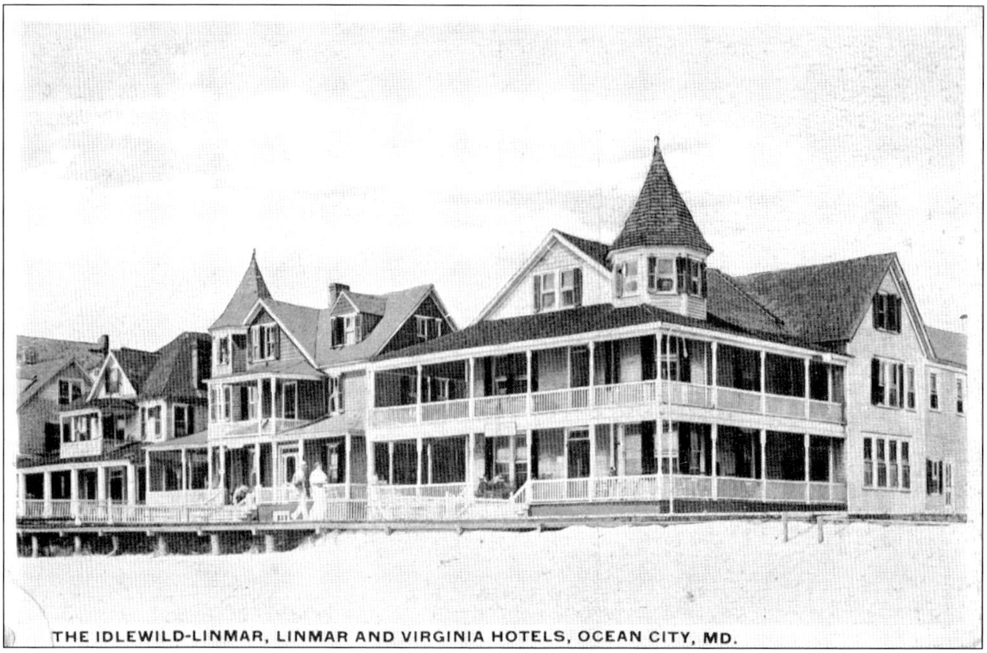

As guest cottages and small hotels were built along the Boardwalk north of North Division Street, a Queen Anne–styled residential streetscape emerged with verandahs and upper porches facing the beach and ocean and often with corner turrets offering more panoramic views of the sea. Several turn-of-the-century cottages (above) changed names during the early 20th century—the Virginia Hotel is barely visible at the left edge of the postcard; beyond it, from left to right, are the cottage that became part of the Rideau Hotel, the Linmar Hotel, and the Idylwild Hotel (which was originally called the Ocean Swell Cottage). The Idylwild Hotel (misspelled on the postcard above as Idlewild), built before 1897, was almost two decades old when the below postcard was mailed. The Linmar was built between 1897 and 1904.

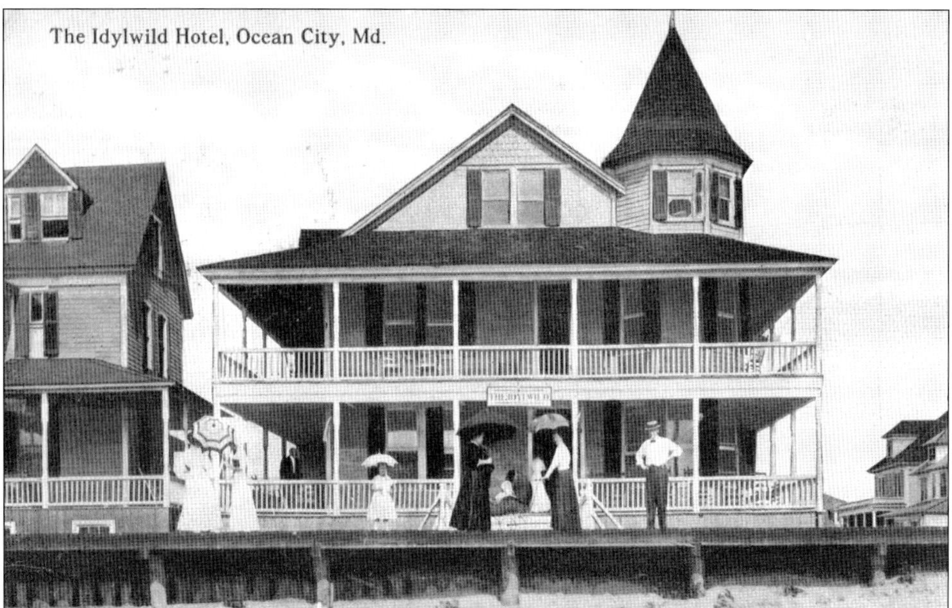

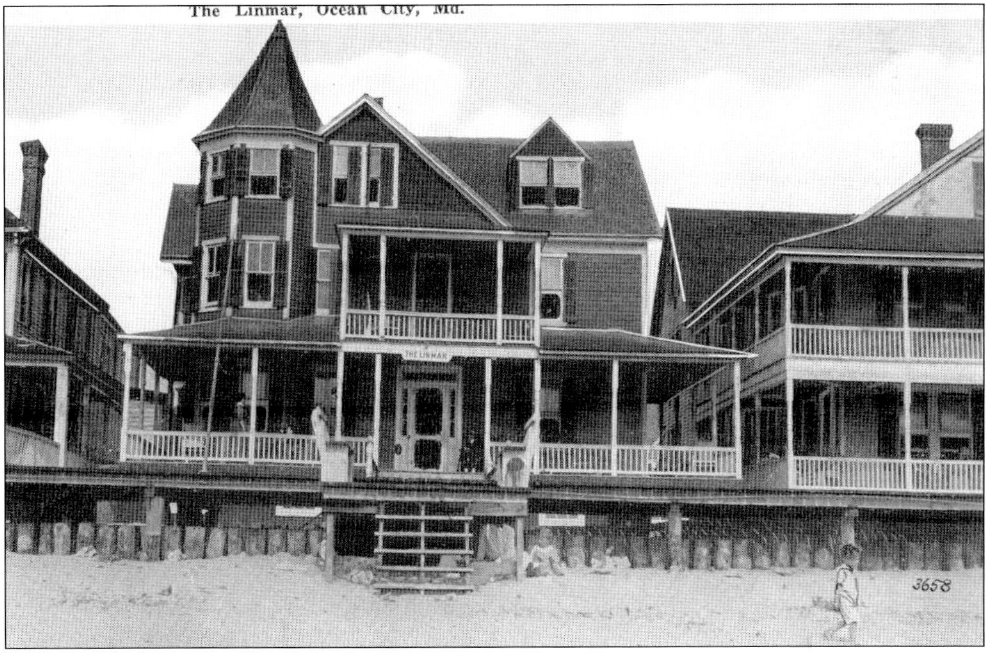

Immediately to the south of the Idylwild was the Linmar Hotel (above) and, two lots south of that, the almost identical Virginia Hotel. Both Queen Anne–styled hotels had triple-height turrets with a candlesnuffer roof at the southeast corner, a broad frontal gable, and an east-facing dormer on the cross gable. Verandahs extended across the full east front of each hotel and wrapped around both the north and south corners. Between the two hotels was a small cottage, the progenitor of the Rideau Hotel. The 1938 photograph of the Rideau (below) shows this cottage (right) joined to the Virginia Hotel (left) by a broad verandah with a striped awning. To the left (south) was the Mount Pleasant Hotel.

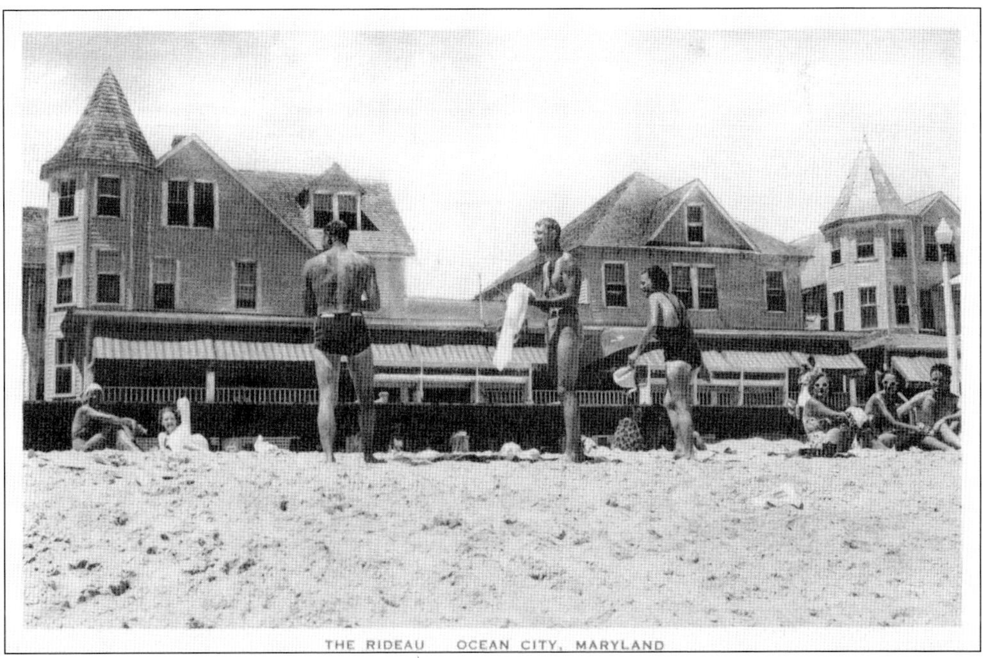

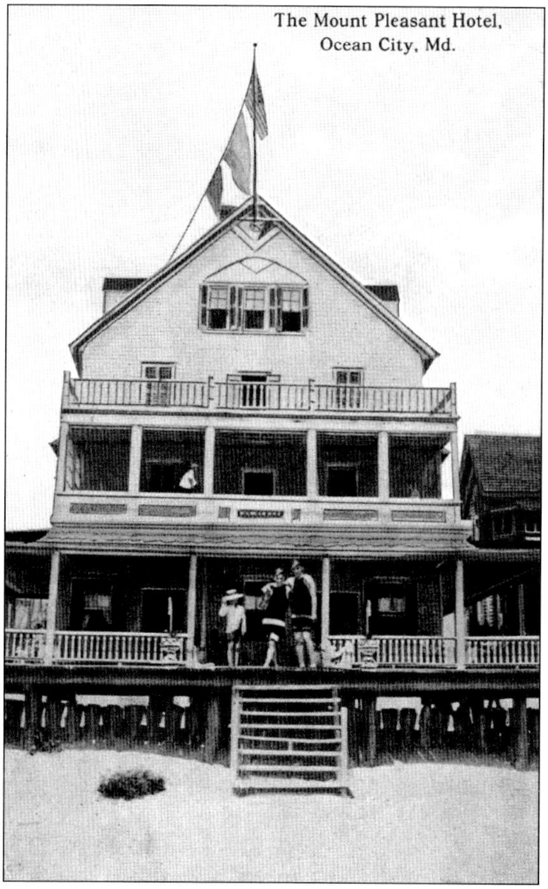

The Mount Pleasant Hotel was built in 1900 by Margaret Campbell Buell and purchased in 1918 by Susan Mason, the author's great-grandmother. The cottage to its south was incorporated into the hotel, and after a fire in 1923, the hotel was rebuilt at twice its original size (see the image at the bottom of page 33) and renamed the New Mount Pleasant. The Masons were forced to sell the hotel in 1932—perhaps the worst year of the Great Depression. The new owners renamed the hotel the Roosevelt to honor the new president, Franklin Delano Roosevelt. The cottage to the right (north) is the Virginia Hotel, which was later incorporated into the Rideau Hotel (see page 31). During renovations in 1970, the Roosevelt caught fire again during one of the town's largest conflagrations, which led to the demolition of the Roosevelt and the three buildings of the adjacent Rideau.

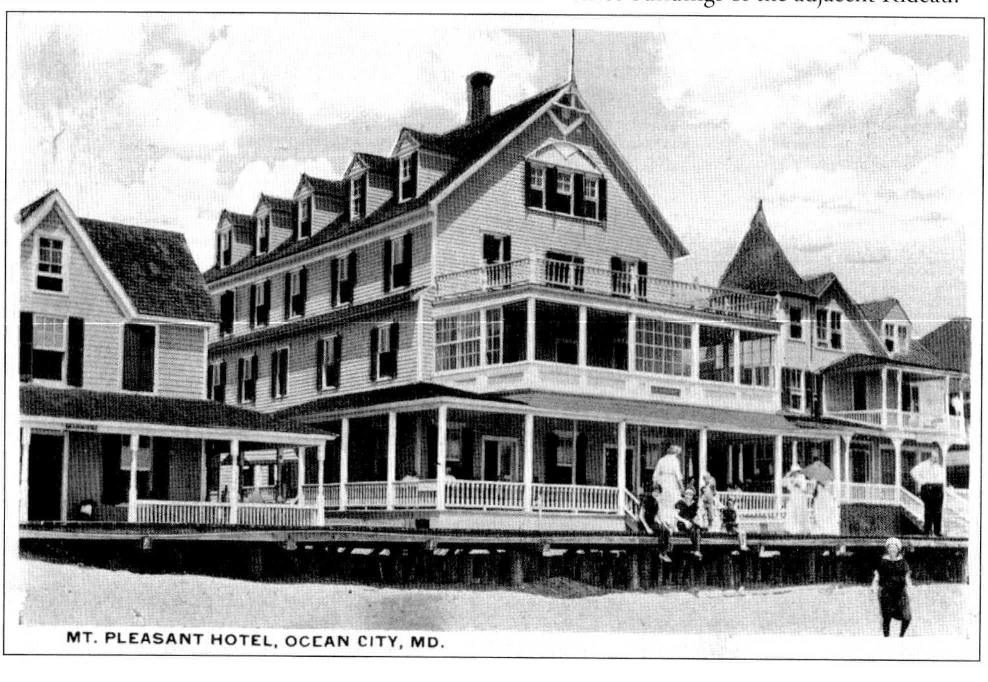

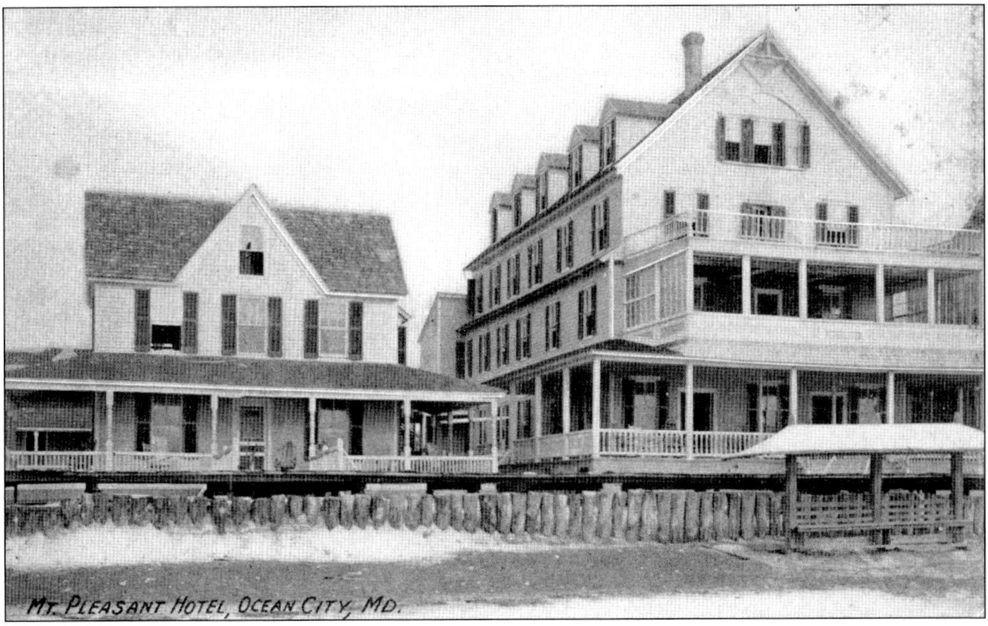

The original Mount Pleasant Hotel and cottage next door are depicted on the above postcard (postmarked 1915). Below is the enlarged and renamed New Mount Pleasant (later the Roosevelt) Hotel. An undated rate schedule during the 1920s, when Susan Mason was managing, highlights "private baths with rooms" and offers weekly rates, including meals, of $17.50 to $25 each for two in a room ($20 to $30 for a single) in June and July, and about 12 percent higher in August. The 1924 New Mount Pleasant rivaled, in scale, the new oceanfront hotels being built during the period, such as the Shoreham (1922), Lankford (1924), rebuilt Atlantic (1925), Royalton (1926), and Mayflower (1926). Interestingly, as noted in the essay "The Petticoat Regime of 1890–1926": "Of the thirty-two hotels and boardinghouses listed in [the] 1926 guide to Ocean City, all but two were owned and managed by women" (www.ocmuseum.org, accessed January 10, 2019).

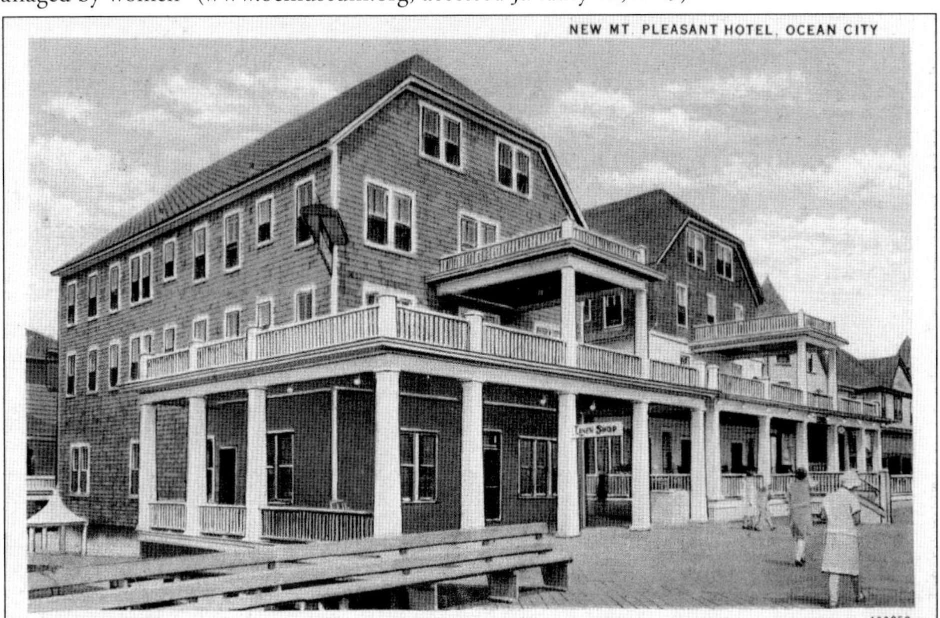

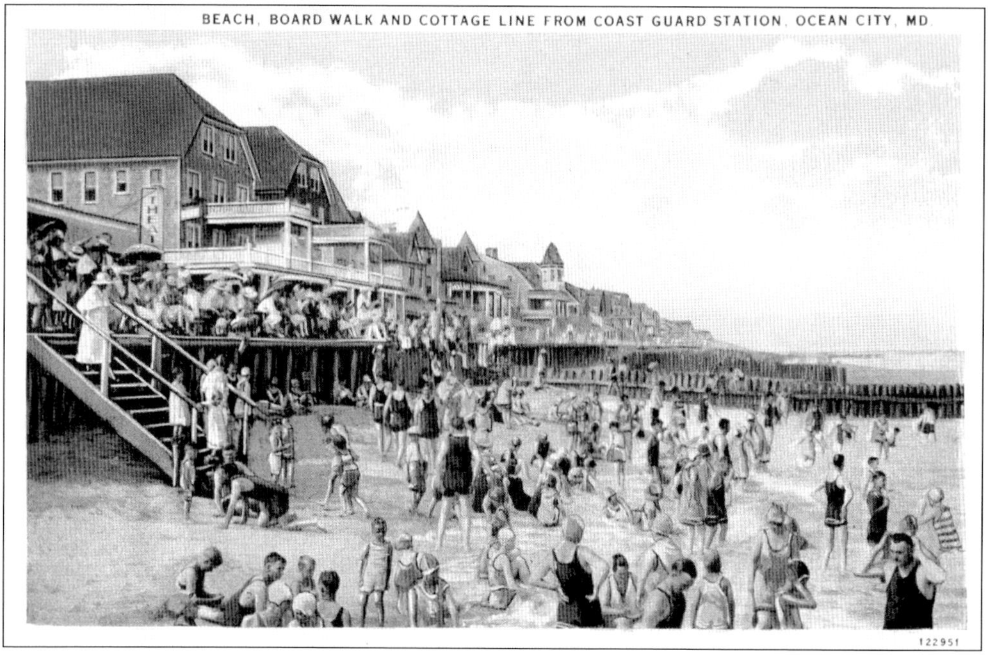

Panoramic views of the two blocks of Boardwalk hotels between North Division Street and Second Street show a parade of turrets, gables, and verandahs. Prominent in the foreground above is the New Mount Pleasant Hotel, with its two jerkinhead roofs, connecting verandah, and second-floor porches. Beyond are the turrets of the Linmar and Idylwild Hotels, and the most prominent tower (in the center of the postcard) is the Plimhimmon Hotel on Second Street.

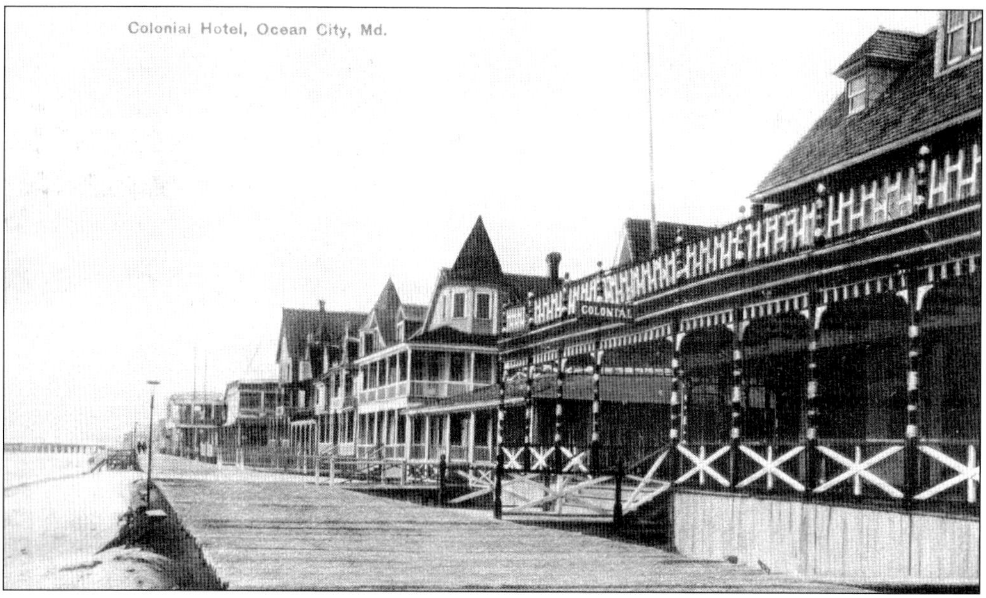

In a view looking south along the Boardwalk from First Street, the Colonial Hotel, with its ornate early porch, is prominent on the far right of this Rinn Publ. (based in Berlin, Maryland) postcard, which is postmarked 1909; beyond are the turrets of the Idylwild, Linmar, and Virginia Hotels. The high frontal gable is the single-block Mount Pleasant Hotel. Beyond is the lower Oceanic Hotel, adjacent to the (recessed and not visible) Ocean City Life-Saving Station.

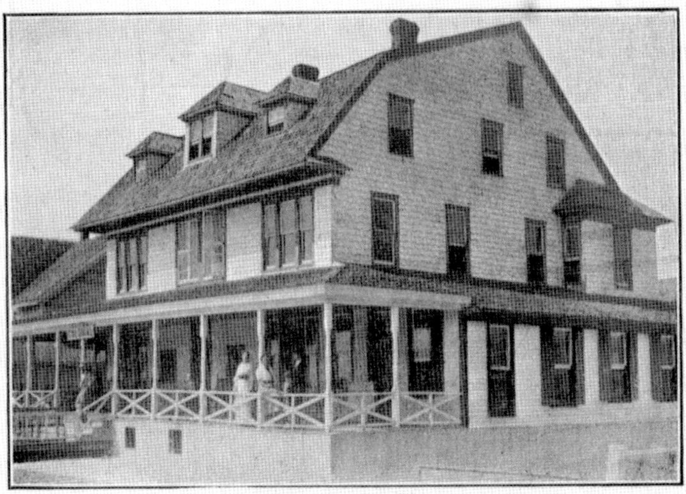

THE COLONIAL, OCEAN CITY, MD.

The Colonial Hotel (pre-1897), located oceanfront just north of North First Street, was a Dutch Colonial Revival building with gambrel roof and dormers and originally had a wide porch with lathe-turned posts just off the Boardwalk. A subsequent remodeling (below) adorned the main building front with a tetrastyle (four columns) colossal portico in the unfluted Roman Tuscan order, flanked by side verandah ends adorned with single-level columns in the same order. The entry door, with its delicate fan light and side lights, is Federal/Neoclassical in style, and the wave-patterned shingle cladding adds an ornamental upgrade to resort architecture that had earlier employed clapboard siding and little classical (or American Colonial) adornment. The Colonial was destroyed by arson in December 1972.

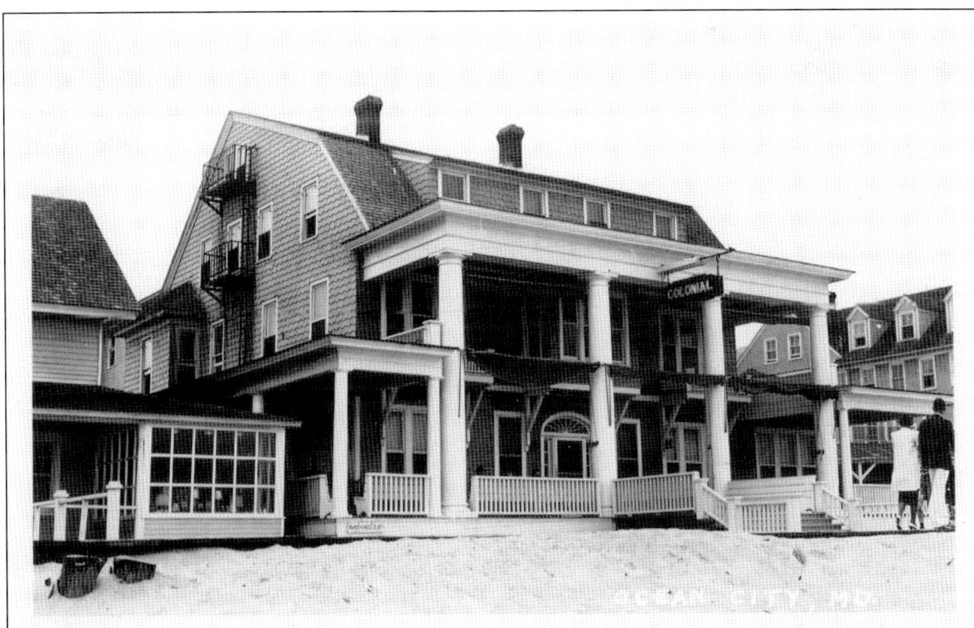

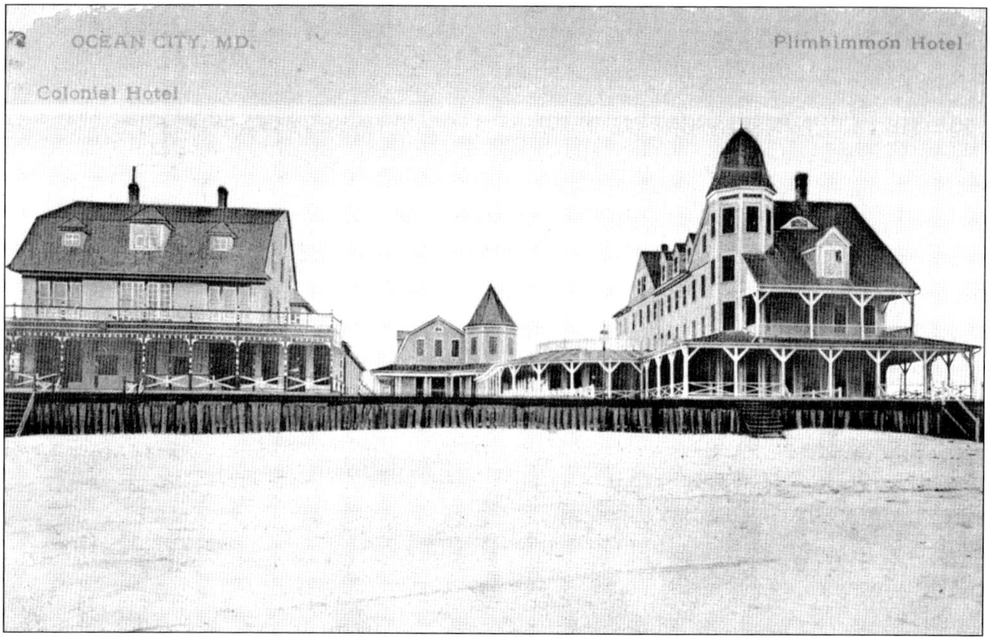

The Plimhimmon Hotel was built in 1894 by Rosalie Tilghman Shreve (when she was about 50 years old) and featured a wood-frame, Victorian-styled main hotel structure with a prominent southeast corner tower and verandah on its east and south fronts, as well as a detached casino, or dance pavilion, connected to the hotel by a covered Boardwalk linked to the south verandah. The main building featured Chattolanee bottled water on the verandah and included a large dining room on the ground floor. The dining room's three-course meal at noon included—according to an account of "local legends" published on March 16, 1997, in the *Maryland Beachcomber*—"soup, local fish, meat, and homemade cake or pie" served while an orchestra played. Evening supper at the Plim featured "broiled spring chicken, corn fritters, butter, fish, cold ham, oysters, poulette, grilled applies, corn pone cake, and peaches."

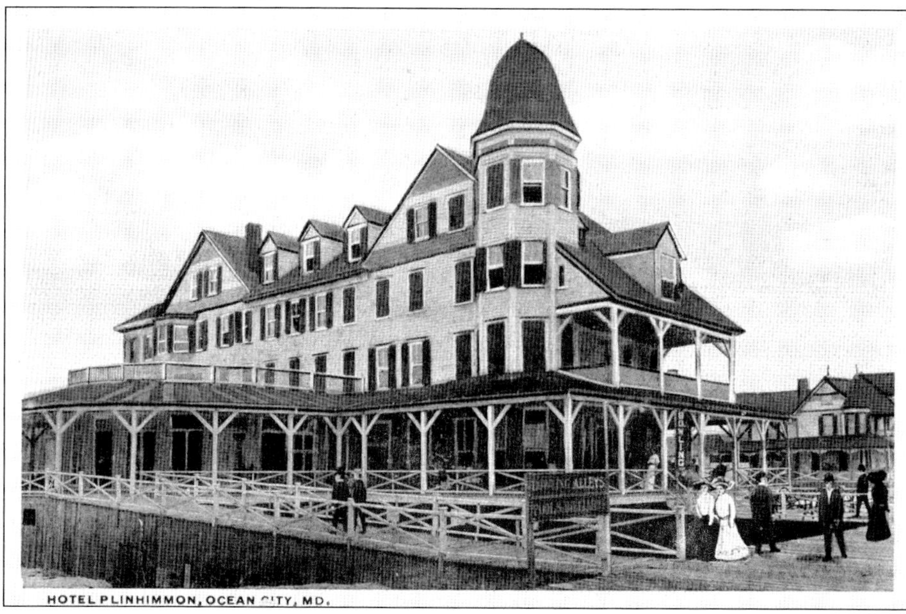

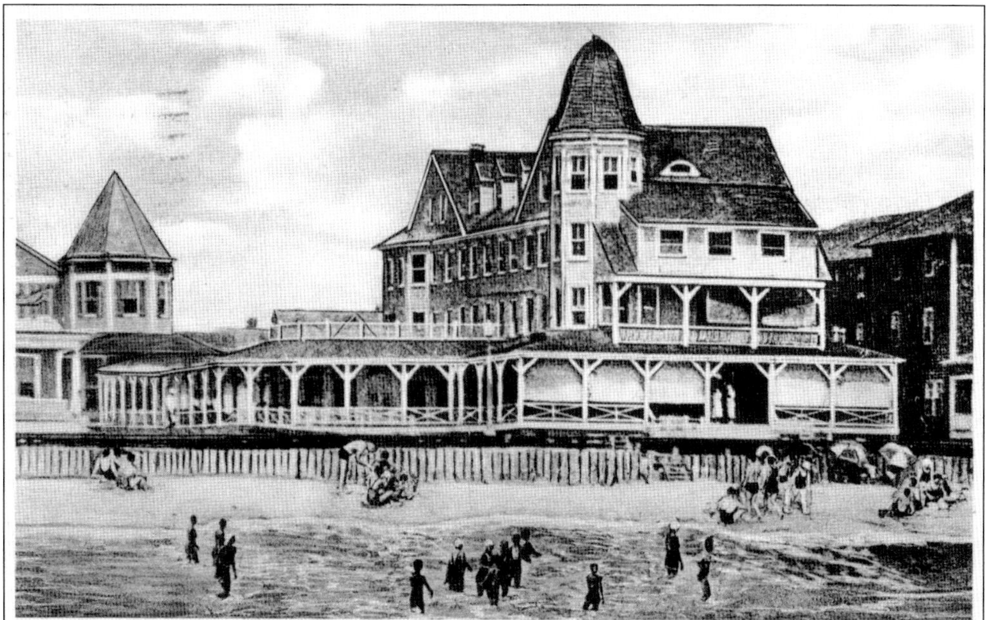

Oceanfront hotels were raised above the beach and ocean level and usually built on poles hammered deep into the sand and connected to the Boardwalk by a short flight of stairs. Pilings ran along the entire frontage of the Plimhimmon to protect against high tides and storm surf. This postcard (postmarked 1937) shows a very narrow beach—unlike the several hundred yards of sand in front of the hotel today.

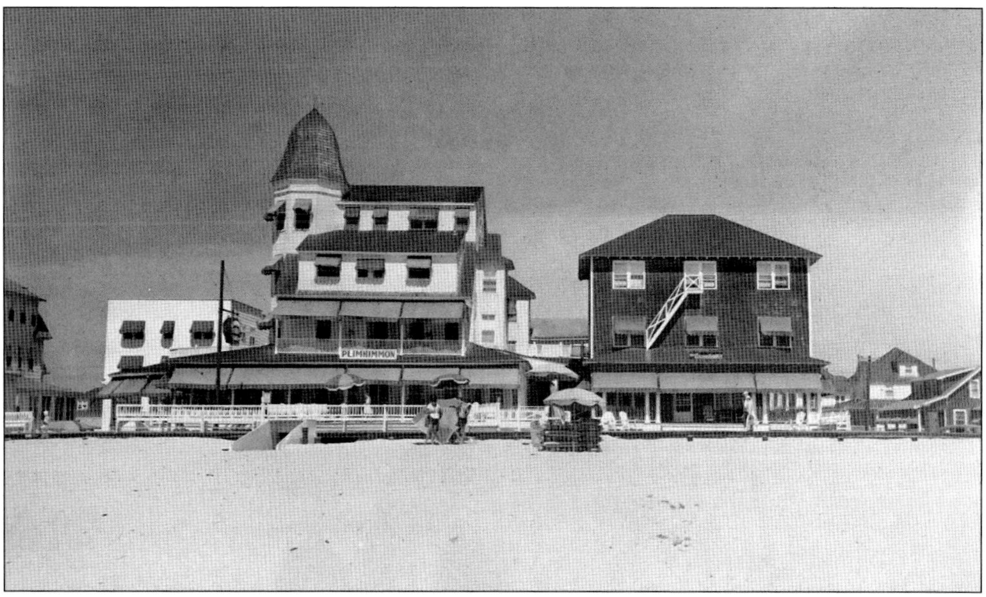

Throughout the first half of the 20th century, the Plimhimmon expanded north and south from its distinctive Victorian building on the Boardwalk. A photograph from the late 1940s or early 1950s shows a hipped-roof and shingle-clad building to the north and a flat-roofed, three-bay rectilinear structure on the former site of the casino to the south, all of which were early steps in the Plimhimmon's expansion. (Photograph by Robert S. Craig.)

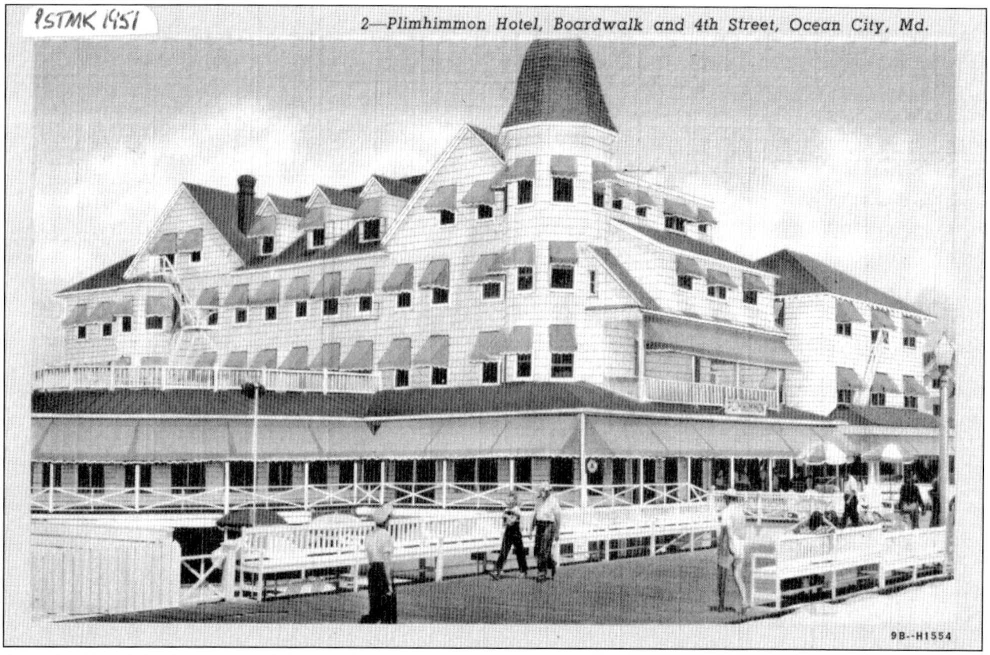

A 1949 Curt Teich postcard shows the Plimhimmon and the adjacent building to its north bedecked in bright green awnings sized to fit each window and matching the new green tile of the roofs, which were originally a brownish-red, if the postcard coloration of the respective periods is to be trusted. The front porches and sweeping verandahs are sheltered by wide awnings in the same green tone.

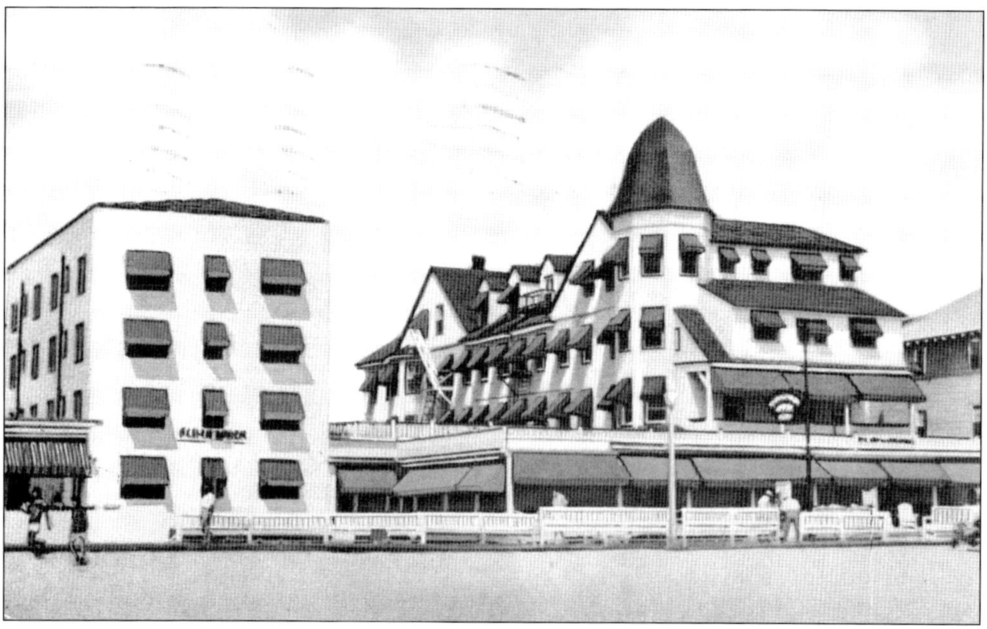

This Curt Teich photochrome (compare this to the image on the bottom of page 37) shows the Plimhimmon's south building rectangle extending forward from the casino site to the Boardwalk and with a fourth level added. The hotel continued to expand while retaining its white surfaces and colored awnings to unify otherwise unrelated building forms.

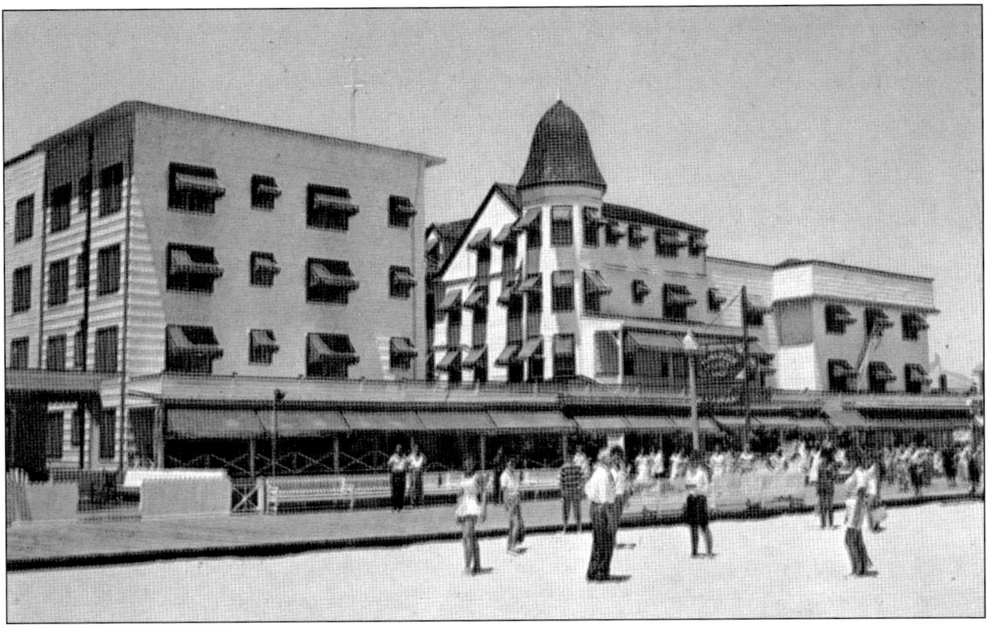

In this photograph by Fred Brueckmann, a producer of local postcards from the Tingle Printing Company in nearby Pittsville, Maryland, the Plimhimmon's south building has been expanded from three to four bays, and the entire composition of the buildings has been unified by color, window awning treatment, and the continuous porch extending the full width of the buildings along the Boardwalk.

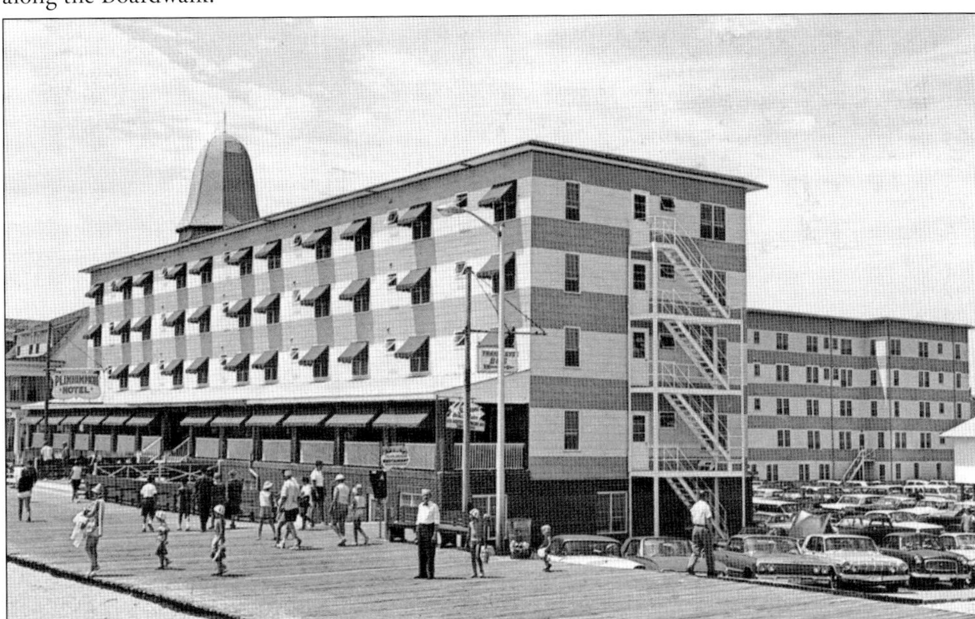

In 1962, during an expansion intended to increase the Plimhimmon's capacity from 280 to 400 rooms, a fire broke out in the north wing and destroyed the entire structure fronting the Boardwalk; only the perpendicular east/west wings were left standing. A complete rebuild as a new Plim Plaza (above) referenced the iconic polygonal turret, striped the entire structure in yellow and green, reinstated green awnings, and lined the Boardwalk with a brick porch.

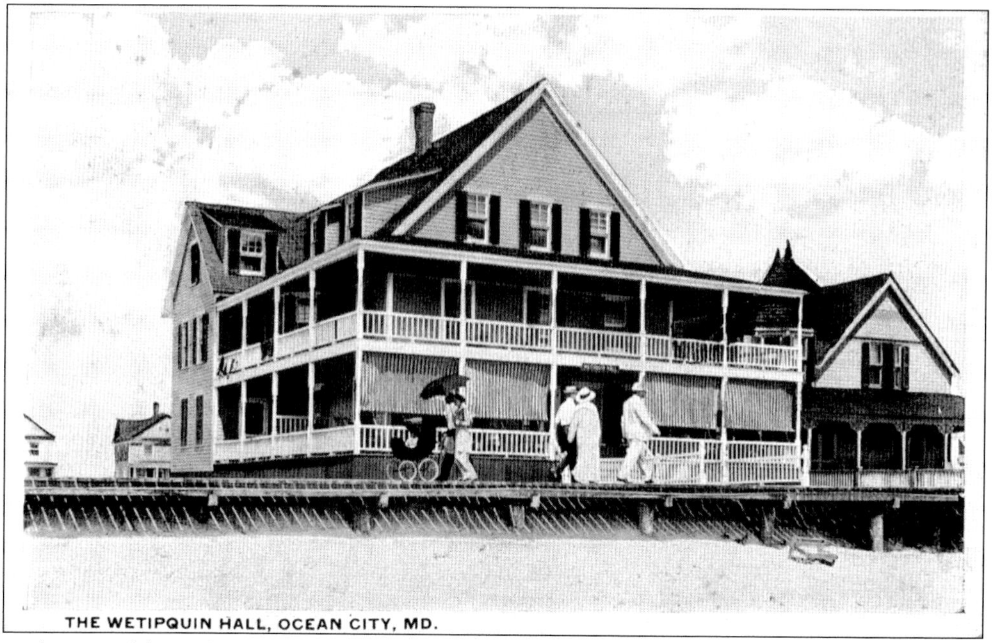

At the start of the 20th century, Wetipquin Hall (later renamed the Purnell) appeared on the Boardwalk north of Second Street. It was a two-and-a-half-story gabled guest cottage with shed dormers and wraparound porches on two levels. During summer days, in the time before air-conditioning, an open window or a rocking chair on a porch captured ocean breezes. The 2007 Somerset Condos structure now occupies this site.

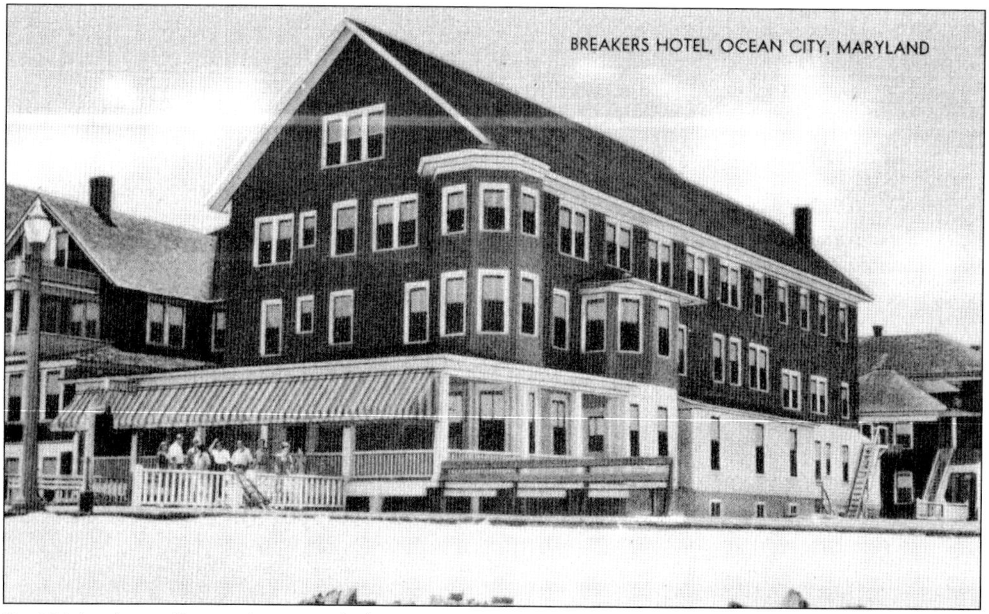

By 1904, a large Queen Anne–styled cottage stood on the south corner of the Boardwalk at Third Street; this was subsequently developed into a cottage hotel and enlarged to become the Breakers. The Breakers was shingle-clad, and the hotel retained the cottage's two-story bay on the north side and three-story northeast corner turret with its original candlesnuffer roof later removed. A full-width porch wrapped around both corners.

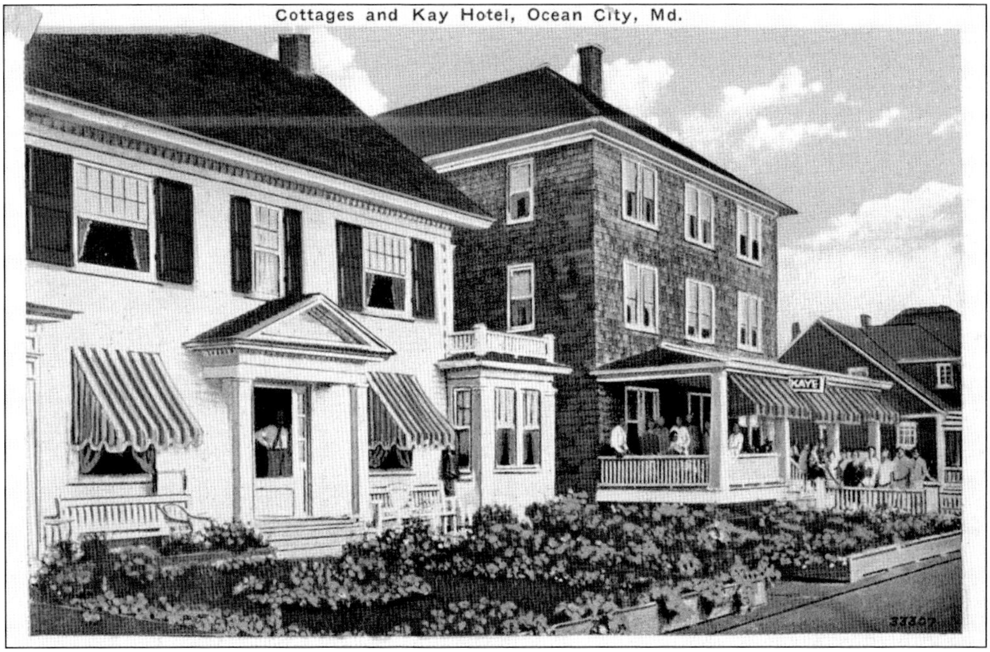

Marie Kaye Kinnamon built the Kaye Hotel (at right in these views) on the southwest corner of Sixth Street and the Boardwalk in 1927. After her death, the property was sold. The hotel opened for the 1945 summer season under its new name, the Hotel Normandy, likely to honor the D-Day landings in Normandy the previous summer. The building was shingle-clad with minimal architectural detailing and had window trim, porch posts, and rails painted white and a striped awning across the full-width porch that accented the front. The below postcard dates to 1945 and shows a marquee high on the northeast corner that was visible from the Boardwalk as well as side streets. After the 1991 summer season, the historic Hotel Normandy was razed and replaced by the Americana Motor Inn.

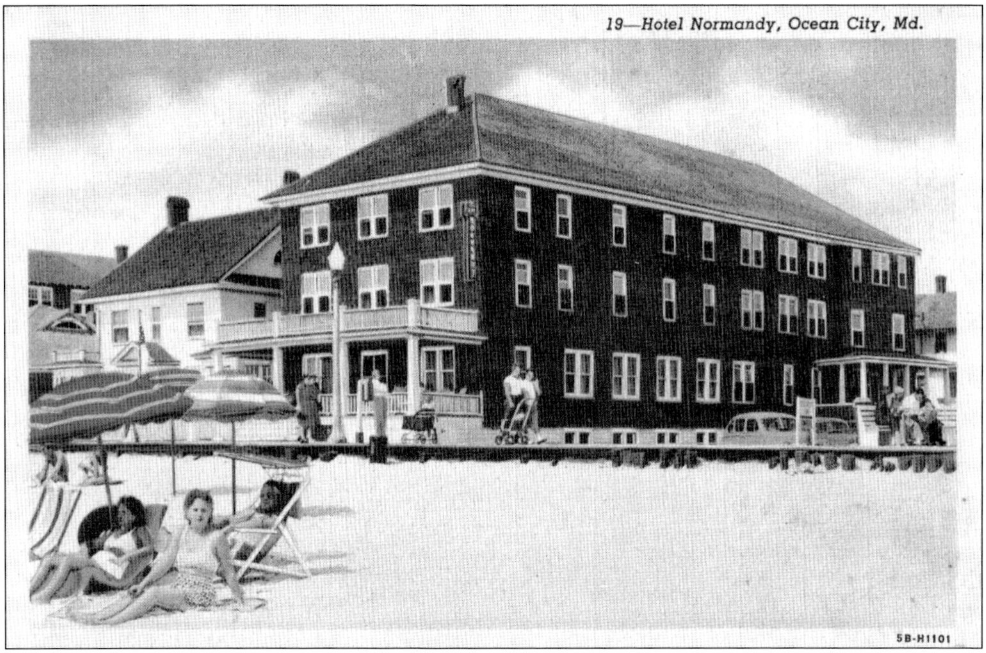

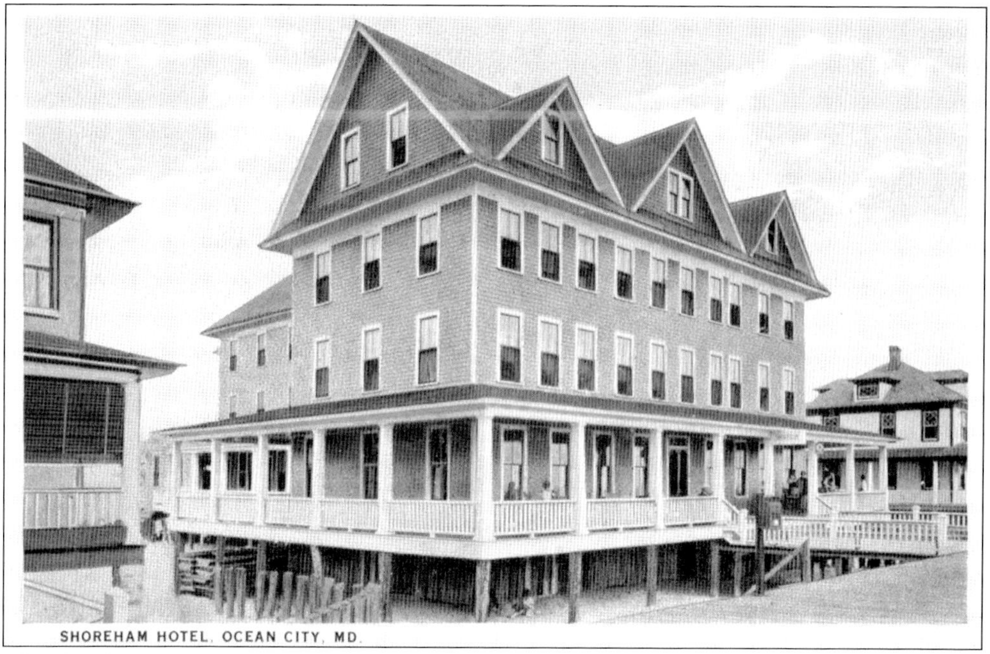

The Shoreham Hotel (a 40-room hotel with 16 private baths) was originally intended to be named the Traymore after the hotel in Atlantic City. Josephine Hastings tore down the old Fox Cottage (also known as the Tourist Inn) on the site at Fourth Street and the Boardwalk and opened the Shoreham on April 15, 1923. An early view (above) shows a three-and-a-half-story block raised on open pilings and connected to the Boardwalk by a balustraded walkway and three steps up to the hotel's broad east and south verandah. A later northeast view (below) shows changes to the east frontal gables at the fourth level, now featuring a long shed dormer with five paired windows. Along the hotel's north flank is the long Fourth Street Boardwalk ramp—a graduated incline that served both pedestrian and bicycle traffic; these ramps were installed at every cross street along the Boardwalk.

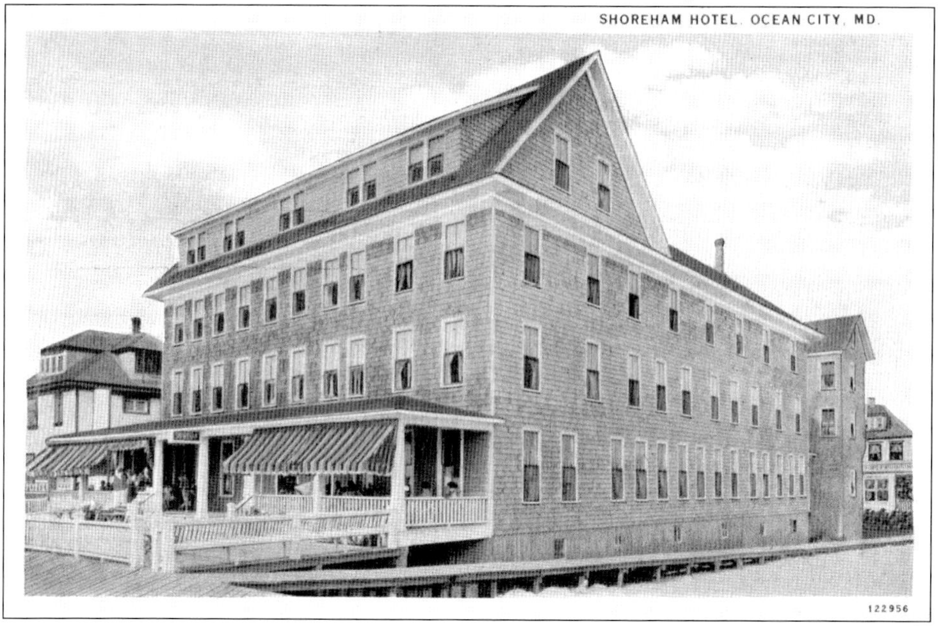

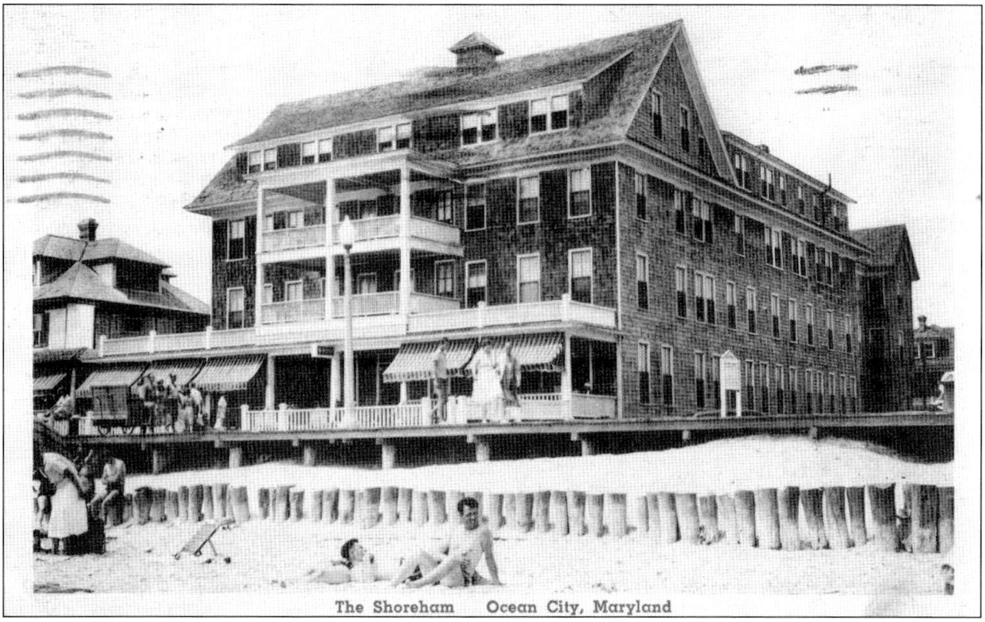

This postcard, postmarked 1940, of the Shoreham Hotel shows additional changes where white balustraded porches were added to the second- and third-floor levels of the hotel's east front (since removed). Owner Josephine Hastings sold the hotel in 1926 to Horace and Amanda Ayres Cropper, who made changes in 1927, 1928, and 1930, enlarging the dining room to accommodate the hotel's American plan. The hotel still stands and is now home to the popular Shenanigan's bar.

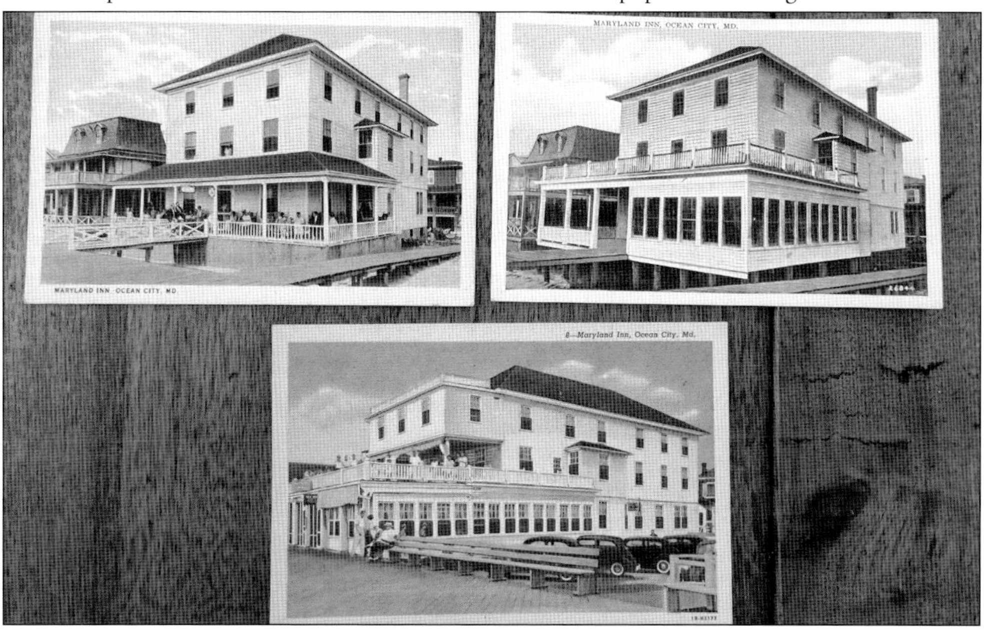

At the Maryland Inn (razed) on the Boardwalk at Caroline Street, hotel alterations and additions were made over time, including ultimately adding attic dormitory space to house the town's lifeguards in the 1960s. The enclosing of the porch, recorded in the c. 1911 view at top right, was made more elaborate by 1941 (the date of the postcard at the bottom of the image) and had additional third-floor rooms projecting forward.

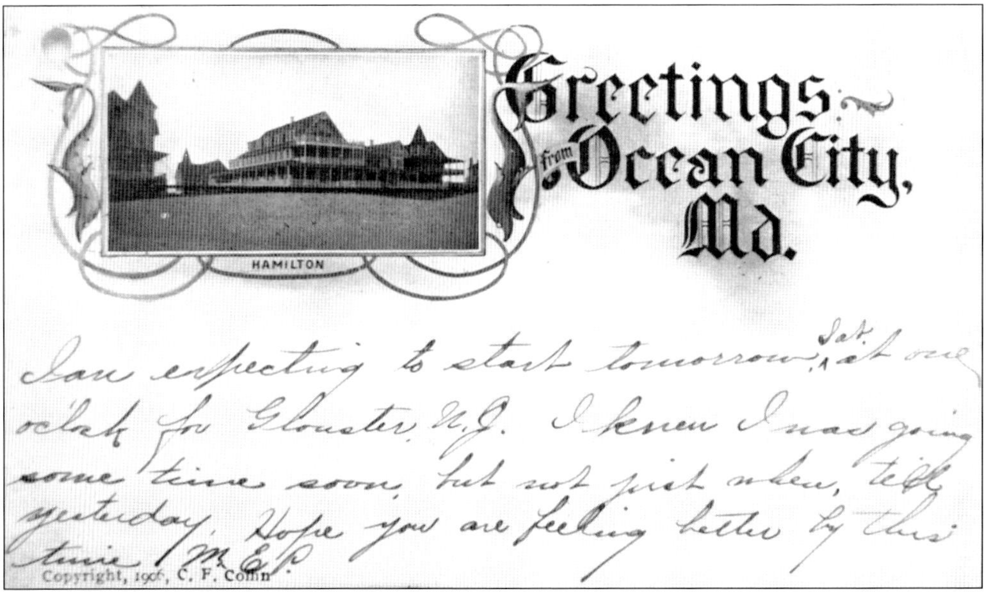

A 1906 postcard by C.F. Coffin includes an insert rich with historic imagery. At the center is the Hamilton Hotel with St. Paul's Episcopal Church behind it. The turret at the left edge of the photograph is part of the Breakers Hotel (see page 40), and the turreted cottage at right is the Mervue Cottage before the alterations visible in the later image of the Sea View Hotel (see page 43).

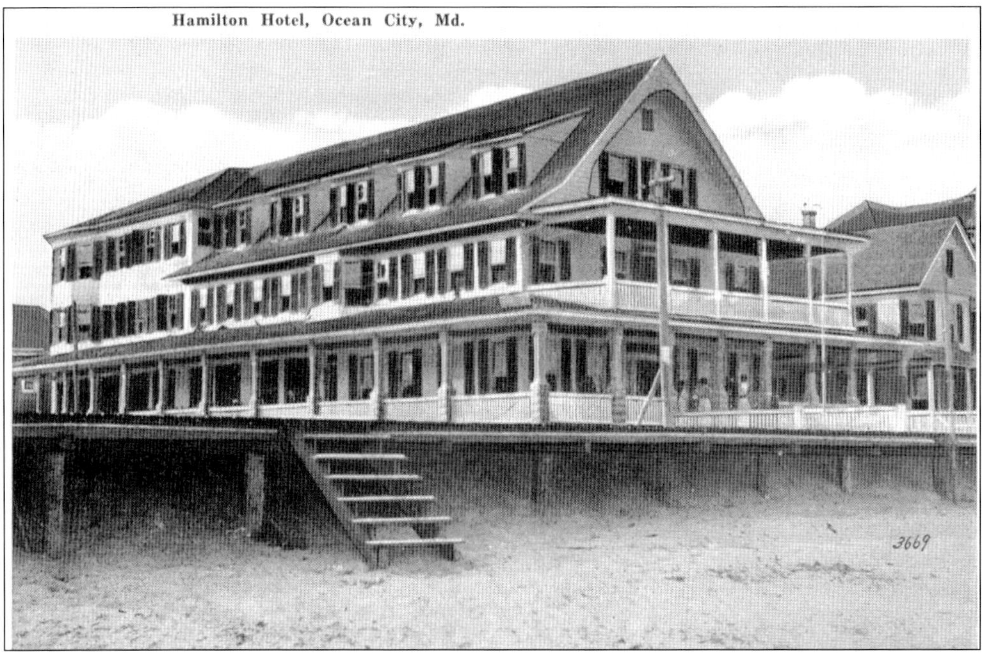

The Hamilton Cottage dates to sometime between 1897 and 1904 (perhaps 1901). By 1911, a wing projecting north from the rear of the cottage was tucked behind the cottage next door. This view, probably taken before the 1920s, shows a west expansion of upper floors and individual shed dormers for five paired south windows. There are two levels of east porches, as shown in the inset on the postcard at the top of this page.

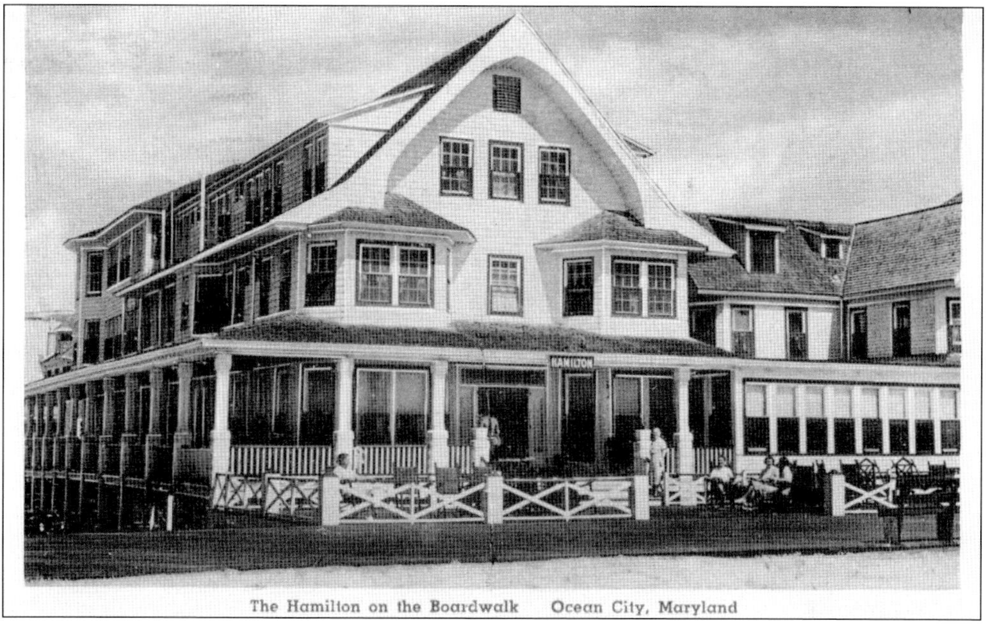

By 1945 (the year this postcard by R.D. Driscoll is postmarked), an elaborate array of window bays and dormers enriched the cottage hotel, creating a more picturesque composition. The southeast view shows two prominent oceanfront bays supporting the original flaring arch under the main gable, while the paired window dormers of the south range are now joined in a continuous shed dormer.

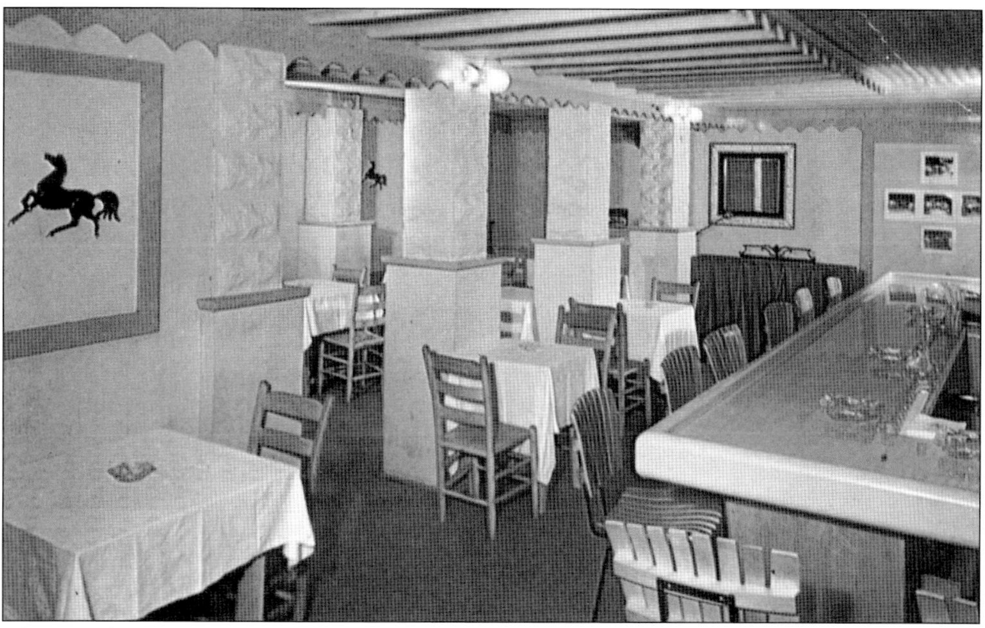

The Hamilton Hotel featured an undercroft café called the Stall, which was crowded with closely spaced encased structural piers supporting the hotel. All along the Boardwalk, these below-deck areas were utilized as rental space for retail, restaurants, or occasionally extra sleeping accommodations, frequently with low ceilings. The Hamilton occupied the north corner of Third Street on the Boardwalk until it was lost to fire in 1969. Polynesian Condos now occupies the site.

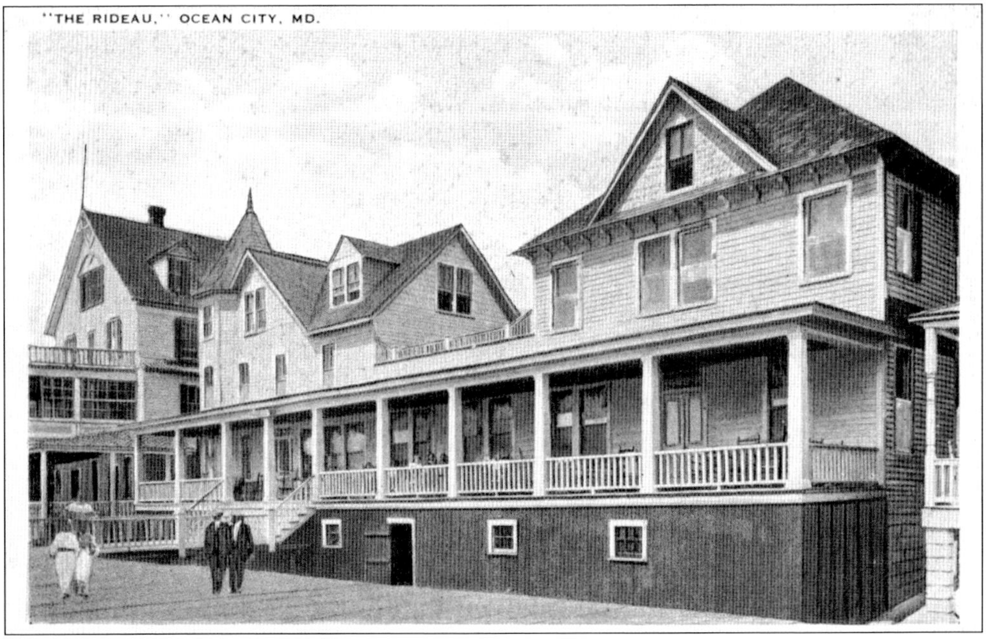

This view shows two Boardwalk cottages joined by a connecting porch to form the Hotel Rideau. At the left edge is the Mount Pleasant Hotel (see pages 32 and 33), which suffered a fire in 1970 that would also prove fateful to the Rideau when these two of its three buildings were also consumed by flames, and water damage was so extensive as to require demolition of all three structures (along with the Mount Pleasant).

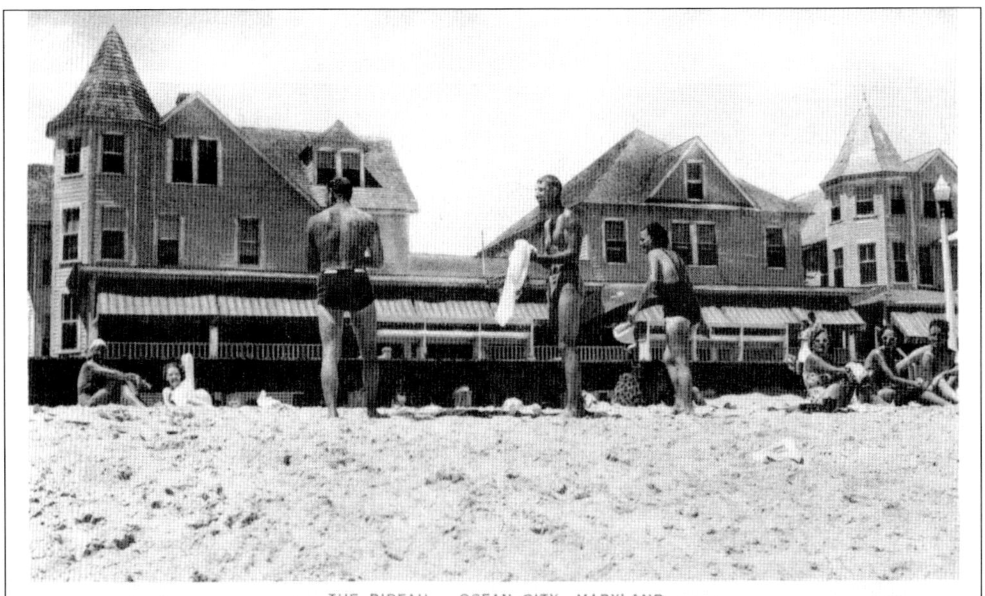

The cottage that would form the historic first structure of the future Hotel Rideau was built prior to 1897. By 1904, two flanking cottages had been built, with the Mount Pleasant Hotel and a pre-1897 cottage to the south and the Ocean Swell Cottage to the north—six structures in all. By 1911, the three cottages between the Mount Pleasant and Ocean Swell were named the Virginia, Rideau, and Linmar (see pages 30 and 31).

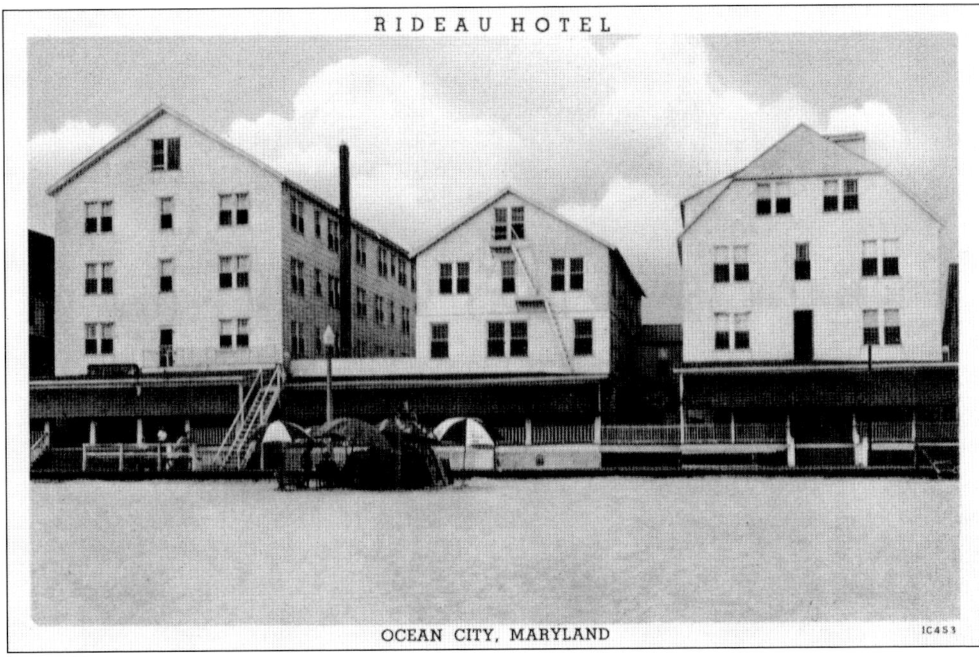

The cottages on the bottom of page 48—(left to right) the Virginia, the Rideau, and the turret of the Linmar—comprised the three joined structures of the Hotel Rideau, which had been expanded and restyled, as shown here, by the time of the fire that destroyed all three in 1970. The owner (the Birch family) immediately built six Boardwalk stores and a restaurant in 1971 and the new 48-room Rideau Motor Inn in 1972 (see page 131).

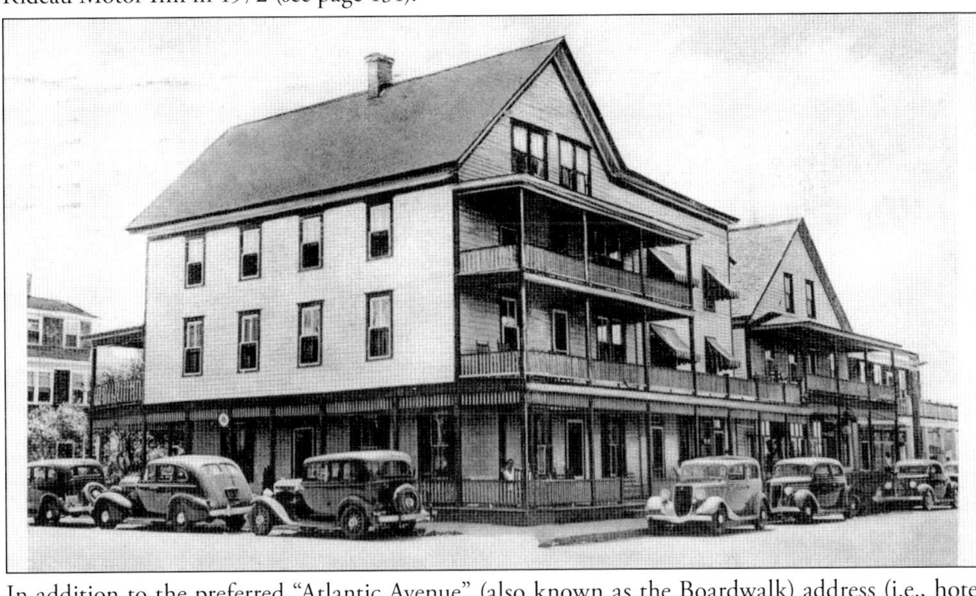

In addition to the preferred "Atlantic Avenue" (also known as the Boardwalk) address (i.e., hotel sites offering ocean views, sea-breezy porches, and direct access to the promenade and beach), side streets and the major north–south thoroughfare Baltimore Avenue were also eventually lined with cottages, inns, and small hotels. As early as 1897, two cottages stood on the southeast corner of Baltimore Avenue and Dorchester Street, with the corner building (possibly both buildings) identified as the Dennis Hotel.

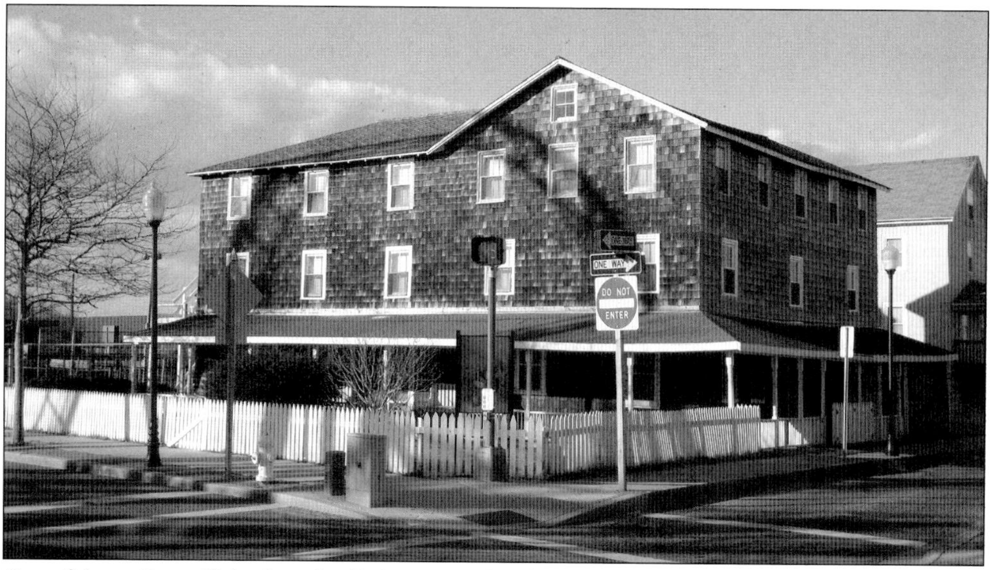

One of the earliest off-the-Boardwalk downtown hotels is the c. 1895 Henry Hotel, formerly Henry's Colored Hotel. Shingle-clad and with a rare surviving picket fence enclosing part of the yard, the extant hotel provided accommodations for Black resort visitors during off-season "Negro excursion days" (Erica Murphy, "The Brightside: Henry's Hotel, WMDT, February 19, 2019, www.wmdt.com/2019/02/the-brightside-henrys-hotel) and for celebrities such as Cab Calloway, Duke Ellington, Lionel Hampton, Louis Armstrong, and Ella Fitzgerald, who performed in town. (RMC.)

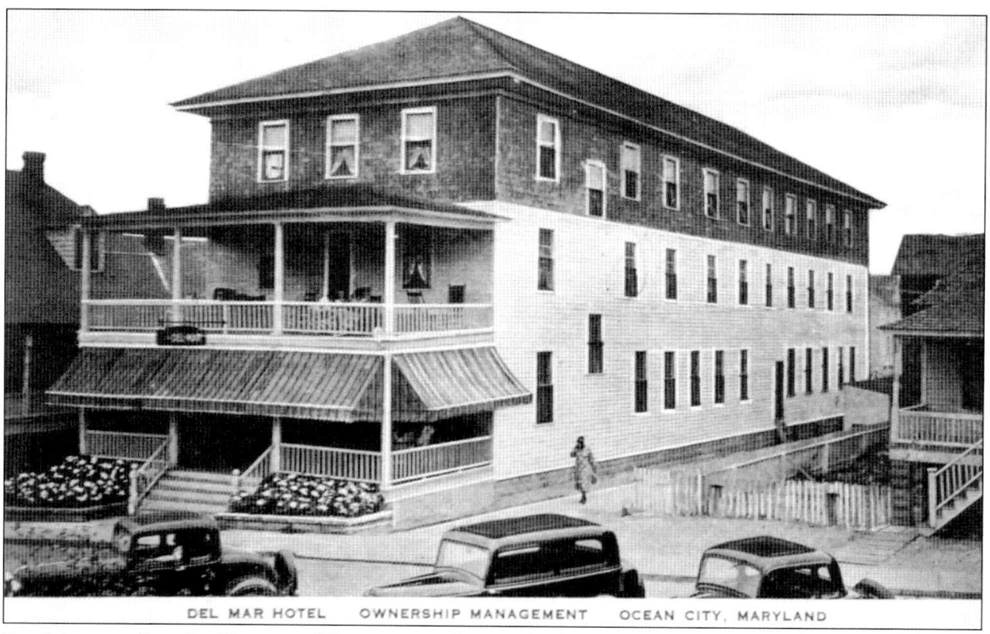

For 50 years after the Henry and Dennis Hotels were built near the end of the 19th century, shingle-clad hotels and inns of simple rectangular form were erected on and off Baltimore Avenue as Ocean City grew northward. The Delmar Hotel, erected between 1911 and 1921 on North Division Street, was sited across from the Hotel Oceanic and midblock between the Boardwalk and Baltimore Avenue. Today, the site is a parking lot.

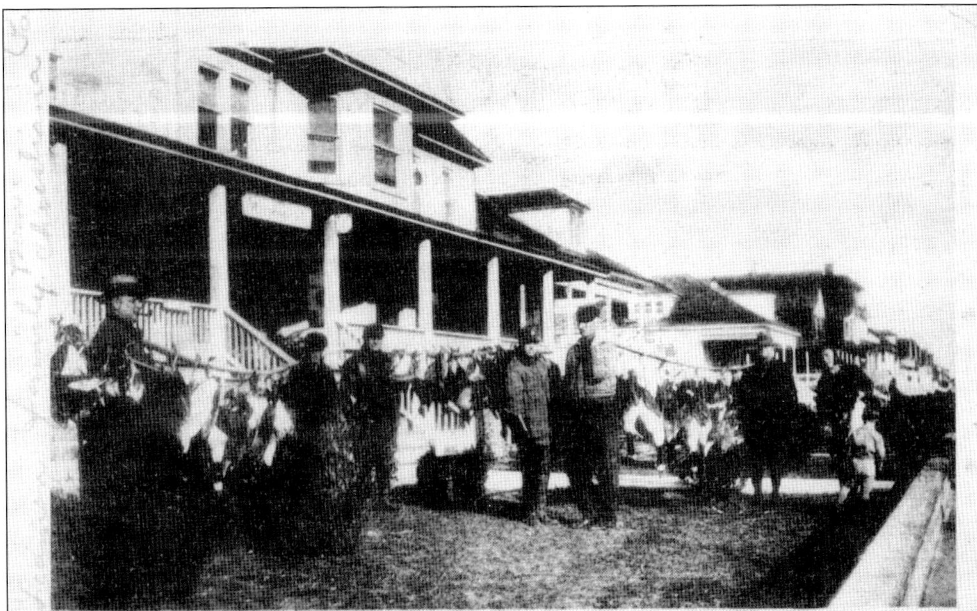

Winter Guests at the DEL-MAR-VA Hotel After a Day's Gunning Trip, Ocean City, Md.

The blocks farther north on Baltimore Avenue would become lined with picturesque cottages; the earliest was the Gables (pre-1897), located next to the Presbyterian church. By 1911, the west side (south of First Street) was fully occupied with eight cottages, each with large east-facing porches. At the north end was the New Avelon Hotel (renamed the Del-Mar-Va Hotel in 1926; see page 27). Operating on the American plan, the Del-Mar-Va's dining room enjoyed a good reputation, even during hunting season, when much of the resort shut down. A few blocks farther north was the shingle-clad Monticello Hotel (1926–1927), with its popular Dinner Bell Restaurant, sited on Third Street opposite the shingle-clad Episcopal church. The Monticello was demolished in 1999 and later replaced by the Hotel Monte Carlo, and the Del-Mar-Va was razed in 2008 and 2009 and later replaced by the Sleep Inn (now Gateway Hotel).

38—Monticello Hotel and Dinner Bell Restaurant, Baltimore Avenue at Third Street, Ocean City, Maryland

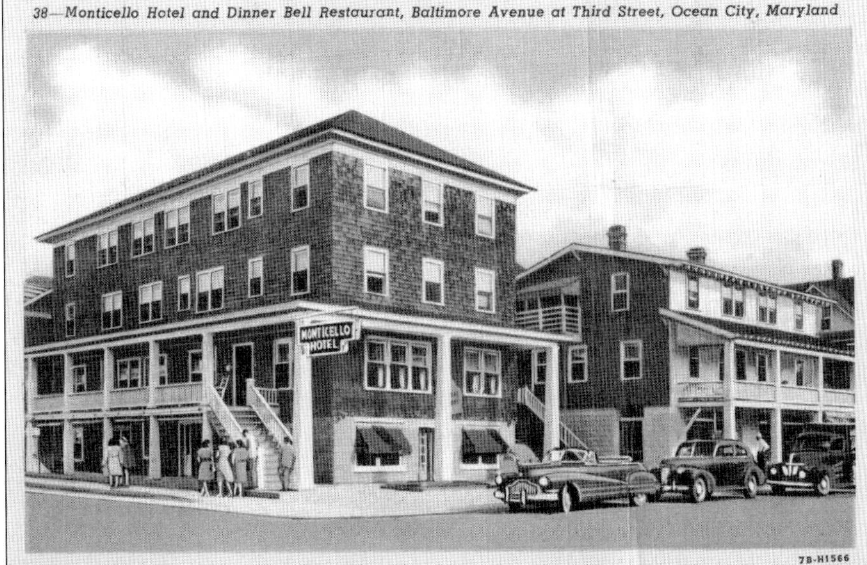

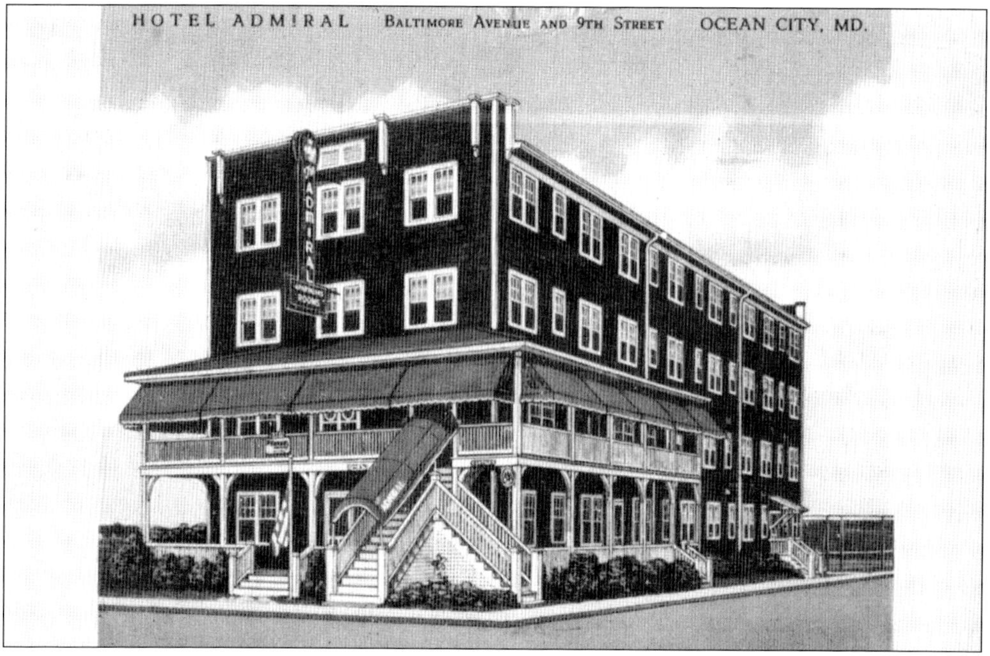

On opposite corners of Ninth Street and Baltimore Avenue are two shingle-surfaced inns from the 1930s: the Admiral Hotel (1937) and the Benson (a rooming house later renamed the Wellington)—both survive today. The Admiral advertised itself as the "Place of Happy Moments and Pleasant Memories." The hotel's unusual corner staircase accessing its main public entry extends exterior flights of steps from both front and side streets. Throughout the late 20th century, the hotel expanded with motel units behind it, extending the complex to Philadelphia Avenue. The Benson was owned by Mayor Hugh T. Cropper Jr., who annexed the land between Forty-First Street and the Delaware state line in 1965, significantly contributing to the development of Ocean City (see chapter four).

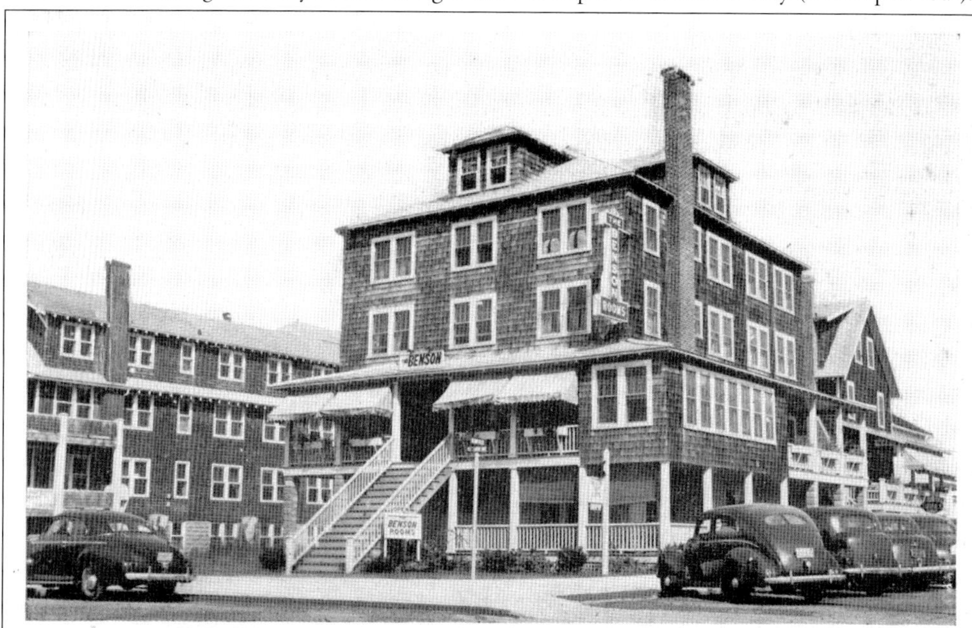

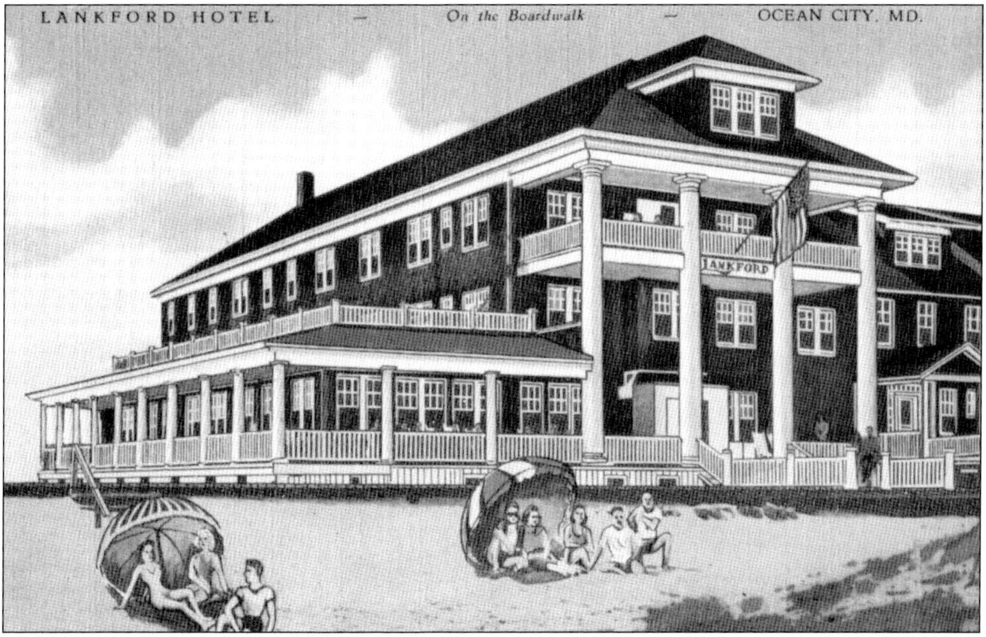

Hotel development continued apace on the Boardwalk, with major hotels built between Seventh and Fifteenth Streets from the 1920s to 1950s. The nobly porticoed Lankford Hotel was erected between Eighth and Ninth Streets by Mary B. Quillen and opened on June 27, 1924. Mary's niece Betty Frame and Betty's husband, Warren, acquired the hotel in 1962 just four days before the Ash Wednesday storm that filled the undercroft of the hotel with sand and wreaked havoc citywide. The Frames remodeled the hotel, built a retail and apartment block extending to Eighth Street, converted the hotel dining room to a cross-stitch and crafts shop, and filled the hotel lobby with antiques and wicker. Both the Lankford and adjacent Ayresbilt (a contemporary three-story apartment building to the north) are slated to be razed in 2023. (Below, RMC.)

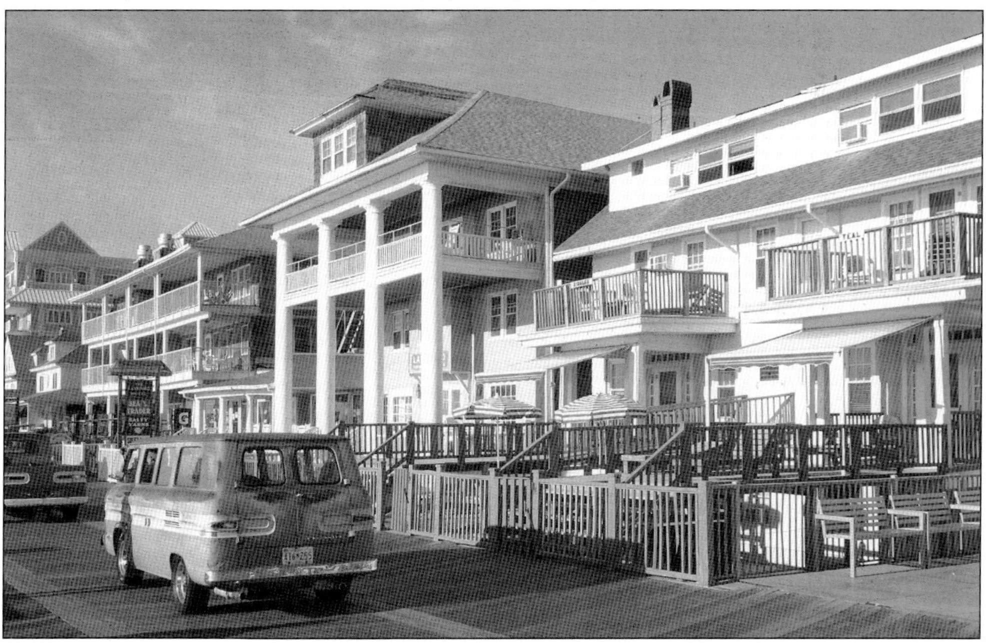

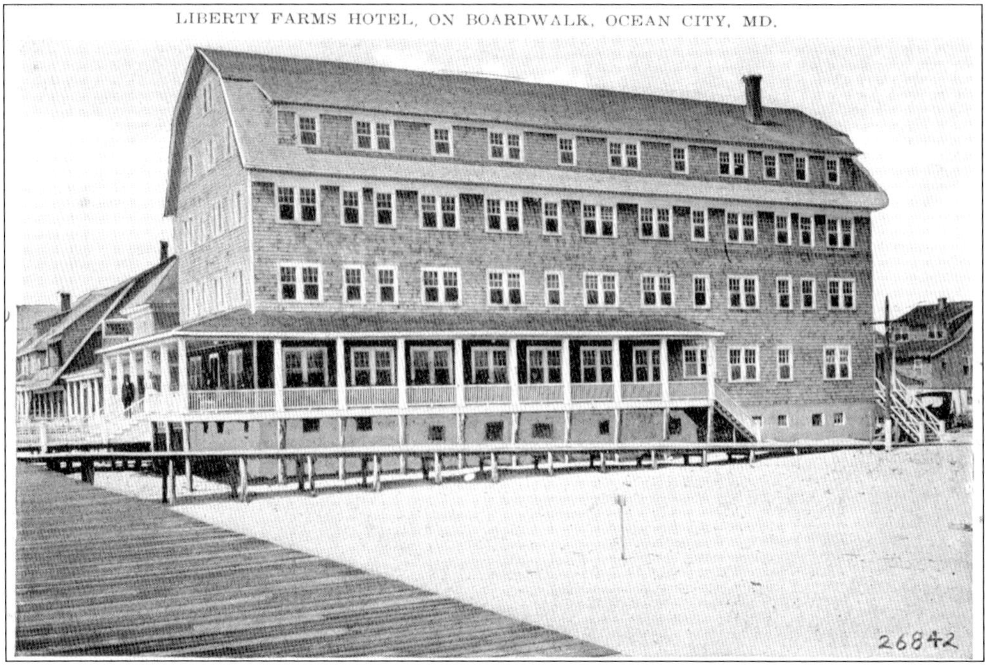

Built by the Bassett family, who owned Liberty Farms just south of nearby Berlin, the Liberty Farms Hotel featured the farm's fresh produce in its dining room. Gum trees, cultivated from Liberty Farms, were employed in the hotel's construction—an unusual material for frame buildings. According to George Hurley, who was in college when he worked with his father on the hotel's construction, "the gum turns almost to concrete over time." Opened in 1926, the hotel was renamed the Majestic in late 1929 and still operates on the Boardwalk at Seventh Street. The below postcard is postmarked 1938.

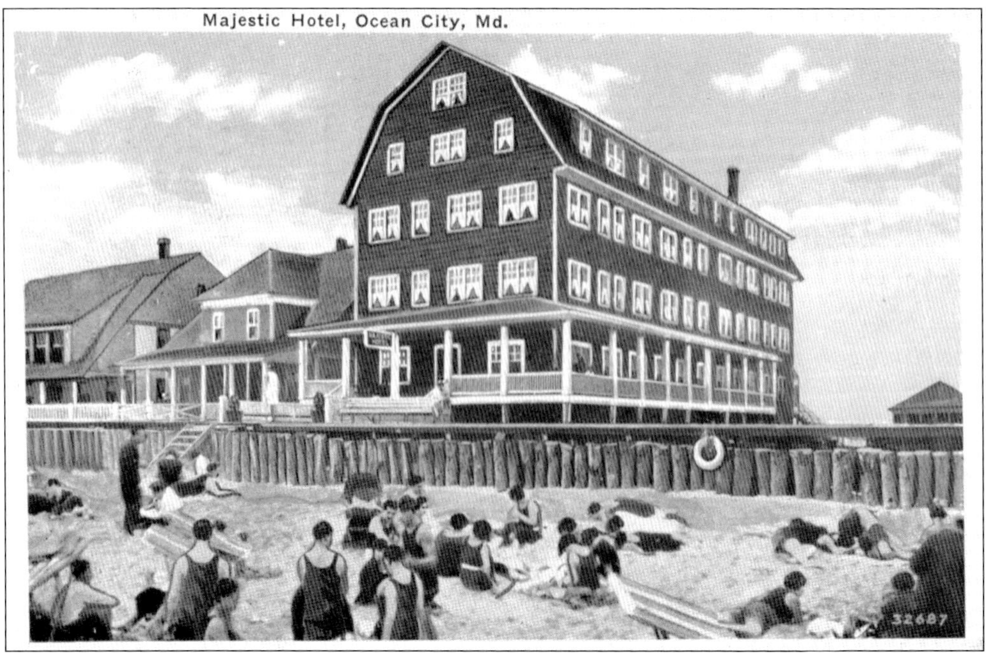

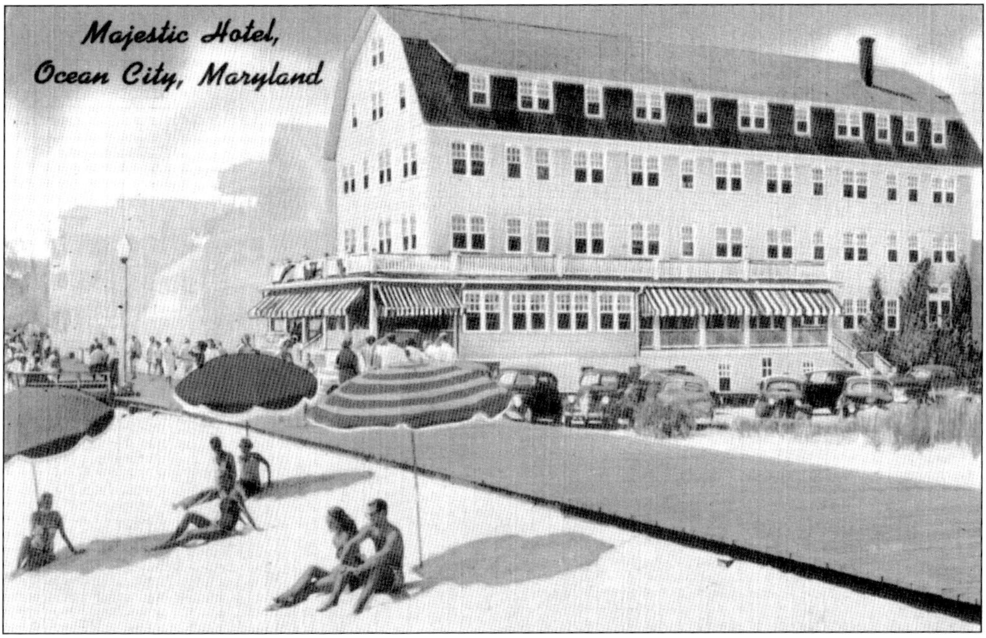

The Majestic Hotel changed little over time. In the 1950s, its north verandah along Seventh Street was first enclosed and then crowned with a full-height addition of rooms, which also replaced the continuous north shed dormer of the original hotel. The above postcard is postmarked 1951. The Majestic's popular coffeeshop operated for many years beneath the front porch and lobby, utilizing crawl space reclaimed from the undercroft—as so many hotels did—to maximize income-producing real estate. The hotel porch was expanded to the Boardwalk, creating additional space for rocking chairs and people-watching. The two-view postcard at right (with the swimming pool on the bottom) is postmarked 1971.

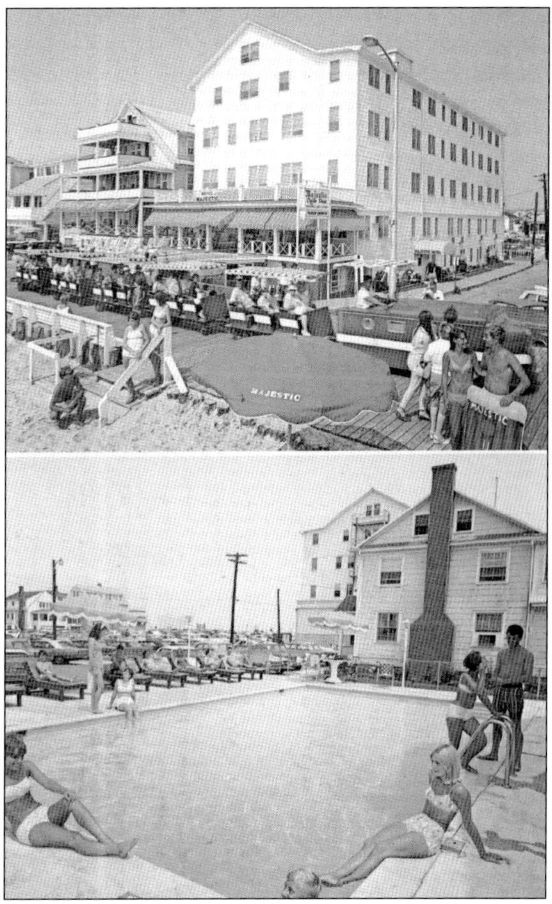

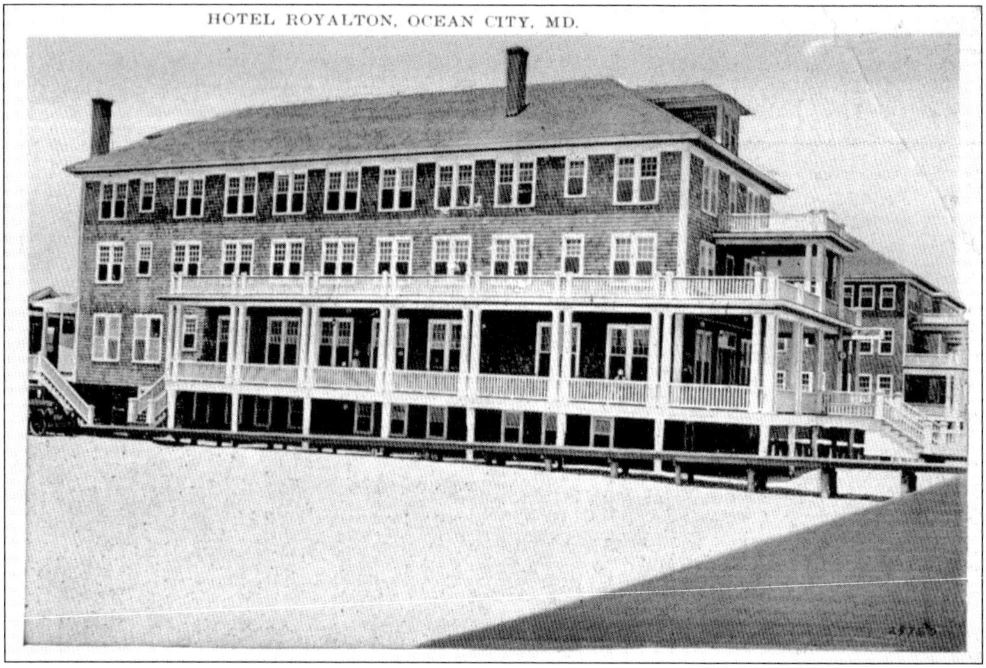

The Royalton (on Eleventh Street) and the Mayflower (on Twelfth Street) were built at approximately the same time (1926) as the Liberty Farms Hotel. The Royalton began as a 38-room shingle-clad building under a hipped roof with a front porch wrapped and extended most of the way down the south wall. A rhythm of paired piers and balusters organized the bays of the verandah, a second-floor porch above, and a smaller third-floor porch on the east front. The Royalton was built by Harry and Ethel Kelley, initially in partnership with Ethel's aunt and uncle, Minnie and John Lynch. In 1930, an identical building was erected and attached to the first one (below). That year, the Lynches sold their interest to Ethel and built the Commander Hotel (see pages 60 and 62–65). A third building was added in 1949 (see page 57).

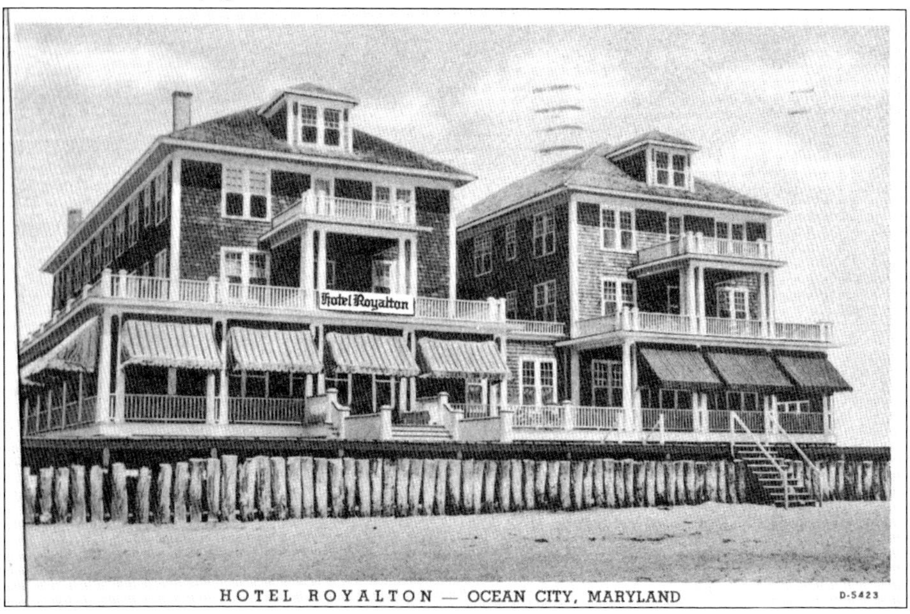

The first two buildings of the Royalton were subsequently split into two entities, the Hotel Royalton (in the left block in the below image) and the Journey's End Hotel (pictured at right and in the middle block in the below image). As the hotels began to deteriorate, a swarm of signage became affixed like barnacles across the hotel frontages, turning the Boardwalk streetscape into a junkyard of advertisement and chaotic commercialism. In 2016, the Royalton (south block) was carefully dismantled, and the following year, a postmodern pastiche of the historic hotel, with a rooftop indoor pool, was opened as the 57-unit Hotel Monte Carlo Oceanfront. The middle and north blocks of the Royalton threesome remain, although they are still overdressed in signage, and despite owner Ethel Kelley's reputation for elegance at the original Royalton, the northern block now houses the more rowdy and indelicately named Bad Ass Café and Brass Balls Saloon.

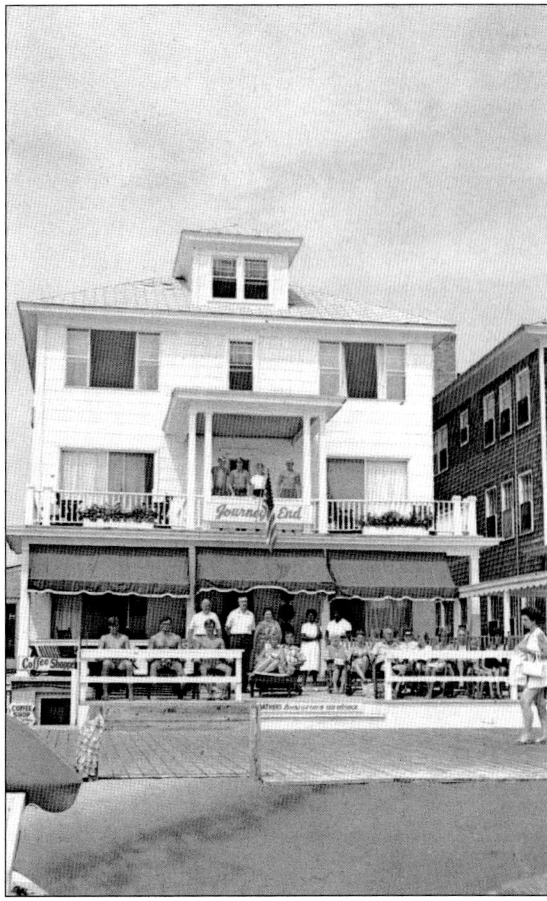

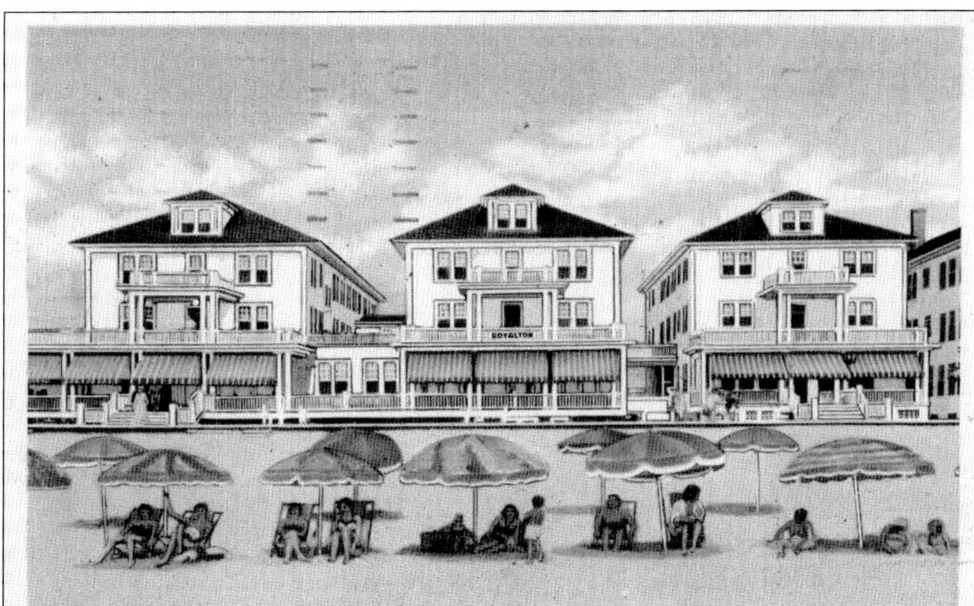

HOTEL ROYALTON — OCEAN CITY, MARYLAND 9B-H1555

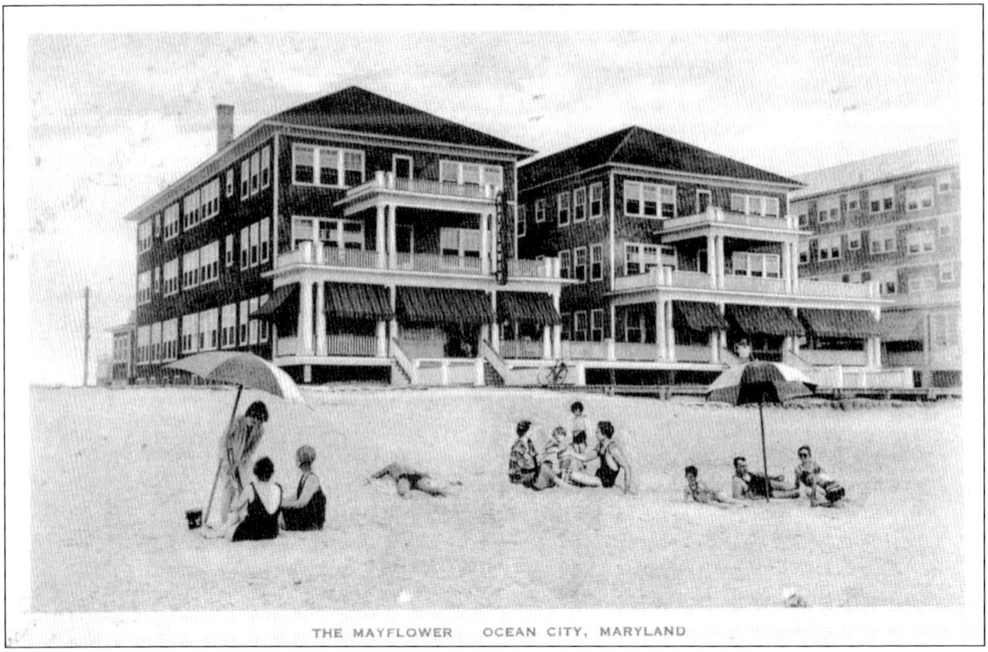

Located in the same block along the Boardwalk and contemporary with the 1926 first phase of the Hotel Royalton was the Mayflower Hotel at the southeast corner of Twelfth Street. Similarly organized in two building blocks under hipped roofs, the Mayflower was surfaced in shingles, featured oceanfront porches with paired piers and tightly spaced balusters, and—like the Royalton—capped the outdoor spaces with a narrower second-floor porch. Oceanfront six-over-six windows were grouped in a 3-1-3 pattern. The above postcard, postmarked 1934, shows a vacant lot to the left of the hotel, which was later filled with the third unit of the Royalton (see page 57); the below postcard was postmarked 1960 and shows the hotel little changed. However, after 60 years of existence, the Mayflower was damaged in a storm and razed in 1987, then replaced by the Howard Johnson Oceanfront Plaza.

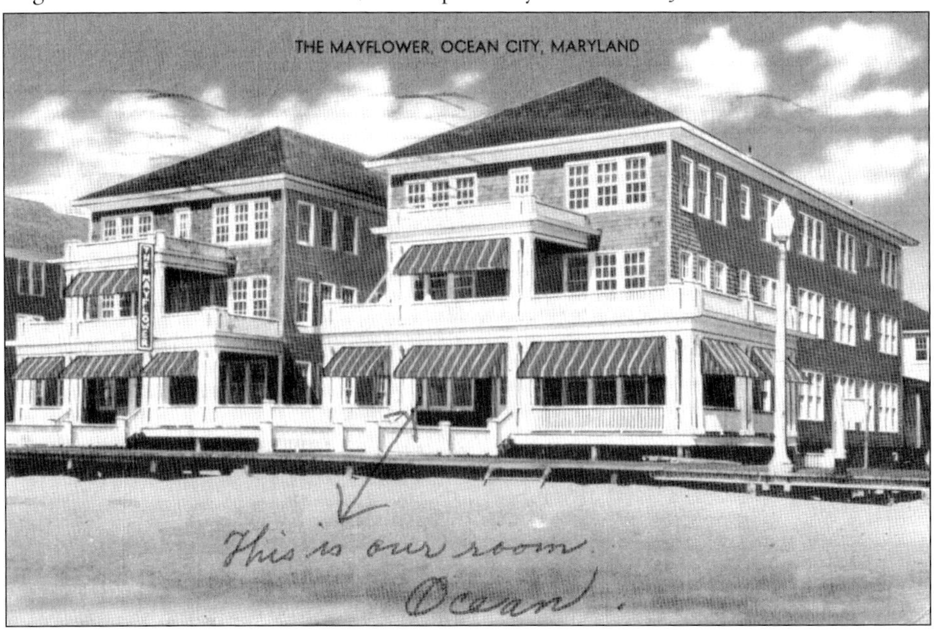

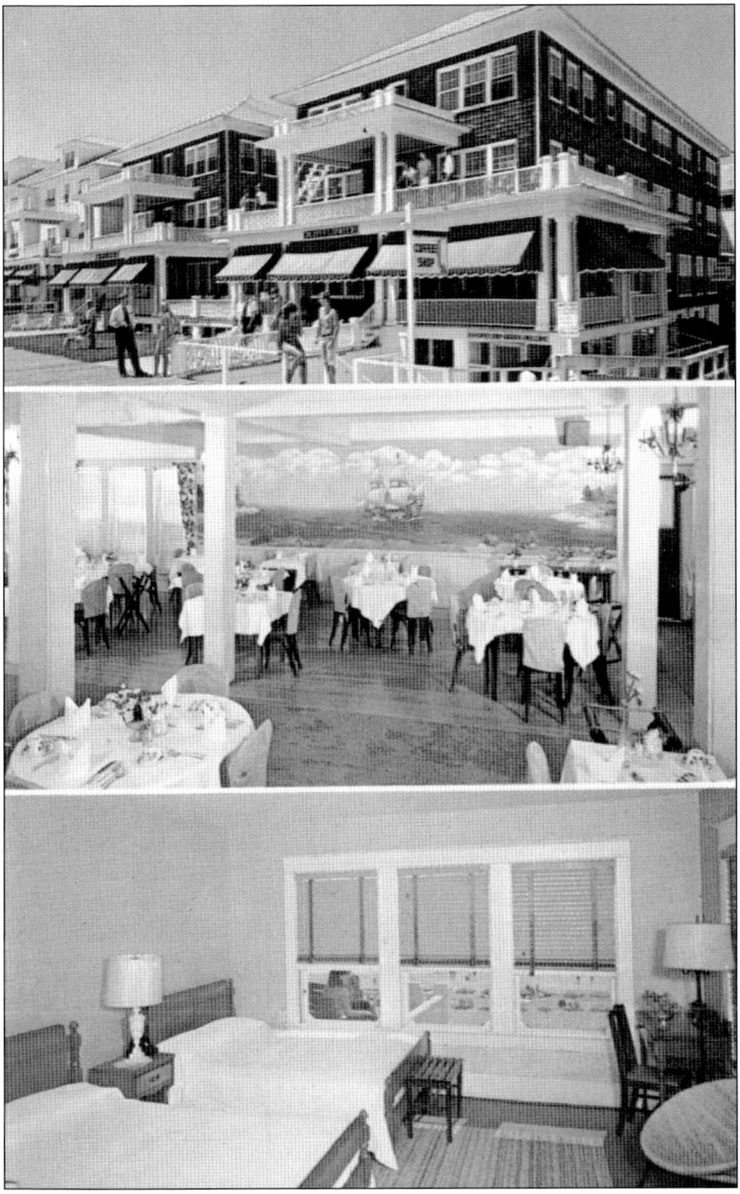

Postcard publishers often combined two or three views in a single card, as in this one from the 1950s showing the Mayflower (top) with the 1949 second unit of the Hotel Royalton in the distance. In the middle is the Mayflower hotel dining room, and the bottom part of the card shows an oceanfront room with a triple window to maximize ocean breezes. The Mayflower hotel's American plan offered breakfast and dinner in its dining room, and the Jo Mar Gift Shop was a favorite for decades, selling seashells, driftwood items, and souvenirs. When the Royalton and Mayflower were built on beachfront lots north of Eleventh Street in the 1920s, there was no organized lifeguard system in place anywhere on the beach. The Ocean City Beach Patrol (OCBP) was not established until 1930, and the few lifeguards hired during the early 1930s were watching bathers farther south. When Robert S. Craig was hired by the OCBP in 1935, he often took over Harry Kelley's beach stand, because the future mayor was frequently called off the beach to help his mother at the Royalton. Kelley served as OCBP captain in 1936 and 1937; Craig captained from 1946 to 1987.

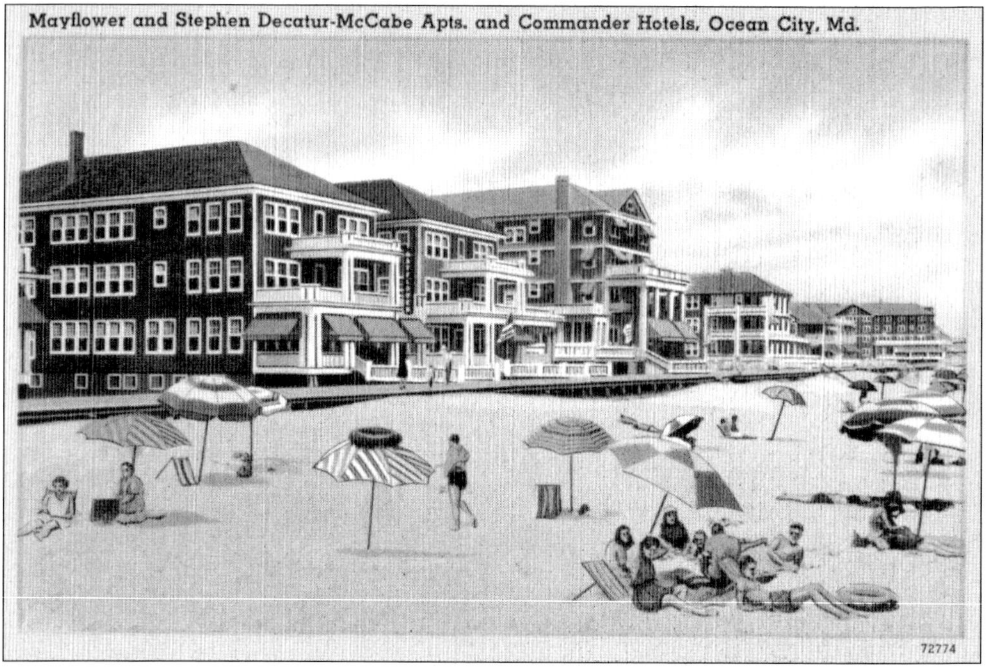

Together, these postcards show the extent of northern development along the Boardwalk during the 1920s and 1930s. The above postcard records the vista from (left to right) the Mayflower and Stephen Decatur Hotel to the McCabe Apartments and, in the far distance, the first (1930) block of the Commander Hotel. The 1940 postcard view below shows the Boardwalk from the columned Stephen Decatur Hotel (1930) porch in the foreground to the cubic George Washington Hotel (1930), with its rooftop pavilion, in the far distance. A common spatial setback from the Boardwalk, columnal porches, and shingle cladding remained the norm for early resort hotels. Ocean City had an aesthetic of weathered grey architecture and white trim mixed with wafts of Eastern Shore cooking smells, cool and salty ocean breezes, and resort holiday spirit—a character now largely lost except to nostalgic memory.

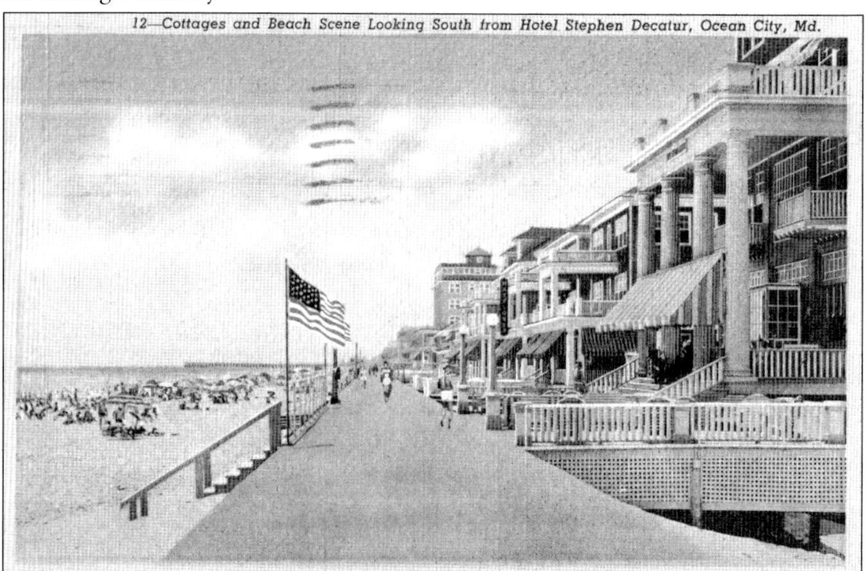

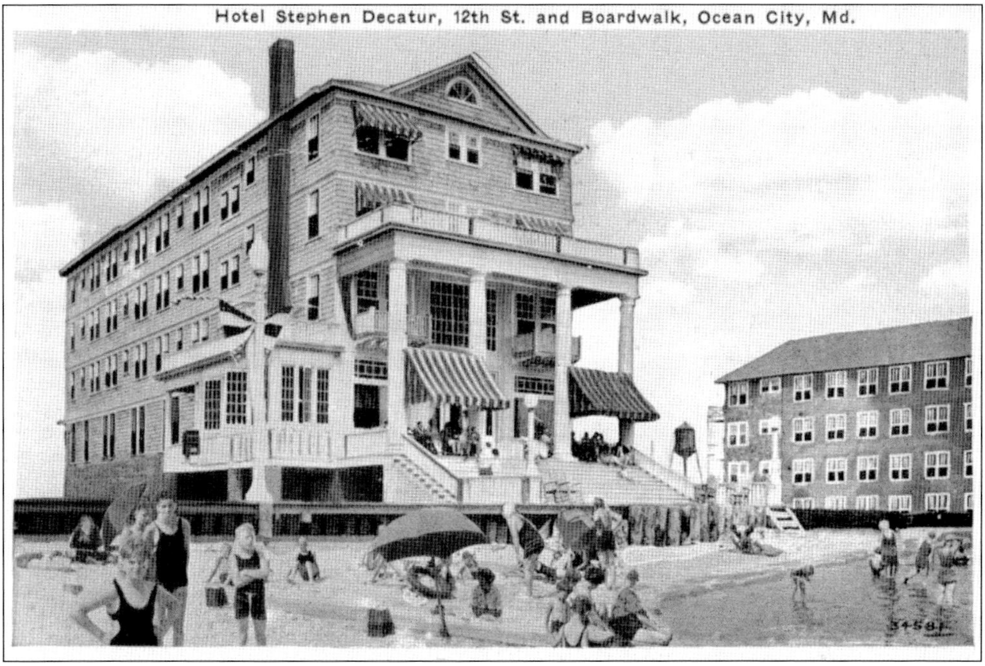

The Stephen Decatur Hotel (1930) was uptown and upscale, with a monumental front elevation ennobled by a wide staircase leading to four colossal Tuscan columns and featuring two large fireplaces in the lobby (note the brick chimney stack in these postcards, with the above card postmarked 1933). The southeast porch is enclosed, the roof of the portico offers a third-level balustraded deck, and individual balconies extend under the portico from second-floor oceanfront rooms. The Albertype Company image below is postmarked 1940 and shows pedestrians in stylish suits, hats, and shoes—a far cry from the fashion of today's Boardwalk perambulators. After the Stephen Decatur Hotel was damaged in a March 1962 storm, the hotel revived and reopened only to be demolished in 1977 and replaced by Decatur House Condos in 1978. The War of 1812 naval hero Stephen Decatur (1779–1820) was born in the nearby but no longer extant village of Sinepuxent, Maryland.

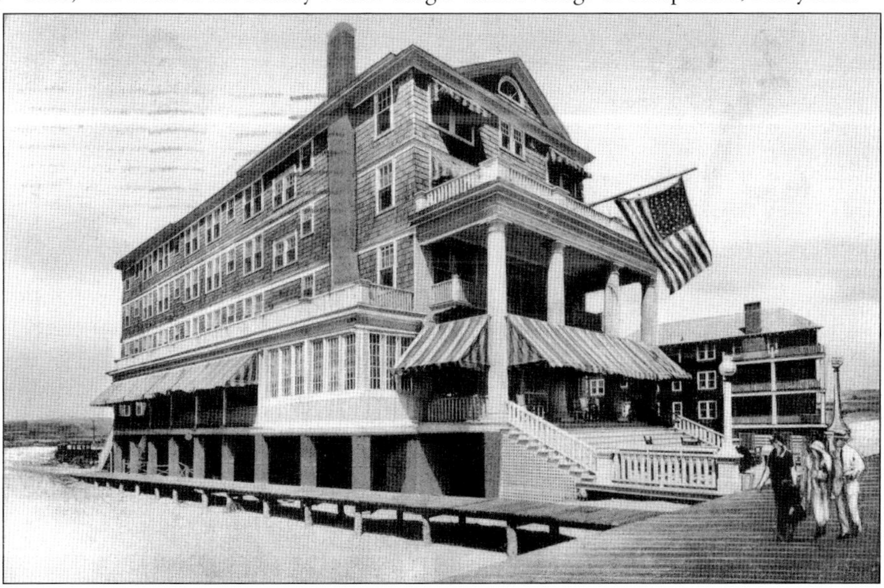

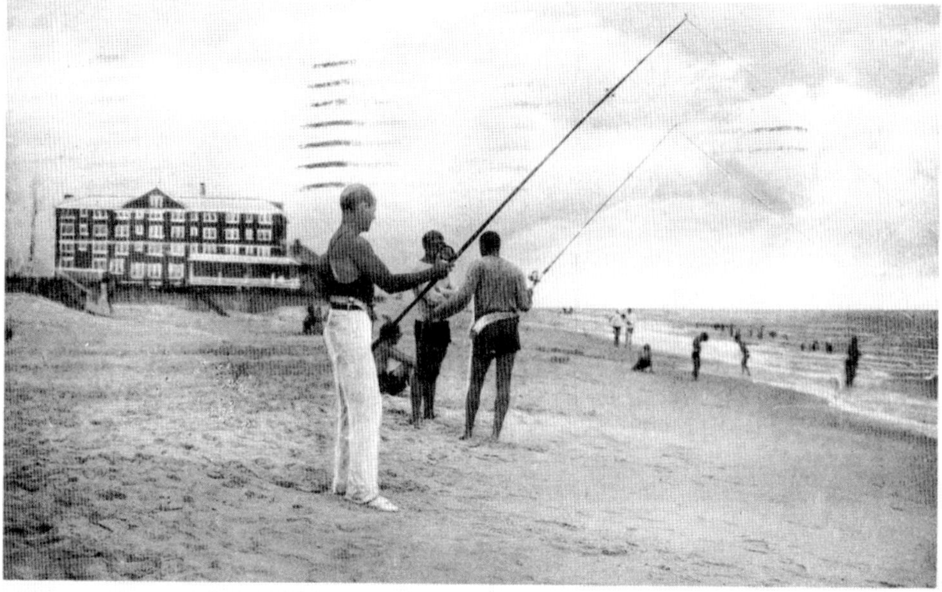

SURF CASTING AT COMMANDER HOTEL OCEAN CITY, MARYLAND

Siting the Commander Hotel on Fourteenth Street in 1930 appeared to be a leap of faith—the property was "way out of town," where only surf fishermen and seashell scavengers spent time among the dunes. Nevertheless, Minnie and John Lynch sold their half of the interest in the Royalton and, on Memorial Day 1930, opened the Commander Hotel's first unit of 62 rooms, for which they charged guests $95 per week (the price included three meals per day).

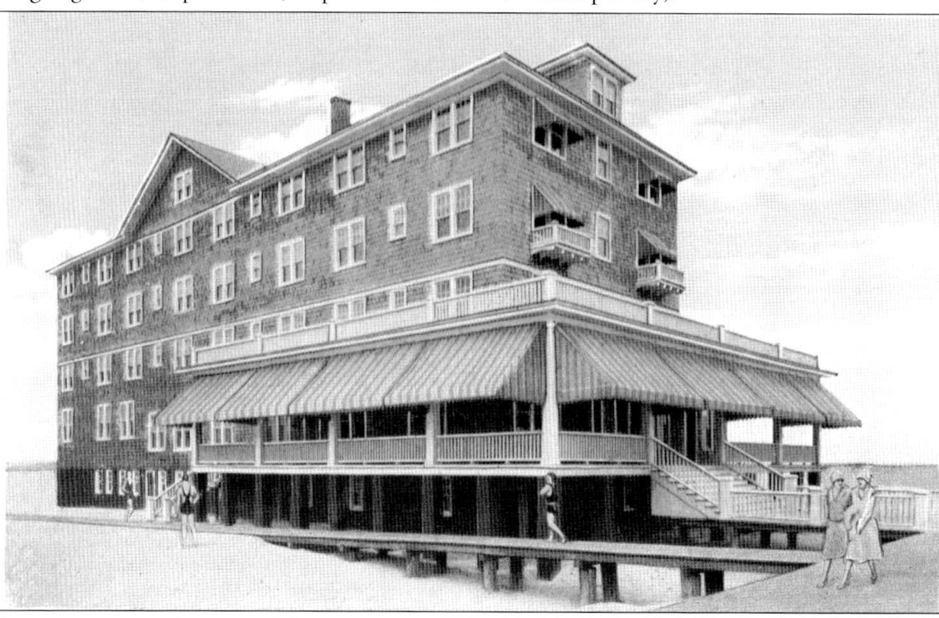

This 1931 Curt Teich postcard illustrates the first unit of Minnie and John Lynch's Commander Hotel, which was built on pilings and raised some eight or nine feet above the sand. It left barely enough headroom for what became one of the most unusual uses of hotel crawl space among Boardwalk hotels—the Commander Boardwalk Dinner Theater, which ran from 1979 to 1993 and featured local talent, including some who became future stars of stage and screen.

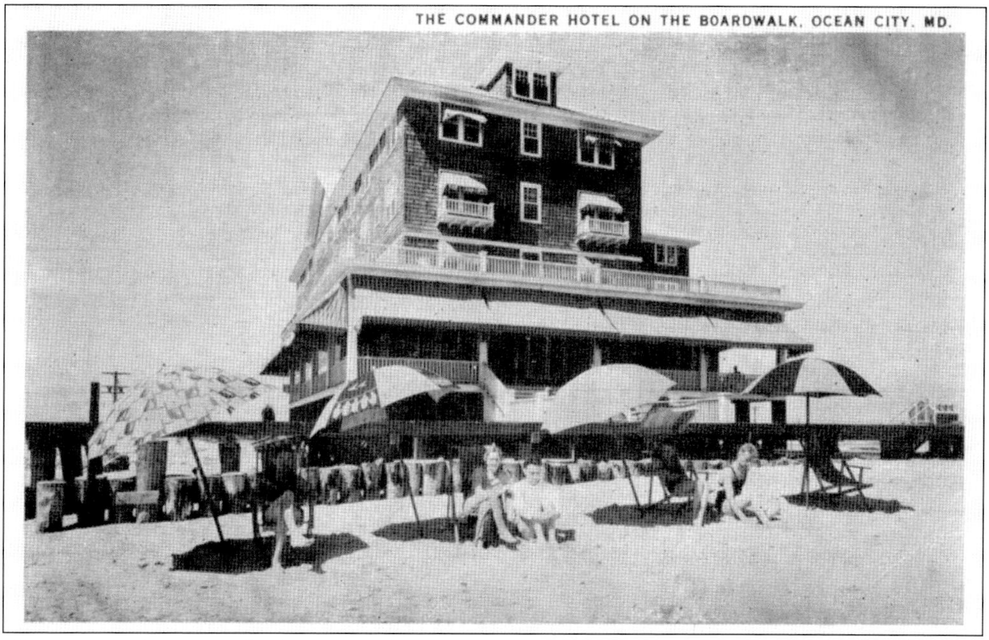

This postcard, postmarked 1933, with vacationers posed for publicity, conveyed that both the Boardwalk and the typical beach amenities of umbrellas and canvas-slung wood-frame chairs had arrived in even this desolate Fourteenth Street northern wasteland. Moreover, the Commander Hotel followed accepted design protocols with its broad wraparound verandah approached by wide welcoming steps, striped awnings, and an upper balustraded deck, above which are individual balconies for two third-story oceanfront rooms.

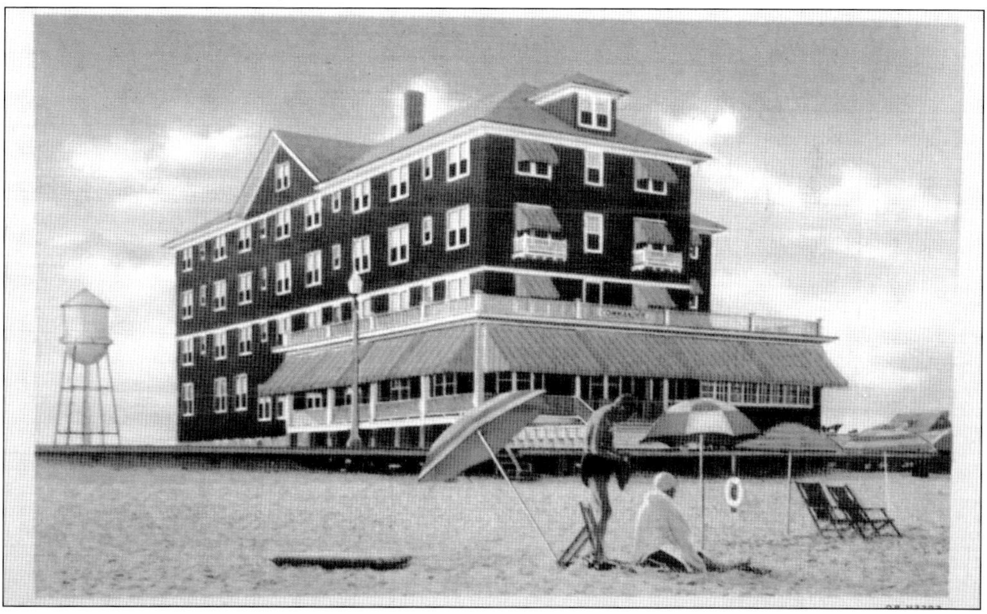

By 1940, the date of this postcard, the north end of the Commander Hotel's front porch had been enclosed, and a streetlight offered an evening glow for the Boardwalk. Within a few years, World War II protocols would require that each hotel room be equipped with blackout curtains for use at night in order to block all window lights and protect the hotel from enemy shelling from offshore submarines.

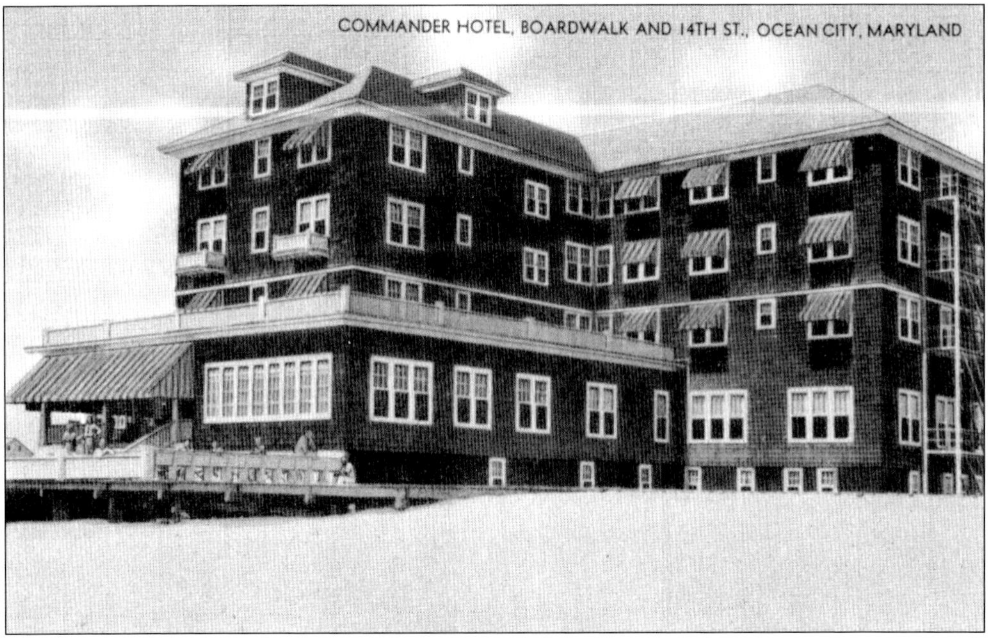

From the start, Minnie and John Lynch, the owners of the Commander Hotel, looked to the future. The hotel featured the city's first elevator and provided in-room telephone service. Its rear wing formed an L-plan (as shown above), anticipating a potential north wing, which the Lynches added during the prosperous postwar years. The 1950 postcard below illustrates this development, which included a more spacious dining room for up to 400 guests, including hotel guests on a modified American plan and locals who were familiar with the kitchen's reputation, the hotel dining room's Eastern Shore menu, and the waitstaff's elegant service. During the 1950s, the hotel sponsored Commander Clambakes, sometimes attracting up to 1,200 guests "who feasted on lobster, corn on the cob, and steamed clams cooked in a coal pit on the beach" (www.commanderhotel.com/our-history.htm).

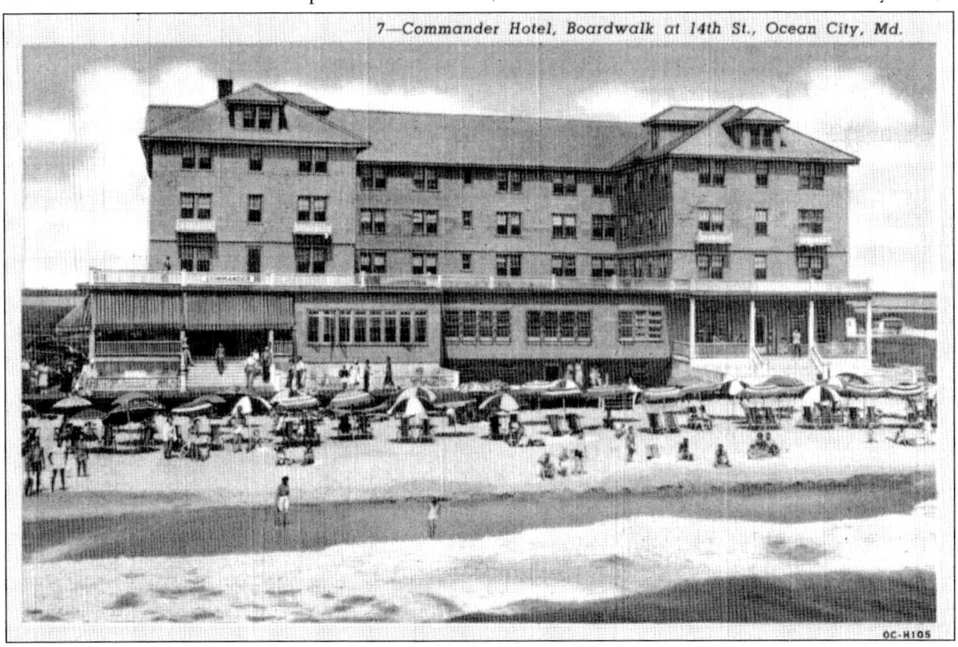

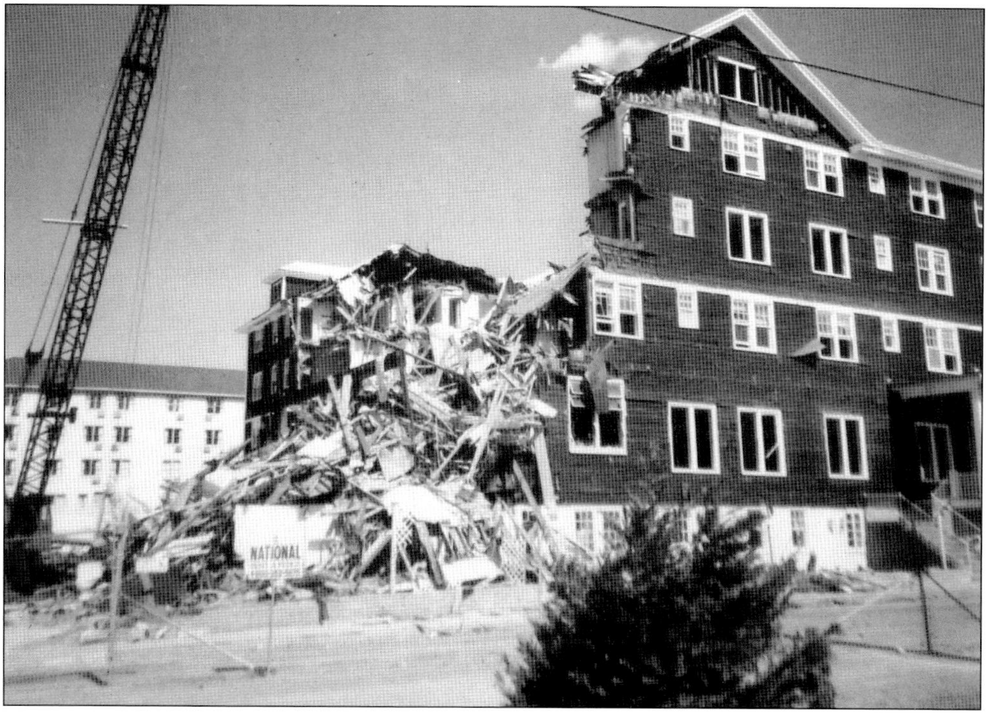

The 1960s saw the expansion of Ocean City's limits to the Delaware state line, and the shingle-clad Commander Hotel was soon considered old school, resident among buildings of a historic downtown. Even the youthful Motel Row of the 1950s and 1960s was being supplanted by condominium development and high-rises. Condo Row sprang up overnight in the 1970s way out in the dunes of Ninety-Fourth to 118th Street. Competing developments provided vacationers with more modern accommodations. In the spring of 1997, like so many shingle-clad "grand dames" before her, the 67-year-old Commander was demolished. In its place, in an innovative turn from east-facing frontality on the Boardwalk, the New Commander angled its stepped eight floors of balconied rooms to face southeast, opening the site and positioning low-scaled retail/restaurant amenities and pool terracing to the pedestrian scale of the Boardwalk. (Below, RMC.)

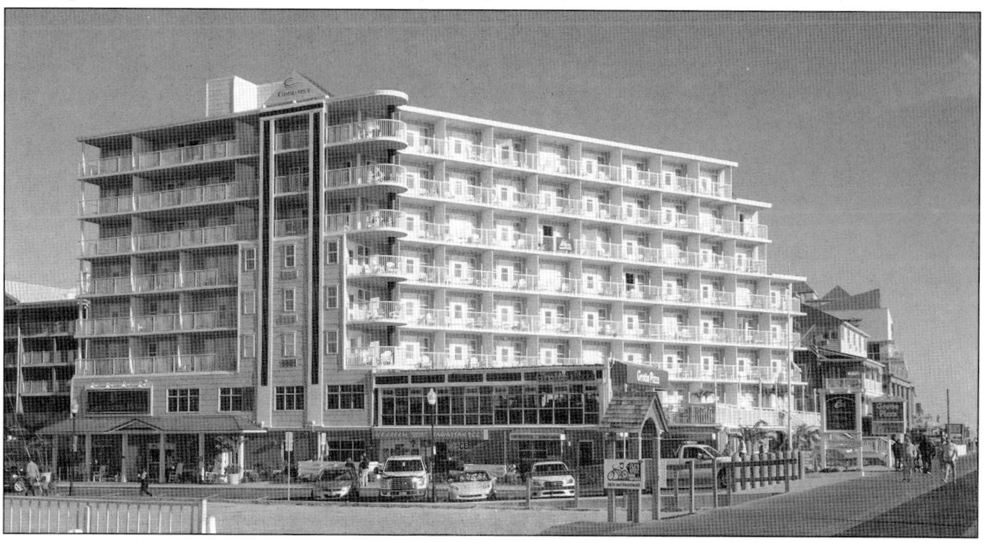

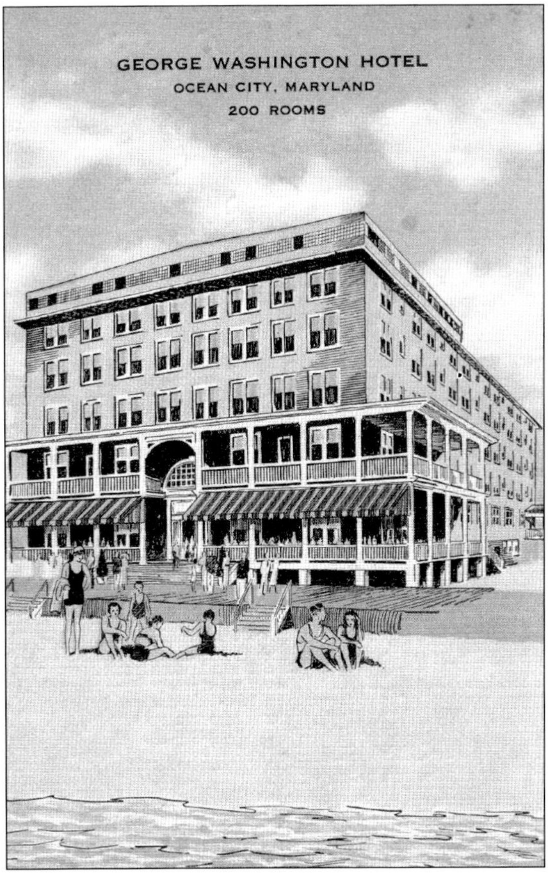

When the 120-room George Washington Hotel opened in 1931, it was the tallest building in Ocean City. When it was torn down in 1990, the *Washington Post* wrote that it is "believed to be the largest wooden structure in Maryland." Indeed, the eight-story hotel long served as a landmark for returning fishermen. Its rooftop ballroom was renowned. However, the hotel's only sprinklers were in the basement, and the city inspector found it in violation of numerous fire codes. The owners decided to replace the building with a steel-and-concrete structure of similar height containing 95 efficiencies and a pool. This would become a pattern of displacement repeated by hotel owners whose clients inexplicably came to the ocean to swim in a pool. Built in 1991, the new hotel, first named the Mirage, was eventually renamed the Americana (see page 148).

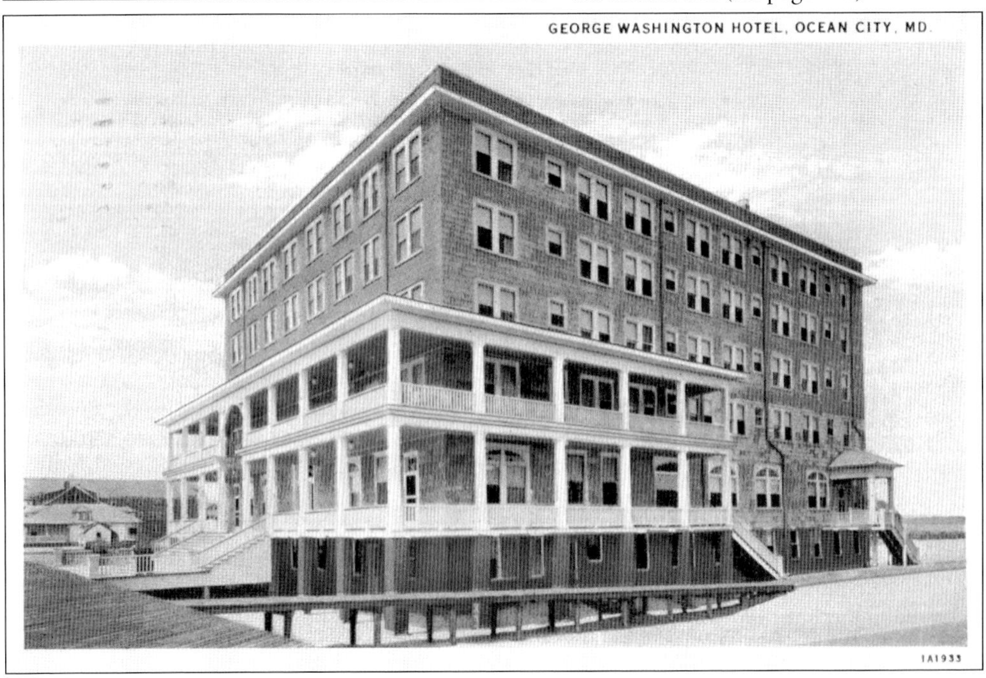

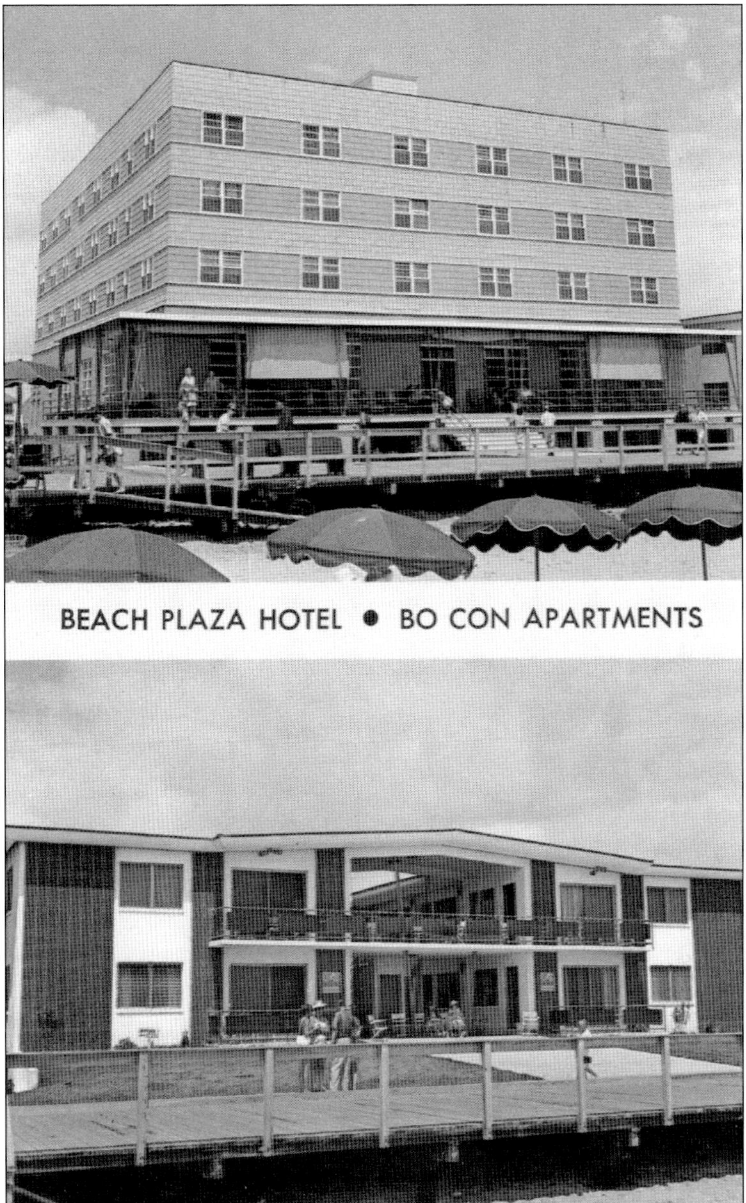

The 1953 Beach Plaza Hotel and adjacent 1959 Bo Con Apartments brought a Modern architectural aesthetic to Ocean City that had been unseen in any local building of its time with the exception of the 1949 Collins House at Baltimore and Surf Avenues. The style involved pipe columns and abstraction, evidenced at the hotel by the building's taut skin (promoting a volumetric, if also boxy, quality), the hotel's horizontal striping of aligned windows reminiscent of Modernist ribbon windows, and the hotel's insistent flat roof. The Bo Con's open courtyard and exposed, angular, minimalist pipe columns (splayed even wider than the hotel's porch columns) promoted an ambiguity and a simultaneity of interpenetrating interior and exterior space that is reminiscent of Cubism. The industrial materials, yellow brick, and unorthodox porch window lines and ship's railings at the hotel were self-conscious gestures of innovation and modernity. The hotel was built by Ethel Kelley, proprietor of the Royalton Hotel and mother of future outspoken town mayor Harry Kelley.

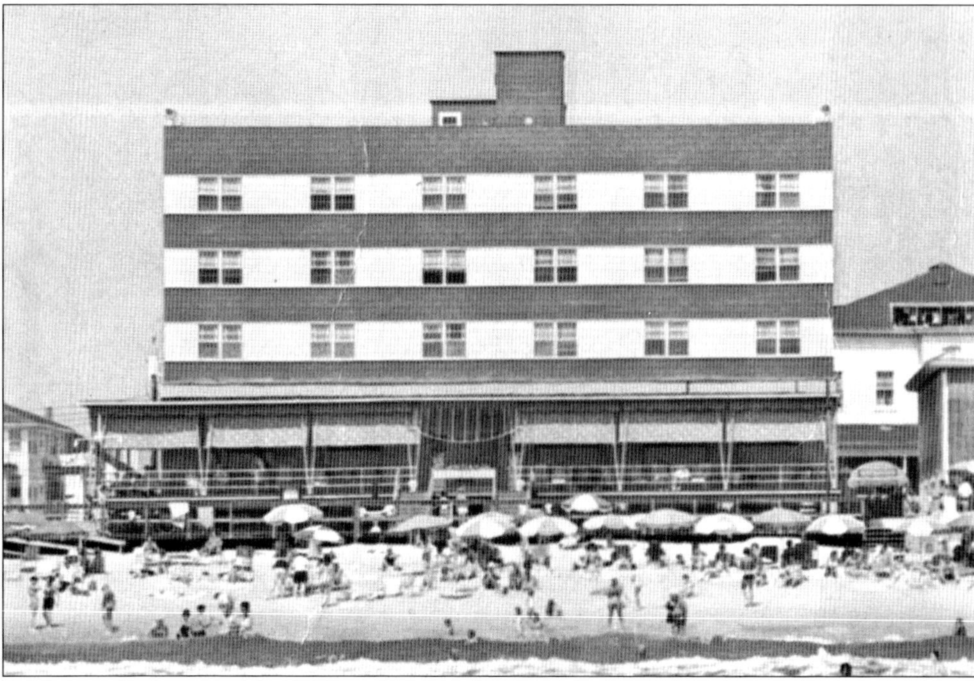

Transformations of the Beach Plaza Hotel have been dramatic since its original construction in 1953. Later views of the hotel show a reversal of dark and light tones in the horizontal composition. Originally, the horizontal bands above and below the window bands were lighter in tone but later turned dark green (above), with slightly projecting stringcourse trim for a shadow line unintended in the planarity of the original elevations. When the Phillips family purchased the hotel, Shirley Phillips waved her magic wand inside and turned the lobby and dining room into Victorian interiors accented by classical statues and chandeliers. In a gesture likely inspired by the Beach Plaza Hotel in Miami Beach, the exterior horizontal striping became vertical striping—a total pastiche in which the white vertical bands are actually applied horizontal clapboarding and the panels between windows are artificial fishtail shingles.

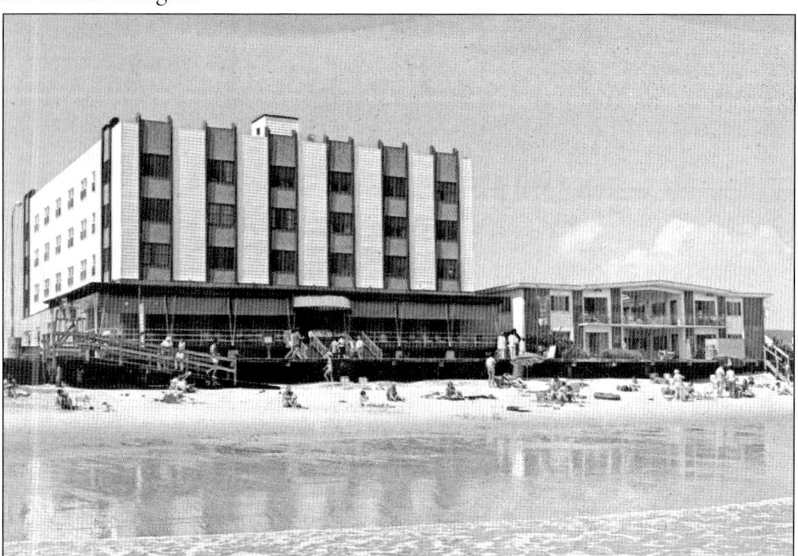

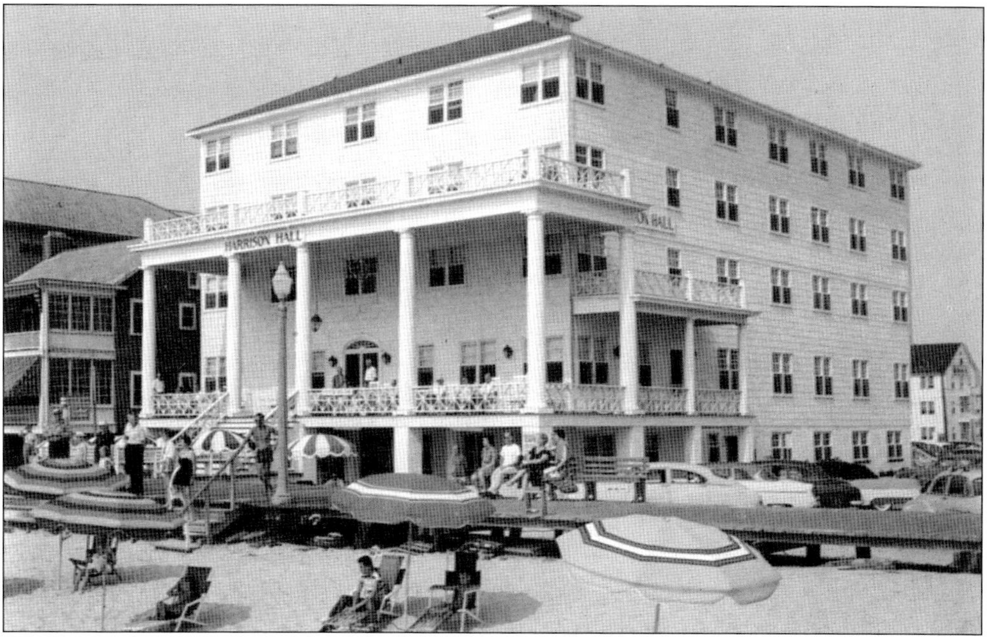

When the Boardwalk ended at Fifteenth Street, Harrison Hall, built in 1951, was considered "the last hotel"—a Colonial Revival with a Federal entry door, paired windows across upper floors, and a misinformed hybrid Tuscan portico (Tuscan is not fluted, as here, and Roman Doric has no base). The porch appears to suffer from a seismic shift to the north. The A-B-A-A rhythm of portico bays accommodates a shallow north porch, and Chinese Chippendale-inspired railings on several porch levels reference the 18th century, but the first-floor windows offer no balanced relationship to the windows above them. Alas, it is an architectural jumble claiming ancestry from Mount Vernon, perhaps, which has windows that display a similar mishmash. The below advertisement from the late 1960s illustrates expansion of the hotel to the west and advertises the new pool, which helped Harrison Hall compete with Motel Row to the north.

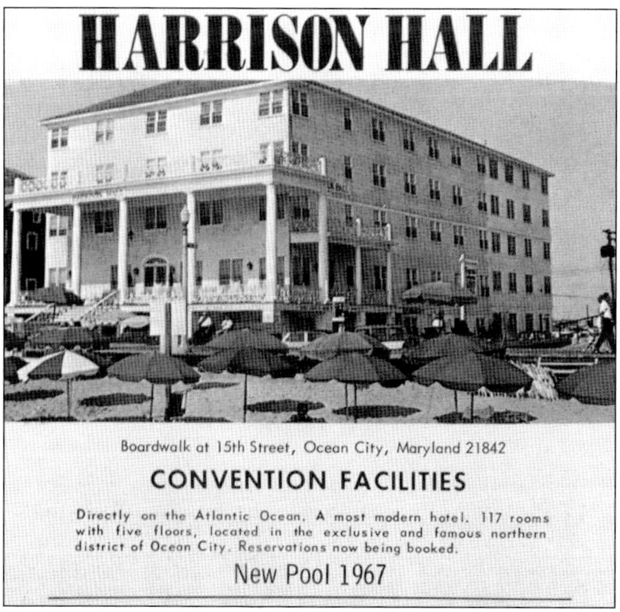

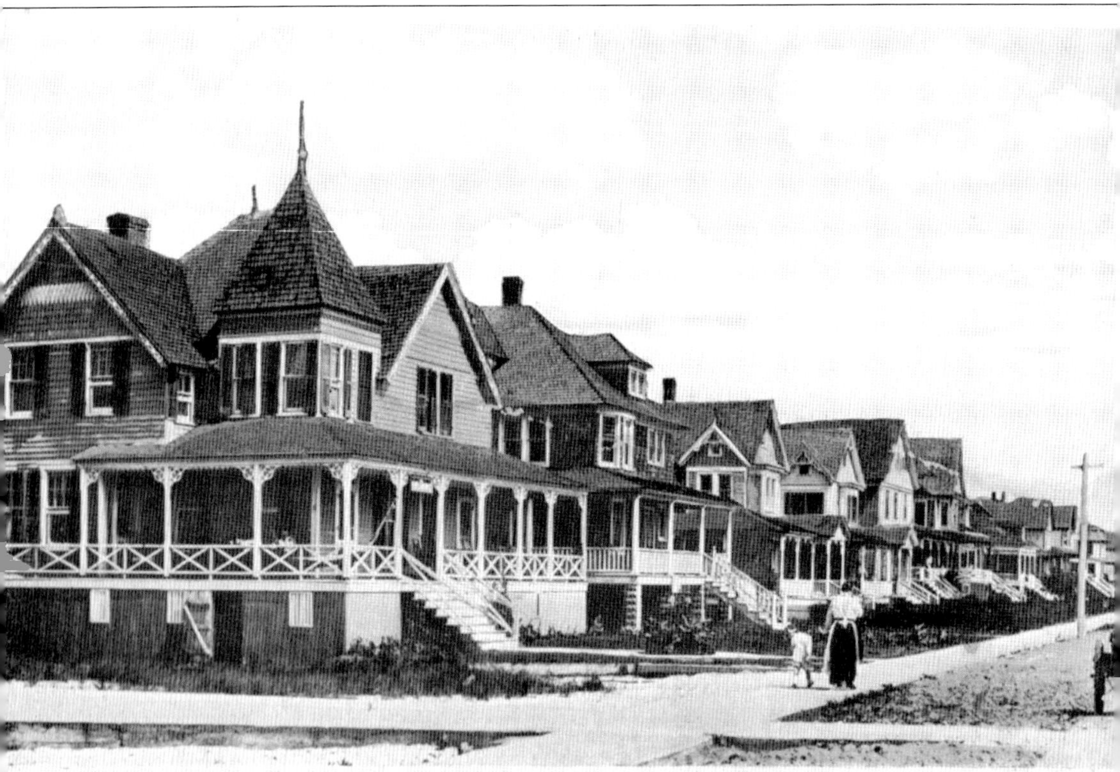

The cottages aligned on Baltimore Avenue north of the Presbyterian church at North Division Street created a picturesque streetscape of gables, porches, and stairs leading up to principal floors above potential storm surge levels. The first (left) and earliest was the Gables, from the 1890s, a Queen Anne turreted cottage with Eastlake porch-post ornament and scalloped shingles. Pedestrian walkways were boardwalks, and for many years, the street was sand and dirt.

Two

Cottages, Cabins, and Tourist Camps

In their classic study *The Motel in America*, historians John A. Jakle, Keith A. Sculle, and Jefferson S. Rogers outline the evolution of lodgings during the early automobile age as developing from auto camps to motels and evolving from mom-and-pop establishments to franchised national chain motels with distinctive phases and building types: tourist homes, cabin camps, cottage courts, and finally, motels conceived as motor courts, motor inns, and highway hotels. This typology began with tents and shacks and shifted to arrangements of the simplest vernacular domestic forms in early roadside collections of white cabins and cottages for tourists. Then, romantic, historicist, and even exotic styles were in evidence in early postwar motels until early chains like Holiday Inn and Howard Johnson became common and could be recognized by their standardized signage or appearance. The history of Ocean City's lodgings similarly includes examples of cabin camps and rows of cottages built in side yards and backyards of farms along the road. In addition, private homes and small cottages offered guest rooms to weekend tourists, especially when the town's hotels were filled.

Tourist homes were popular in the east, especially in resort areas where private guest rooms could supplement the limited hotel accommodation. In 1935, for example, *Hotel Monthly* reported that there were about 1,000 tourist homes licensed in Richmond, Virginia. Licensed or not, private cottages in Ocean City answered a need—on a busy summer weekend during the 1950s, tens of thousands of tourists filled the town's hotels to capacity, and it was not unusual for a homeowner to answer a knock on the front door to find a desperate individual or family, lacking reservations elsewhere, inquiring if the homeowner had a spare bedroom for the night. The homeowners' children were warned not to be noisy too early in the morning, because there was a Mr. Smith sleeping on the couch, and the rest of his family was in the guest room.

Cottages offered charm and intimacy not available in larger hotels. In Ocean City, the original town plan was interspersed with striking Queen Anne–styled houses on prominent sites. Properly preserved, they would be city landmarks today. A notable example was the 1905 Taylor house on Lot 54 of the original plat; it was razed in 2018. Some residences were built as guesthouses, such as Tarry-A-While, which was constructed in 1897 at 8 Dorchester Street and later moved to 108 Dorchester Street, where it continues to house ocean lifeguards. Some smaller hotels were run like more intimate guest cottages or boardinghouses.

At 4 Dorchester Street, just off the Boardwalk, a cottage built in 1897 was bought in 1902 by Elizabeth (Lizzie) Harper Hearne and converted to the Belmont Hotel. In 1910, Hearne built the Hearne next door, and for four generations, her female descendants owned and managed the Belmont-Hearne Hotel. Seventy-two years after the small hotel opened, it was described by Theresa Humphrey in a June 4, 1992, article in the *Washington Post* ("A Hotel Where Tradition Never Checked Out") as a "throwback" with a "musty lobby" whose hostess was a "55-year-old chain-smoking and sometimes ornery owner" named Kate Bunting, "who is determined to keep the hotel open." By 1992, the Belmont-Hearne was one of only two hotels in town still providing the American plan (a room rate that included breakfast and dinner). Bunting maintained a fading card file and pictures of guests, some of whom had been coming back to the hotel for 40 years. "You can't beat the woman's personality," remarked one repeat guest. "It's like visiting your aunt. It's the homey touch." Another guest, who had been returning to the hotel for 25 years, remarked of the homespun proprietor, "She *is* this hotel. I can't imagine this place without Kate. . . . It's like being in someone's home." In 1997, Bunting died at the age of 60, and in 2004, the Belmont-Hearne was demolished to make way for the Belmont Towers, a behemoth condominium block completed in 2006.

Cottages like the original Belmont created picturesque streetscapes as they lined the town's avenues and Boardwalk—some displaying Victorian turrets or bays, and most with porches—with each contributing to a domestic scale as they settled in comfortable alignment along the beachfront or on pre-1930s Baltimore Avenue. Every cottage featured a unique expression of domesticity, sometimes with classical accents or Colonial Revival styling, displaying gables, porches, white curtains in windows, white picket fences, window shutters with marine cutouts (such as boats, birds, or anchors), yard furniture, and welcome signs.

Beyond individual cottage lodgings in town, the roadside architectural development that directly led to motels was the cabin camp and cottage court. In West Ocean City, on homesites along the old bridge road, on flanking streets, and along US Route 50 (as well as north of town along the Coastal Highway), enterprising property owners built small cottages in rows, cabin camps, and the town's earliest motels. Some local farmers, aware of jokes about the farmer's daughter, preferred not to invite strangers into the family home but allowed travelers to pitch tents in side yards, and from this emerged the first phase of this development—auto camps. The landowner then erected small cabins (geometric boxes standardized on square or rectangular plans and capped with a plain gable roof) and rented them to tourists. Porches, and especially screened porches, were added amenities. Inside, there was room for a bed, table, and chair.

Groups of such minimalist cabins might be built adjacent to a tourist home or sited independently, and roadside arrangements varied. Many such cabin groups were lined in single or double rows, some were L- or U-shaped, and others formed crescents or clusters. Neither the Brown House Cottages (north of town on the Coastal Highway) nor the Fisher and Harbor Court cottages (on Harbor Road) survive, and in recent years, many others west of town were abandoned and lay derelict in woodlands awaiting new development. Such was the fate of Blue Top Cottages and Rooms on Grays Corner Road (formerly Ocean City Road), which, by 1940, offered look-alike gabled cabins with screened porches extending back from the road. These were usually adjacent to the owner's house, offering bedrooms. The Elk Horn Cottages on Elm Street in West Ocean City still exist, having been incorporated into the Francis Scott Key Motel complex. Long Acres Motel and Cottages, along Old Ocean City Road, also known as Old Bridge Road (at Route 50), illustrates the transition to motels as a motel block, flanking the farmhouse, is combined with surviving cottages.

Also located west of Ocean City on Old Bridge Road are the Villa Nova cottages, which form a U-plan open to the road and have a roadside bar/restaurant conspicuously sited inside the U. The farmhouse flanks the composition. The individual cabins (aligned and offering just under 500 square feet of space) were named for states (from left to right) Maryland, Pennsylvania, New York, Virginia, DC, Delaware, Vermont, South Carolina, New Jersey, Connecticut, Maine, West Virginia, Rhode Island, Massachusetts, North Carolina, New Hampshire, Kentucky, Tennessee, Georgia, and Florida; then larger units Ohio, Indiana, New Mexico, Colorado, Texas, and California; and then two apartment blocks. The Villa Nova group is the area's most developed survivor of the pre-motel era of cabin/camp-type lodgings.

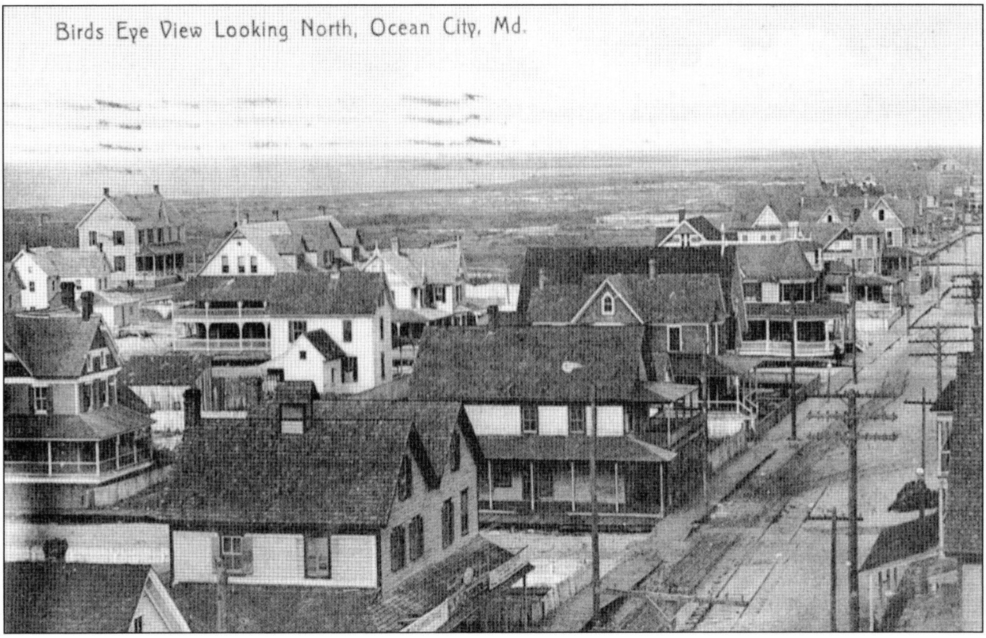

This bird's-eye view of downtown shows an array of wood-framed Victorian cottages from T.J. Cropper's property at Somerset Street (located in the lower center part of the image) northward. Most are gabled with ample porches, sometimes adorned with corner turrets with candlesnuffer roofs, and each represented a Queen Anne vernacular architectural style that persisted during the early years of the resort. This postcard, postmarked 1907, shows virtually no development north of Talbot Street on the bay side.

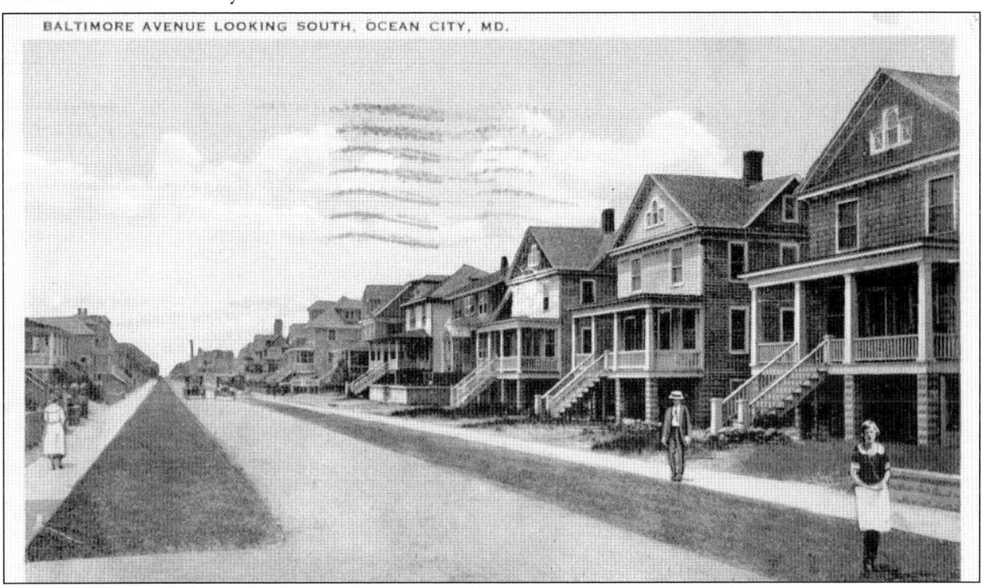

In this postcard view looking south and postmarked 1944, the tall chimney on the horizon is part of the Eastern Shore Gas and Electric Company, where the 1925 fire began (see page 15). Almost 40 years after the previous postcard was sent, relatively similar two-story frame cottages raised on concrete blocks line Baltimore Avenue in this view looking south. Today, such houses are extant only north of Fifth Street on Ocean City's stylish Edwardian avenue.

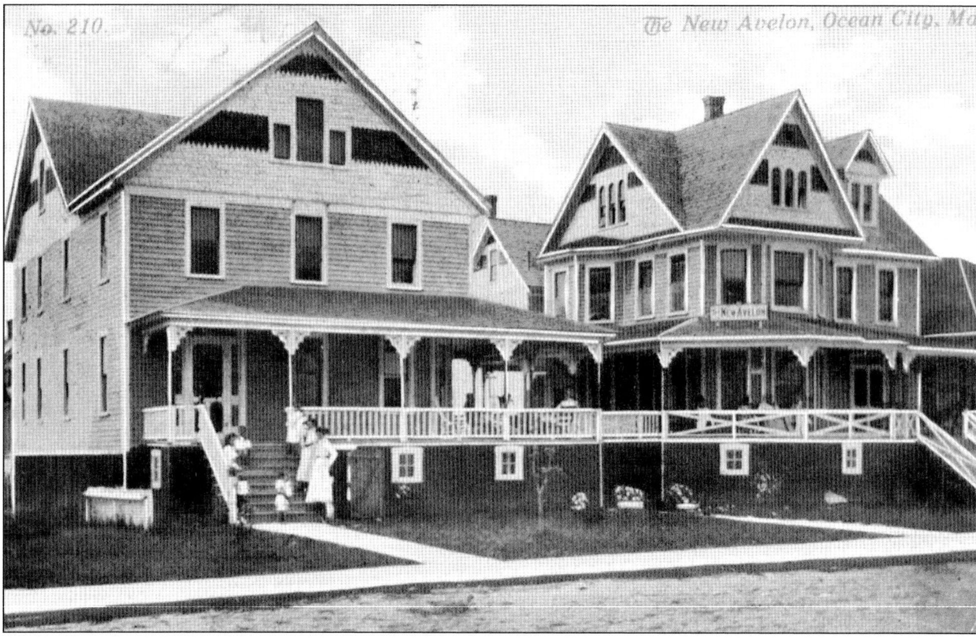

The five cottages on these facing pages represent residential structures erected along Baltimore Avenue during the early 20th century. Only Dr. Francis S. Townsend's cottage at 105 South Baltimore Avenue (pictured below) remains extant—although in altered form, with its porch and substructure enclosed and now wrapped in vinyl siding. Some cottages were joined to form inns and small hotels, as on the avenue near North First Street, where Josephine Hastings joined a flanking cottage to her own house to form the New Avelon Hotel (above). The cottages displayed period ornament in the gables (shingle) and on porch posts, where stenciled brackets flanked upper posts.

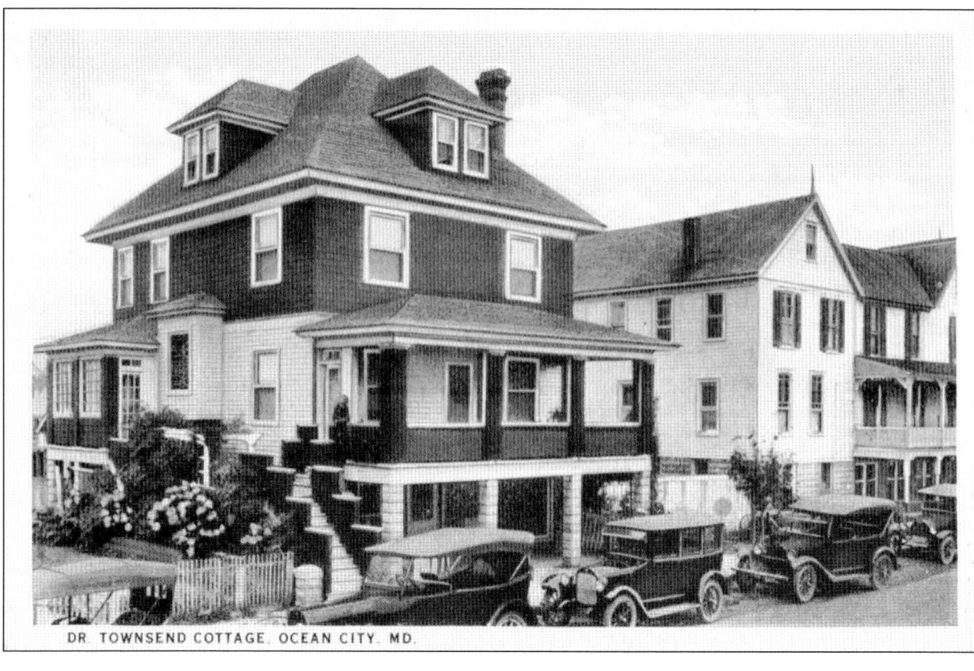

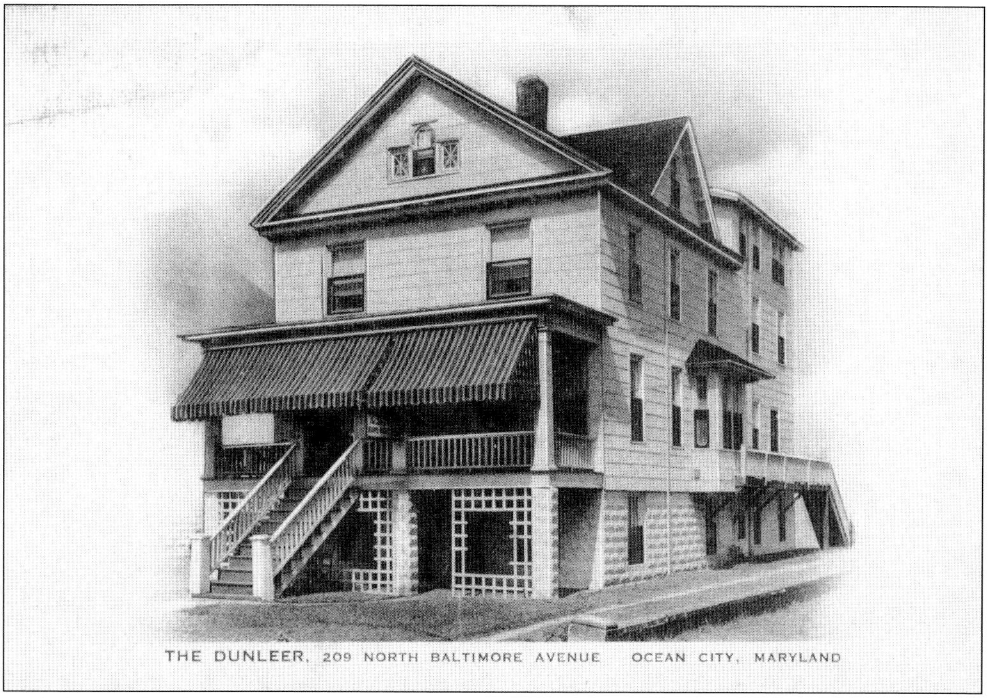

Both the Dunleer (at 209 North Baltimore Avenue; above) and the Smith Cottage rooming house (at 401 Baltimore Avenue; below) have been demolished. Today, the Smith Cottage site is a municipal parking lot. Such cottages were raised approximately six or seven feet above the ground as a precaution against flooding, and the popular material for such piers and crawl space enclosures was a rusticated concrete block intended to appear like more expensive stonework. Pamela H. Simpson described this do-it-yourself CMU (concrete masonry unit) material in her book *Cheap, Quick, & Easy: Imitative Architecture Materials, 1870–1930.* Surviving examples can be found on Baltimore Avenue at No. 503, No. 603, the 1937 Davis (Shuster) Cottage at No. 607, the Surf Villa Hotel at No. 705, the 1930 Burbage Home at No. 711, the apartment building at No. 807, and the 1926 Harrison Apartments at No. 904.

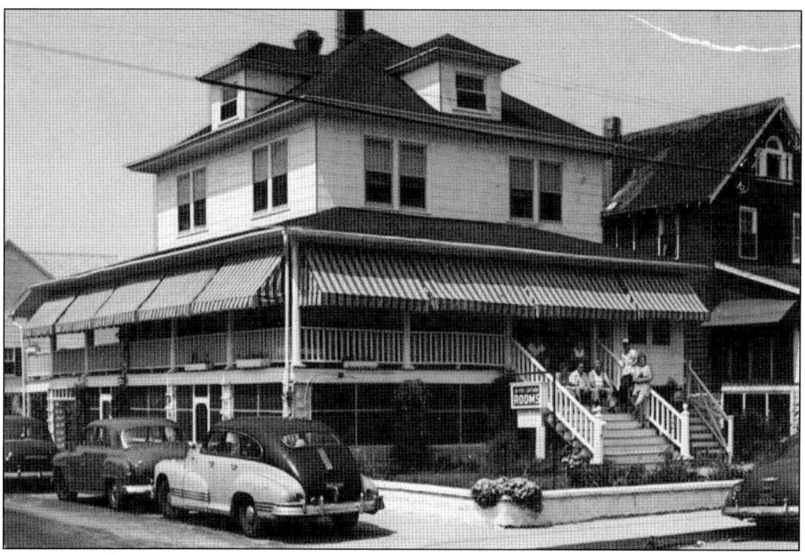

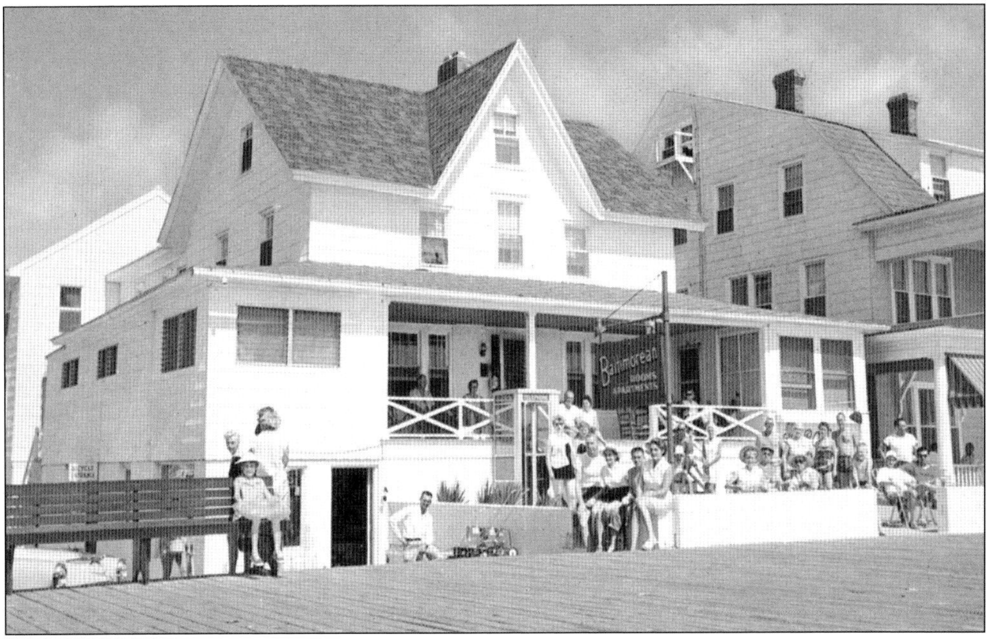

Oceanfront cottages offering rooms and apartments formed similar streetscapes along Atlantic Avenue (the official street name for the Boardwalk), although only two or three survive south of Tenth Street. The Baltimorean (above) offered beachfront rooms and apartments on First Street next door to the Colonial Hotel. The site is now a five-story hotel and suites mid-rise (timeshare) called Ocean 1, with Boardwalk frontage that is no longer a cottage porch but comprises all-too-typical garish Boardwalk shops such as Sunglass City, New York vapes, ear piercing and T-shirts, and TLC Polish Water Ice, which sells a product invented by an aeronautical and astronautical engineer of Polish descent "freshly made and fat free." Perambulating tourists will not find another Boardwalk cottage until beyond Fifth Street—Eugenia's (later Maria's) Guest House at No. 511, now refaced as the Kite Loft.

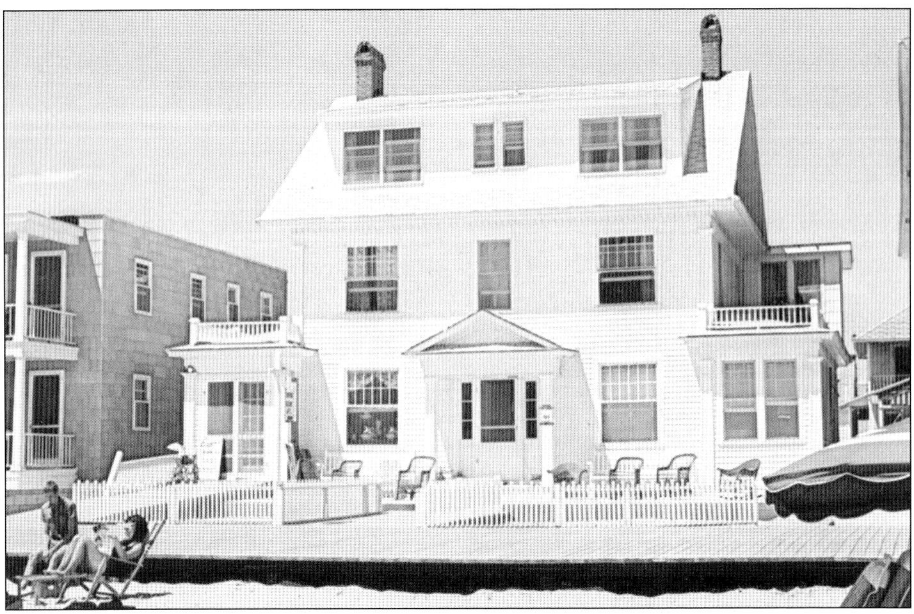

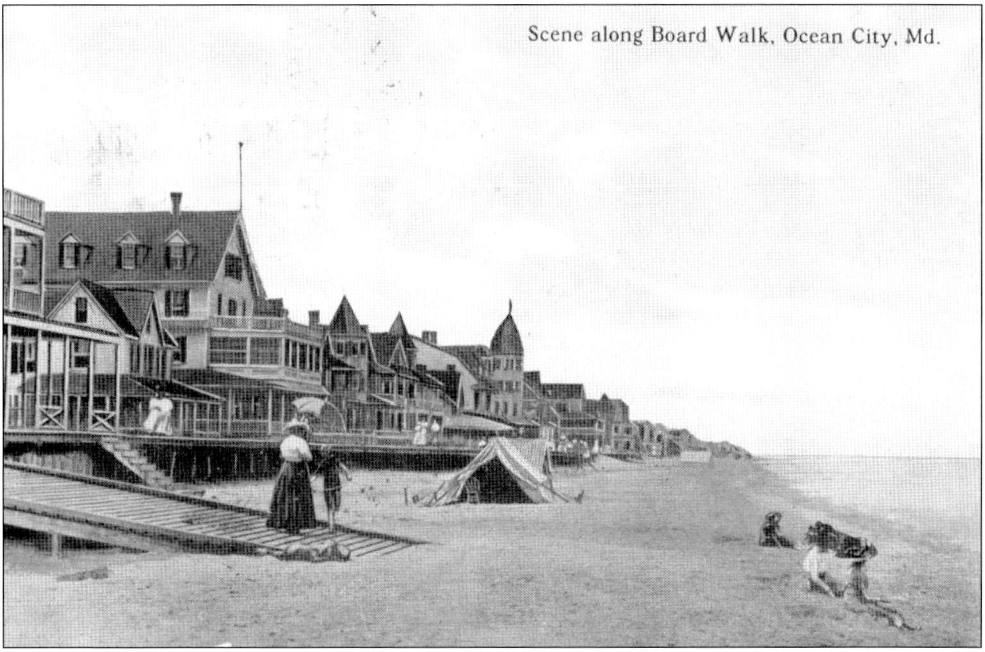

The contrast between today's flat Boardwalk facades and yesteryear's variegated architectural forms could not be more startling. The historic lower Boardwalk frontage (above) and the "upper end" Boardwalk (below) comprised a parade of familiar domestic forms: gables, porches, dormers, corner towers, window shutters, and awnings. Phenomenologists understand these to be signs—conscious and experiential indicators—of home, comfort, and rest. The cottages were vacation homes that offered holidaymakers more than today's monotony, more than concrete cell-like habitats for cellphone-toting "down for the week" revelers, more than pastel walls decorated with beachy imagery intended to counterbalance the vacuous architecture. The pair of surviving Boardwalk cottage residences still extant between Surf Avenue and Eighth Street are dinosaurs as well as irreplaceable treasures of a lost time.

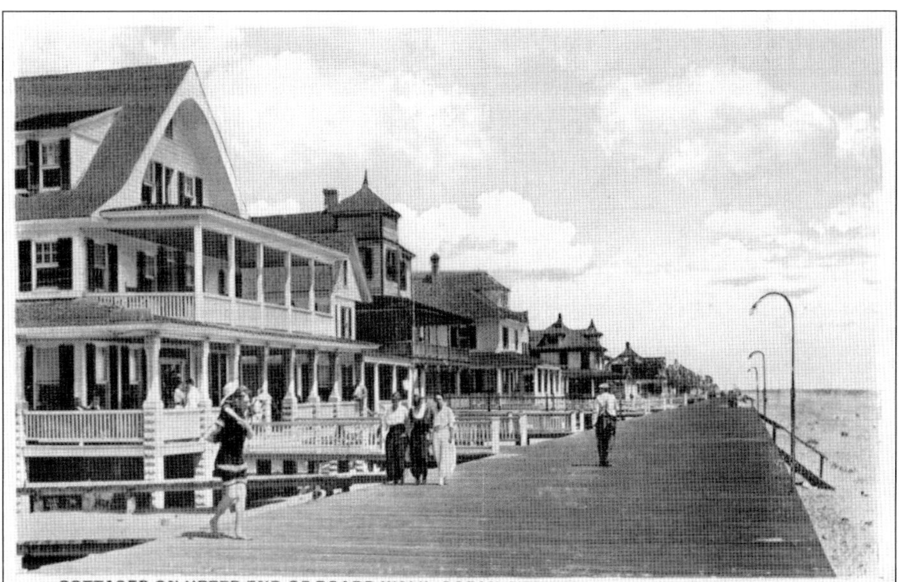

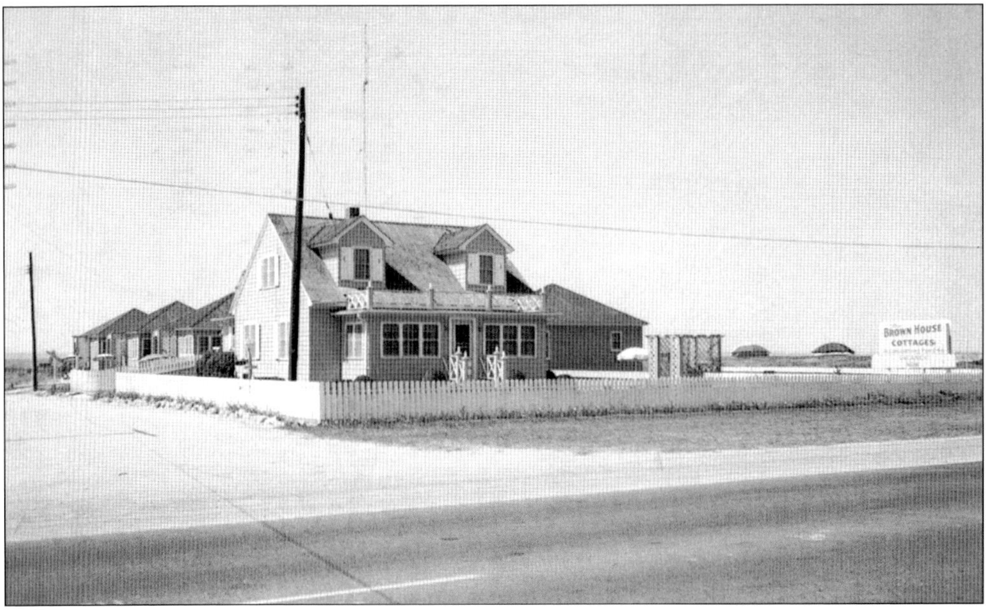

During the early years of hotels and rooming houses, vacationers accessed summer resorts by railroad. As more Americans acquired automobiles, a transition in the architecture of accommodation reflected their increased mobility. Outlying cottages, tourist cabins, and motor courts began to populate the roadside along major thoroughfares. This pattern followed similar developments nationwide along roads such as Route 66, the Dixie Highway (en route to Florida), and—in Ocean City—along the old Ocean City Road in West Ocean City and the Coastal Highway north of town (as shown above and below). The above postcard, postmarked 1955, shows the Brown Cottages built along Route 528 (Coastal Highway). In a typical layout, the backyard of the owner's house contained small, look-alike rental cabins, usually plain white and gabled, sometimes with porches, as well as private and detached.

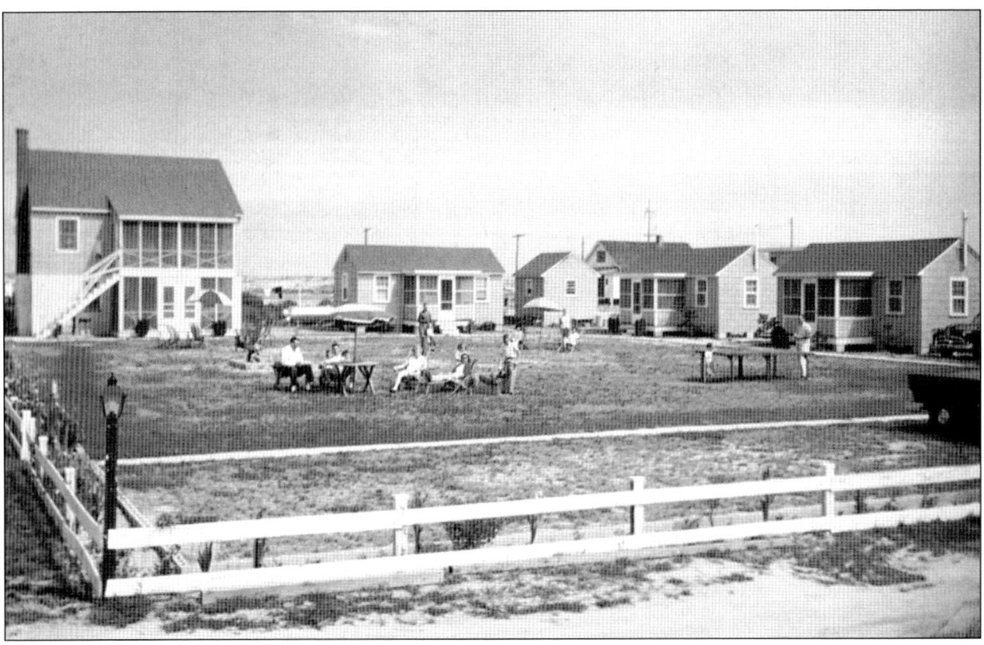

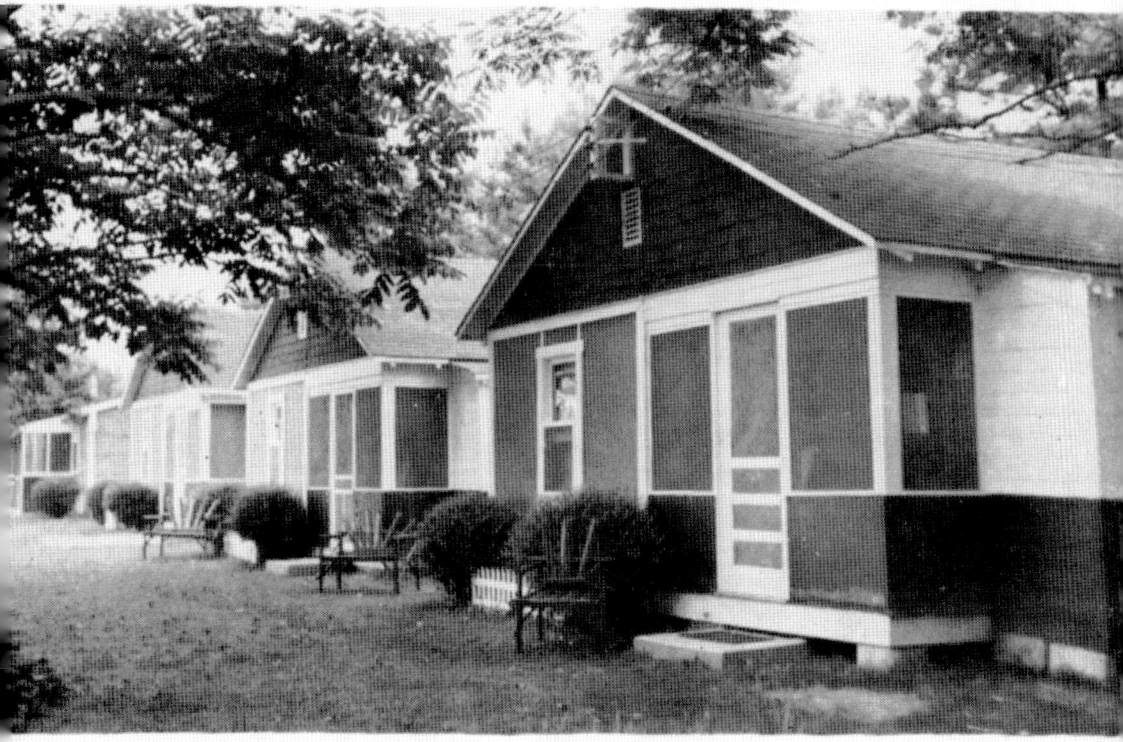

This view of Keystone Cottages is representative of many cabin groups built in West Ocean City during the 1930s and 1940s—the era before motels, when American mobility was on the rise, and vacationers sought simple and private accommodation without hotel tipping, extra amenities, and crowds. Among the early cottages built on the mainland roads approaching Ocean City were the Bird's Nest Cottages (since razed) at Herring Creek, which date from the early 1930s; the 10 Delmarva Cottages built in 1935 on Route 611 at Route 707 (old Ocean City Road); Costopolis Cottages, built around 1942, about the time Route 50 opened in the area; Crest Cottages (page 82); Capital Cottages, built around 1946 on Route 707 near Route 50; and the Kruger Cottages on Route 707, built in stages (two around 1946, two around 1948, and two around 1952). The Kruger Cottages had solid blue, pink, and green roofs; three others were striped blue, pink, and green. Four former slave quarters were moved here in 1976 from fields near Pocomoke, Maryland.

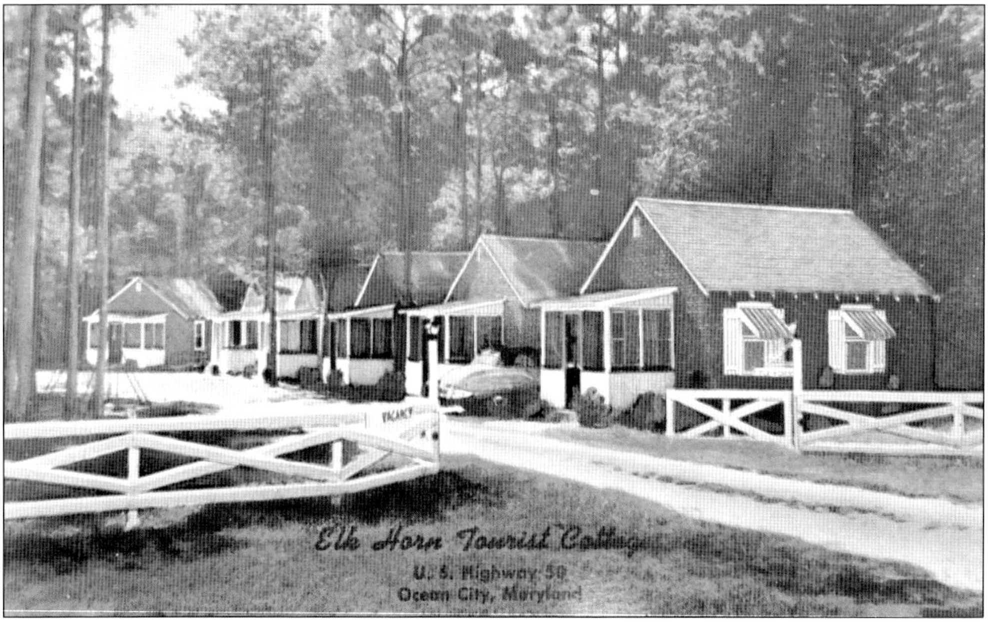

In a configuration different from parallel rows facing one another or along the roadside, the L- or U-plan arrangement of inward-facing cottages is illustrated here at the Elk Horn Tourist Cottages (above) on Maryland Route 611 just south of US Route 50 and at Wyatt's Cottages (below) on Old Bridge Road. Wyatt's Cottages are a remarkable survivor of the 1940s/1950s tourist cabin tradition that is still active today in restored and updated units renamed the Bungalows. These larger hipped-roofed units enjoy wider screened-in porches and more ample interior space. The shutters (since removed) brought a homey character to these unsophisticated cabins in their roadside clearing, and such tourist cottage groups became the accommodation of choice for travelers wishing to avoid downtown hotels. Cottage guests could enjoy either one-room units or one bedroom with a den; upgrades have added kitchens, essentially anticipating motel or suite-type units.

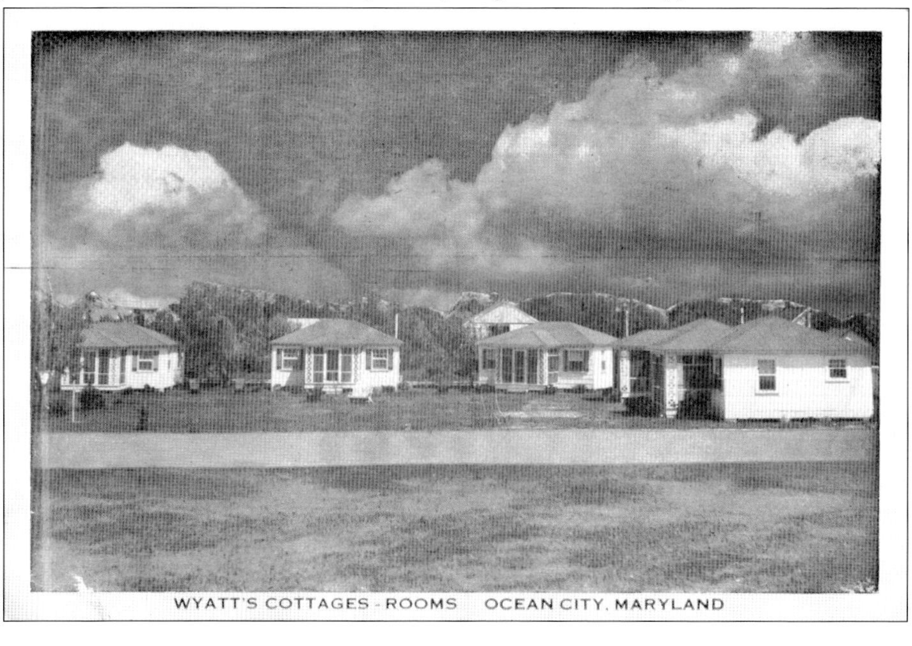

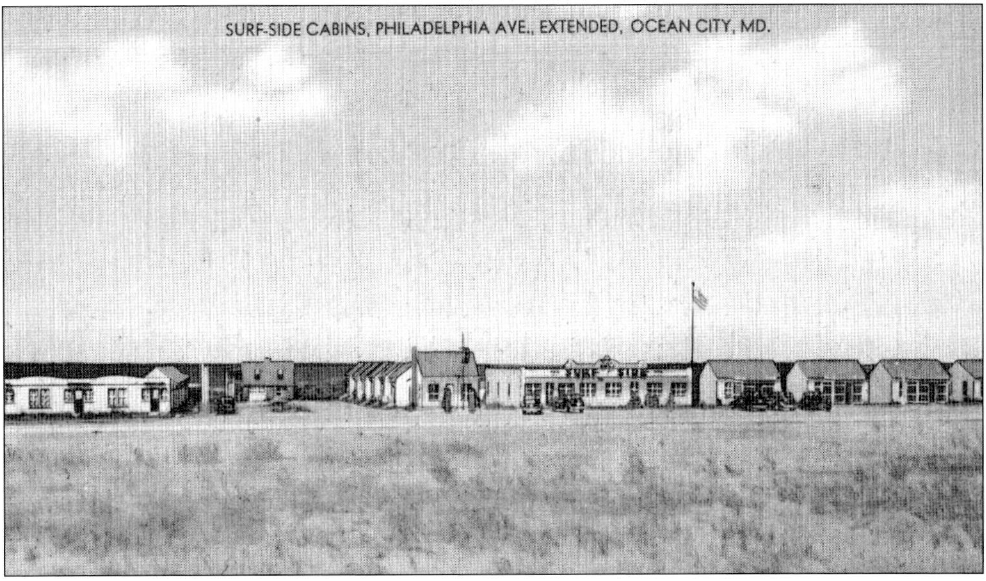

Tourist cabins and cottage groups were also built along the Coastal Highway (an extension of Philadelphia Avenue) north of town. The Surf Side Cabins had units parallel and perpendicular to the road and even joined some units (at far left) into a primitive motel block. The central building offered other amenities (likely a café), and the gas pumps outside completed this classic piece of roadside architecture.

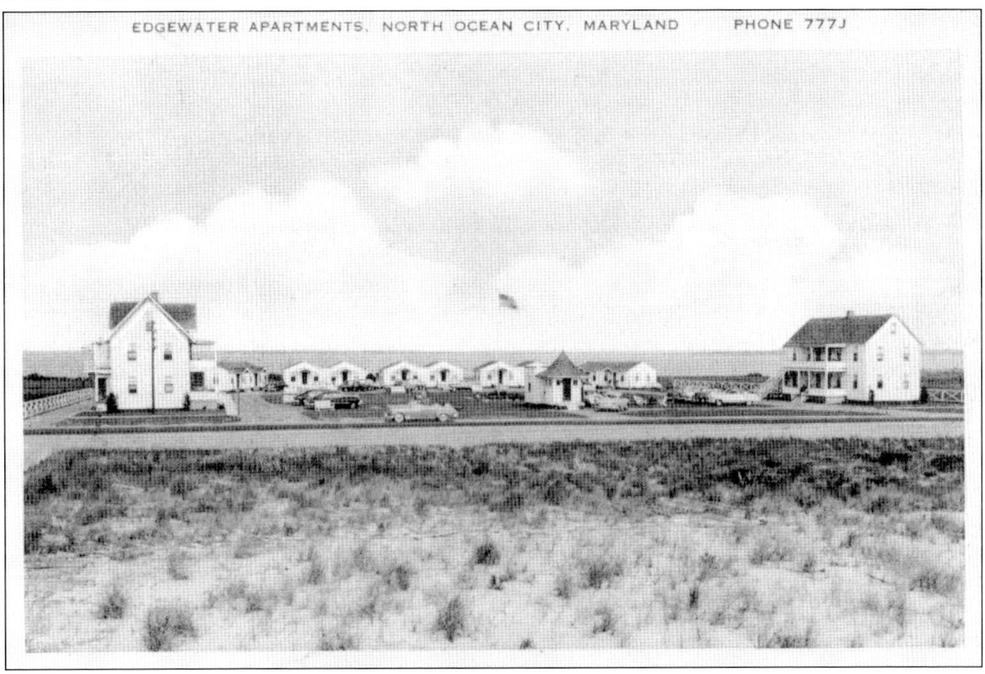

The Edgewater Apartments framed its composition of rental units with flanking two-decker apartments with single-story duplex cottage units aligned bayside deep on the property. The owners added corner paired units that were angled to form a U-plan ensemble preserving extensive open space within it. In lieu of signage, the American flag served to mark the site—much as golden arches on 60-foot steel poles would later do along interstate highways.

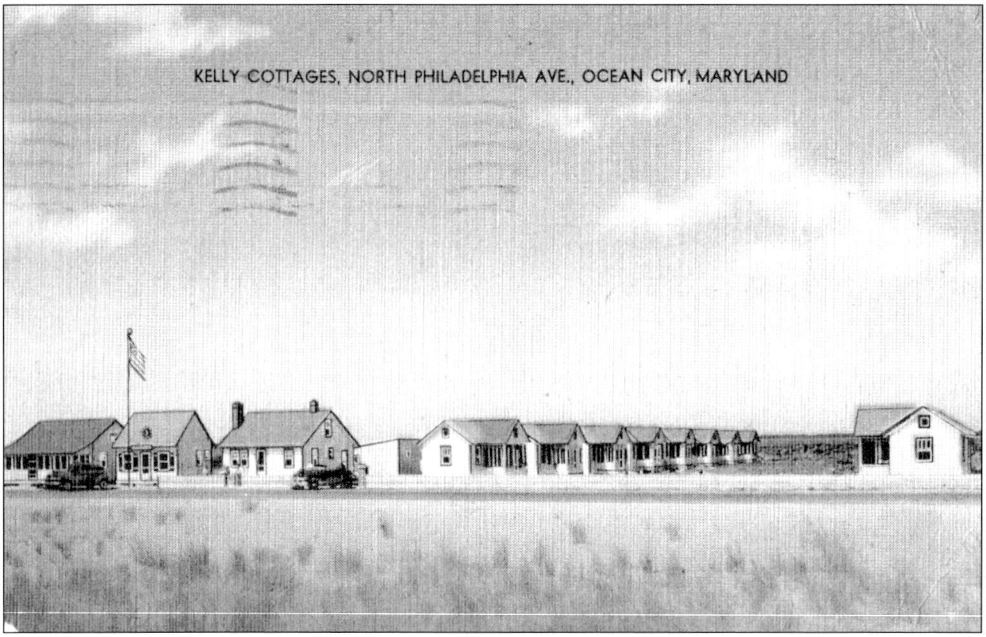

The Kelly Cottages (above) and Crest Cottages (below) represent two developments in cabin groupings. The Kelly complex was built on an undeveloped site just north of town on North Philadelphia Avenue, an empty two-lane highway passing through duneland to Delaware. Crest Cottages were built west of town on the mainland in the rear yard of a farmhouse; the site was on the old Ocean City Road (Old Bridge Road), also known as Maryland Route 707, just east of its intersection with US Route 50; the latter became the main road to the resort once the new bridge was completed in 1942. Mainland farmers and other property owners could supplement their income by erecting such tourist cabins, which were cheap to build and popular with travelers during the era before motels.

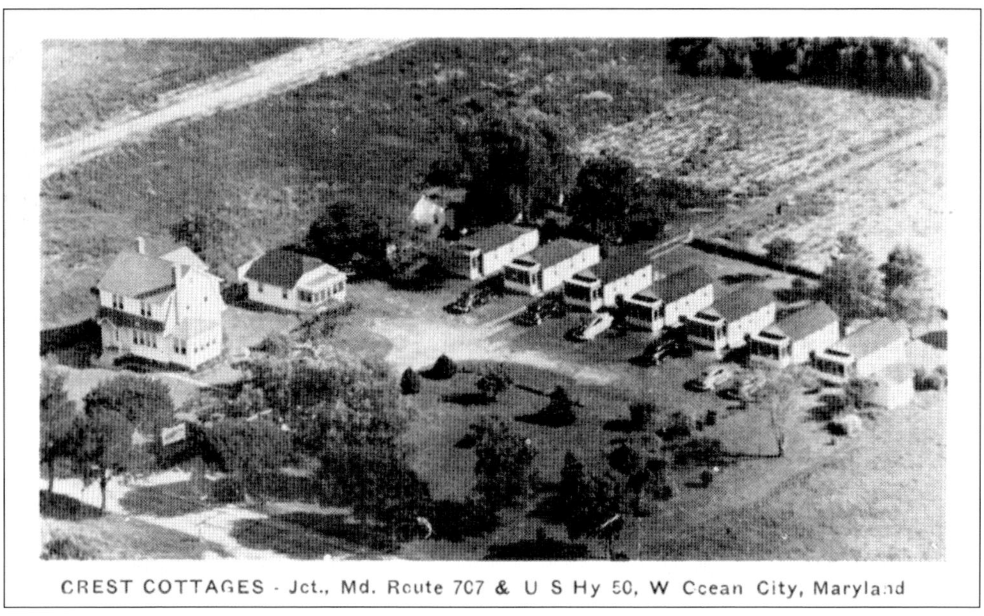

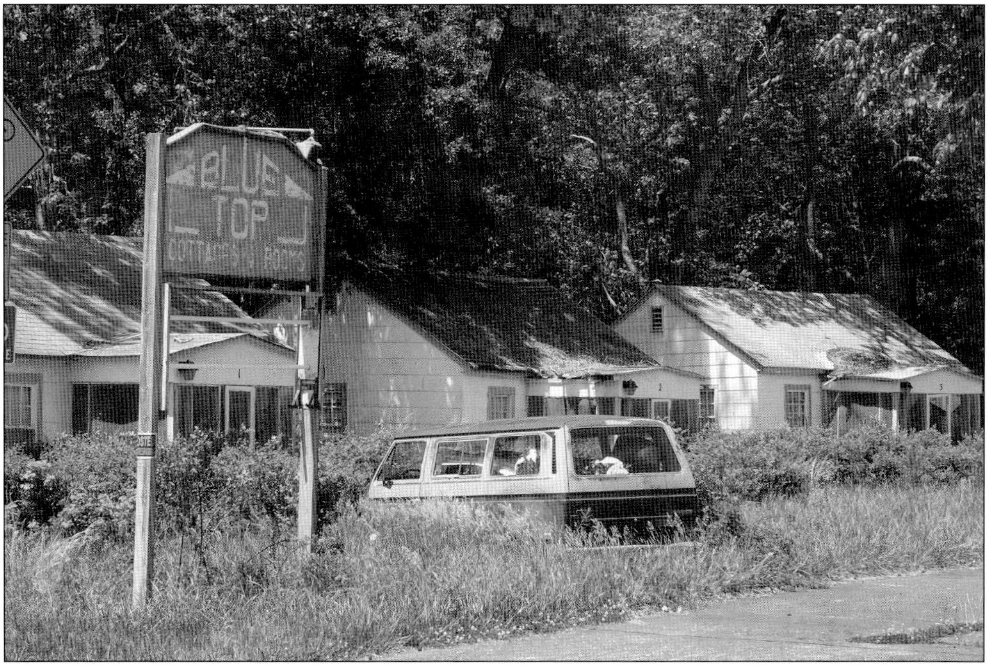

US Route 50 and the old Ocean City Road west of town still harbor a few ghosts of the tourist cottage tradition with long-abandoned cottage groups behind owners' dwellings. A few are still occupied with tenants, while others are abandoned, overgrown with foliage and high grass, with a faded sign still announcing its former life as "Blue Top Cottages and Rooms." The main house served as a tourist home offering travelers overnight rooms, while the detached cabins provided homes away from home for traveling vacationers who could, if they liked, interact with other cottage-dwellers in the small community. (Both, RMC.)

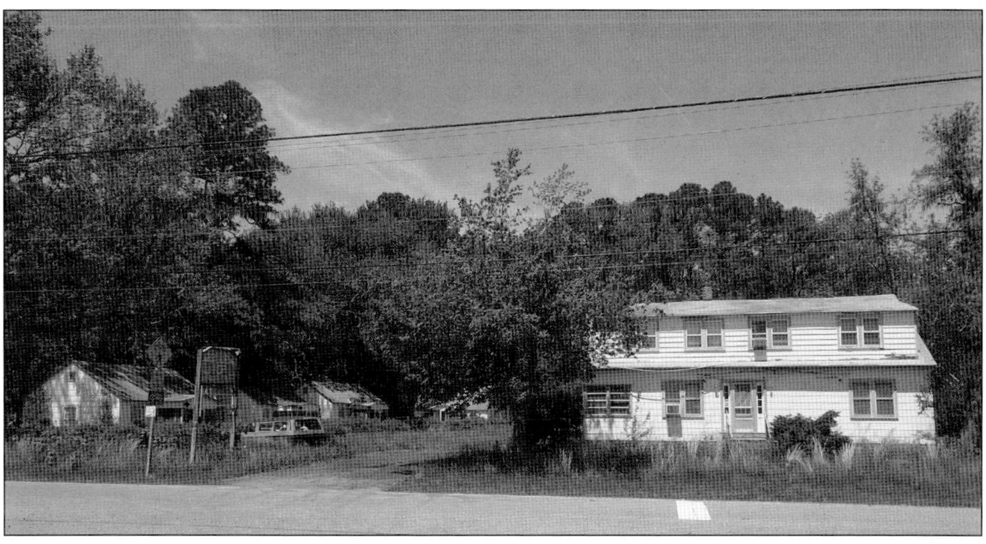

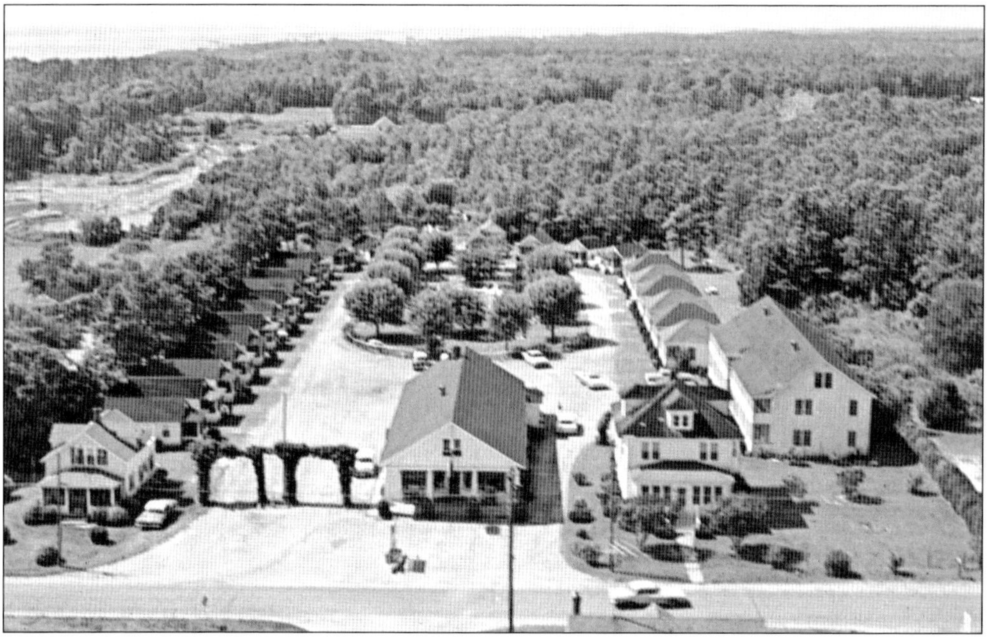

A fully developed example of the tourist cottage ensemble is on view at the extant Villa Nova Cottages on Old Bridge Road in West Ocean City. The above photograph shows the owner's house and restaurant/bar facing the road in front of a U-plan of variously sized cottages and apartments arranged around an open space behind the public house. The Maridel Motel and Cottages (1954, below) took the final step in a little-disguised transformation by facing the conjoined cottage units with a continuous (likely Permastone) screen in front, and the motel was born. On Route 50, six cottages were built around 1945, with two more added in 1947 or 1948 and three more added around 1949 on a site eventually occupied by the Maryland Motel, which offered identical sleeping rooms in a motel block. Nearby were the Pines Motel (1948, razed) and Green Gables Motel (now Toast Restaurant).

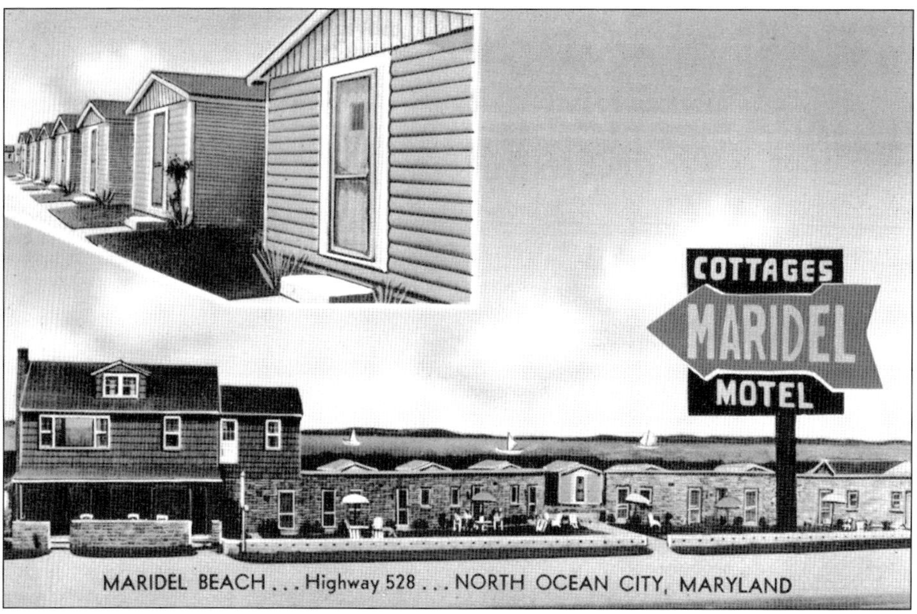

Three

Motels

In the late 1960s, when architect Robert Venturi drew public attention to ordinary roadside architecture, advertisement signage, and commercial buildings in "A Significance for A&P Parking Lots, or Learning from Las Vegas," an article written by Venturi with Denise Scott Brown in the March 1968 issue of *Architectural Forum*, Ocean City had already built much of its Motel Row north of Fifteenth Street. What attracted Venturi in his study of the Las Vegas motel strip were the forms, signs, and symbols of a commercial vernacular (the lighting, urban patterns, and architectural language of "decorated sheds")—imagery that brought meaning to non-elite, "ordinary and ugly" buildings. Contemporary theorists articulated their sometimes esoteric responses to the ordinariness of the ubiquitous American commercial strip by advancing heady monologues of semiotics. Likewise, pop-culture scholars appreciated that ordinary objects of American material culture offered a broader understanding of the national culture and society than that afforded by traditional histories that once proclaimed that the past was solely a story of heroic individuals and landmark architecture and that architectural history was limited to architect-designed buildings and high art. In his studies of the strip architecture of Las Vegas, roadside architecture (from diners to motor courts), and ordinary commercial buildings, Venturi opened the door to an appreciation of postwar commoner architecture such as that found on Ocean City's Motel Row.

Scholars began to look beyond the famed architects of a heroic Modern architecture; they gathered at societies such as the Vernacular Architecture Forum and the Society for Commercial Archeology to present academic papers on ordinary (not architect-designed) buildings, and publishing houses printed books on the history of gas stations, roadside diners, Googie drive-ins, and jet-age motels. Ocean City's Motel Row—with its earliest Boardwalk motels like the Santa Maria, its exotic Castle in the Sands Motel set among northern dunes, and its contemporary-styled Eden Roc Motel—became a modern architectural district of historical significance, although few recognized it at the time.

The shingle-clad hotels—and indeed, hotels in general— became "old school." By the late 1950s, the Jetsons, Tomorrowland, and the space race were shaping a futuristic formalism in design. For instance, Sputnik inspired Ocean City's Satellite Motel. Referential buildings were dominant; movie Westerns were recalled in motel names such as Westward Ho, while patriotic national and regional pride was evident in the Southern plantation imagery of the Francis Scott Key Motel. The increasingly mobile American tourist could visit such far-reaching locales as Miami and Texas, so Ocean City's white, neo-Spanish Miami Court and Alamo Motel appealed to the romantic side of well-traveled vacationers. Motel nomenclature and styles varied, with each trying to entice the arriving tourist to "stop here and register"—the King's Arms and Princess Royale suggested nobility, while the Riviera and French Quarter implied upscale fashion and partying, and references to the sea (Sea Scape, Sea Cove, Ocean Mecca, New Beach, Ocean Park, Sandyhill, Dunes) were used to advertise motels in neon and supergraphics. One local motel was named Shangri La, a mega-inn was called Paradise Plaza, and a certain escapism was implied by the name the Stowaway. The old hotels had been named for historic figures—George Washington, Stephen Decatur, or King Charles—while others borrowed the names of the homes of founding fathers or kings, including Monticello Hotel, Mount Vernon Hotel, and Windsor Hotel. All of that had become old-fashioned or downright stodgy. The latest victim of vacationers' expectations is the forthcoming demolition of the 1924 Lankford Hotel, brushed aside because tourists demanded more oceanfront rooms and a swimming pool.

In the transition from the large hotel to the mom-and-pop motel, it also became evident that more affordable rates made motels less elitist, implying that the American motel promoted social equality.

There were no dress-up dining rooms, serving Eastern Shore fare, where the elite could be served by a team of obsequious, bow-tied staff in black suits with white linen draped over their forearms and where haute society customers paid a premium to be seen. At the motel, the Everyman character, typical and ordinary to a fault, arrives by car, parks anonymously in front of a row of similar units, and—having stopped earlier at a roadside diner for a platter and two sides—enters a standardized motel room with two beds, a television, a bath, and more affordable rates.

Moreover, the modern motel was youthful, liberating, and perhaps a little risqué; as with the sartorial transition from black-tie attire to Hawaiian shirts and bikinis, motels were full of color. A 1957 Chevy or surfboard-toting Woodie parked outside the Eden Roc Motel became a new iconic image. Mid-century Modern motel architecture (what author Kirk Hastings has called "Doo-Wop motels") conjures up images of *Gidget* (the first of several Gidget movies appeared in 1959), the new California aesthetic (the Beach Boys formed in 1961), and teenage cruising. The postwar roadside motel was the architecture par excellence of the automobile culture and is quintessentially American. In *The Motel in America*, historians John A. Jakle, Keith A. Sculle, and Jefferson S. Rogers wrote, "Our modern nation would be difficult to imagine without motels, a fact forcefully reflected in their nearly ubiquitous presence in the American landscape." What is peculiarly "American" about Ocean City's historic lodgings? This author would argue the motel.

However, the mom-and-pop motels of Motel Row and in West and North Ocean City have almost all disappeared, and Mid-century Modern motel blocks, inns, and motor courts, as well as romance-styled smaller motels, face constant threats from massive motel and hotel chains ready to tear down and enlarge building fabric. Always ready to overpower the early traditions of motel design, new developers build undistinguished concrete megastructures bearing national franchise signage and able to accommodate more and more numbers of clientele.

Ocean City's motel history unfolds with illustrations of Spanish casas, adobe blocks, and ranch-inspired overnight sleeping units. Postwar motels lined the right side of the highway as vacationers approached the 1942 bridge to enter Ocean City; there was no point in trying to attract overnight stays on the road heading west out of town. The Francis Scott Key Motel is a rare survivor in this once-extensive Route 50 roadside motel group. One's eyes are drawn deep into the roadside site—beyond framing trees reminiscent of Oak Alley in Louisiana to a grand portico of columns, an image of the Old South, and a promise of hospitality, fine food, and Southern comfort. Not far away is the Alamo Motel; its new owners, in an unconscionable act of vandalism, removed the motel's 75-year-old roadside sign (with its neon and iconic sombrero) and repainted the once adobe-white motel units Prussian blue.

During the 1950s and 1960s, Ocean City's motels were "signs of our time." But like the shingle-clad hotels, the town's motels increasingly became victims of changing times. Despite significant loss, Motel Row preserves a fraction of its original postwar collection and remains a significant ensemble of a strikingly American building type. Still extant are period advertising signs at the Majestic and Harrison Hall Hotels and motel signage at the Dunes and Flamingo Motels, and the surviving historic motels themselves are signs of a democratic and mobile American life. Let us conserve what remains and enjoy the value in retro.

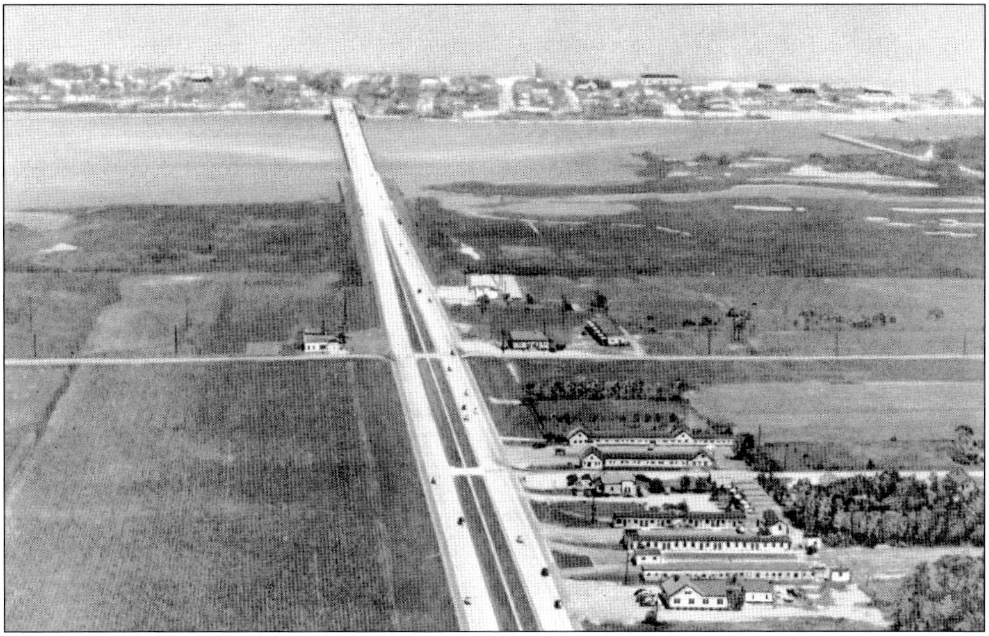

An aerial view (above) looking east toward the new bridge into Ocean City shows development of early motels and cottages on the right (south) side of US Route 50 attracting visitors as they arrived at the resort, with no development except a filling station on the north side of the highway where traffic is leaving the resort. Of the group of motels at the bottom of the photograph, the motel at the top is the still-extant Green Gables (now Toast Restaurant). Others along this highway included the Pines Motel (pictured below; now razed), the Maryland Motel (now razed), the Francis Scott Key Motel, and—predating them all—the Alamo Court Motel. Some of these motels included individual cottages as part of the transitional motel complex. Two Quonset huts remain extant east of the Pines Motel site and west of Elm Street (the road leading south in the lower part of the above image).

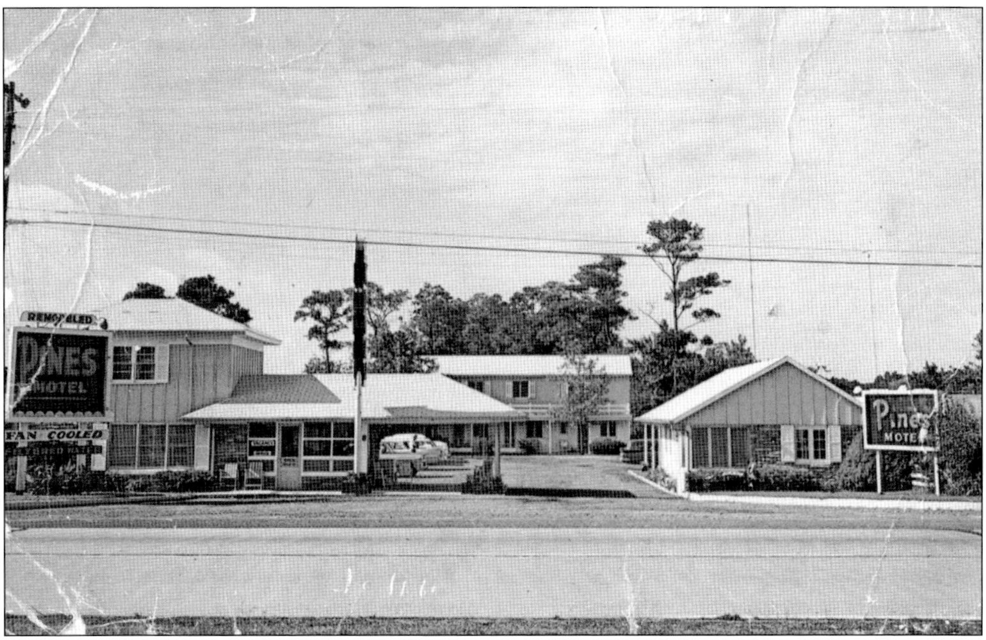

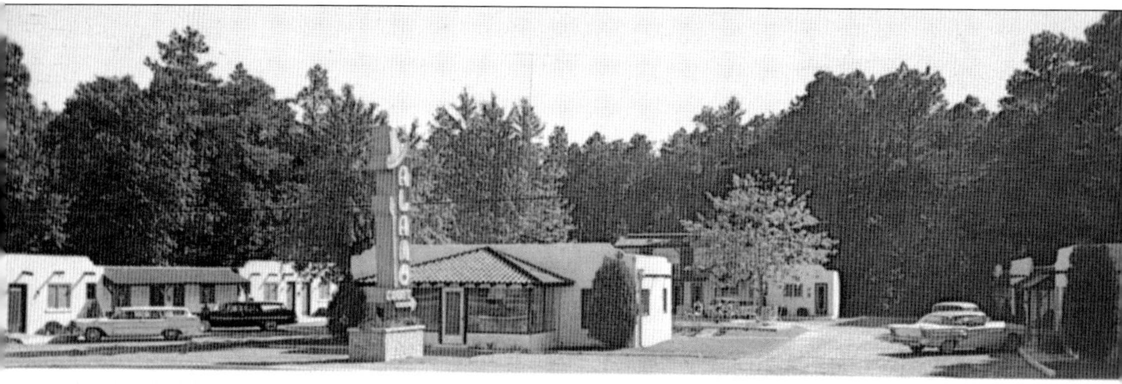

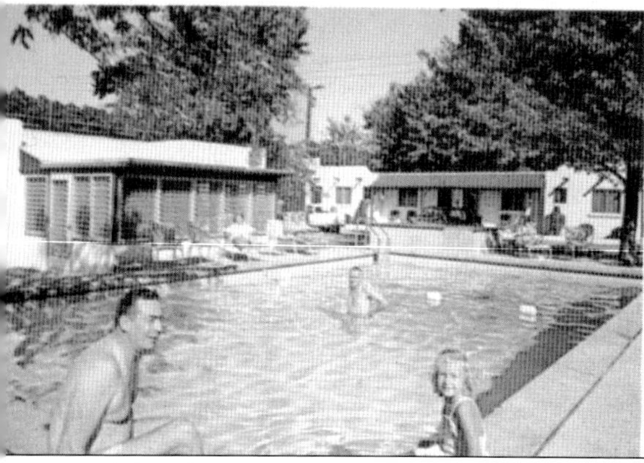

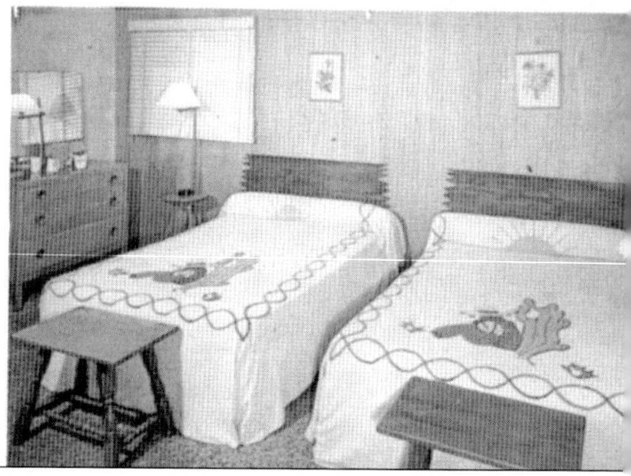

The Alamo Court Motel, built in 1946 on US Route 50 west of Ocean City, was the first motel in Worcester County. It was not affiliated with the regional chain of Alamo Plaza Hotel Courts, which historians identify as the first motel franchise, founded in 1929 in Waco, Texas; by 1955, Alamo Plaza Hotel Courts had spawned more than 20 similar and affiliated motels with Alamo forms and stuccoed false fronts throughout the Southeast. Surviving examples can be found in Savannah, Atlanta, Augusta, and elsewhere and can be recognized by their Spanish mission parapet profiles and off-white appearance. The chain set the standard for postwar motels' competition for clientele by dressing their buildings in revivalist and exotic architectural styles promising an ambiance beyond the ordinary. Ocean City's Alamo Court Motel, originally with uniform white stucco exteriors and projecting vigas, evoked a similar image of the Southwest, displaying a prominent neon sign topped by a sombrero. In one of Ocean City's worst acts of wanton desecration, in 2022, the Alamo Court Motel sign was removed and trashed after marking the site of the area's most historic motel for over 75 years.

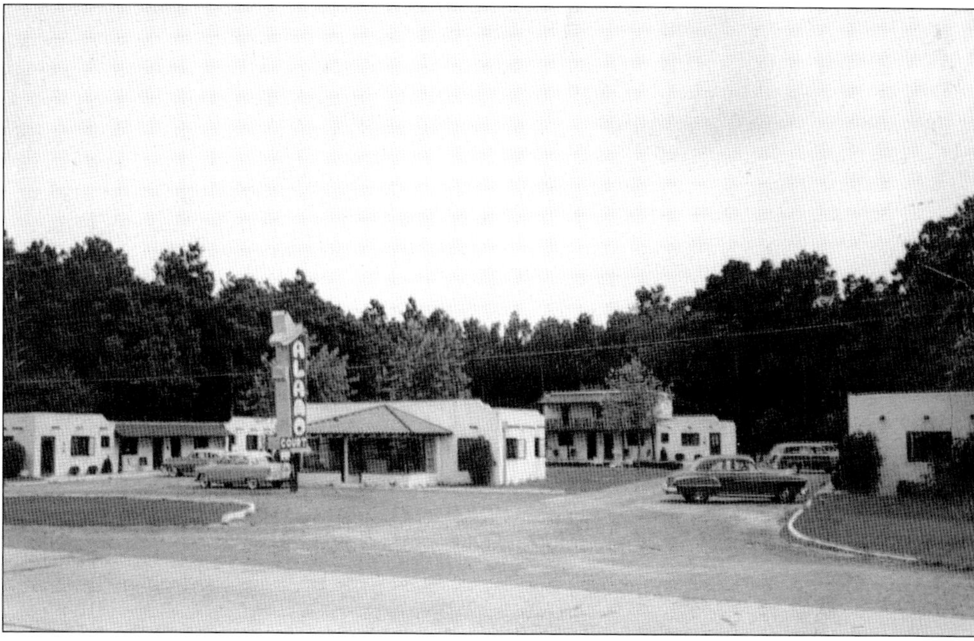

The original layout of the Alamo Court Motel sited a roadside office centered between a flanking row of connected units on each side and a detached two-story block with one-story wings centered deep on the property with open lawn between them—in all, a detached U-plan (as shown above). Soon, the lawn was replaced with a swimming pool (below), an increasingly necessary amenity in motel accommodations. In later years, the center-rear block (at left in the below image) was converted to a pool bar and grill. Recent renovations gave the sleeping units a striking postmodern tropical Deco palette of pastel colors, which were regrettably lost in 2022, when the entire complex was painted a dark midnight blue, irreverently destroying the motel's referential and exotic character.

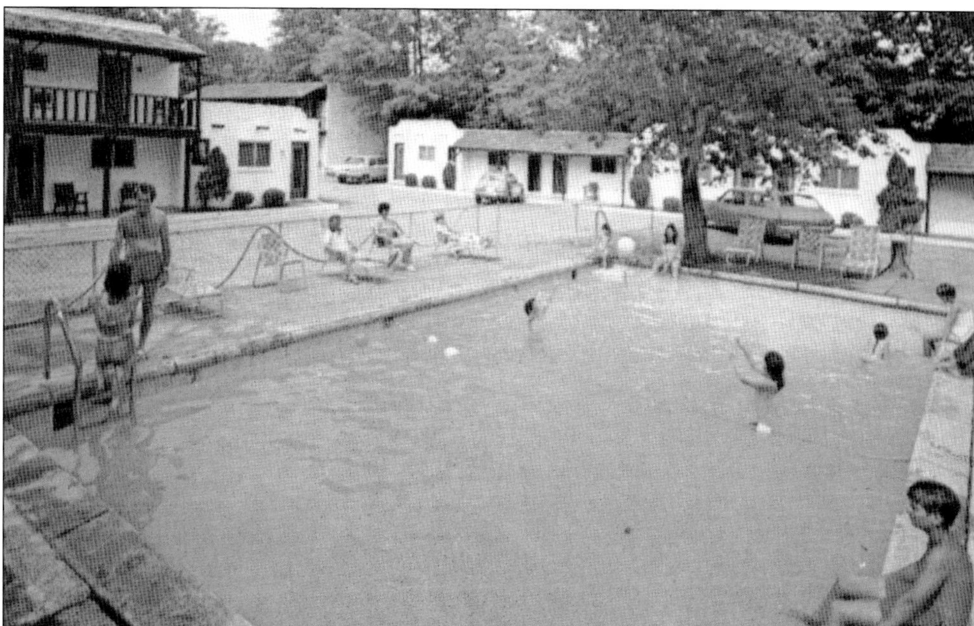

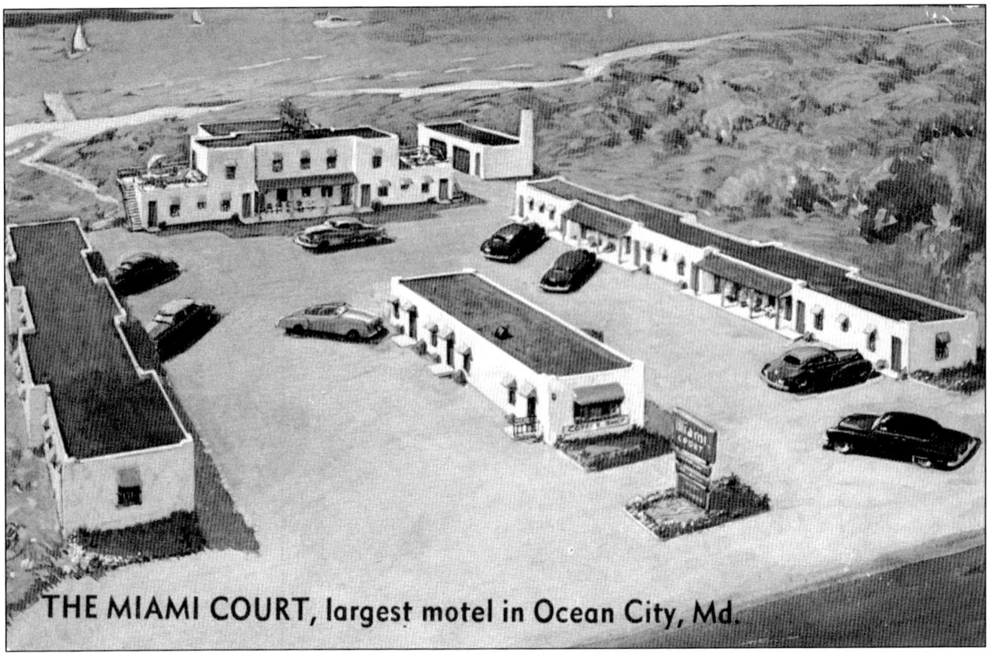

The first motel built in Ocean City proper was the Miami Court, which was constructed in 1948 and opened in 1949 and located on Philadelphia Avenue at Twenty-Second Street. For several years after competing motels opened, it advertised its 72 rooms as the town's "largest" motel. Adopting a flat-roofed, stucco, adobe architectural style and a layout similar to that of the Alamo Court Motel, the Miami Court featured a roadside restaurant, two parallel blocks of attached units running west from the Coastal Highway toward the bay, and a detached two-story block sited deep in the property. The one-story wings on the latter provided roof terraces as an additional amenity. Its builder, Ridge Harmon Sr., later built the Sea Scape Motel in 1952—this was the town's first Boardwalk motel and the start of Motel Row.

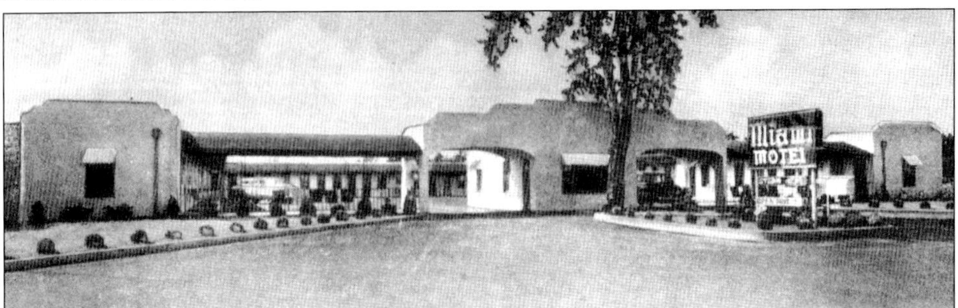

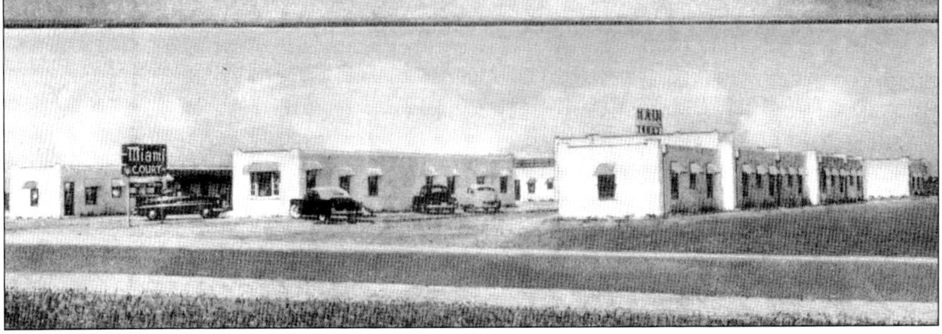

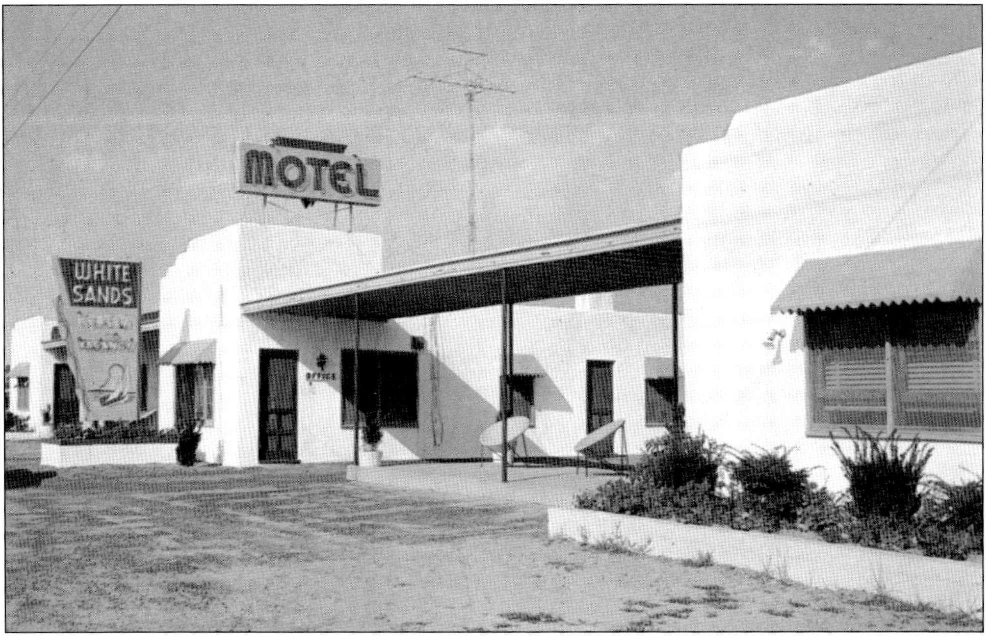

Some motels, while drifting away from the explicit stylistic reference to adobe or Spanish Colonial Revival architecture, nevertheless maintained stark white exteriors to suggest the accommodation was clinically clean. The White Sands Motel (above) conveyed such an image while referencing the powdery blanched sands of the resort's well-maintained beach. Indeed, motel names soon adopted a host of references to the ocean, beach, dunes, and bay (unlike the hotels named for Stephen Decatur, George Washington, the *Mayflower*, or local property owners such as Dennis or Harrison). Cashmyer's Ocean City Motel, located on the beach/Coastal Highway at Thirty-Second Street (10 blocks north of the Miami Court), simply borrowed the town name before anyone else did. Along with the Miami Court and some other postwar motels, Cashmyer's advertised heated rooms so the lodging could be open year-round.

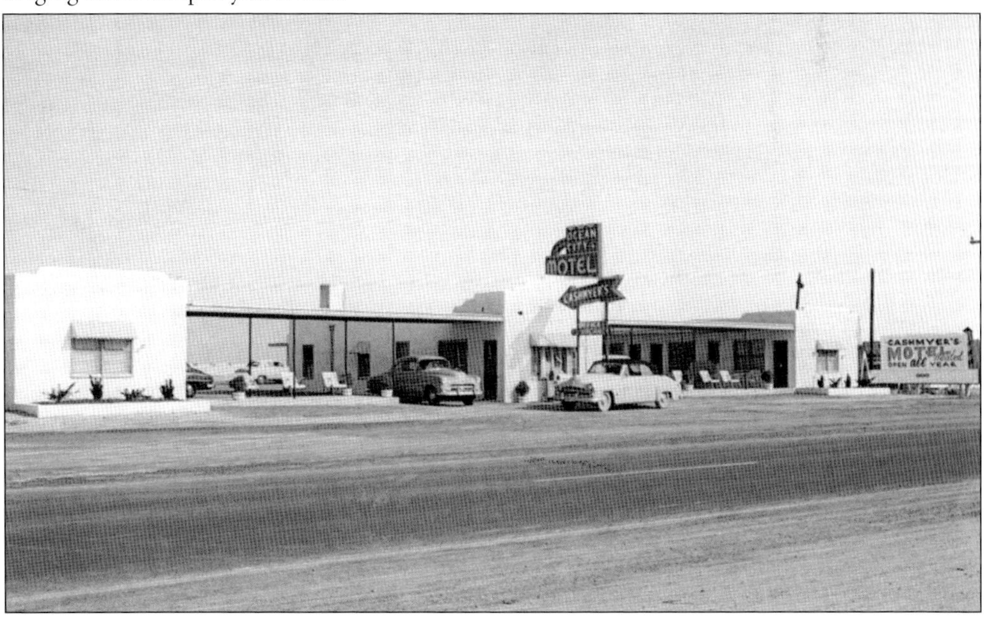

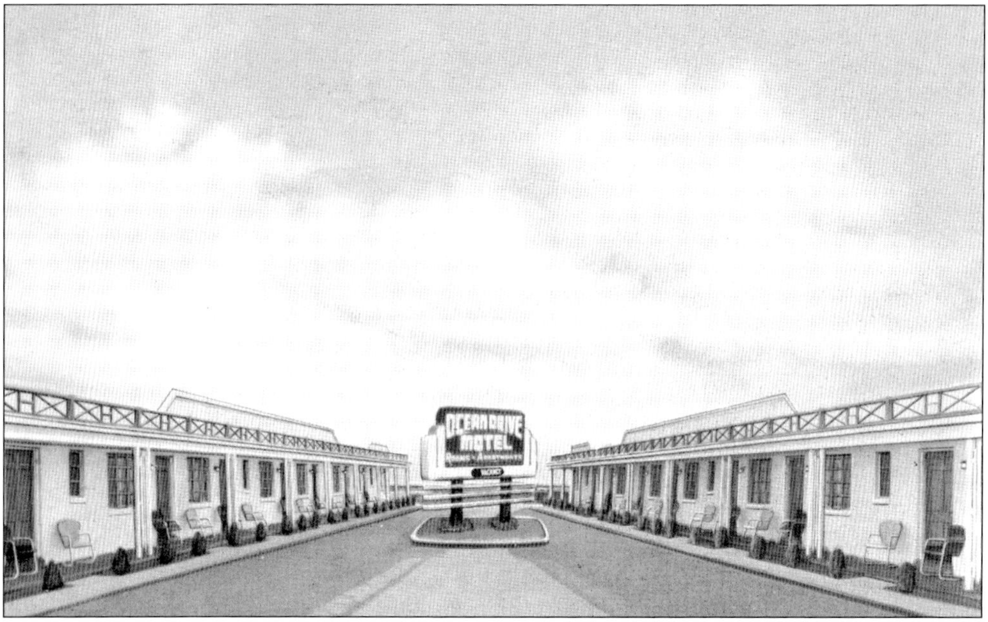

The Ocean Drive Motel maintained a whitewashed appearance, homogenizing units to a repetitive sameness and offering identical doors, windows, outdoor metal armchairs, and plantings on the outside, while on the inside, identical beds, drapes, bedspreads, side tables, televisions, mirrors, and pictures awaited visitors. The motel was becoming the quintessential embodiment of democratic architecture for a mobile middle class, with identical units, equality for all, and blocks of rooms mirroring their opposites in parallel rows.

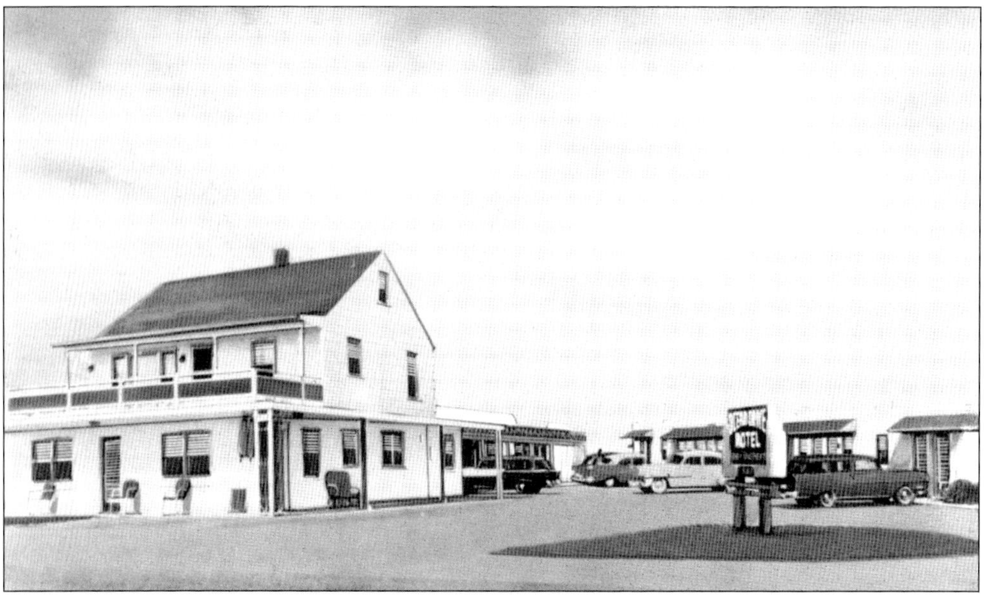

As in earlier cabin and cottage camps, the domestic forms of a private residence served as the vacationer's first point of contact and where interior space offered additional rental rooms, apartments, or restaurant facilities. A roadside café or restaurant on the grounds of the cottage group or motel was increasingly sought by travelers as an alternative to more expensive hotels with dining rooms, including those offering the American plan (meals included with room rates).

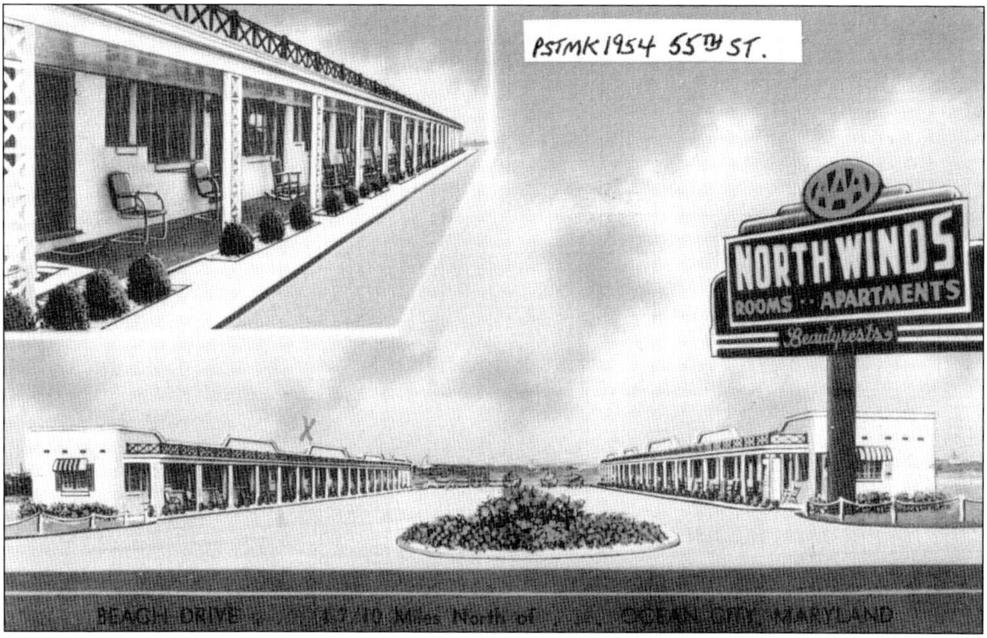

The North Winds Motel was erected in 1952 on the beach highway at Fifty-Fourth Street, where it stood for 50 years before being razed to make way for the Sunset Bay condominiums. Its original character (above) recalled individual cottage units from the 1940s, now styled as white adobe units linked by a continuous *portal*, or porch. In its remodeled form, two new developments were significant. The first was the provision of second-floor units atop each sleeping room block. The second was the conscious effort to display a modern image rather than a romantic image of the historic past, whether it was colonial, Spanish Southwestern, or Southern plantation. The porte cochere, with its structurally expressive angular supports, and the prominent Moderne motel sign slicing into the building like the abstract plane of a De Stijl sculpture were purposefully modern.

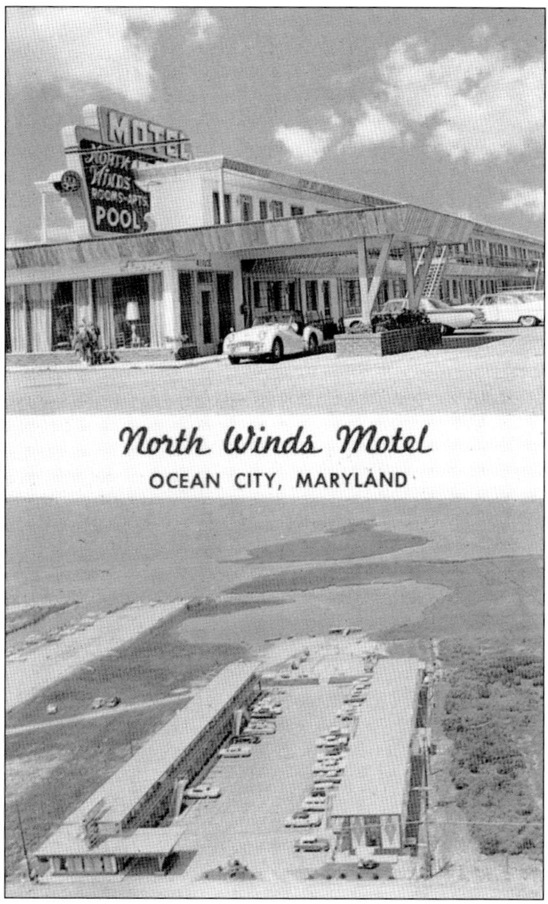

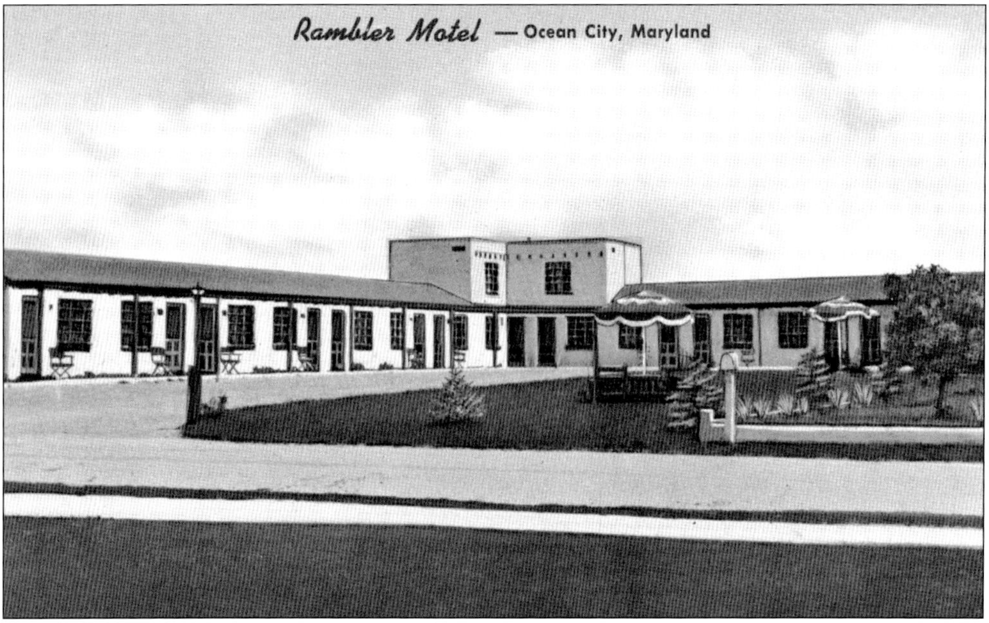

The Rambler Motel on Elm Street in West Ocean City began with a distinctive Spanish Colonial or Pueblo aesthetic with single-story wings in an L-formation and a two-story block with exposed vigas at the intersection of the wings. A second story of units was subsequently added to the left (north) wing. A pool walled off from the street was also added. The motel remains extant.

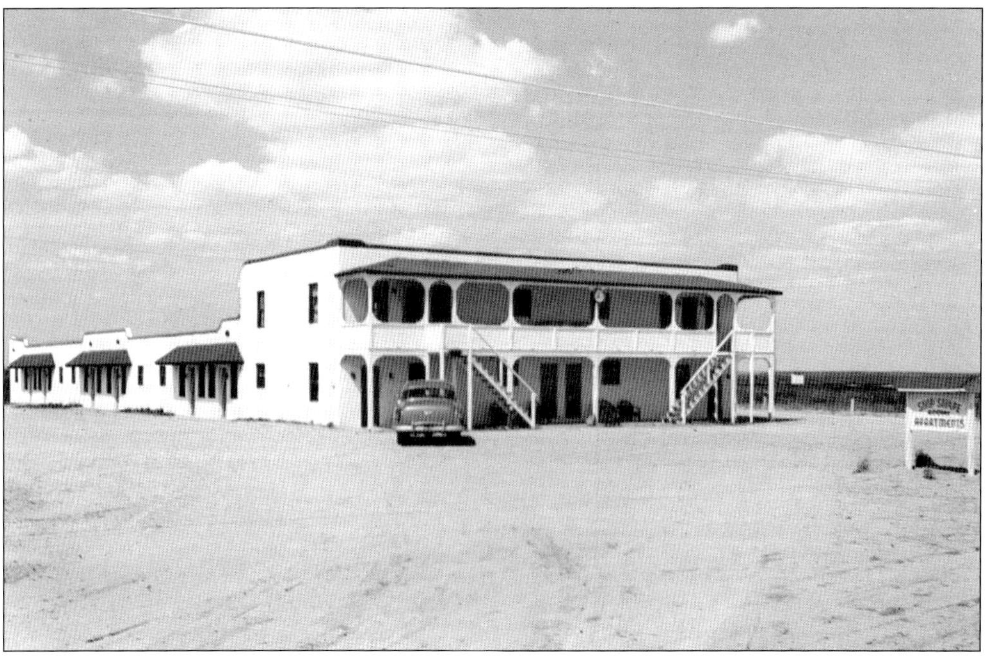

One of Spanish California's best known works of colonial domestic architecture is the 1835 Larkin House in Monterey, a frame building with full-width porches on each of its two floors. Such an image, with adobe forms behind it, characterized the Ship Shape Apartments on the Coastal Highway at Sixty-First Street, another pseudo-historicist tourist accommodation.

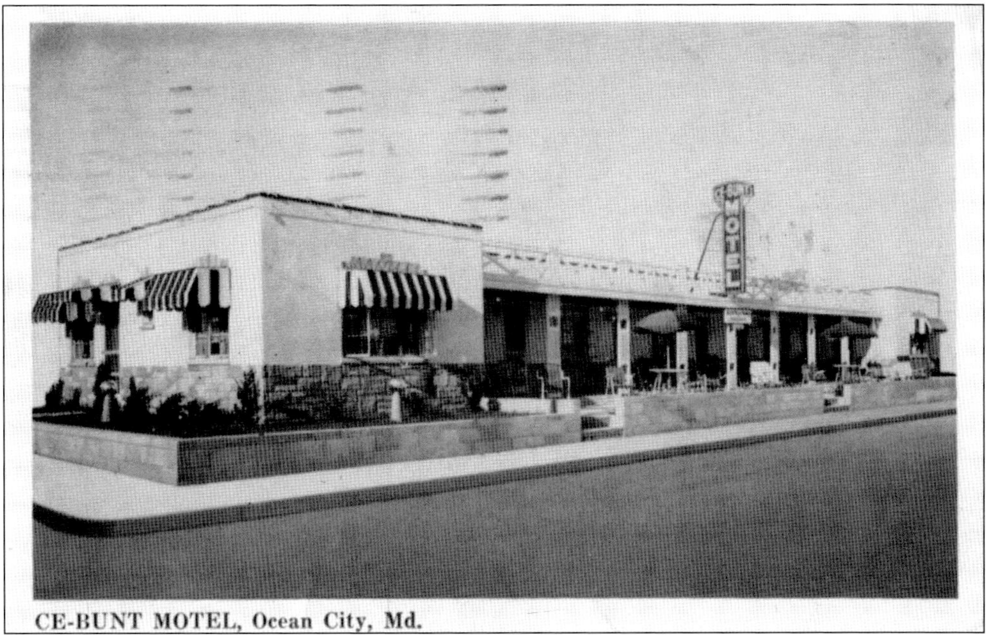

Downtown, at the bayside docks, ship captain Talbot Bunting built the CE Bunt Motel to accommodate fishermen chartering party boats on regular excursions out of Ocean City, often seeking marlin. The form of the early single-story motel calls to mind the Governor's Palace in Santa Fe, New Mexico, with its long portal (porch) extending between two adobe end blocks (see page 93). At the first CE Bunt Motel, windows in the stuccoed end blocks are adorned with Permastone lintels (visible above the striped aluminum awnings), and a broad Permastone base extends from the ground to the windowsills. This type of faux stone siding surfaced buildings across the country in the 1940s and 1950s with an artificial variegated rusticated cosmetic. When a second floor of units was added to the CE Bunt Motel, the Permastone remained. Today, the three-story Talbot Inn occupies this site.

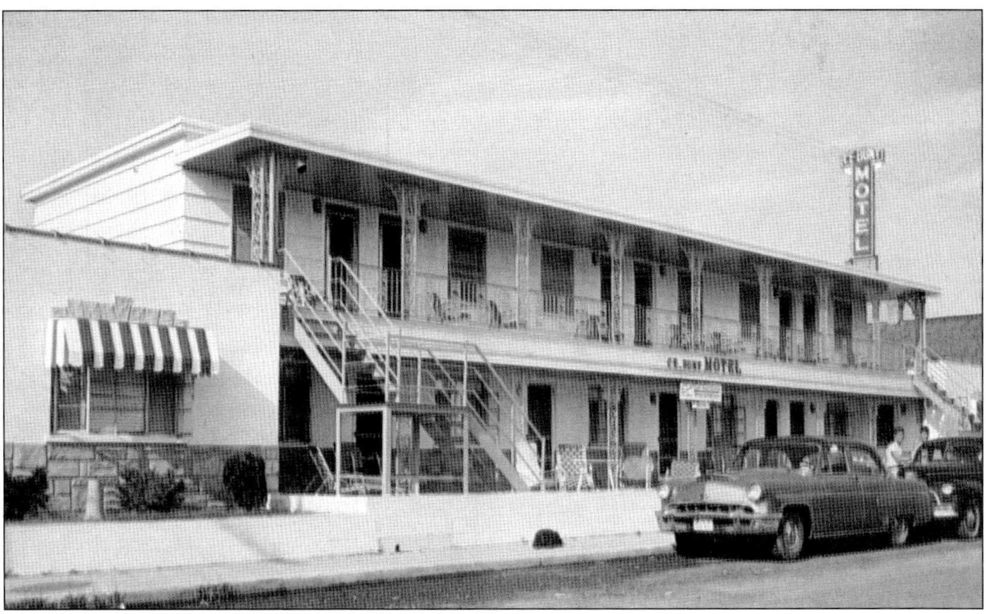

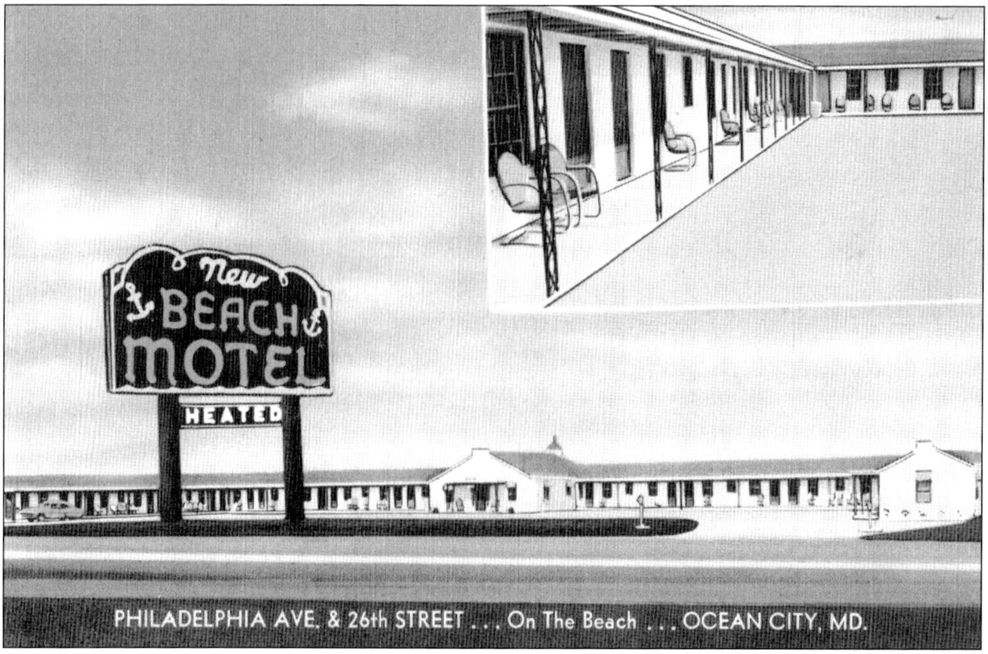

Larger motels expanded single or double parallel blocks of motel units into U-plans open to the road—a pattern that recalled cottage groupings in the 1940s (see page 84). Opened in 1951, the New Beach (later renamed Misty Harbor) Motel spread its wide arms along Philadelphia Avenue at Twenty-Sixth Street in a broad gesture of welcome, opening on a large court where numerous automobiles could be seen as indications of the motel's popularity in front of a seemingly endless array of available units. The gabled ends of the central office block and the two arms conveyed a domestic image, while the long continuous porch connected the units, each furnished with identical Mid-century metal rocking lawn armchairs, and offered outdoor space where guests could enjoy ocean and bay breezes before retiring for the night.

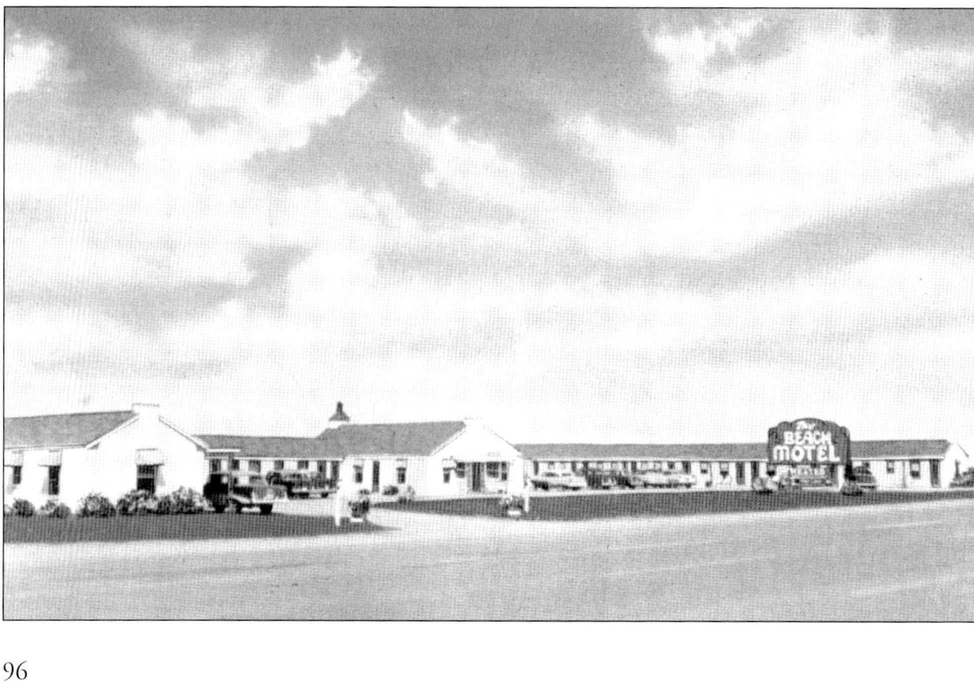

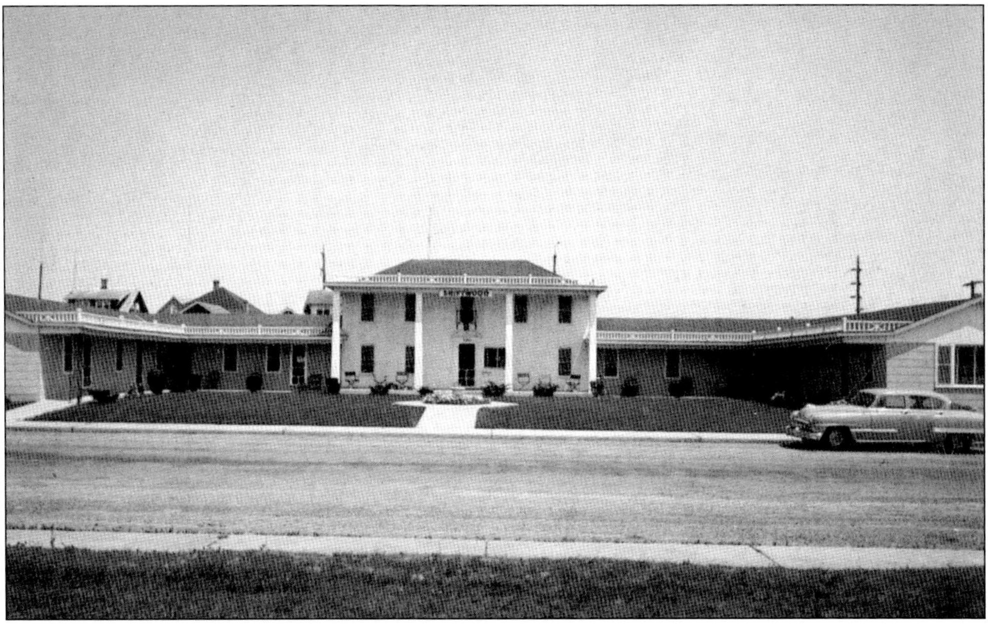

A variation on the U-plan was evident at the Driftwood Motel (above), located on St. Louis Avenue north of the US Route 50 bridge and no longer extant. Its prominent hipped-roof central block was fronted by a portico of widely spaced two-story classical columns, calling to mind Mount Vernon but combined with side arms in a Palladian villa layout. An unusual note about the Driftwood Motel is the fact that the units are reused and joined shacks from a mainland camp of the Civilian Conservation Corps (CCC), a 1933–1942 New Deal agency. A not particularly authentic borrowing of a colossal portico also adorns the Burgundy Inn Hotel, which is still extant on Philadelphia Avenue between Twelfth and Thirteenth Streets. Here, the portico is weak, and the flanking staircases to second-floor units crowd the temple porch. The cladding calls to mind historic shingle-clad hotels but contradicts that nostalgic evocation with burgundy paint on the siding.

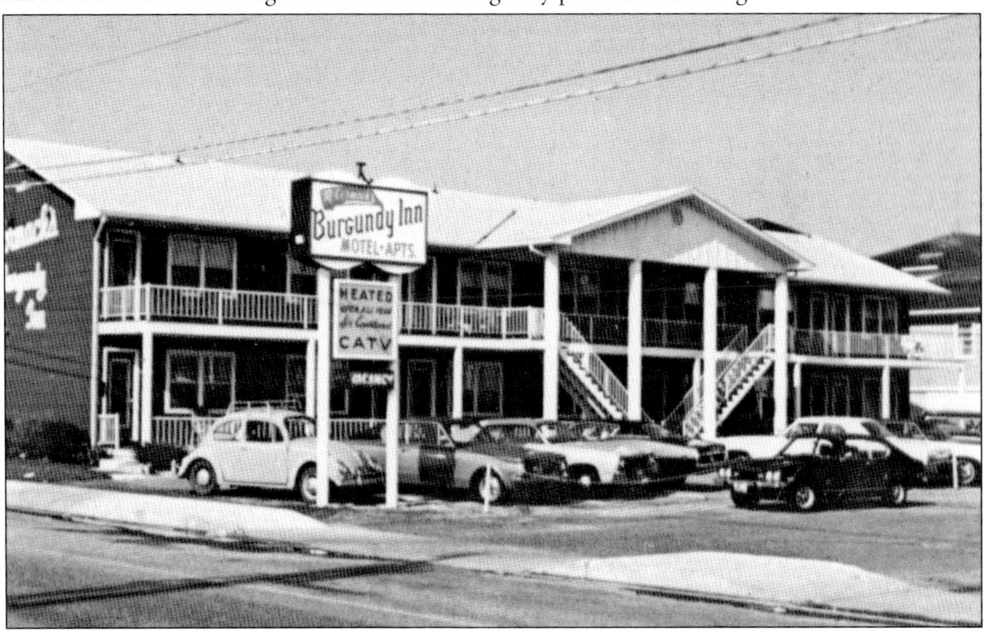

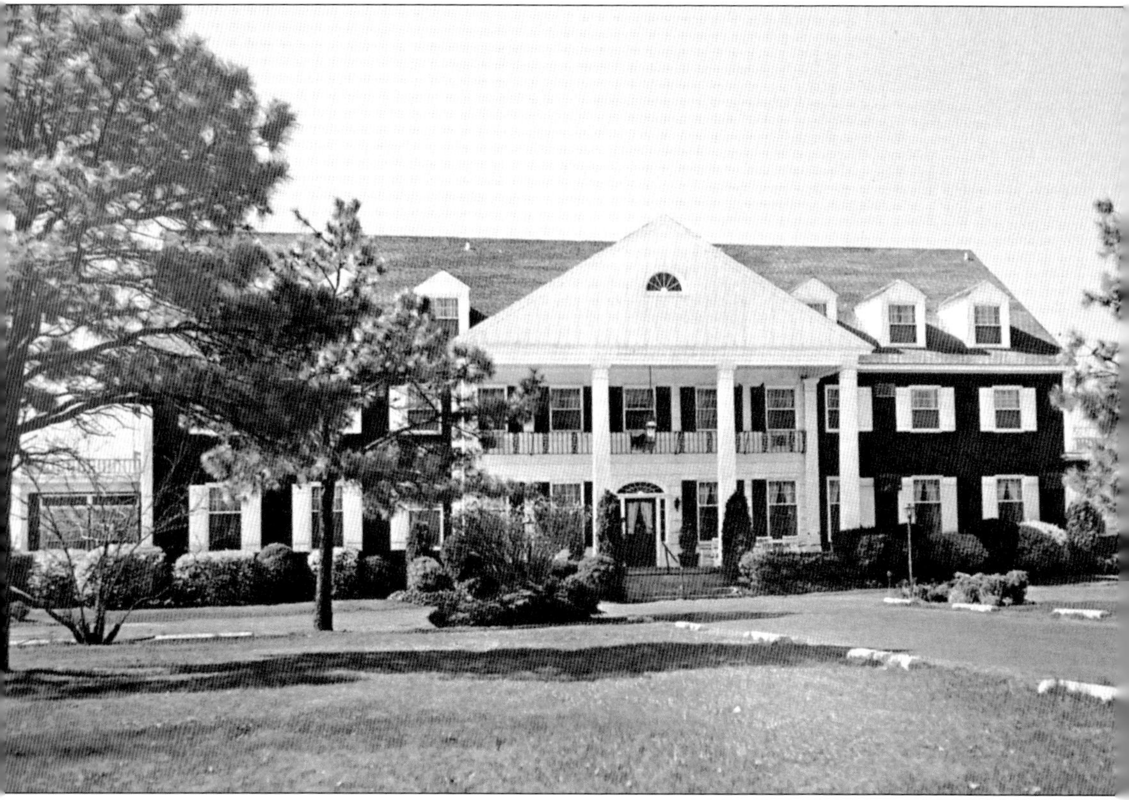

From the beginning of Ocean City's motel development, competition encouraged individuality in architectural design, and as elsewhere throughout the country, motel operators sought romantic imagery in order to attract travelers off the road for the night or a longer holiday stay. One of the most striking postwar motels in Ocean City was (and remains) the Francis Scott Key Motel (1953–1954), later Family Resort, with its flanking "ranch" and cottages and with larger motel blocks (32 units in 1986 and 40 units in 1989) and additional cottages added behind the lodge. The plantation imagery, sited at the far end of a tree-lined avenue and presenting a well-proportioned tetrastyle (four piers) portico, is highly evocative. Travelers are invited to admire the dormers fronting the sheltering gable roof and pass beyond the classical piers and through the inviting Federal-styled (fan- and side-lighted) front door into the big house. This is old Southern charm; a complex today enlarged to a family resort with an outdoor swimming pool, a Putt-Putt course, playgrounds, and restaurants, it is one of the success stories from the motel era.

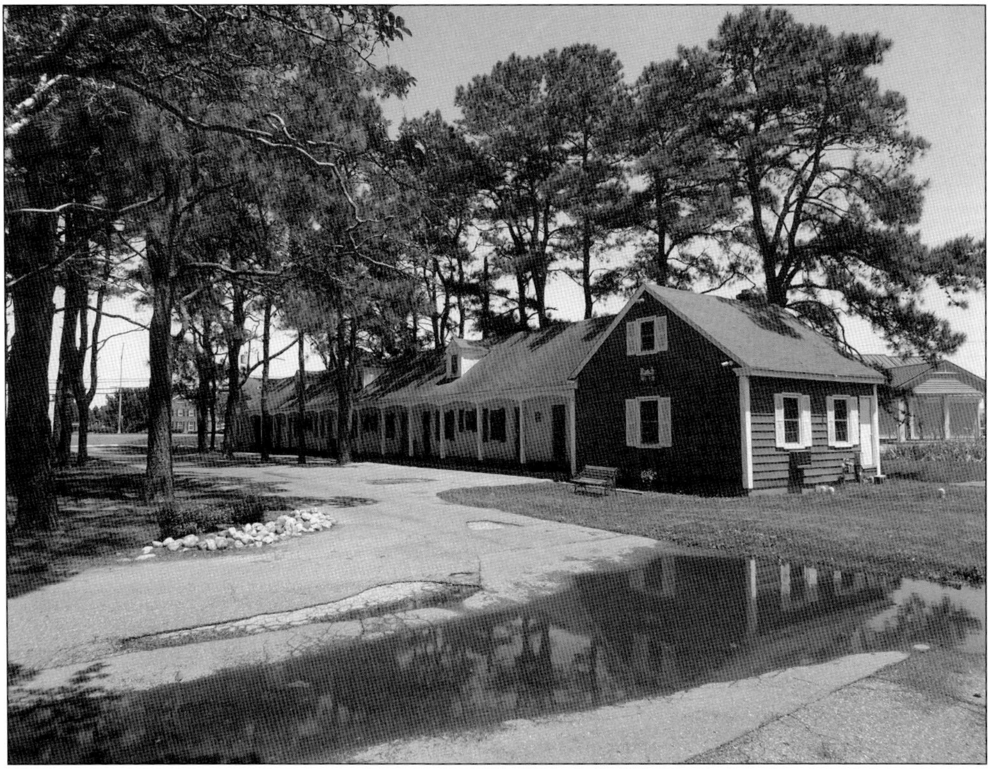

The more traditional motel units flanking the east side of the approach to the Francis Scott Key Motel were identified as a ranch block (above). As the complex grew southward, larger two-story motel blocks of units were added behind the lodge. These were named for US states (as were the cottages at the Villa Nova), and the below image shows the Maryland and Delaware blocks. Scattered among these larger motel blocks are the Shipwreck Cove (an outdoor swimming pool), with its huge "beached" ship with deck-top refreshments, and the adjacent Peg Leg miniature golf course with a pirate theme; there is also a Caribbean Key indoor pool. (Both, RMC.)

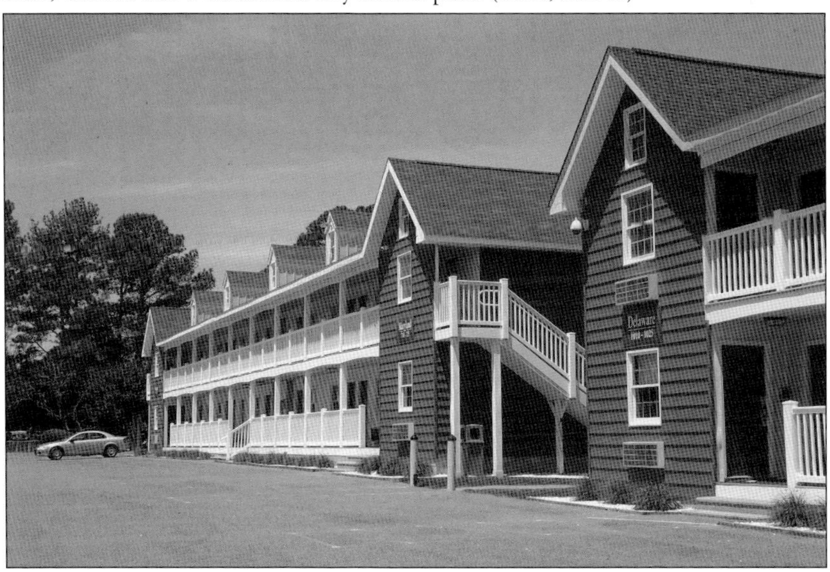

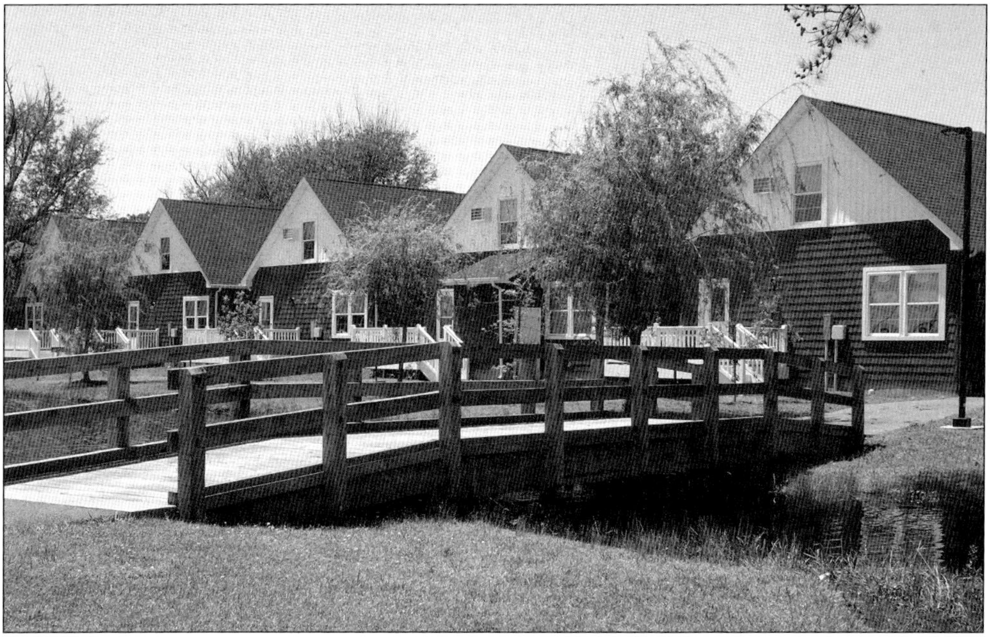

The expanding Francis Scott Key complex also moved to its grounds the Elk Horn Tourist Cottages from US 50 (and other cottages) and built new cottages in the old tourist cottage-camp tradition. Today, the complex preserves all three traditions—the hotel lodge with a dining room, the individual tourist cottage group, and the motel. With all of its buildings painted a rustic barn red with white trim, the facility is also well landscaped. While the view from Route 50 is not quite that of Boone Hall Plantation in Charleston, South Carolina (the possible model for the Francis Scott Key complex's design), the motel's nostalgic historicist styling and evocative romantic imagery nevertheless recall times when automobile excursions were adventures and overnight stays did not yet suffer from the standardized ordinariness of one-ounce soap bars, flat-screen televisions, and chain-motel three-star ratings. (Both, RMC.)

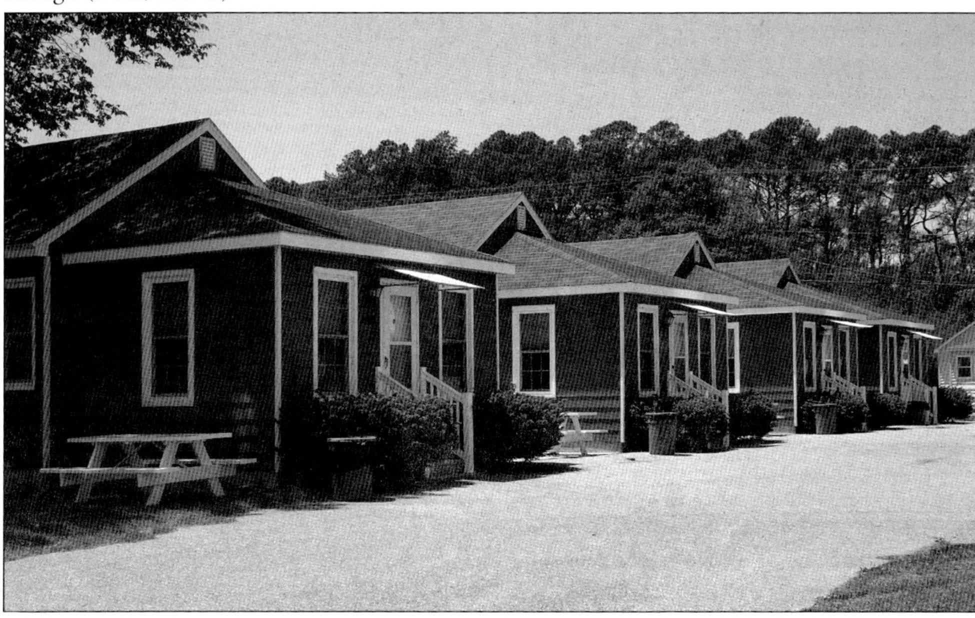

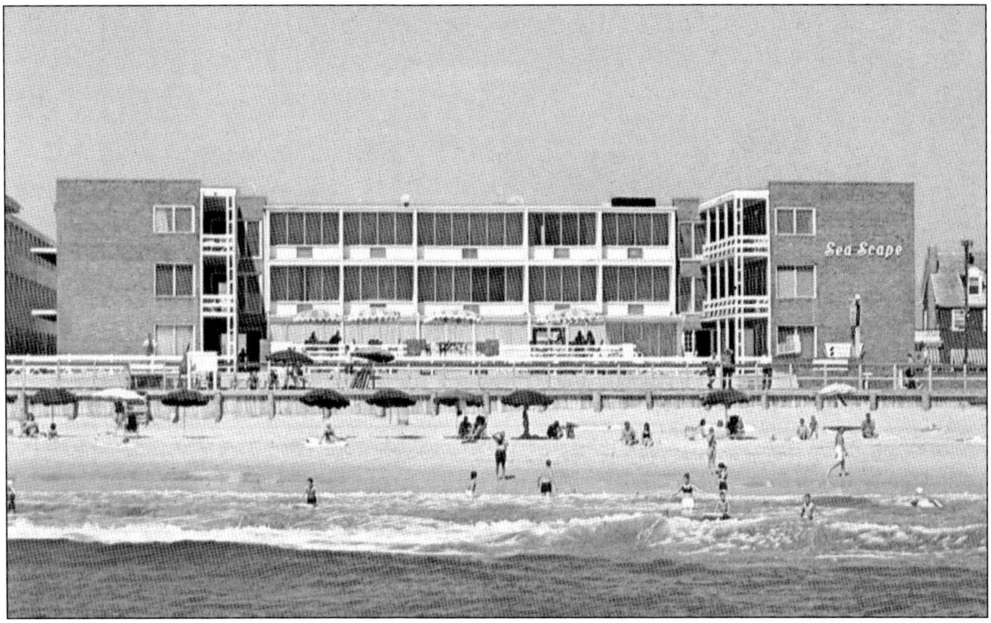

Ocean City's "Motel Row" dates from the 1952 opening of the Sea Scape Motel (above) at Sixteenth Street, the town's first Boardwalk motel, and the first Boardwalk motel swimming pool. Oriented east, toward the ocean, the Sea Scape wrapped its three levels of 95 motel rooms around the Boardwalk-fronted swimming pool. After more than six decades, the motel was demolished following the 2016 summer season and replaced by the Hyatt Place Hotel. At the north end of the motel district was the Thirty-Second Street Ocean City Motel (also opened in 1952), which was later renamed the Charm and then Budget Beach Motel. The Ocean Park Motel (below) soon followed (1954–1955) at Seventeenth Street on the Boardwalk with a swimming pool and on-site parking. Two-story blocks of motel units overlooked both the beach to the east and an open green space between the two motel blocks.

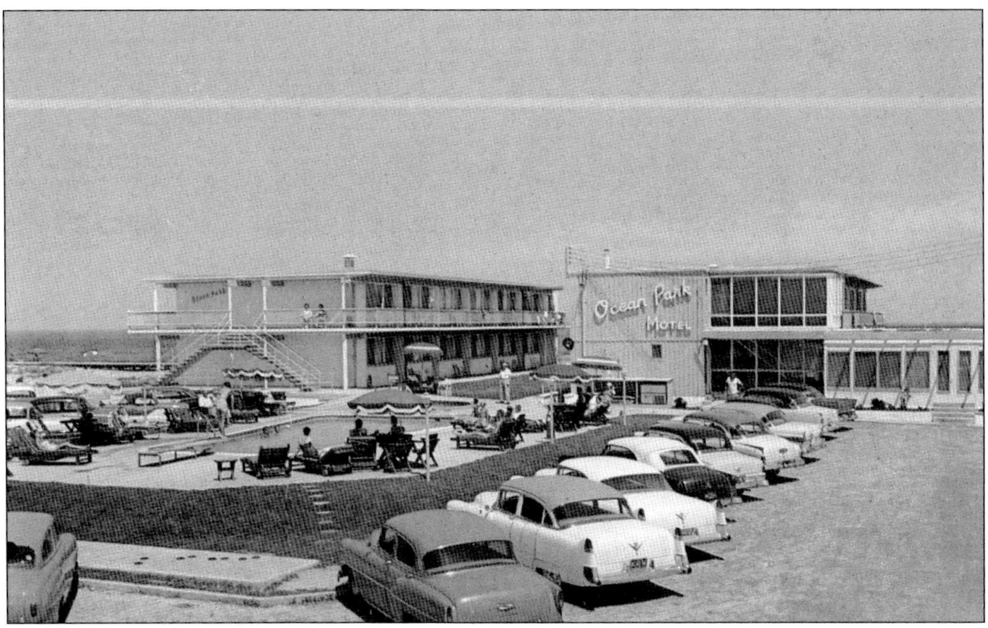

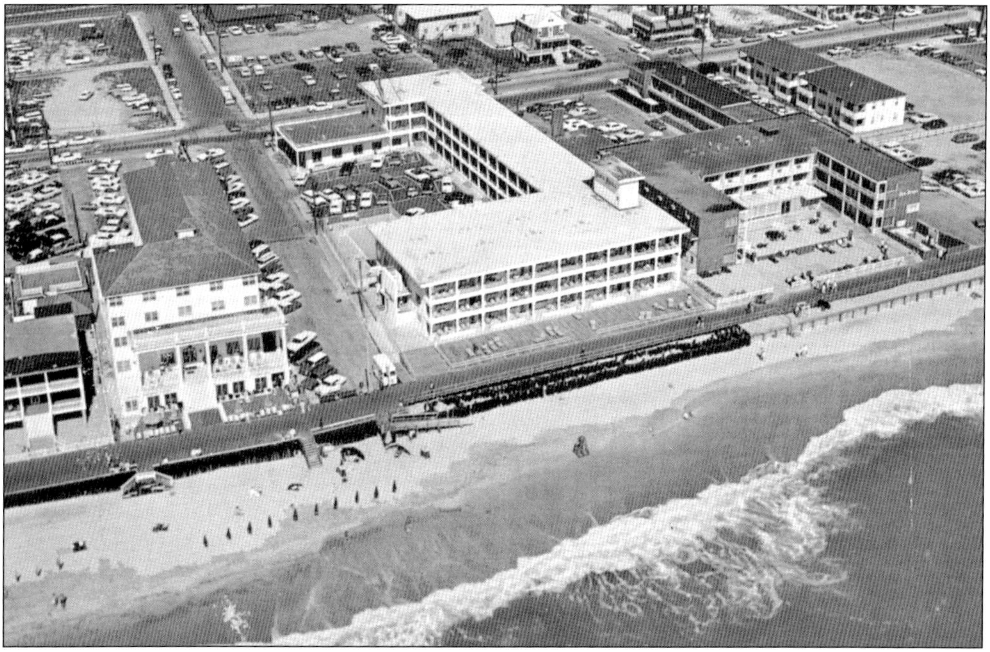

During the mid-1950s, Mid-century Modern motels were constructed on and off the Boardwalk north of Fifteenth Street. The Boardwalk had earlier ended at Fifteenth Street; Harrison Hall, the northernmost hotel of an earlier era, was sited on the south corner of Fifteenth Street, and motel architecture was the order of the day farther north. The three principal buildings along the Boardwalk at Fifteenth Street shown in the aerial photograph above are (from left to right) Harrison Hall, the Santa Maria Motel (1956), and the Sea Scape Motel (1952). Farther north, between Seventeenth and Eighteenth Streets, were the 1955 Ocean Park Motel (page 101) and the 1959 Sandyhill Motel (below). An inflatable tent covered the Sandyhill pool during off-season months so the motel could advertise an indoor pool and heated water.

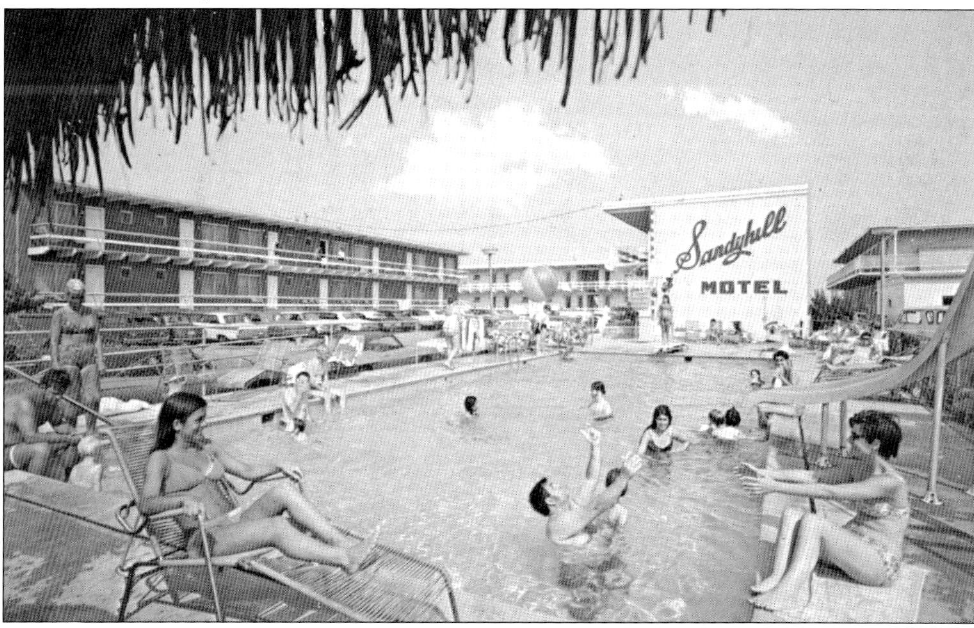

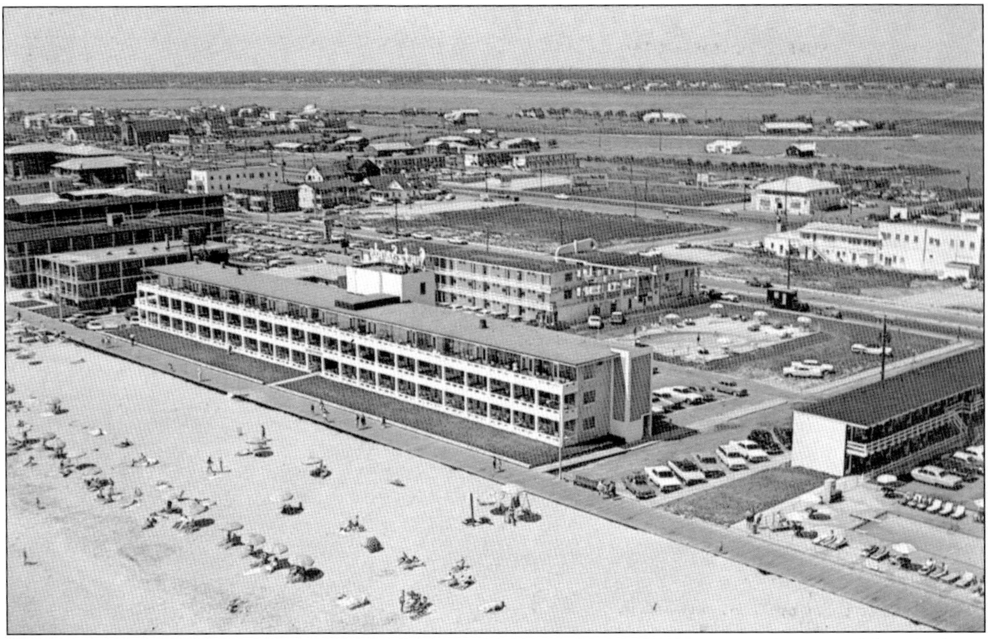

The Surf and Sands Motel, which opened in 1955, extended its 24-bay ocean frontage (above) along the full block between Twenty-Second and Twenty-Third Streets on the Boardwalk, with the motel office fronting Baltimore Avenue. The motel advertised "every room with private porch," providing each beachfront motel unit with a private balcony and view of the ocean. A twin-bedded beachfront room rented for $16 per night. Initially erected with two stories, the motel later added a third level, continuing the CMU (concrete block) construction with walled balconies. On the west side (below), a kidney-shaped outdoor pool and smaller circular children's pool were surrounded by ample terraces with lounge recliners and promised sunshine for recreational sunbathing. The Surf and Sands logo used a seahorse for the capital S in "Surf." Enlarged to five levels (with a sixth adorning the ocean front's center bays), the motel is now a Days Inn.

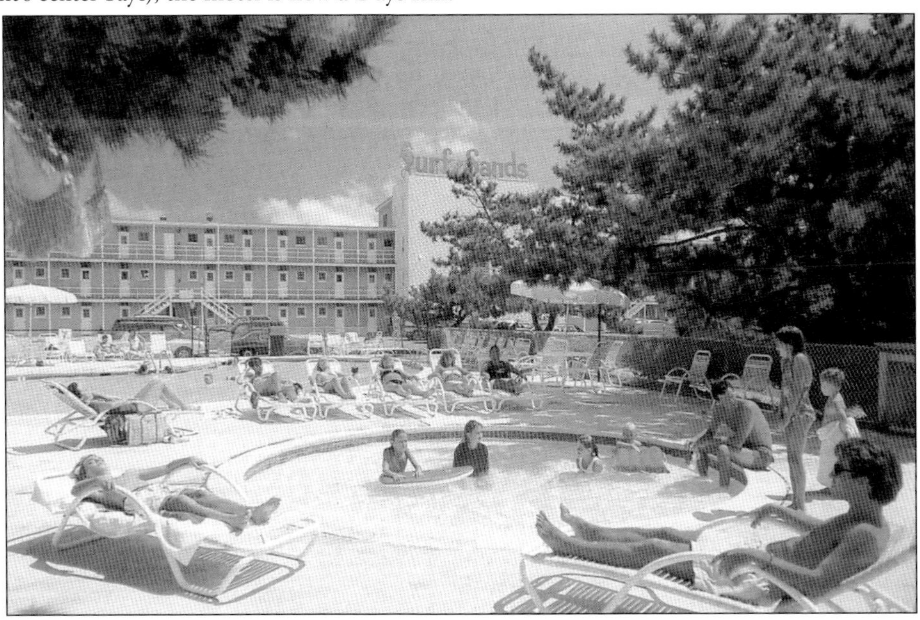

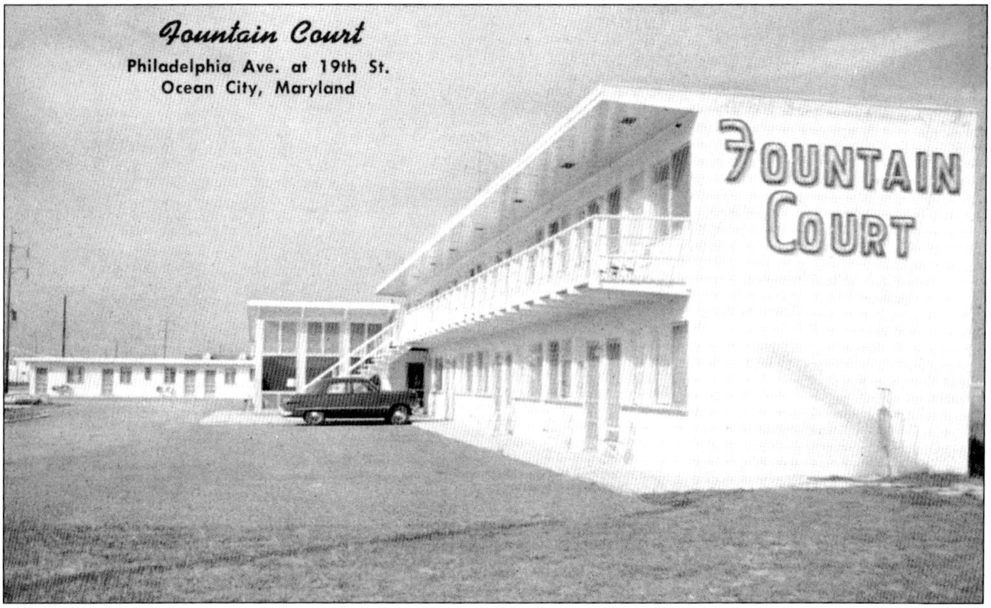

Contemporary with the Surf and Sands Motel is the Fountain Court Motel, built in 1955 on Philadelphia Avenue at Nineteenth Street. Soon after its initial summer seasons, the motel was enlarged and given a Mid-century Modern office with a distinctive "butterfly" roof (inverted slopes converging in a valley rather than gable ridge) that has been linked to Modernist Marcel Breuer's introduction of the inward-sloping roofs in 1944 in what he called binuclear houses. The form reaches back to 1930 in Le Corbusier's unexecuted Maison Errazuriz project, appropriated in 1933 by Antonin Raymond for his house in Japan and published in *Architectural Record* in 1934. It was William Krisel's use of the butterfly roof in California houses in the mid-1950s that popularized the roof form. Ocean City's iconic example is at the Fountain Court, which was renamed the Cabana and is still extant today.

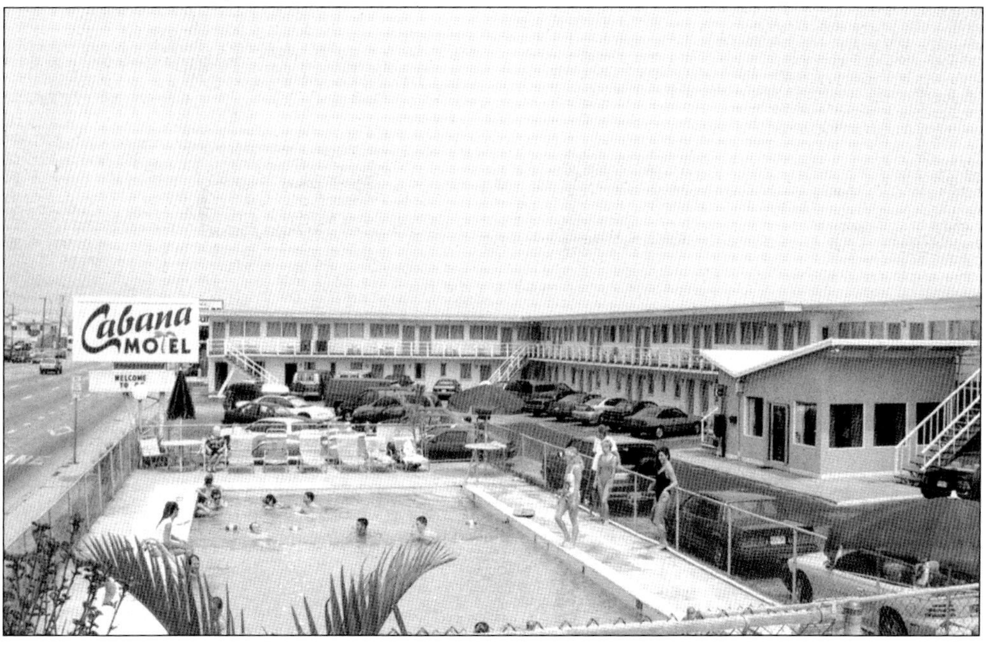

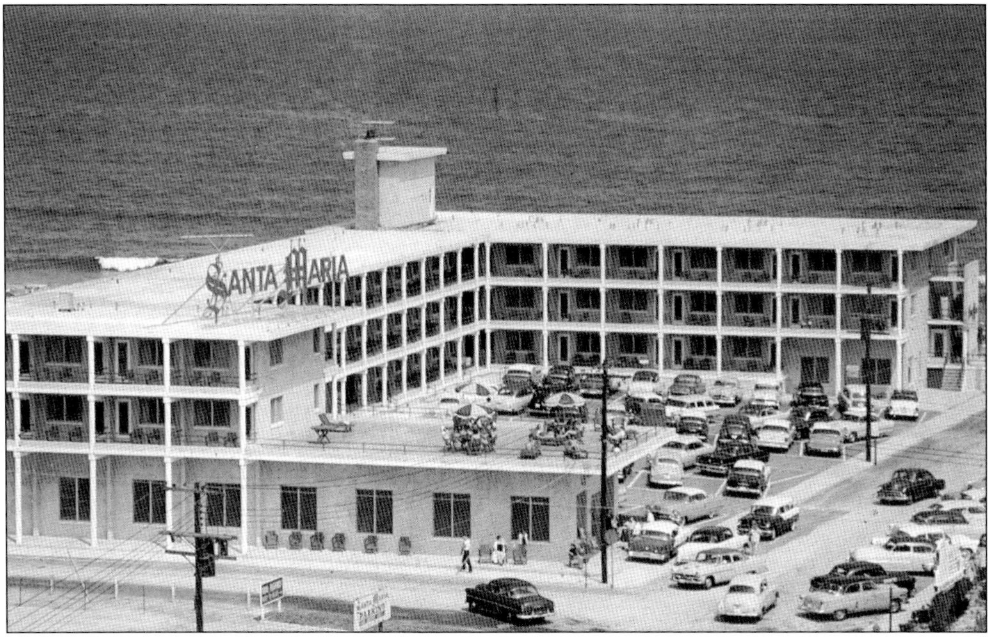

The Santa Maria Motel opened in 1956 and was a classic; its replacement by the current Courtyard by Marriott may be viewed as symbolic of the displacement of mid-century mom-and-pop motels by the franchised megastructures of today's Motel Row. What might have been preserved as a unique mid-20th-century historic district now instead features an epidemic of chain motels—Quality Inns, Holiday Inns, Marriotts, and a swanky Hyatt. In today's Motel Row, it is rare to see motel names referencing the ocean, beach, surf, sand, waves, or even familiar names from US history. Indeed, few of today's down-for-the-dayers could tell you what "Santa Maria" references. The homey Captain's Table restaurant in the original motel was a local favorite and also crowded with tourists in the know, but today it is an upscaled, upper-floor designer dining room offering "cuisine."

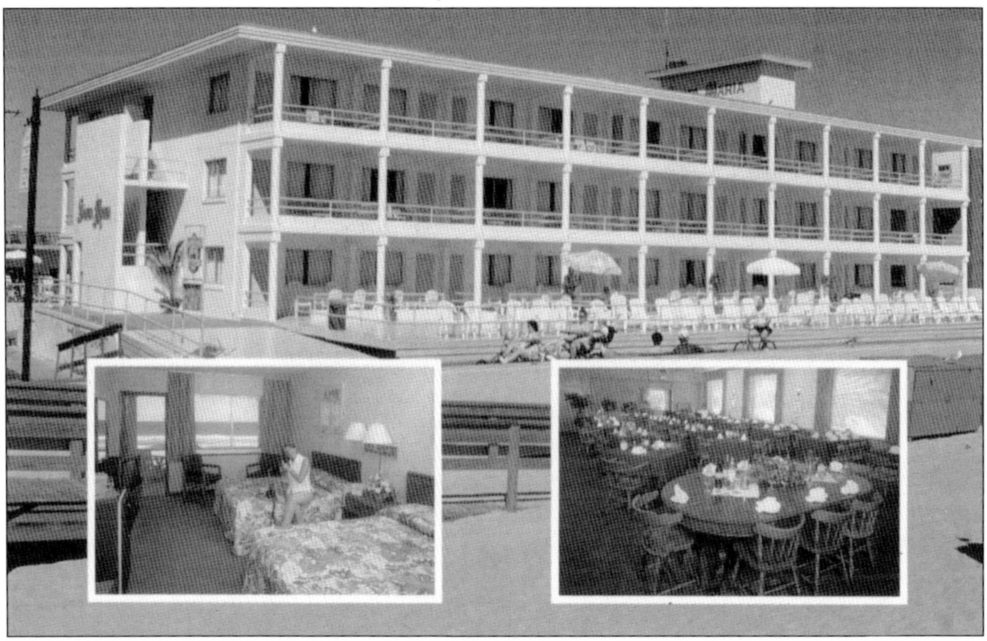

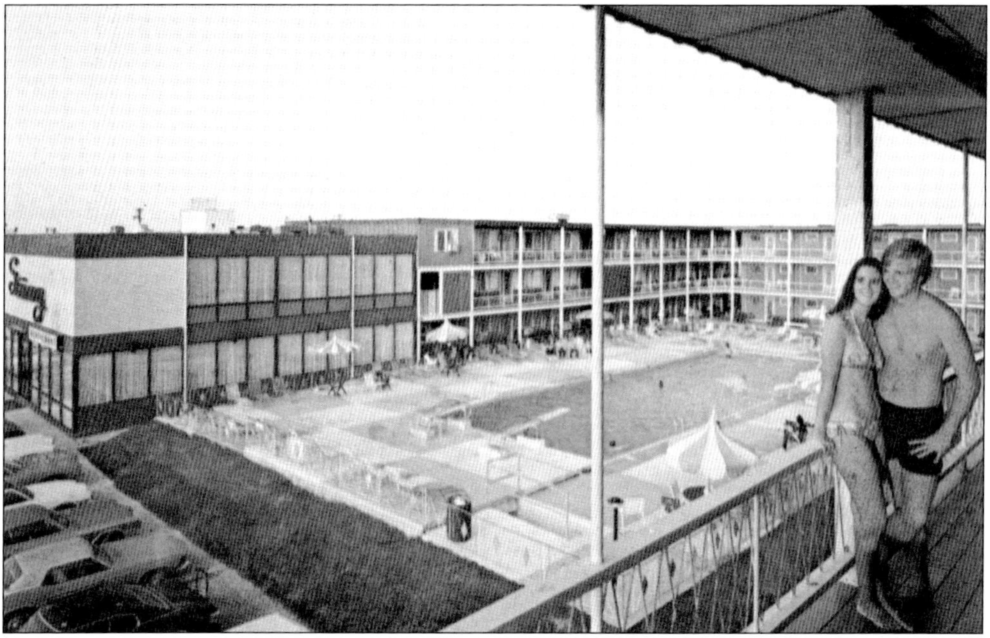

The town's largest motel for the 1960s, the Stowaway (above), appeared on the scene in 1956 fronting the Boardwalk and extending the entire block between Twenty-First and Twenty-Second Streets. The 120-unit motel offered the largest swimming pool in Motel Row, and its Hide-A-Way Lounge was popular. However, after 40 years, the Stowaway was torn down following the 1995 season, and in 2001, the semicircular 12-story Stowaway Grand Hotel and Spa opened on the site. Another Motel Row classic is the Ocean Mecca Motel (below), which was recently rebranded as a "retro vintage property . . . [whose] nostalgic renovation . . . brings back the charm of a long gone area when Ocean City was only motels at the beach" (vymaps.com/US/Ocean-Mecca-Motel). Renamed the Ocean Mecca Motel and Fish Tails Boardwalk Inn, the motel still displays classic features of Mid-century Modern architecture.

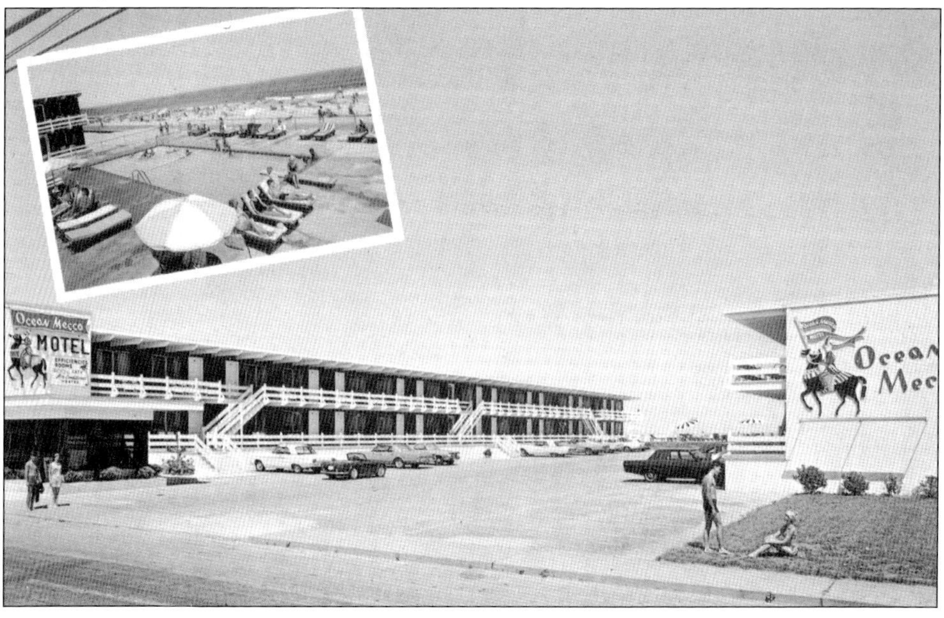

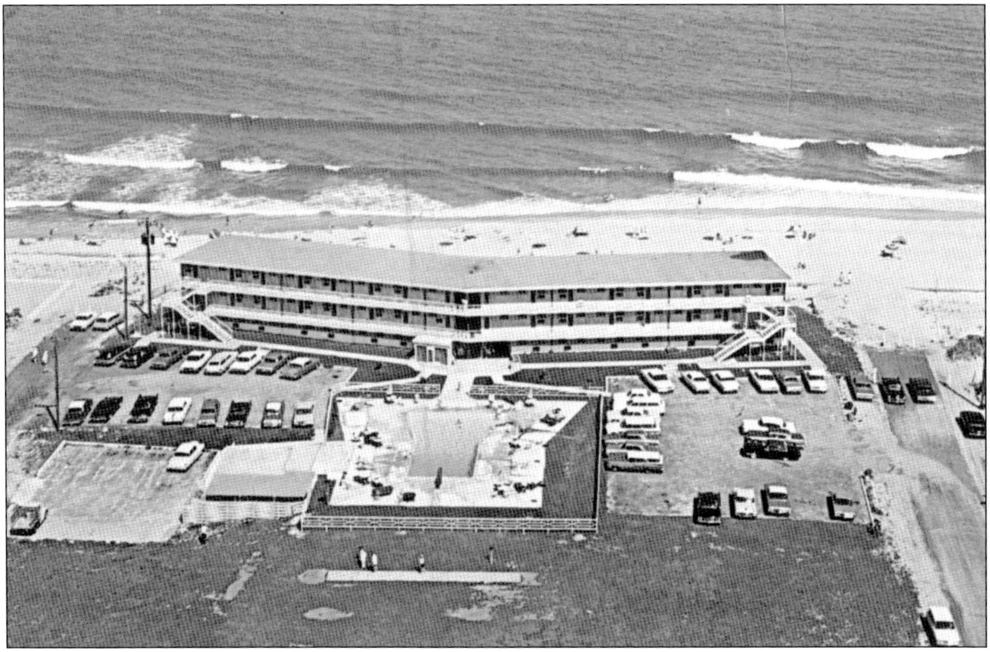

In 1958, at the time when oceanfront land was conveyed between Fifty-Fourth and Fifty-Fifth Streets, the site of the future Park de Ville Motel (above) was outside Ocean City's limits and well beyond the developing Motel Row. Investors, however, were counting on the continuing northward growth; just as the Commander Hotel, built on Fourteenth Street in 1930, seemed isolated in open dunes beyond the range of the lodgings market, so 40 blocks farther north was considered remote in 1958. In 1962, the Carousel Motel (below) opened on 118th Street, and in 1965, the city limits were extended to the Delaware state line. The Park de Ville's original obliquely splayed wings are still visible from the west (poolside), but its open arms were blocked by a five-story oceanfront block of rooms when it was expanded in 1981 and converted to a Quality Inn.

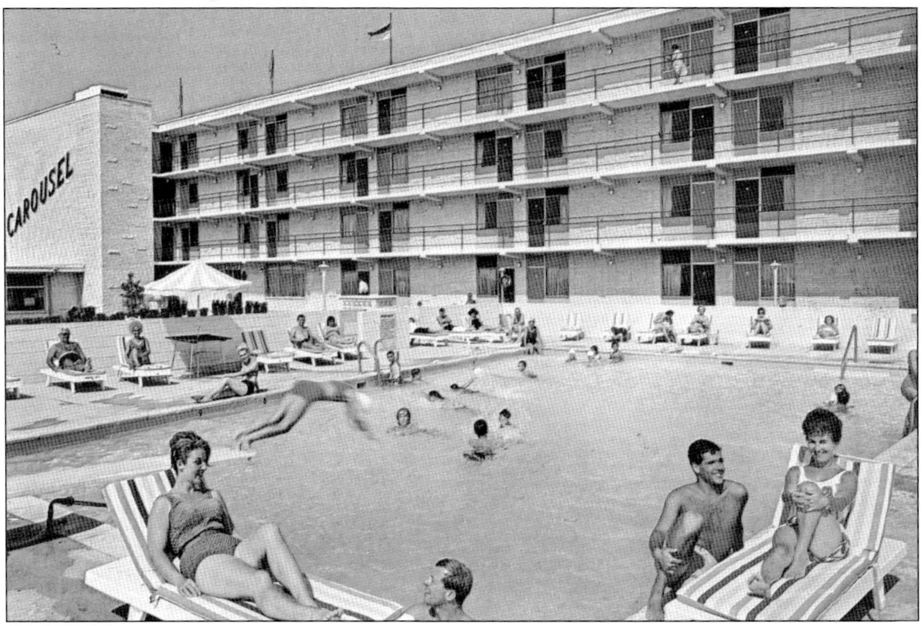

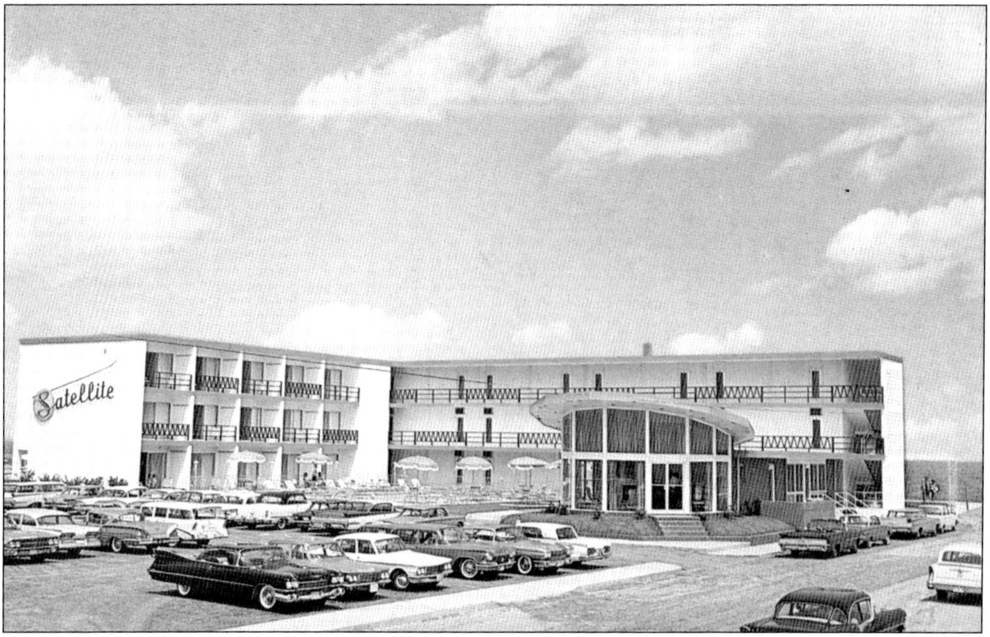

On October 4, 1957, the Soviet Union launched *Sputnik I*, the first artificial satellite, and the space race was on. Ocean City's Satellite Motel, which opened in 1961 on the Boardwalk at Twenty-Fourth Street (above), was one of numerous architectural reflections of this event, shown here in the motel's name and—to a degree—in the more kinetic lines of the polygonal glazed office. In Anaheim, California, industrialist Al Stovall created four cosmic-themed motels (Space Age Lodge, Inn of Tomorrow, the Galaxy, and the Cosmic Inn); another of his Space Age Lodges in Gila Bend, Arizona (now a Best Western), employed a flying saucer in its signage. Elsewhere in Ocean City, the Stardust Motel (below) featured signage with tiny bursts of atomic fireworks, or space-age "stardust," in its futuristic meandering three-story motel block.

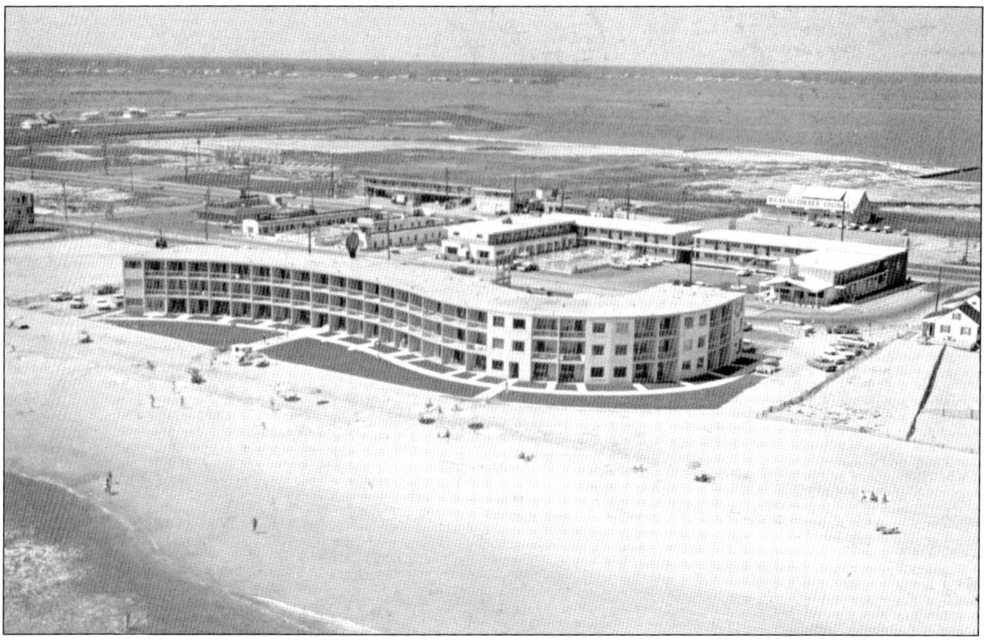

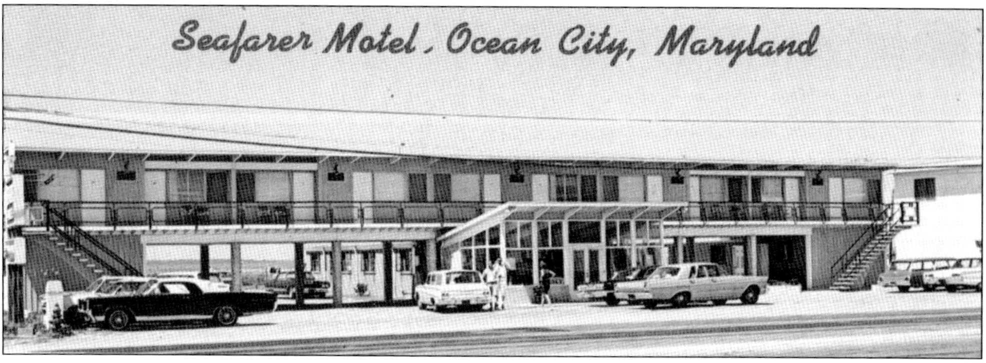

The Stardust Motel on Thirty-Third Street (see page 108) marked the northern edge of the Motel Row district, and nearby motels of the time included the White Sands, also known as Charm Motel (now a parking lot for the Hilton); the 1964 Yankee Clipper, also known as the Voyager (which was razed in 2013 for a La Quinta Inn; see page 156); and the Seafarer (above; now the site of Jolly Roger Amusement Park). The acute angle of the Seafarer's office roof, with the uplift of a Frank Lloyd Wright–styled Usonian house, is a sign of its 1950s origins. The Stardust was razed and became the site of a Hilton. Survivors in the district include the L-plan Sun 'N Fun Motel on Baltimore Avenue at Twenty-Ninth Street (below), the King's Arms on Baltimore Avenue at Twenty-Fourth Street, and the Empress Motel on Baltimore Avenue at Twentieth Street.

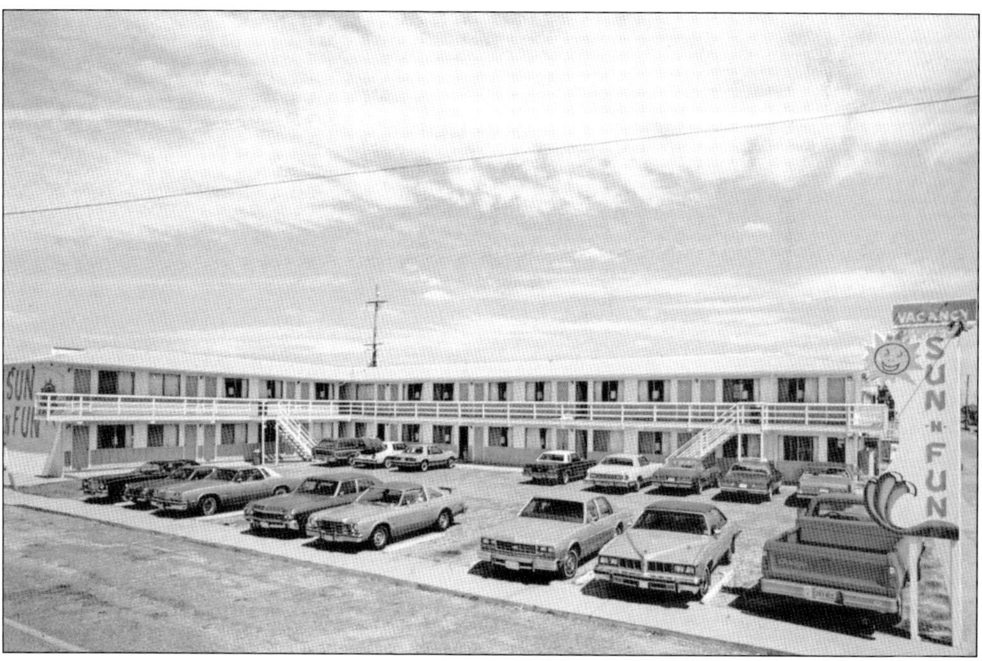

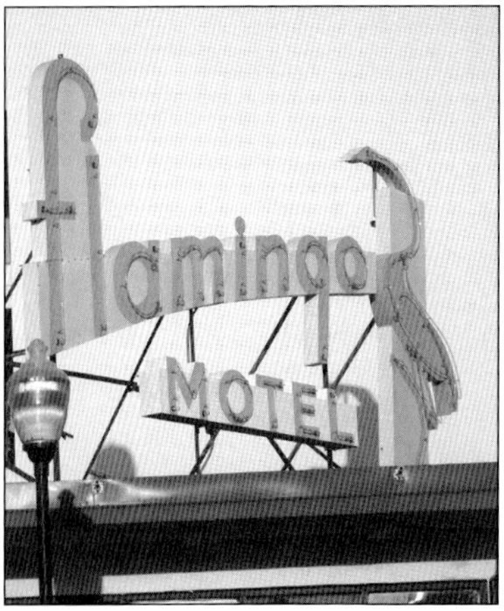

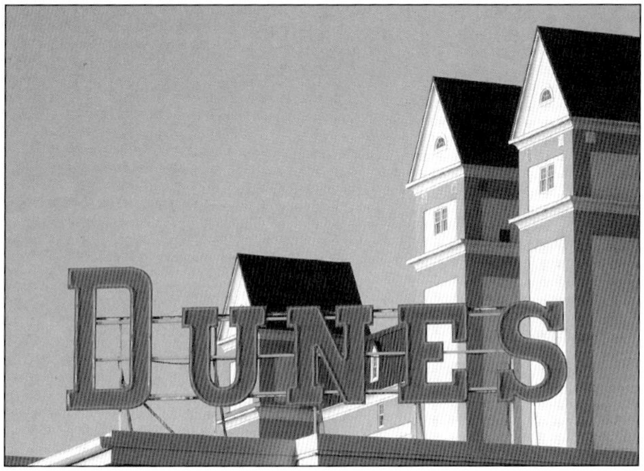

Four landmark motels are especially notable for their signage and survive as significant examples of 1950s and early 1960s design: the Flamingo, the Dunes, the Eden Roc, and the Seabonay. Motels relied on signage, often delineated by neon calligraphy or decorated with a recognizable symbol such as a pink flamingo. Both the name and the symbol were intended to be memorable, and at a beach resort, the simplicity of "Dunes" was enough. While so much of Motel Row has been lost, it would be a further travesty to replace these signs, which are historic in their own right, with modern commercialism. They are quite literally signs of our times. (All, RMC.)

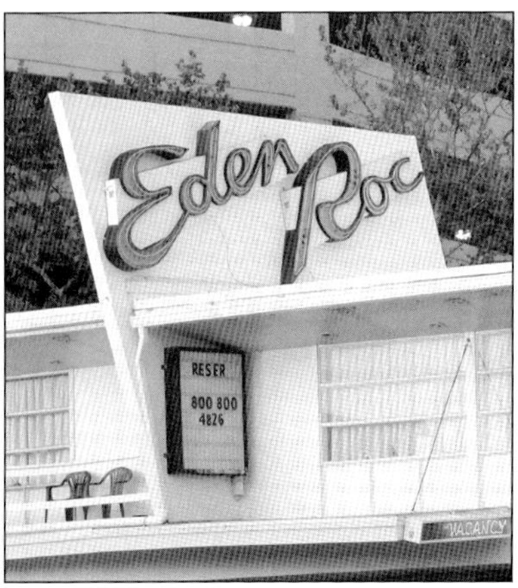

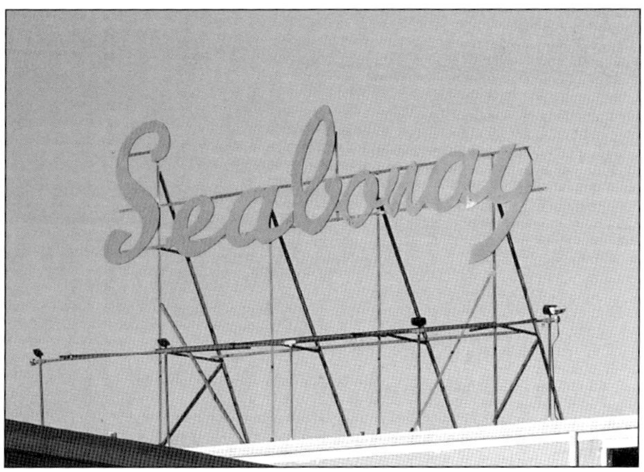

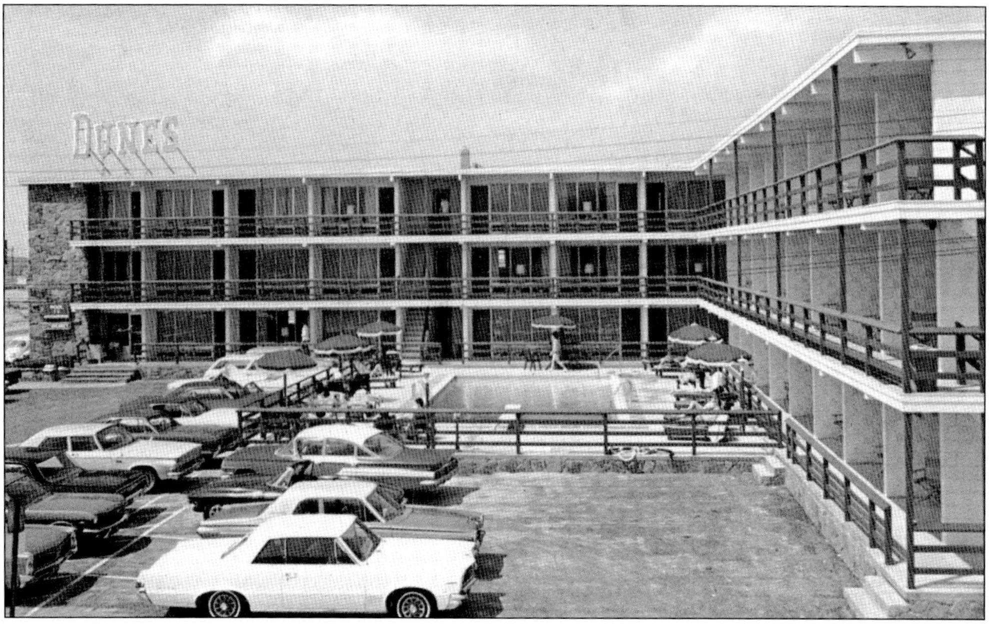

The Dunes organization recognizes its red rooftop sign as iconic, describes the 49-room Dunes Motel (now called Dunes Court) as "retro chic," and defines its motel experience as a "step back in time." Thelma and George Connor bought the Dunes Motel in 1965 and later added the Dunes Suites at the Boardwalk's north end. At the age of 75, Thelma Connor opened the Victorian Dunes Manor Hotel on April Fools' Day in 1987 (see page 149).

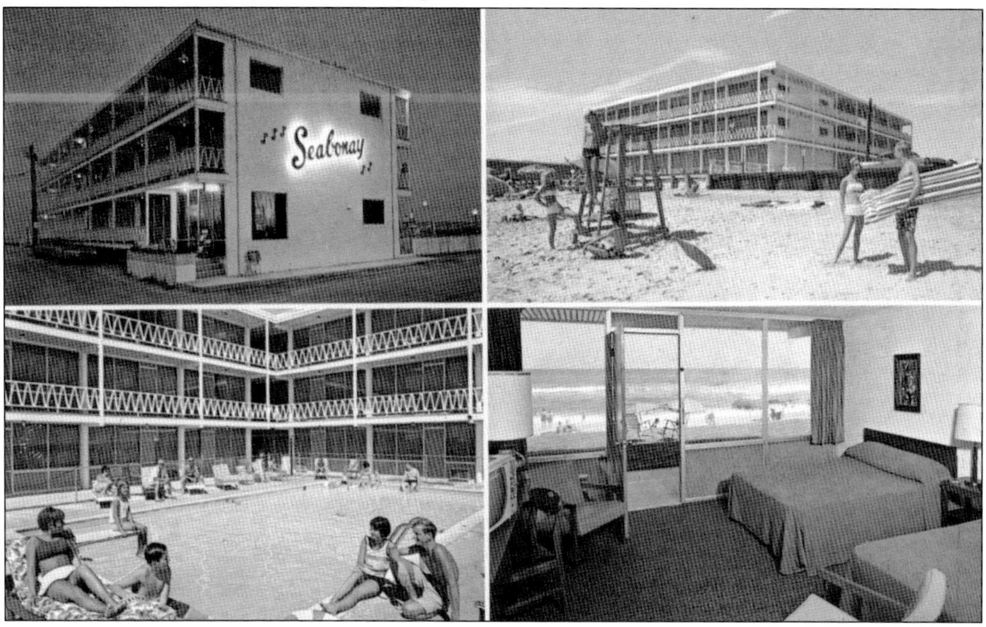

Overlooking the dunes line at Twenty-Eighth Street is the Seabonay Motel, an oceanfront motel built in 1965 with 55 rooms. Its three levels of rooms form an L-plan with an inner southwest side that embraces a small swimming pool. The 1960s-scale motel is overshadowed by the 12-story Dunes Manor Hotel to its north and the five-story Dunes Suites block stretching southward to Twenty-Seventh Street. Nonetheless, Seabonay's rooftop sign holds its own.

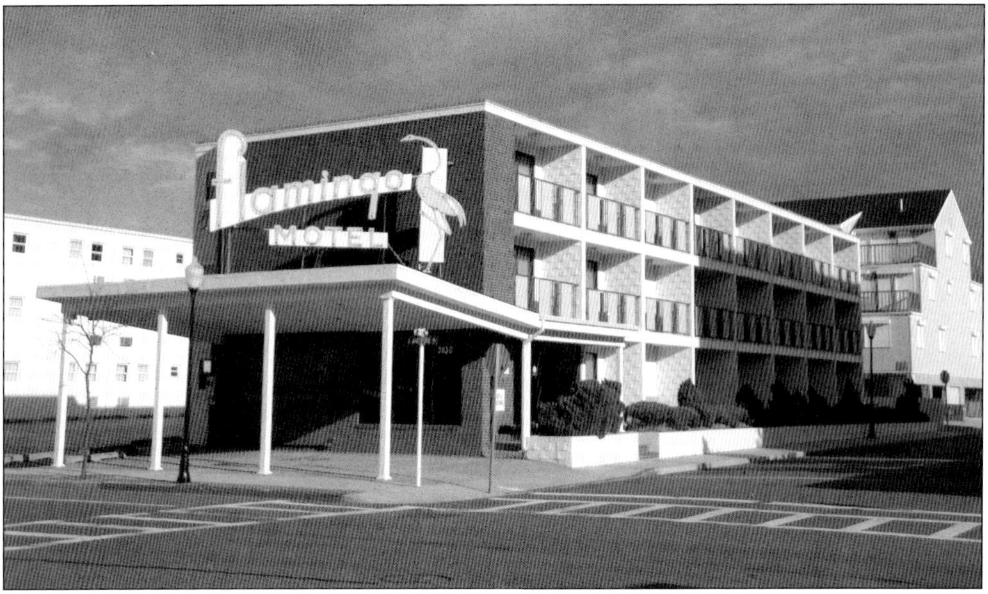

The Flamingo Motel was built in stages. It started as a classic mom-and-pop motel that was owned and operated for nearly 60 years by the Brous family. The original 1962 motel at Thirty-Seventh Street contained 30 units on three levels fronted by an angled slab–canopy porte cochere entry; that building is now the Simple Life Motel. Following this initial construction, two Flamingo towers were built at each end of the block to the south, at the Baltimore Avenue corners of Thirtieth and Thirty-First Streets, with each five-story tower having south-facing balcony corridors. The motel's 12-foot-tall pink flamingo sign is an original piece of the resort's "Tropical Deco" imagery and a landmark of Motel Row. Beyond borrowed flamingo motifs, business owners' wintering in subtropical Florida also encouraged the yearly importing of palm trees to adorn restaurants and miniature golf courses throughout Ocean City. (Both, RMC.)

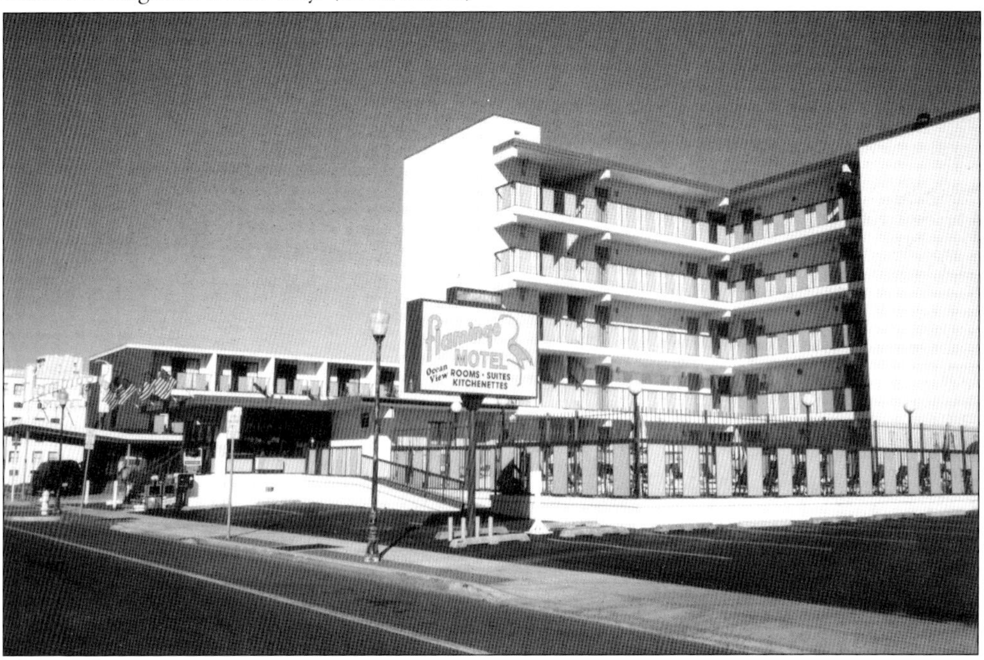

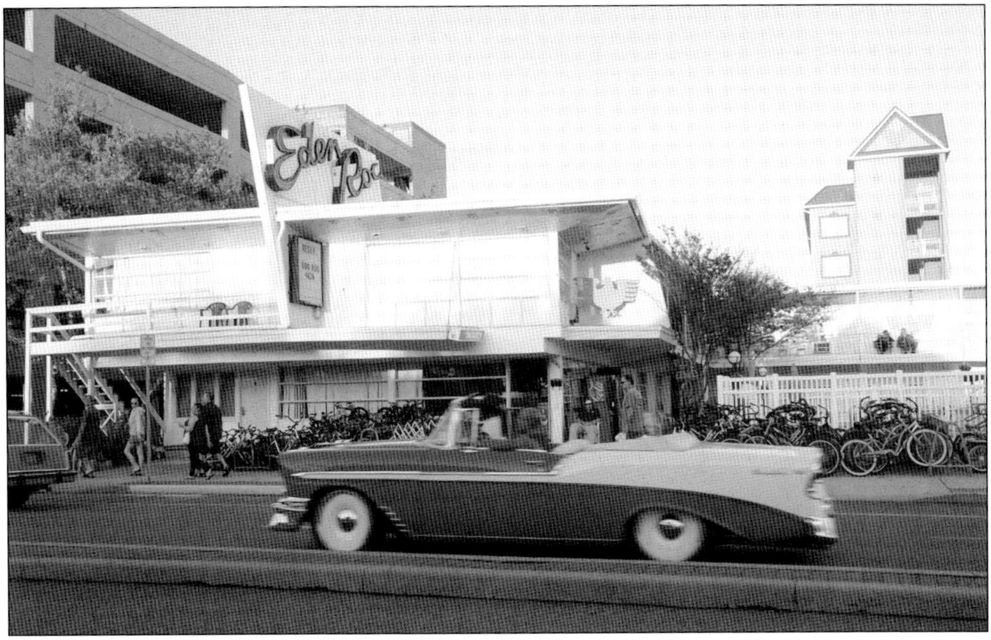

The Eden Roc Motel's distinctive modern style dates from 1960, and the motel has retained its mid-century character—relatively unchanged—for over half a century. Large horizontal windows, flat planar roof slabs, and thin balcony floor slabs with minimalist support posts and abstract geometric porch rails emphasize a volumetric architecture of open voids rather than formal masses. The angular plane of the motel sign slices through the flat roof plane like a De Stijl "counter construction," with the exposed parallelogram rooftop simply adorned with "Eden Roc" in cursive longhand. Signage and architecture are thus joined in the uniquely coordinated design of one of Ocean City's most significant buildings, which is worthy of listing in the National Register of Historic Places. (Above, RMC.)

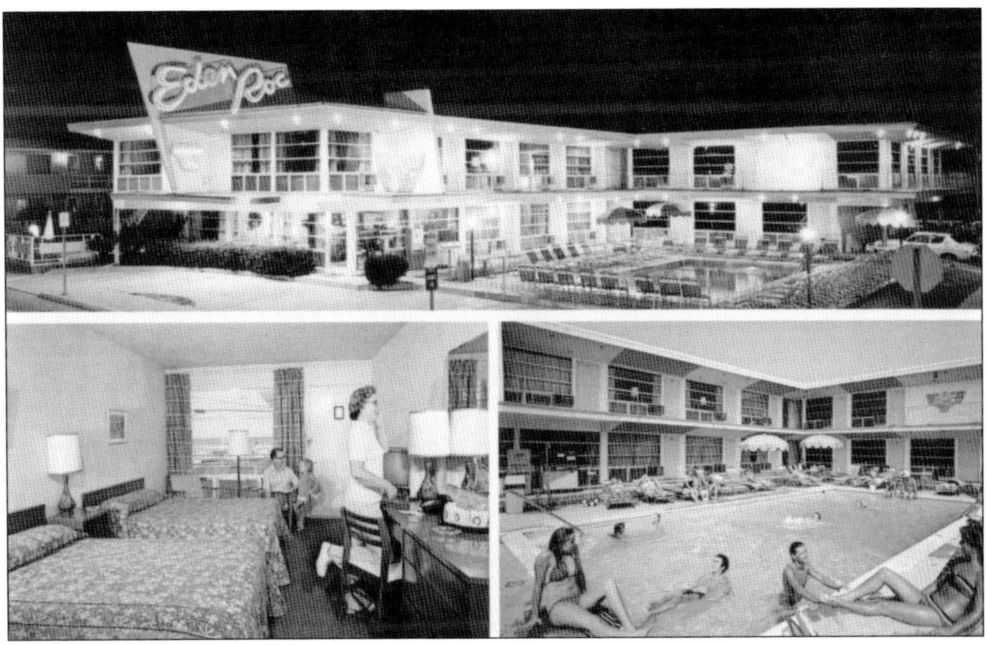

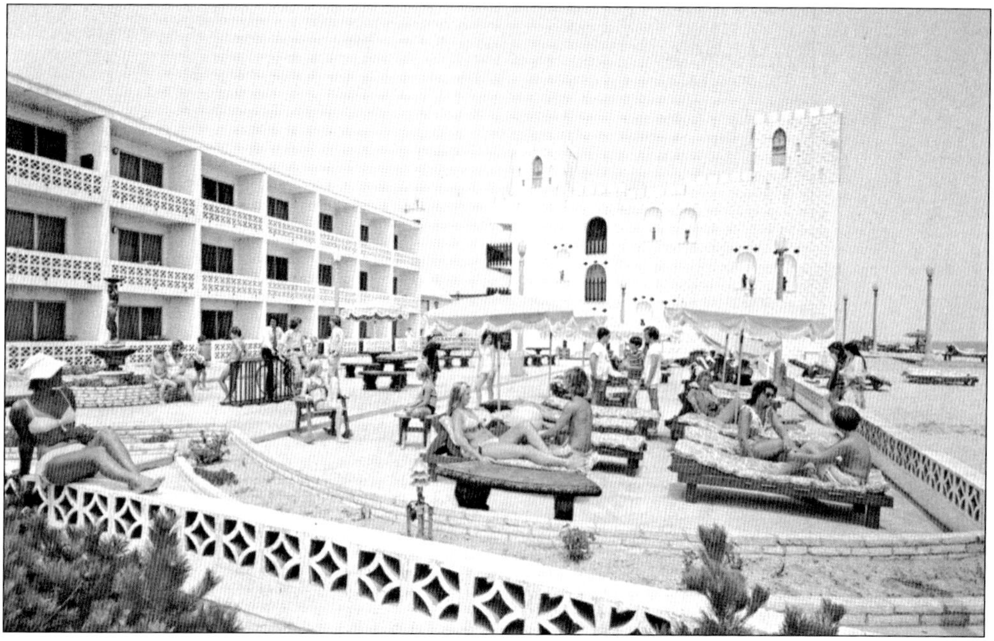

Contemporary with the Eden Roc Motel is the Showell family's Castle in the Sand Motel, which was built on beachfront land purchased in 1958, with the motel opening in 1960. The Castle could not be more different from the Modernist Eden Roc. By harkening back to the romantic imagery of stage-set motel design, the Castle moves beyond the adobe forms of the Miami Court and Alamo models and sidesteps the Southern planation imagery of the Francis Scott Key Motel. Nonetheless, the Castle in the Sand was dressed in the same tradition of picturesque, evocative, and historicist motel garb with its painterly crenelated medievalism. The motel even offered a King John Suite and a Queen Anne Suite, paying tribute to both British monarchs and proprietors John and Anne Showell. The Showell family has been in Worcester County since 1683.

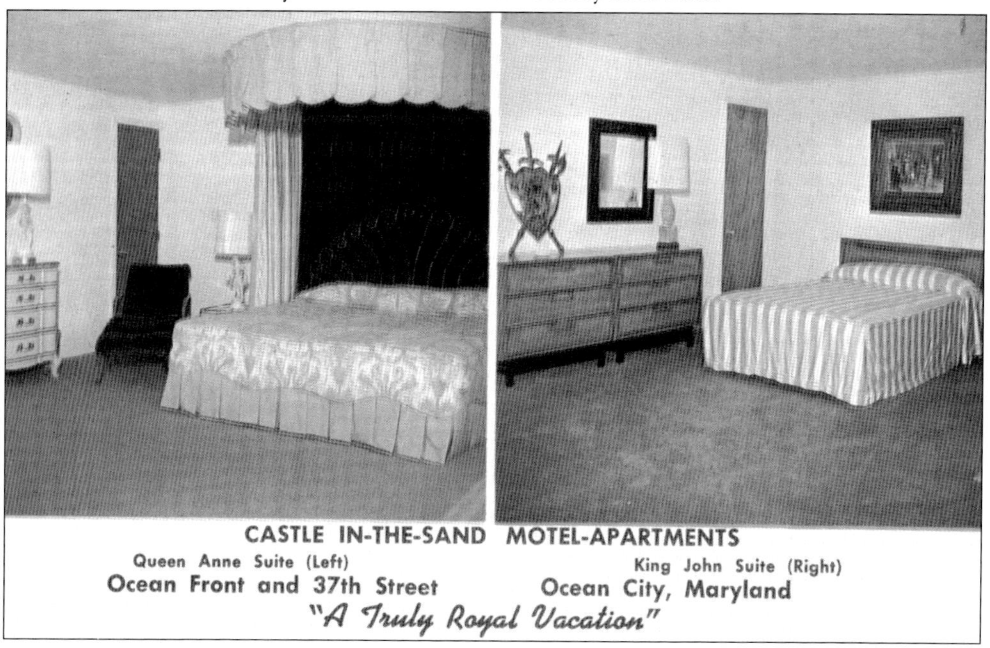

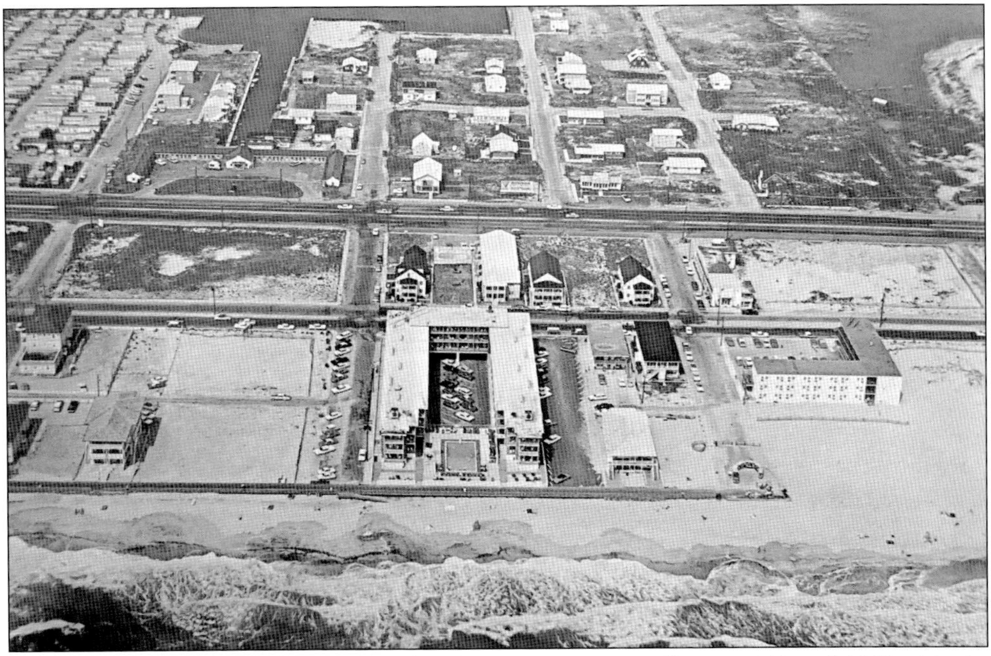

An enlarged scale was brought to motel architecture in Ocean City in 1959 and 1960 with the building of the 93-unit Diplomat (now Flagship) Motel on the oceanfront at Twenty-Sixth Street. The Diplomat was a vast U-plan of four-story blocks enveloping a large outdoor pool and raised terrace at the Boardwalk, as shown in this aerial photograph. It was soon considered the resort's most luxurious motel, although when built, it was thought to be at the northernmost edge of town. As the above photograph shows, the Boardwalk ended at Twenty-Seventh Street, and even scattered development appeared not to disturb vacant land to the north. The L-plan motel at right is the Dunes Motel (see pages 110 and 111).

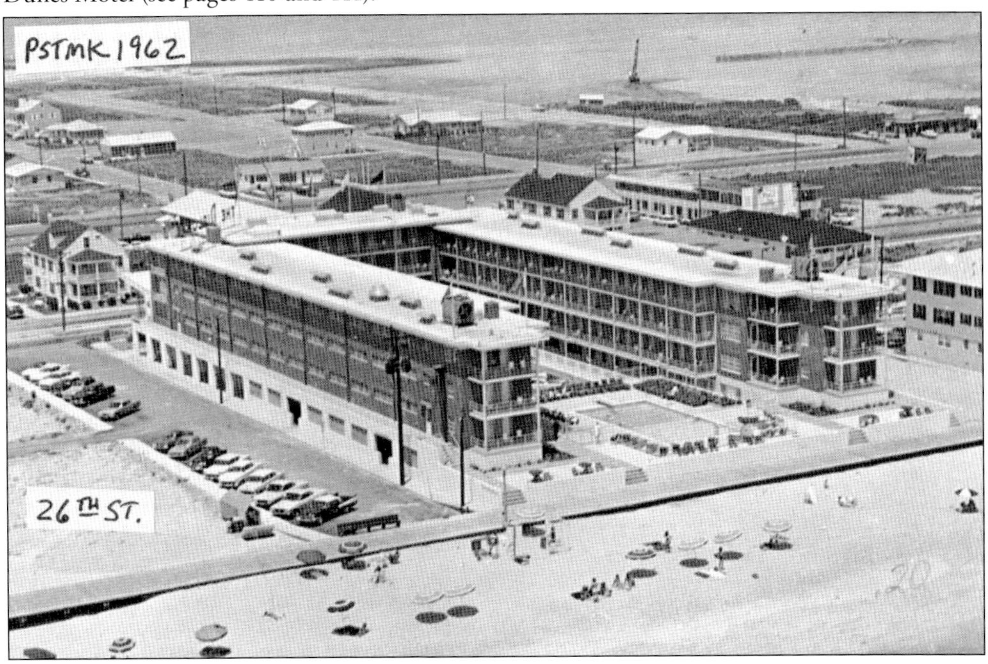

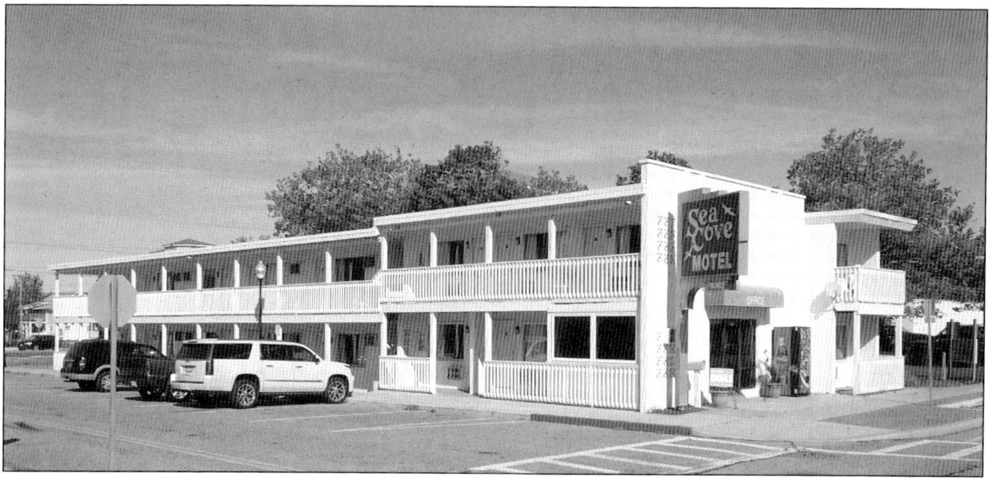

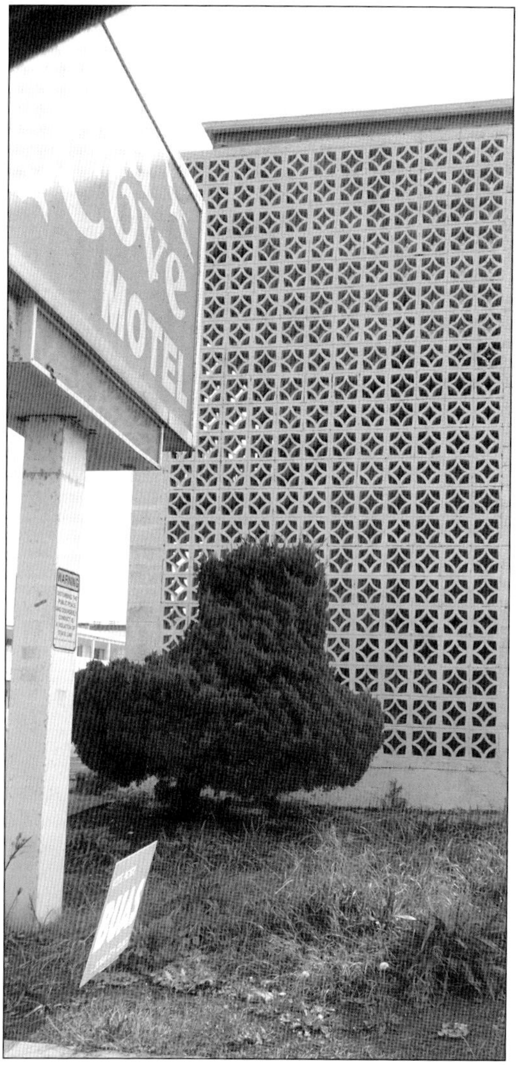

Another motel dating from the turn of the 1960s is the Sun and Sea Motel, comprising a two-story block of units on each side of Twenty-Seventh Street between Baltimore and Philadelphia Avenues, with the first likely built before 1959 and the second added in 1962. Still extant, and renamed the Sea Cove Motel, the two motel blocks are notable for their pierced concrete block walls—a part structural, part decorative device made popular in the mid-1950s by Modernist Edward Durrell Stone. Such pierced concrete blocks were widely employed in motel design in the tropics, where both light and air can filter through the patterned screen walls. (All, RMC.)

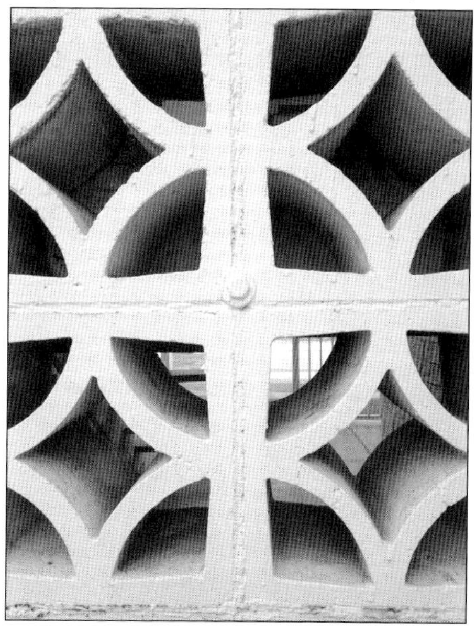

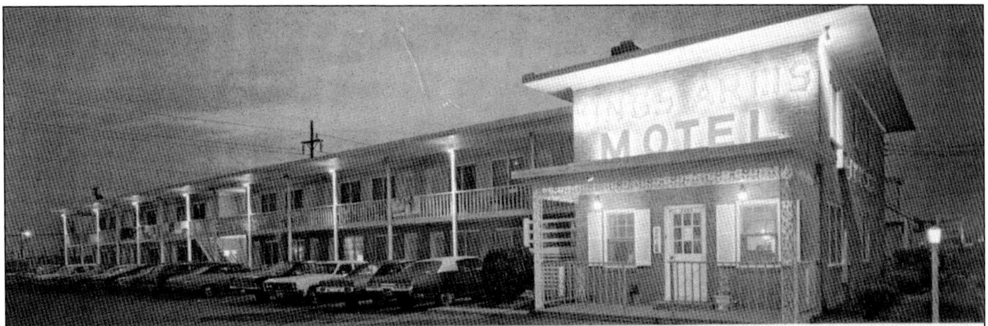

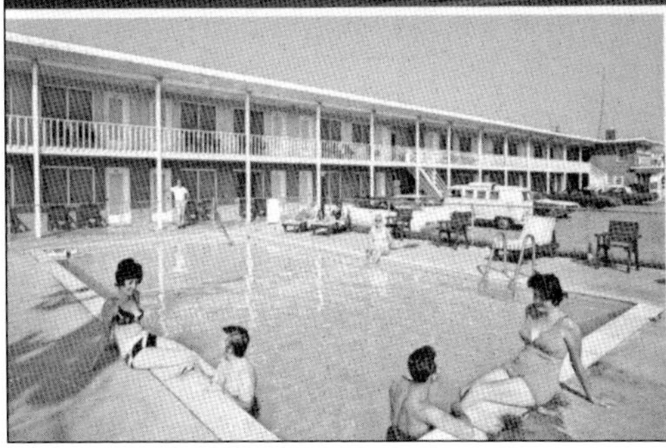

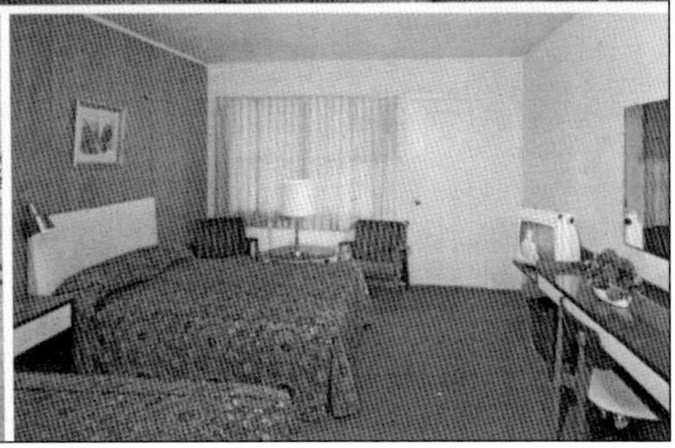

By 1960, the Salty Sands Motel was on the Forty-Sixth Street oceanfront. The Salty Sands is no longer extant, but the Windjammer Motel (by 1961) remains on the south side of Forty-Sixth Street at the beach. The Maridel Motel was on the Coastal Highway at Forty-First Street, and the King's Arms Motel opened on Twenty-Fourth Street at Baltimore Avenue in 1960. The flat roof of the King's Arms office, which appears to angle upward in the above postcard, is reminiscent of similar office blocks at the Fountain Court (page 104) and Seafarer Motel (page 109), as well as the porte cochere of the Flamingo Motel (page 112). The above postcard is postmarked 1972. (Below, RMC.)

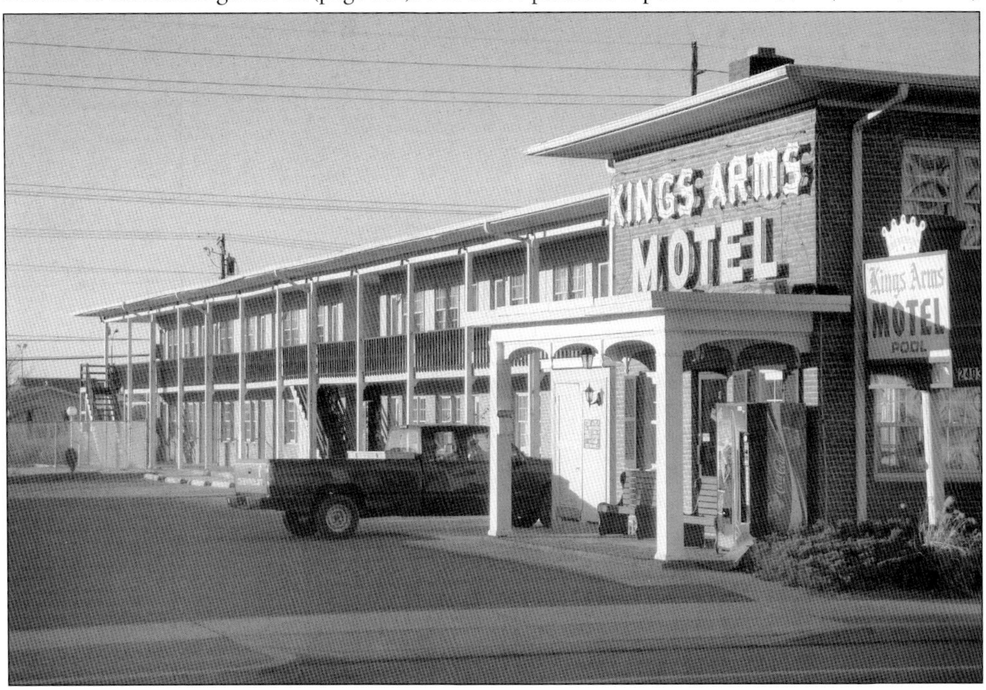

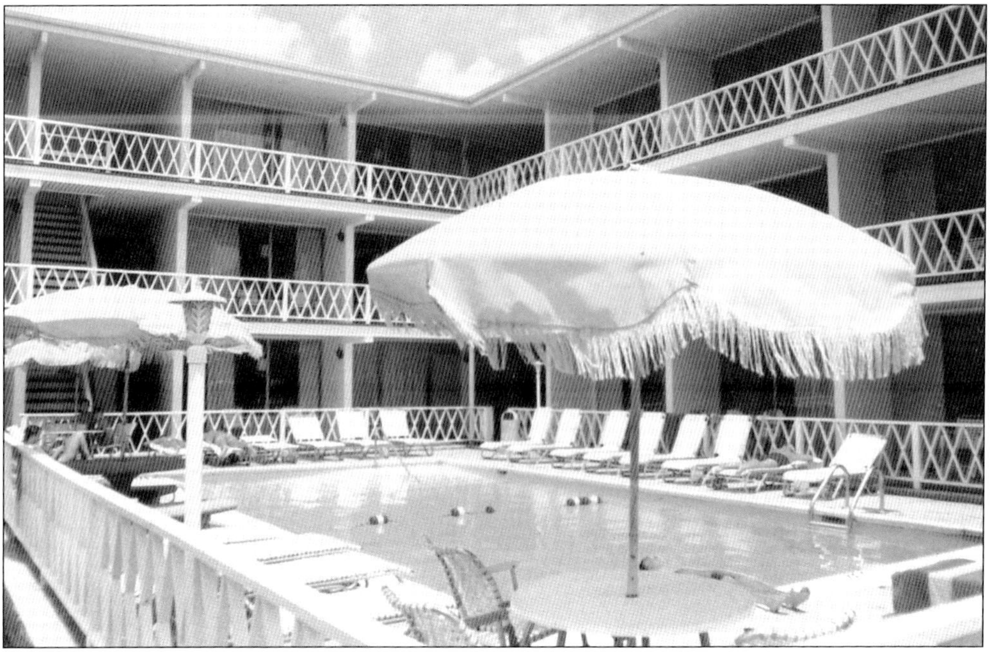

In 1965, three motels appeared in the Motel Row district—the Seabonay (pages 110 and 111), the Empress Motel at Baltimore Avenue and Twentieth Street (pictured above and below), and the Sahara Motel (page 119). They were typical L-shaped blocks on two or three levels, with parking and/or a swimming pool in the inner space of the L, as at the Dunes Motel. When the long leg of the L aligned with a side street (as was the case with the Seabonay), balcony corridors were in evidence. Sometimes, however, as at the Empress along Twentieth Street, the rear of the motel displays a repetitive arrangement of blank walls, small windows, and air-conditioning units, with the elevation lacking distinction, and here, apparently little disturbed by the public exposure of the Empress's backside. (Below, RMC.)

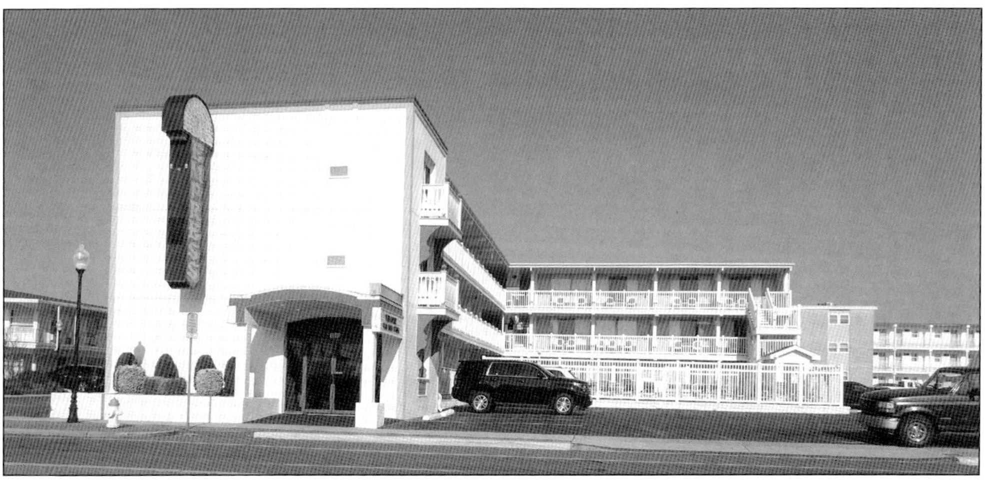

The Sahara Motel had an L-shaped arrangement that opened its inner south and west elevations of three levels to overlook the swimming pool, on-site parking, and Nineteenth Street and treated the corridors connecting adjacent units as semiprivate balconies with short partition walls open at the continuous rail. A post was later added to strengthen the support of the floor and roof. A second block, situated on the oceanfront and also L-shaped, reversed the L to provide a northwest exposure but also opened individual balconies on the dominant south and east fronts, with the latter overlooking the beach. Finally, a tower block with a café and "west building," both along Baltimore Avenue, completed the enlarged Sahara, now comprised of four distinct motel buildings united by kelly green signage, white building surfaces with red brick accents, and pale sky-blue doors. (Below, RMC.)

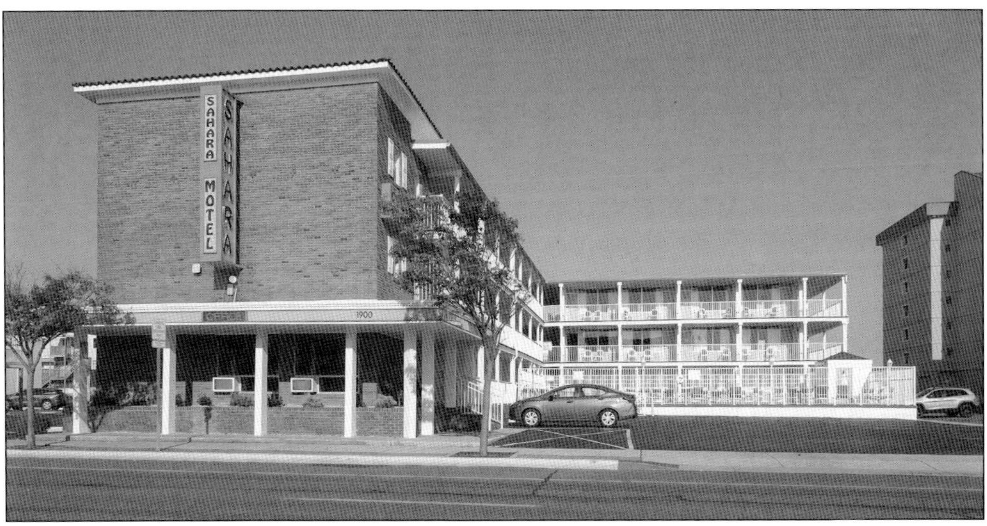

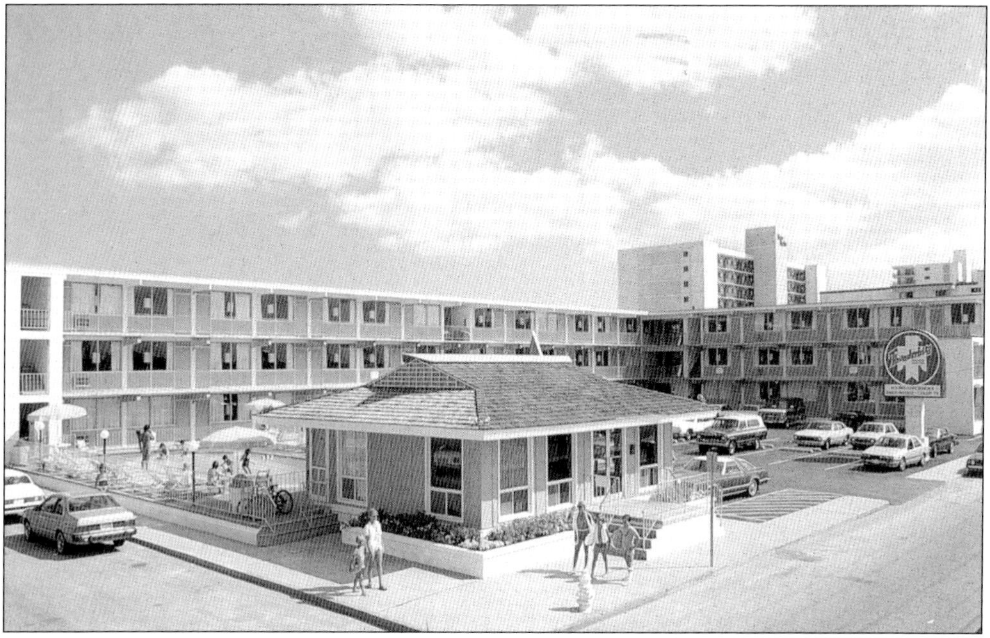

As the 1960s ended, motel owners continued to build L-plans open to the main thoroughfare of Motel Row along Baltimore Avenue with the intention of displaying uniform room units overlooking a swimming pool and of advertising the availability of on-site parking. The Thunderbird Beach Motel (1968) followed this pattern at Thirty-Second Street, consuming two-thirds of the block shared only by the original Flamingo Motel to the south.

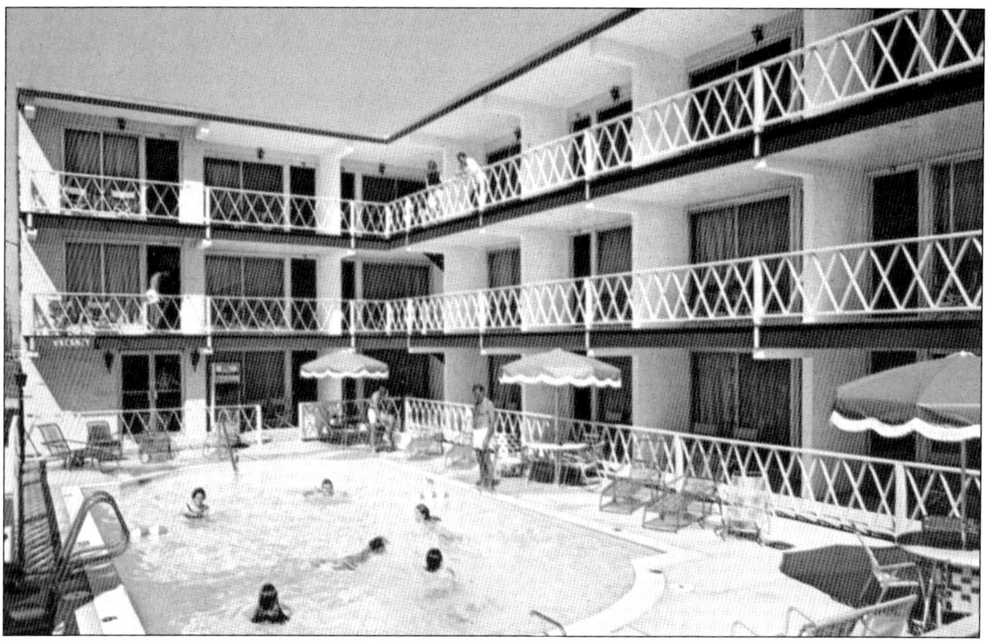

The Shangri La Motel (1969) took the giant leap of building in the dunes of Eighty-Fourth Street on land that had been recently annexed by the town after its city limits were extended to the Delaware line. With parking available north and south of the small motel, the Shangri La cradled its small swimming pool within its L shape with little more than empty sand dunes beyond the motel.

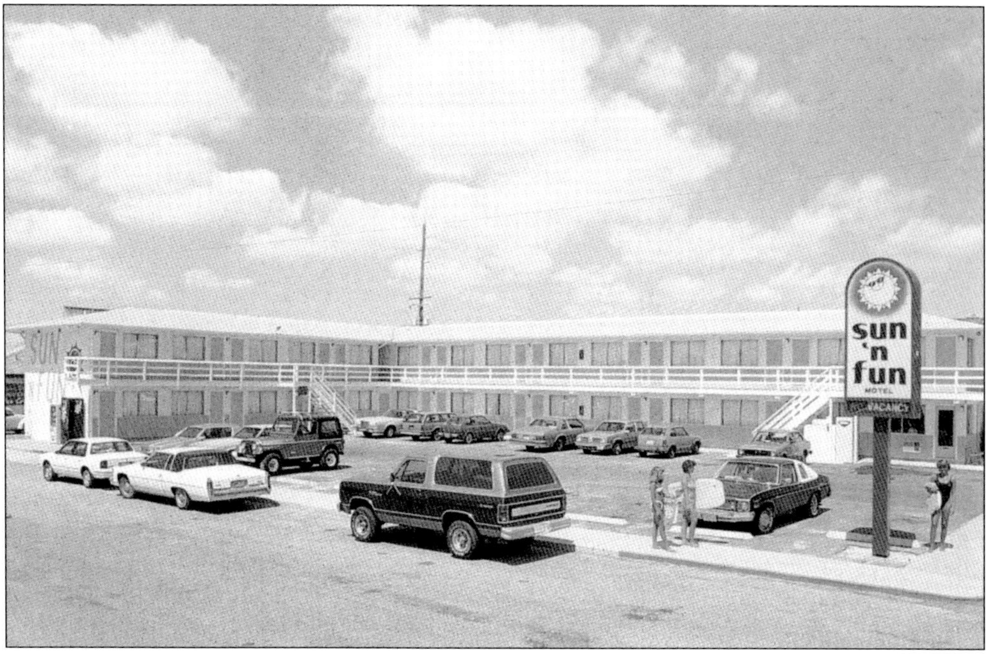

The Sun 'N Fun Motel (see page 109), a smaller motel from 1970 that still stands on the west side of Baltimore Avenue at Twenty-Ninth Street, lacked a swimming pool but offered on-site parking within its L-plan layout. The much larger Casablanca Oceanside Inn (also opened in 1970 and also still extant on Baltimore Avenue but just south of Twenty-Fifth Street) stacked five levels of motel rooms in an L-plan overlooking a pool and open to Baltimore Avenue, with off-site parking across the street. As motels grew larger, increased parking space was required, and Ocean City began to suffer from perceived hardscape overdevelopment: the conversion of large acreage to concrete or asphalt parking lots. (Below, RMC.)

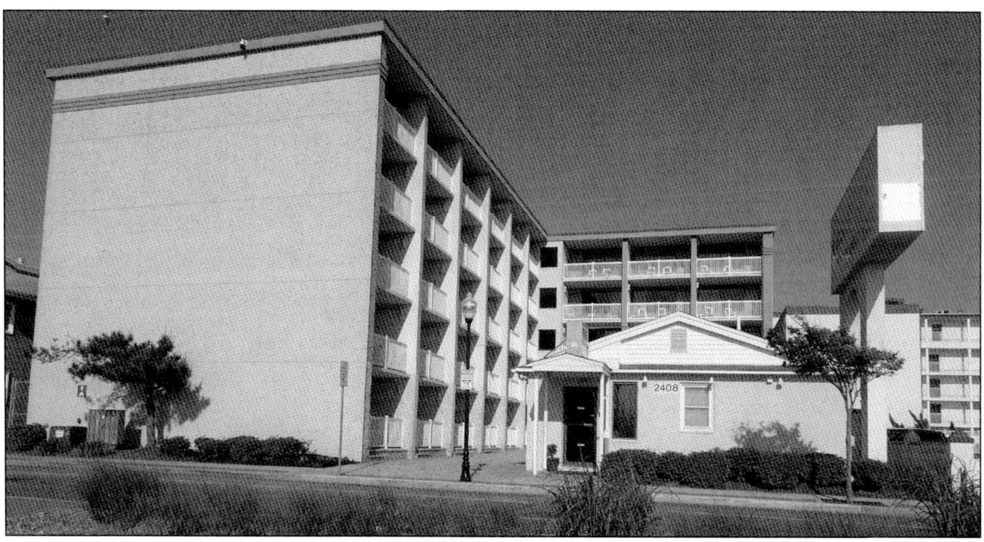

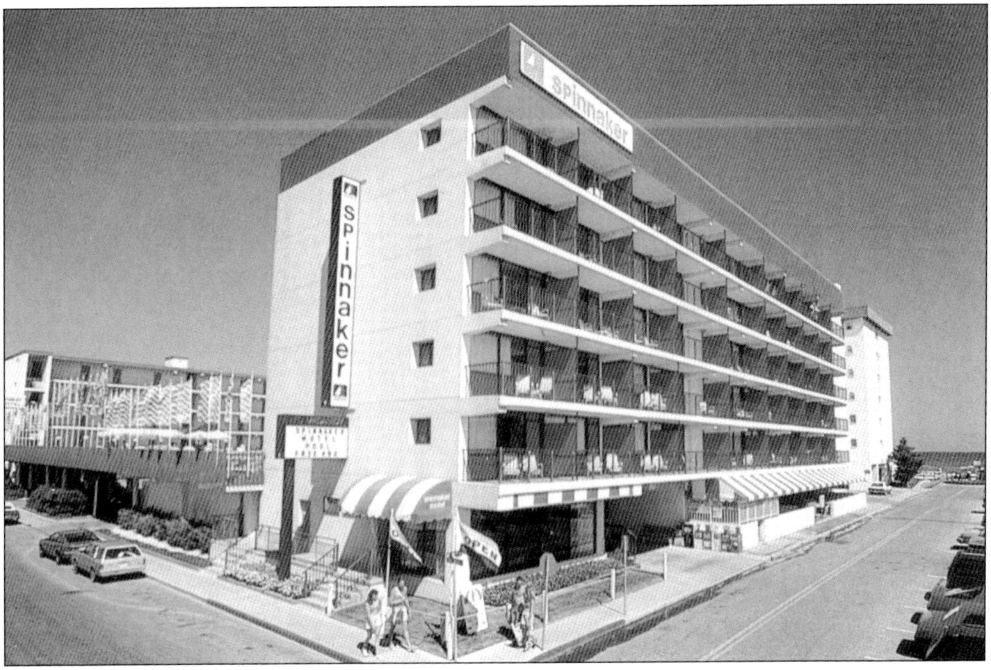

With the 1973 Spinnaker Motel on Eighteenth Street and the 1975–1976 Fenwick Inn, sited 120 city blocks farther north, the scale of motel architecture changed dramatically. The Spinnaker features two five-story blocks of 50 units each, with the blocks connected by a raised sundeck and a swimming pool fronting Baltimore Avenue (below) and on-site parking between the north and south blocks. Each unit provides a private balcony and kitchenette, and the bright orange doors, balcony partitions, ground-level awning, and upper parapets on the south building present striking accents that are highly noticeable in the streetscape. (Below, RMC.)

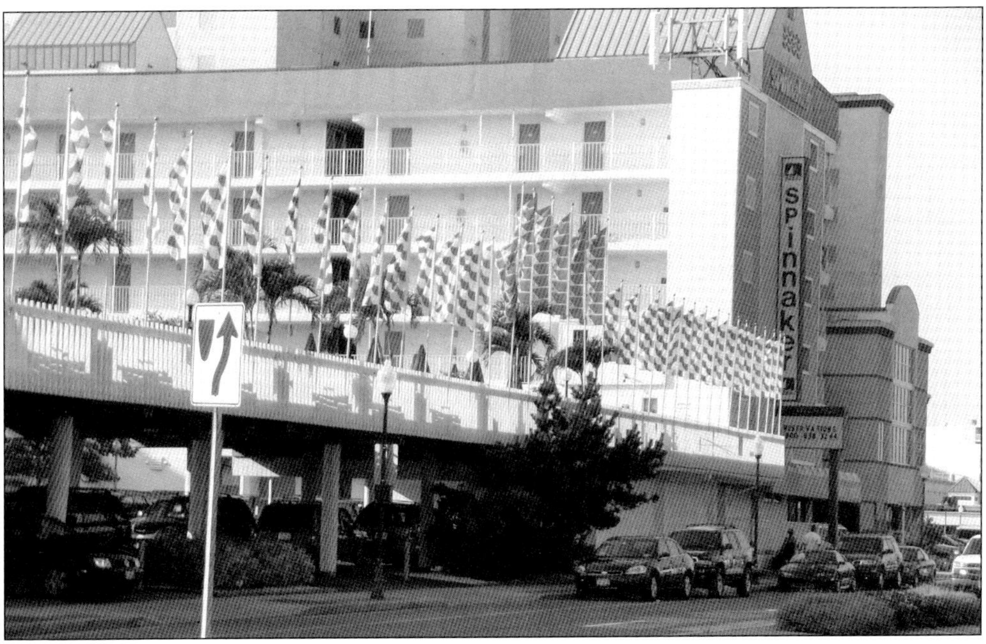

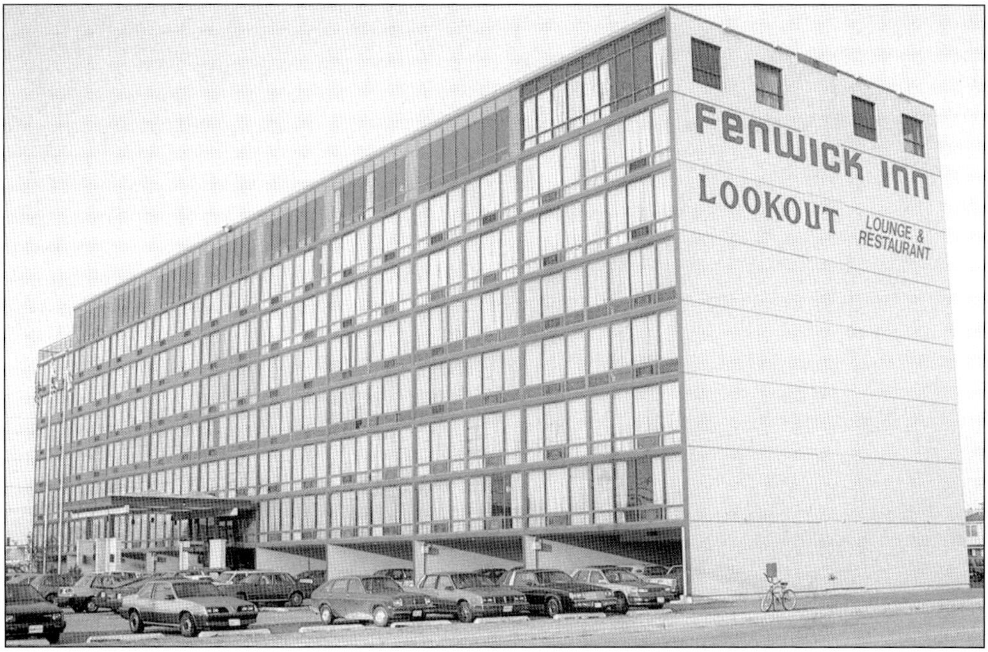

The 200-room Fenwick Inn was built at 138th Street, bayside, rising eight stories along the Coastal Highway and featuring an indoor pool. Its original architectural detailing (above) was almost Miesian, with its unadorned end walls and open front facade of glass surfaces in metal framing. For many years, the Fenwick Inn featured the Admirals and other bands at its rooftop restaurant, which has been converted to a wedding venue. Today, the originally unadorned motel block, with its sharp-edged rooftop, sports a new look—an all-too-common postmodern paint-accented parapet and cornice. The Fenwick's 2022 renovation included colorizing the inn's exterior surfaces with a facade cosmetic, including navy-blue vertical bays and an inexplicable film-socket edging on end elevations. (Below, RMC.)

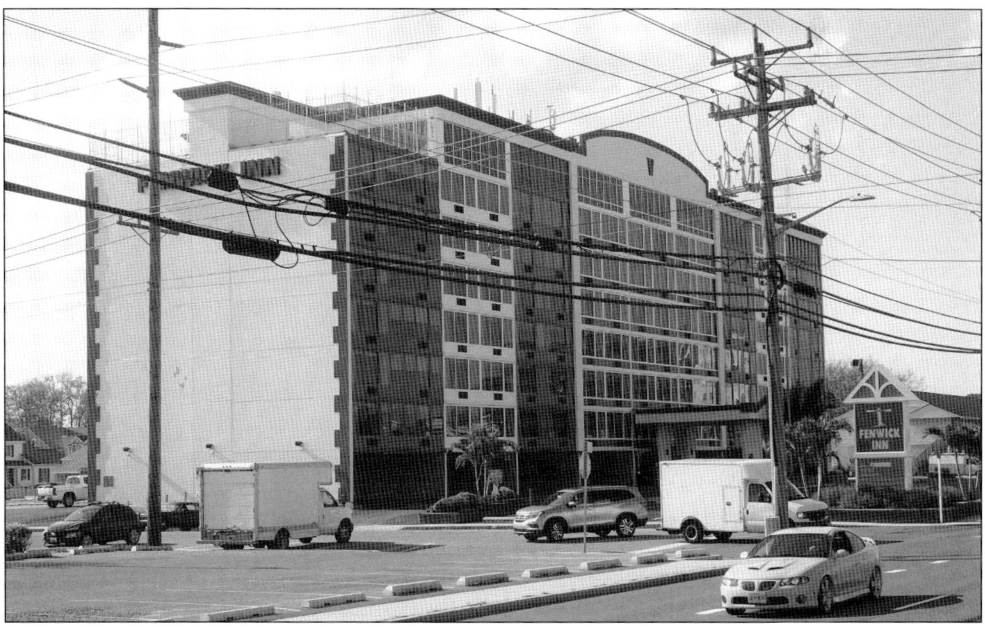

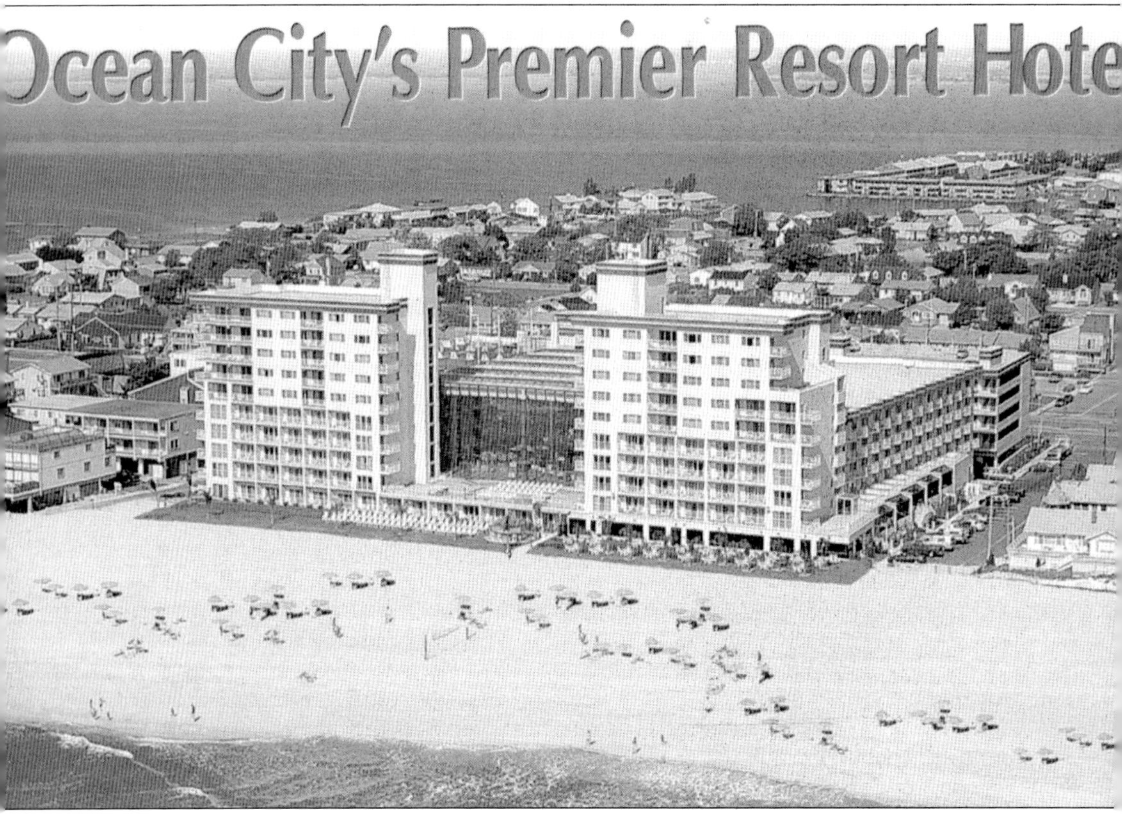

By the time of the 1991 opening date of the Princess Royale Oceanfront Resort, Condo Row had been built, shingle-clad hotels were being replaced on the Boardwalk with concrete cellular slabs (both casting long afternoon shadows over sunbathers on the beaches), and motel chains were swiftly replacing smaller mom-and-pop motels. The Princess Royale was said to have infilled the only remaining oceanfront property in town. The giant resort motel filled the entire block from Ninety-First to Ninety-Second Street and from the beach to the Coastal Highway with its multistory motel units and full-block-width, five-story concrete parking garage, with the garage providing six levels of parking, including on the rooftop. On the beachfront, two 10-story motel blocks frame an enclosed four-story atrium containing an Olympic-size swimming pool and Tropical Tiki atrium bar overlooked by motel balconies. The terrace and "open ocean air dining" allow guests to take advantage of the motel's beachfront site. Rivaled in size only by the enlarged Carousel Motel and Condo, the Princess Royale advertises itself as "the largest oceanfront resort in Maryland."

Four

Condos and Chain Hotels

Although summer vacationers driving automobiles to the ocean resort would today question the ease of access to the beach on a busy weekend, events during the third quarter of the 20th century significantly simplified auto travel to Ocean City. Between 1919 and 1952, the Claiborne-Annapolis Ferry shuttled passengers and vehicles across the Chesapeake Bay from the western shore at Annapolis to the eastern shore at Claiborne and back—a slow process that required meeting departure schedules and offered limited capacity. The Chesapeake Bay Bridge at Kent Island opened in 1952; motorists could now drive across the bay, making the ferry obsolete, and ferry service ceased. At the south end of the Delmarva peninsula, the opening of the Chesapeake Bay Bridge-Tunnel at Norfolk in April 1964 had a similar effect on ferry transport at Cape Charles, where auto-ferries had operated since the 1940s (and passenger ferries had operated prior to that). A second bridge span across the Chesapeake Bay at Annapolis opened in 1973, and vacationers poured into Ocean City in even greater numbers.

With the mid-1960s expansion of Ocean City's town limits northward to the Delaware state line and the construction (started in 1968) of Route 90 and its new bridge into north Ocean City at Sixty-Second Street (the road and bridge opened in 1971), the formerly open dunes and unsettled marshlands—and especially the oceanfront acreage of north Ocean City—were ripe for development.

In 1970, John Whaley built the town's first high-rise, the 15-story Highpoint South, at 112th Street. The major motel in the area, the Carousel Motel at 118th Street, which was built in 1961 and 1962, expanded in 1971 and 1972 to become the town's first megastructure, adding 155 rooms, 189 condos, and an atrium in addition to a five-level concrete parking garage to accommodate 535 cars. Developers salivated at the potential for profit in the untouched area of northern dunes, and Condo Row, located between Ninety-Fourth and 118th Streets, literally burst onto the scene. Loans were quickly secured, permits were obtained, builders were contracted, and realtors lined up to arrange hoped-for presales of condo units that were projected to fill the collection of towers by the hundreds.

In a stampede recalling the Oklahoma land rush, developers hurriedly laid the foundations for numerous concrete towers designed at unprecedented heights and scale for Ocean City. The giant forms were anchored in the sand where only the shingle-clad Isle of Wight Life-Saving Station had once stood isolated amidst sea grass and high-tide marks. However, as the 1973 oil crisis emerged and the national economy slid toward recession, it soon became apparent that Ocean City's condo builders were in trouble—they had overbuilt. They held too many unsold units, and neither builders nor owners could make payments on construction loans or mortgages. Developers lowered condo prices to try to obtain cash for the supplies needed to complete construction or to service their existing debt. One after another, speculators went bankrupt, and more than one Maryland bank nearly failed for lack of revenue from loans that they had provided to developers who were now unable to repay. Thirty-year mortgage rates rose from around 7.5 percent in 1971 to 11.2 percent in 1979 and then to the highest level in modern history by 1981, when they hit an annual average of 16.63 percent.

But Condo Row survived, extending 24 blocks along the coastline to create an unprecedented and unique skyline of towers. However, behind the towers of what became known as Ocean City's gold coast was no longer a two-lane road to Delaware but a Coastal Highway without character, a commercial strip complete with its own suburban "gold coast mall," an attenuated agora crowded with restaurants, fast food drive-thrus, and saltwater taffy shops; sportswear, beach equipment, and T-shirt stores; gas stations, real estate offices, and groceries; and newer and larger chain hotels, multistory motels, and a multitude of infill condo blocks both north and south of Condo Row. North Ocean City had become an all-too-typical American commercial strip development on steroids.

However, Condo Row itself offered new opportunities for laudable and distinctive architectural design—a potential not always reached at each building site but with a certain attraction as a whole. Most notable are the Pyramid and Century I. The Pyramid (1971–1973) was designed by William Morgan and may well have been influenced by the four larger and contemporary pyramidal apartment blocks designed by André Minaugoy at the Marina, Baie des Anges, in Villeneuve-Loubet on the French Riviera between Cannes and Nice. The first building of the huge French seaside development started in 1969. The second, Le Commodore (comprising 333 apartment units in a stepped pyramid rising 21 floors), is formally more comparable to Morgan's Ocean City Pyramid, which was under construction at the same time. The projecting wings of Morgan's Pyramid embrace a swimming pool and form a concave oceanfront cluster of balconied units rising up to 19 floors and containing 170 condo apartments.

Century I pays homage to New Brutalism, a recognized late modern architectural style of raw concrete, steel, and glass. Century I leaves constructional surfaces exposed with board-form concrete and expresses its concrete frame in a strong, narrow slab of full-depth condo apartments with views of both the ocean and the bay to the east and west. Century I's two-story units recall a like composition in section at Le Corbusier's *unité d'habitation* in Marseille, France, where housing units extend from front to back through the building and corridors are on every third level. At 313 feet in height, Century I is the tallest structure in Condo Row.

Other condo towers display features of notable design individuality, including the Moderne-inspired curved corners and horizontal strip windows (*fenêtres en longueurs*) of Atlantis (1975), the full-height open atrium at the polygonal tower of Antiqua (1975–1976), and the multiple balconies spread across the flaring wings at Sea Watch (1975). Less distinguished condos simply fill in space along a high-rise row, collectively maintaining an aligned oceanfront building line arranged like military personnel at roll call. Some building forms spread wide along the Coastal Highway like billboards blocking ocean views from the highway, including the Golden Sands Condos (1975) and the Plaza (1985); others are thin slabs that knife their way between competing condo blocks anchored perpendicular to the ocean and highway, including The Capri (1974), 9400 Condos (1974), and The Quay (1974–1977).

Throughout north Ocean City, other condominium blocks had a more bland architectural character, a tower aesthetic of concrete largeness and a lack of individuality of expression, and sometimes a spirit more akin to Soviet housing superblocks retrofitted in pastel hues but still falling short of vacation-home architecture. The plethora of look-alike mid-rise condos and newer and larger chain hotels offers only rare architectural distinction. Historic hotels were overtaken by a bevy of inns—Holiday Inns, Quality Inns, Hampton Inns, Rodeway Inns, and Comfort Inns. Ocean City lost the Doo-Wop character of Motel Row, and in its place, too much of north Ocean City has become a homogenized nonplace where, as Gertrude Stein once wrote, "there is no there there."

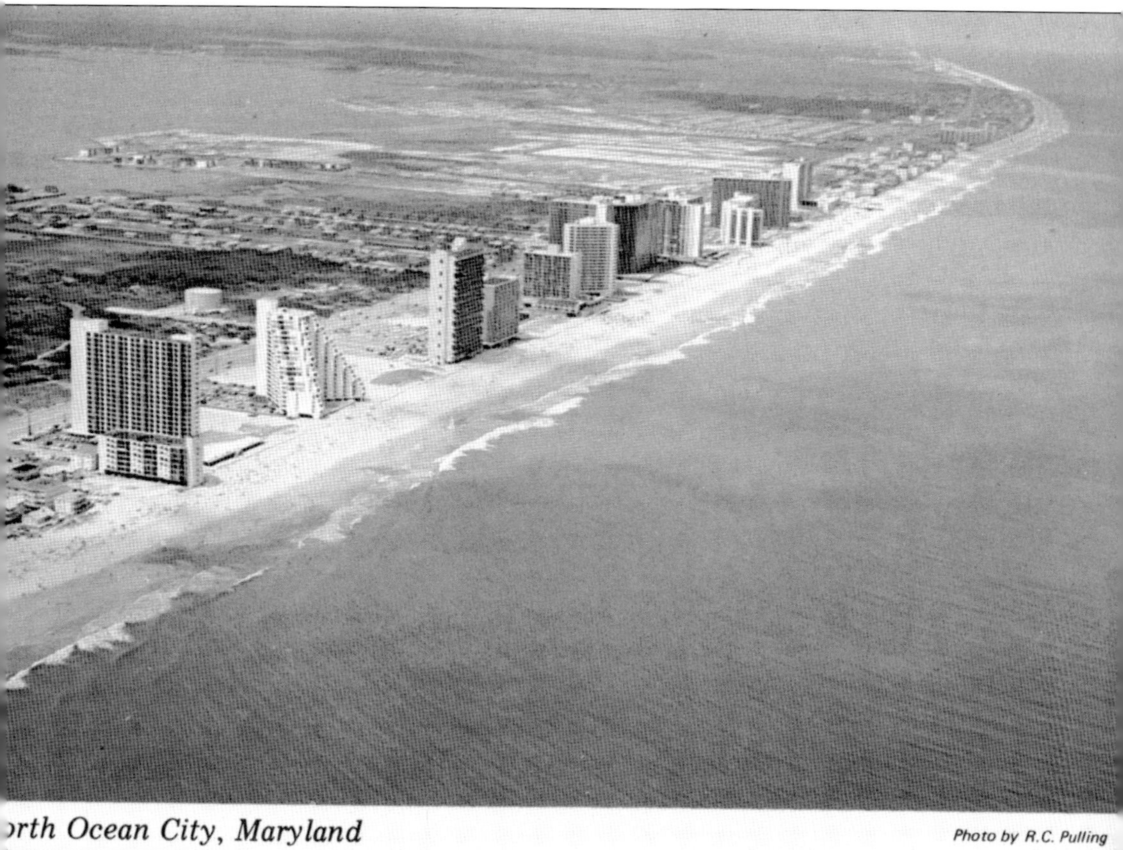

This c. 1975 aerial postcard view of Condo Row, with a photograph by R.C. Pulling, shows the earliest towers from the 9400 block (left) to the Carousel Resort Motel, the last large building at top right. Near the south end of the row, north of the 9400 block, the Pyramid and Century I are distinctive forms, while the Flying Cloud (between 9400 and the Pyramid) and the Plaza (between the Pyramid and Century I) had not yet been built. Visible north of Century I are (from left to right) English Towers, the vacant future site of Marigot Beach Condos, the Sheraton Fontainebleau (now Clarion) Hotel, Atlantis, the unbuilt future site of The Quay, Golden Sands, The Capri, The Irene, the future site of Rainbow Condos, Highpoint South (three vertical light-toned tower forms) and Highpoint North, the broad south face of Sea Watch, the barely visible Fountainhead, and the enlarged Carousel. The photograph illustrates how quickly Condo Row emerged following the construction of Highpoint South, the first high-rise condo in the area, in 1970.

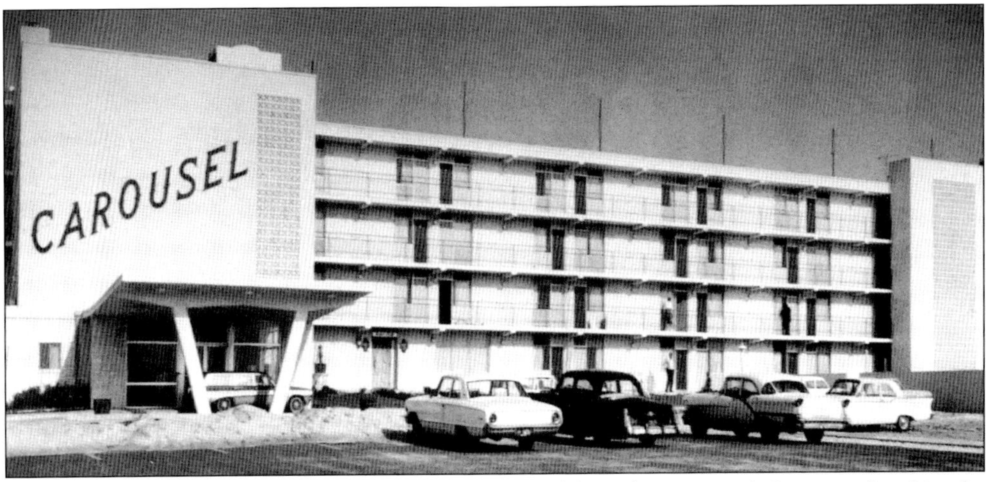

The original 75-room Carousel Motel was built by Bobby Baker on 118th Street, isolated in the northern dunes and reputed to be a retreat for some of the most powerful people in Washington, DC. When the motel opened on July 22, 1962, Vice Pres. Lyndon Johnson and his wife, Lady Bird, arrived by limousine with 200 senators, congressmen, lobbyists, and congressional staffers following in seven chartered busses, "swill[ing] champagne on the way" (*OC Today*). The Carousel Motel was built on borrowed money—Bobby Baker admitted in his 1976 memoirs that he had 51 loans out between 1959 and 1963. A former Johnson protégé and confidant, Baker (described by local newspaper *OC Today* as a "congressional bag man and wheeler dealer") went to prison in 1971 after being convicted of tax evasion, bribery, and fraud. The below photograph shows the original motel's west elevation preserved in the atrium. (Below, RMC.)

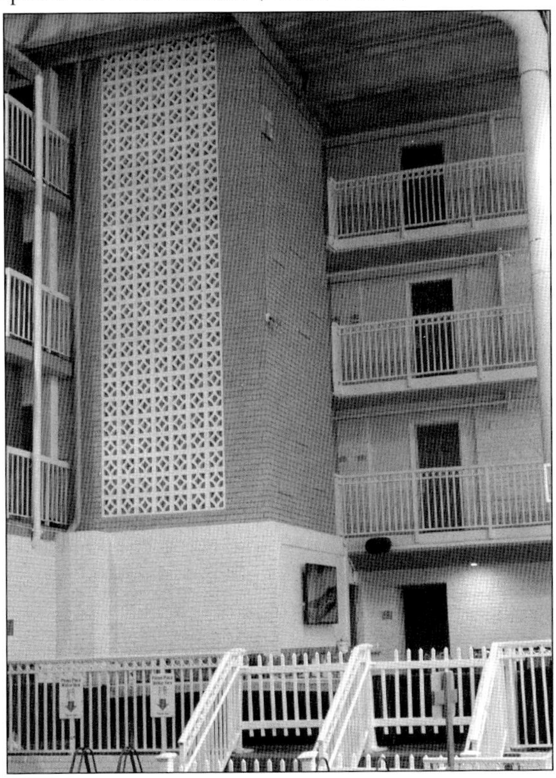

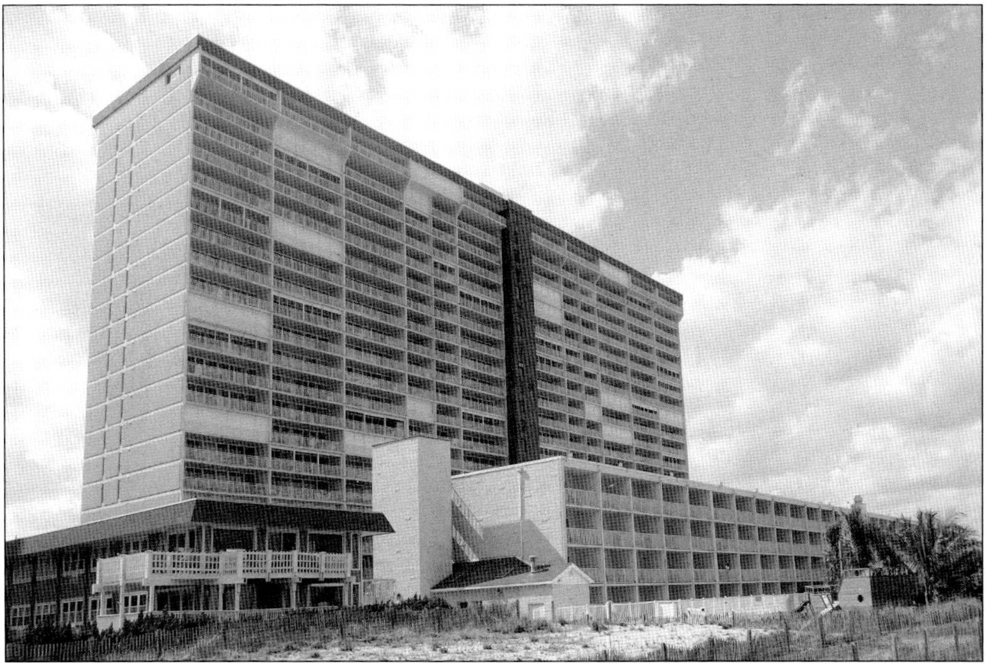

Bobby Baker's Carousel Motel opened the eyes of Ocean City developers to the potential of growth in north Ocean City around the area that became known as Condo Row. Soon after Baker was sent to prison in 1971, Max Berg, an active developer of condominiums during the 1970s, bought the Carousel and expanded its original five stories by adding 155 motel rooms and 189 condo units in a tower block and a 535-vehicle parking deck. Berg then sold his interest and went on to build The Irene condo tower, named for his wife. The beachfront view above shows four floors of the Carousel Motel block with the condo tower rising behind it; the west elevation (below) distinguishes the upper 17 floors of condo units from the motel rooms below them. (Both, RMC.)

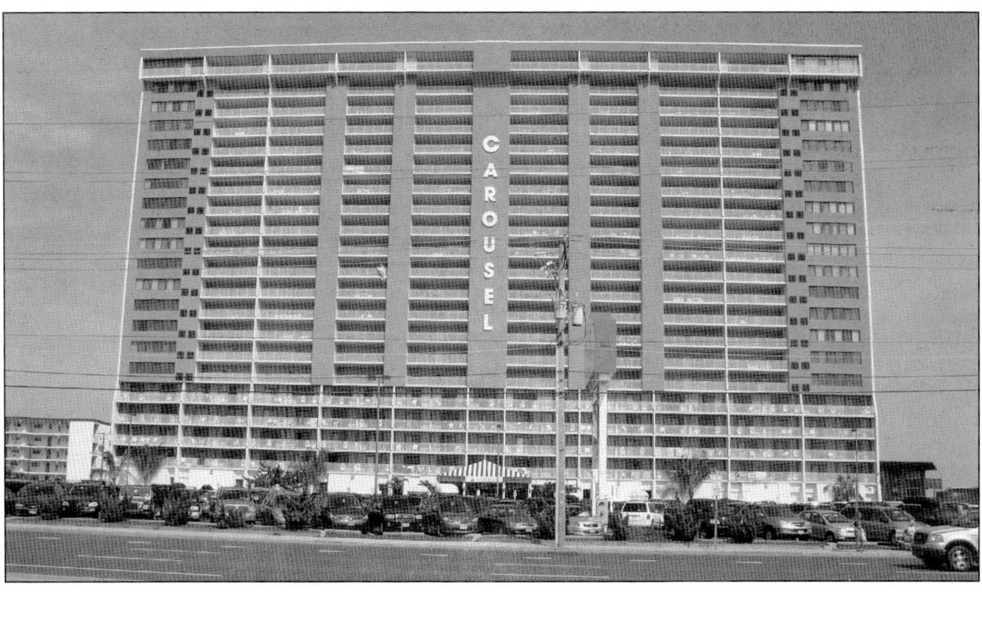

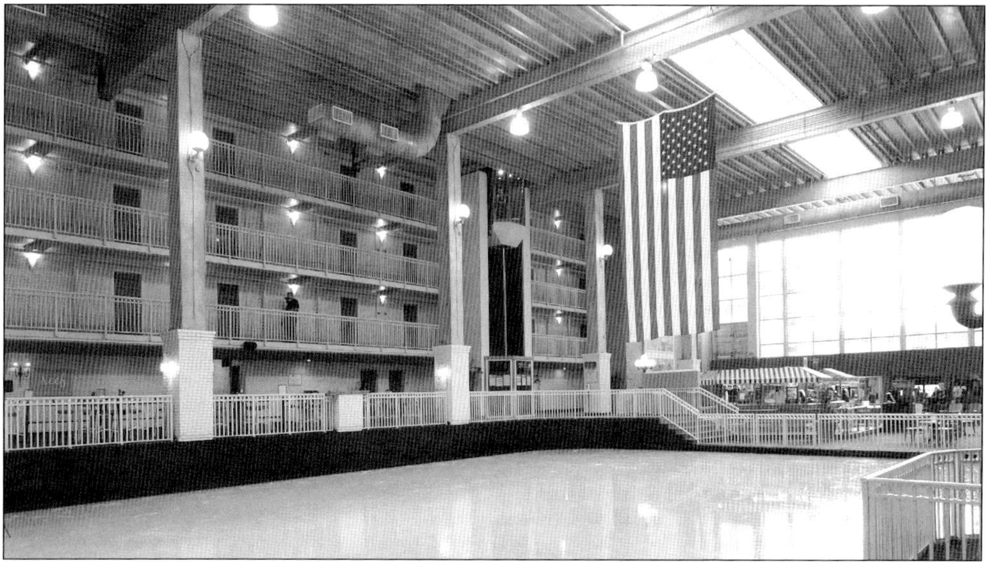

The parallel motel and condo blocks of the expanded Carousel overlooked an indoor swimming pool and an atrium containing an ice-skating rink, and a small theater occupied one of several meeting rooms. The megastructure still stands today despite the Carousel's foreclosures, bankruptcies, and related troubles. Overshadowing these vicissitudes is the fact that the Carousel opened the door for the large-scale developments that became Condo Row. (RMC.)

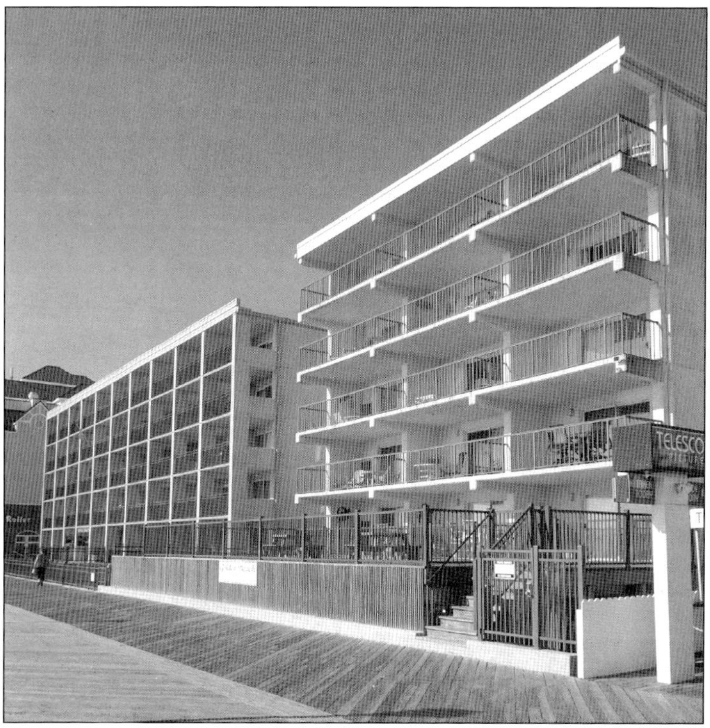

Changes also occurred on the historic Boardwalk. In November 1962, fire destroyed the Plimhimmon Hotel, and a new Plim Plaza Hotel emerged (see page 39). In December 1969, the Hamilton Hotel (see pages 46 and 47) burned down; it was replaced by the Polynesian Condos (left building in photograph at left) in 1972. The Golden Beach Condos were added next door in 1984. Concrete cellular units were becoming the new face of oceanfront/Boardwalk lodgings. (RMC.)

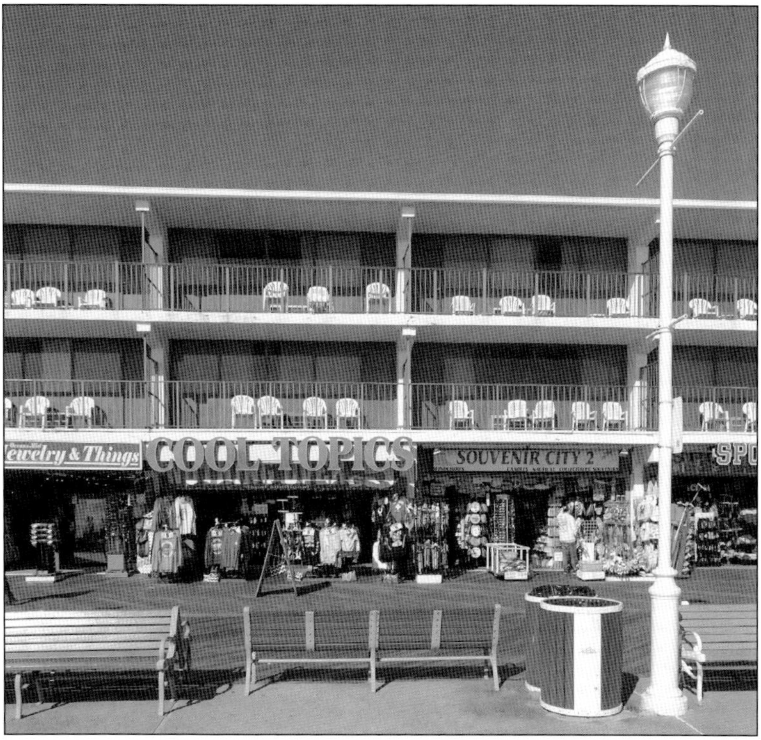

In March 1970, the Roosevelt (also known as Mount Pleasant) Hotel caught fire and also burned two of the three buildings of the adjacent Rideau Hotel (see page 49). The Rideau immediately began to rebuild, lining up a row of six Boardwalk shops and a restaurant with a new 48-room Rideau Motor Inn rising above and behind it. (RMC.)

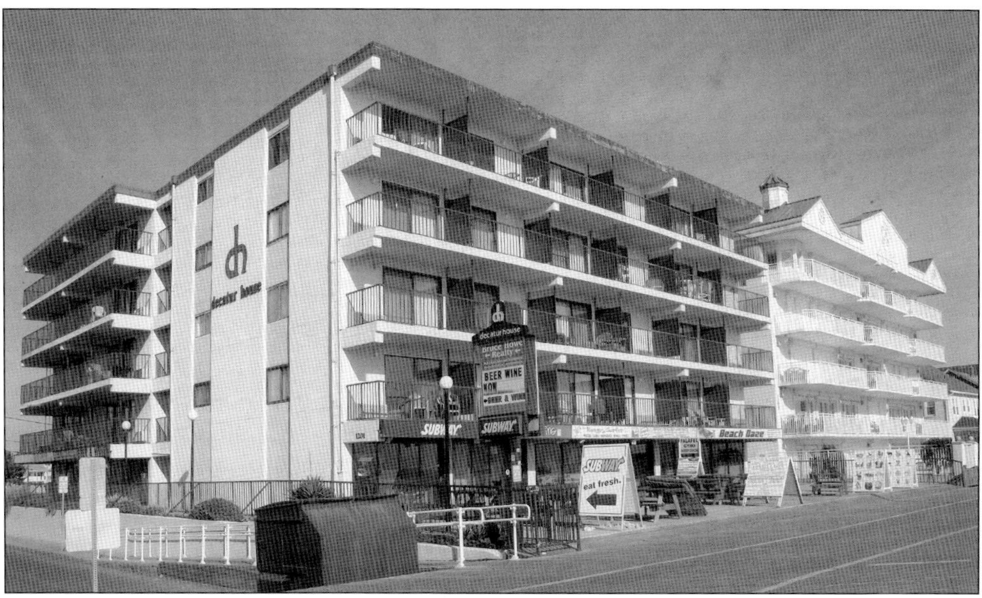

As Condo Row was building up the north beach, historic Boardwalk hotels were being replaced by structures of little distinction. The 1930 Stephen Decatur Hotel (see page 61) was razed in 1977 and supplanted by the bland Decatur House. Next door, in 2004, Ocean's Pointe Condos appeared wearing gabled parapets and silly party-hat mini turrets—both familiar Postmodern appliques intended to mollify the wearisome boxy-balconied aesthetic. (RMC.)

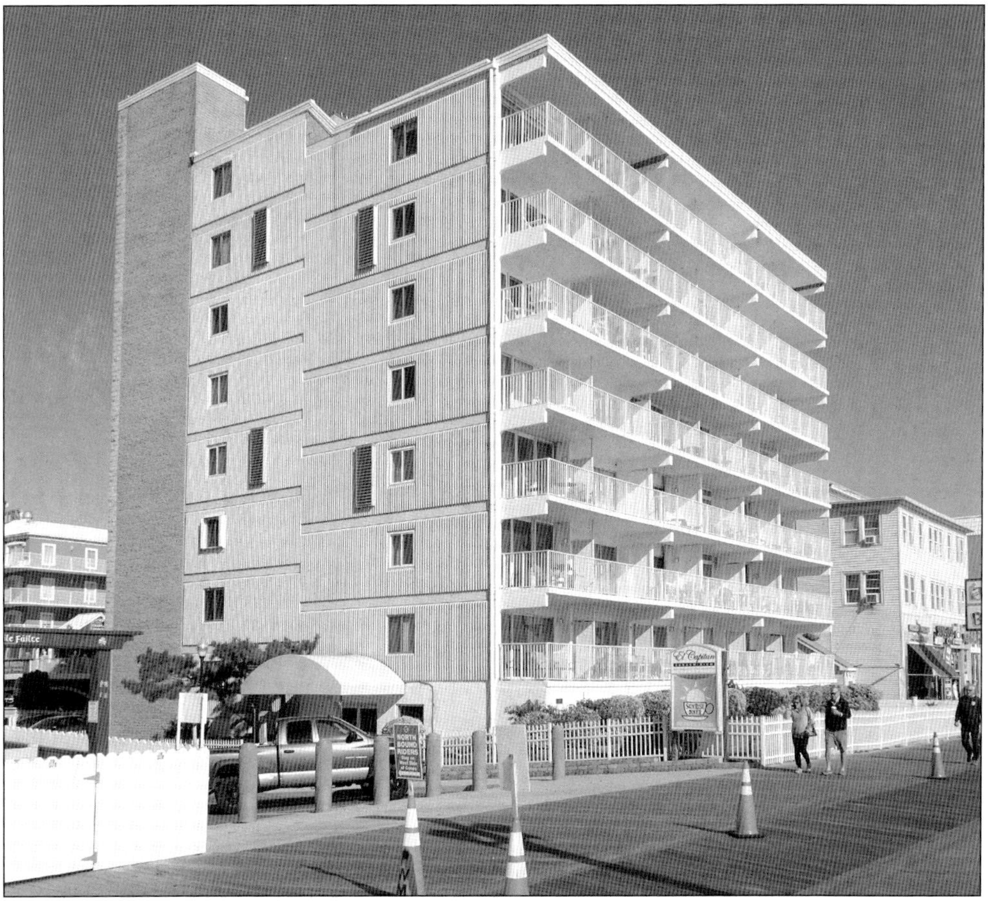

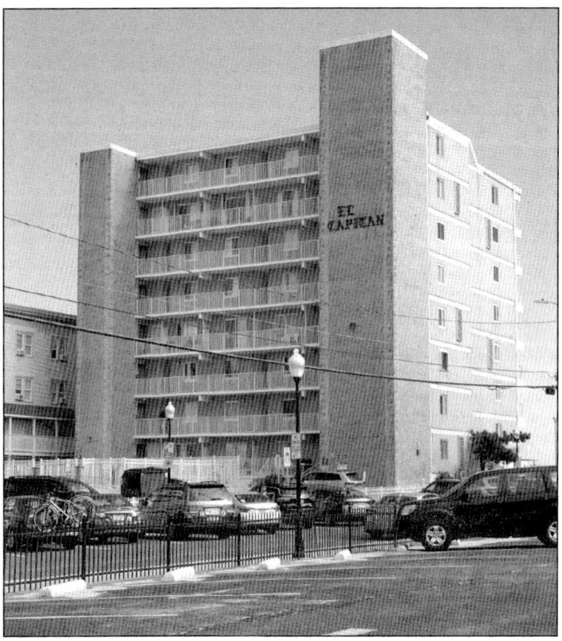

During the height of the Condo Row boom, a seven-story condo block with continuous balcony railings rose above the Boardwalk at the north corner of Fourth Street on the former site of a Boardwalk cottage. Built in 1973 and 1974, El Capitan Condos features 30 split-level townhouses, an interior configuration expressed on the side elevations, giving the unusual impression that two buildings were joined without their floor heights quite aligning. The building is one of the few Boardwalk properties to preserve—or, one should say, create—a foreground of landscaping; it was done here with the highly inappropriate choice of a suburban lawn, clipped hedges, and a flower border. Natural dune grass and sand might have been more native. (Both, RMC.)

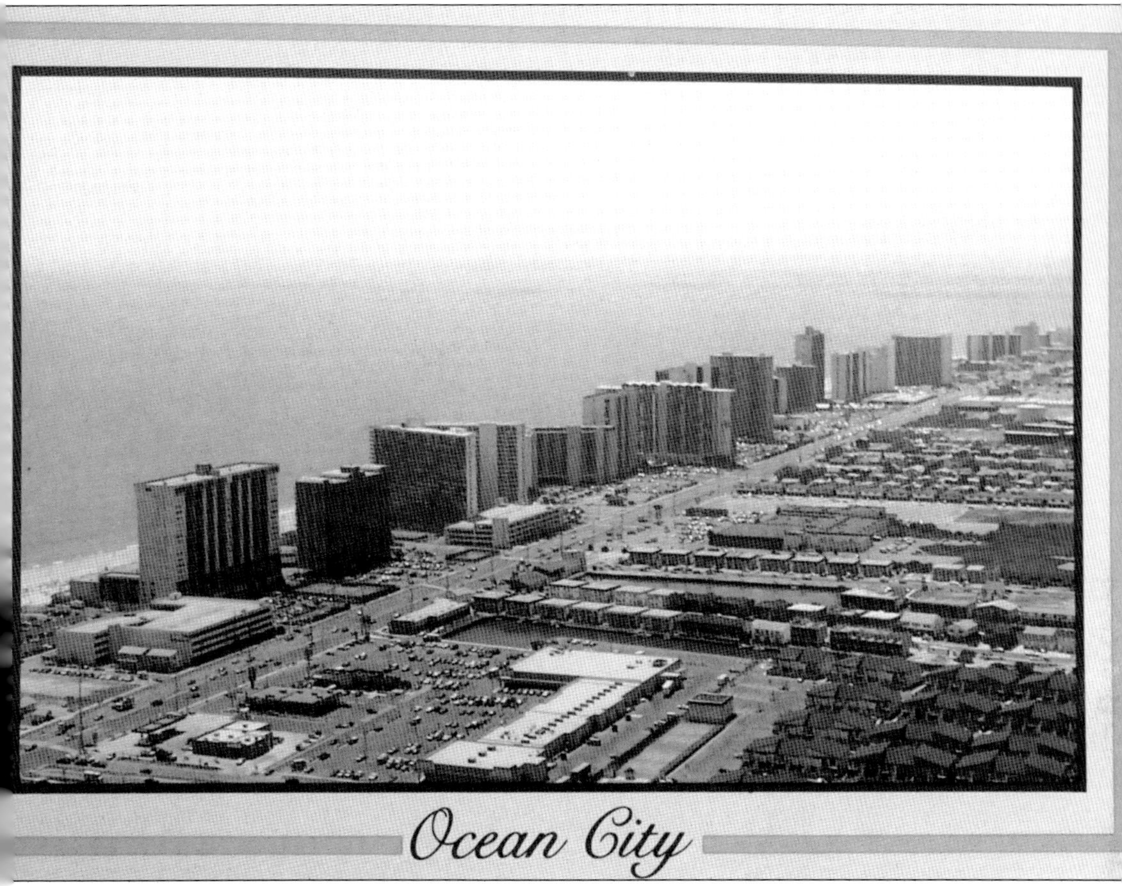

In the more natural environment of the north dunes, extensive construction of condos took place during the 1970s. This frenzy of building occurred throughout scattered northside locations but was especially vigorous within the stretch of 24 blocks from Ninety-Fourth to 118th Street—this became known as Condo Row, where developers were building condos as quickly as construction loans could be secured. This c. 1976 aerial photograph by R.C. Pulling looks south on Condo Row and shows the extent of development in just five years, from the 1971 construction of the first high-rise in the area, Highpoint South, and the expansion of the 1962 Carousel Motel to a condo tower (1971–1972) to the nearly completed Condo Row. The Carousel (on 118th Street) is in the lower left of the picture, and the 9400 Tower (on Ninety-Fourth Street) is at top right, with Sea Terrace (1974) and Antiqua (1976) beyond it. In between, 12 condo towers were erected between 1971 and 1975, with The Quay completed in 1977 and four more added in the early 1980s.

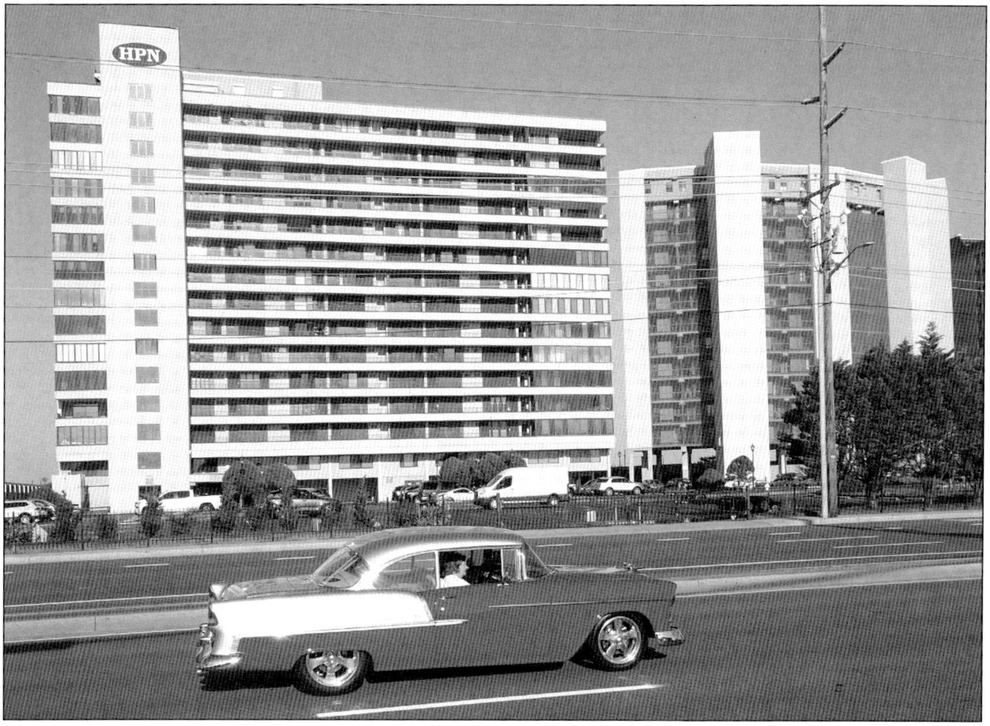

Ocean City's first high-rise was Highpoint South (at right in the above image), a 14-floor tower of 103 units built in 1971 by John Whaley. On its oceanfront side, Highpoint South's curved concave glass facade opens to panoramic ocean views. Slightly askew, the footprint's axis is aligned northeast–southwest rather than due east. Below the building are a polygonal terrace and pool. In 1972, Whaley built Highpoint North (at left in the above image), with 19 efficiencies at mezzanine level and a 4,000-square-foot penthouse on the 14th floor—between these are 65 one-bedroom and 52 two-bedroom units, each with a private oceanfront balcony. The 20,000-square-foot beachfront deck, which extends the full width of the building, is one of the largest among Ocean City's condo developments. In 1973, the 17-story Fountainhead Towers Condo project (below) was completed just south of the Carousel. Its 166 units feature both bayside and oceanfront balconies. (Both, RMC.)

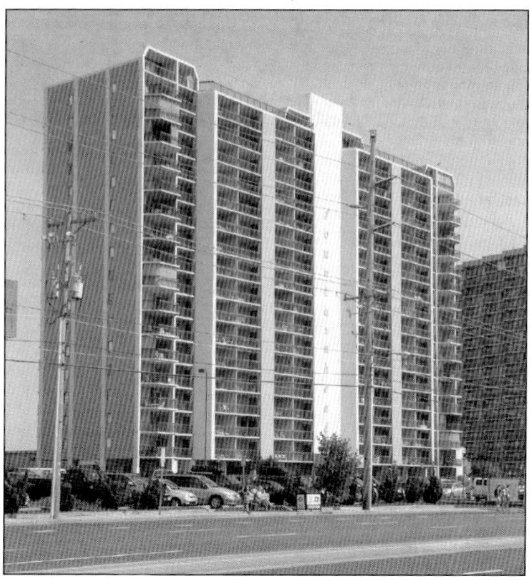

In 1974, the Sheraton Fontainebleau Hotel opened. Long affiliated with Clarion, the hotel was owned for the past 35 years by Leonard Berger. It was sold in 2020 and is being rebranded as the Ocean City Fontainebleau Resort. With 16 meeting rooms, the hotel's 40,000-square-foot conference center hosts executive retreats and conferences and serves as a wedding venue. The hotel has outdoor and indoor pools and an award-winning restaurant called Horizons. (RMC.)

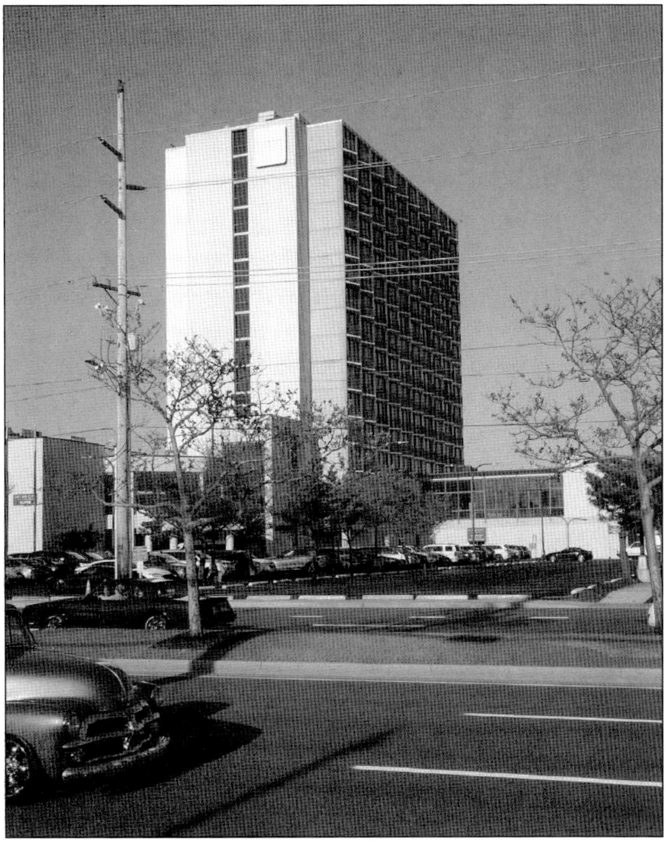

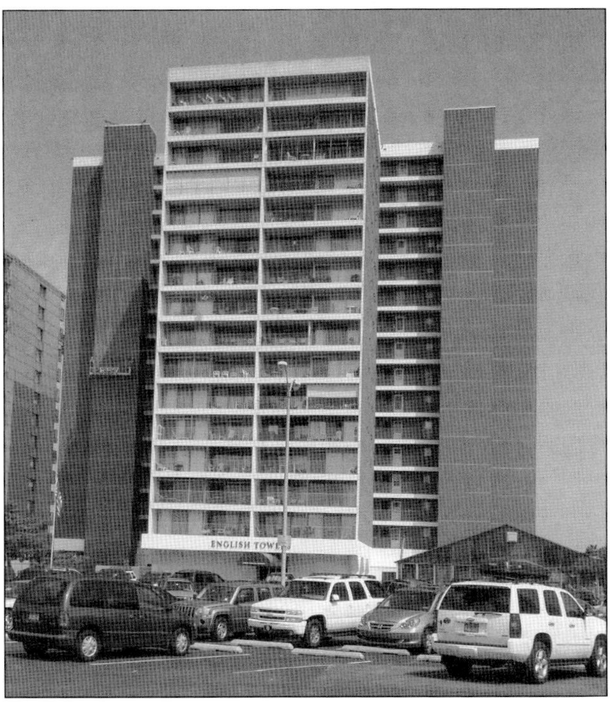

The English Towers rises 16 floors in a T-plan with 90 oceanfront condos and 60 bayside units in the back stem of the T. A wide continuous balcony extends across the living rooms and master bedrooms. The pool is Olympic-size. The crisp building styling, sharp-edged with structural framing of glazed facades, calls to mind apartment blocks by master Modernist Mies Van der Rohe. (RMC.)

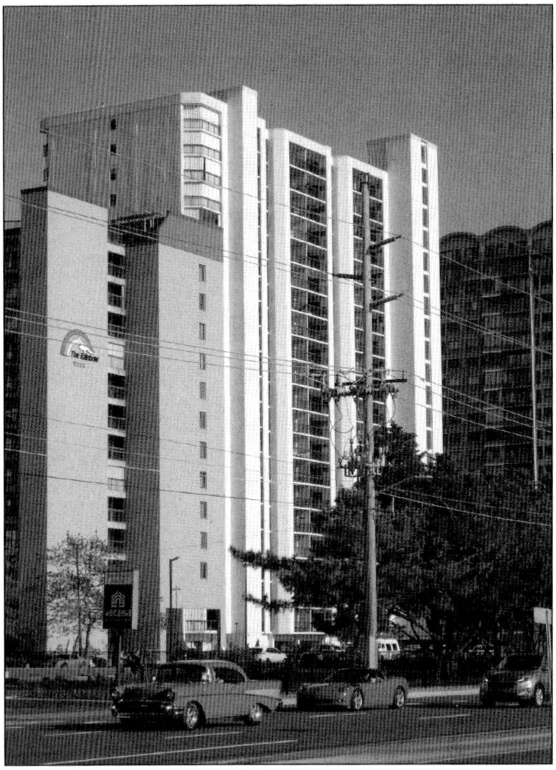

In this photograph, The Irene (1974) looms behind the Rainbow Condominium tower, which was built 10 years later, when new towers were filling in the few remaining gaps on Condo Row. The Irene is named for the wife of Holocaust survivor (and one of Ocean City's premier condo developers) Max Berg, who had previously expanded the Carousel from a motel to a significantly enlarged motel/condo megastructure. (RMC.)

The Irene, at 21 stories, contains 146 condos, some two-bedroom and some three-bedroom units. Amenities include a small, circular heated indoor pool under the dome on the highway side of the building. The round and somewhat futuristic styling of the glass pool building contrasts with the towering concrete block behind it. On the beach side is a large, full-width sundeck with the natural dune line and public beach beyond. (RMC.)

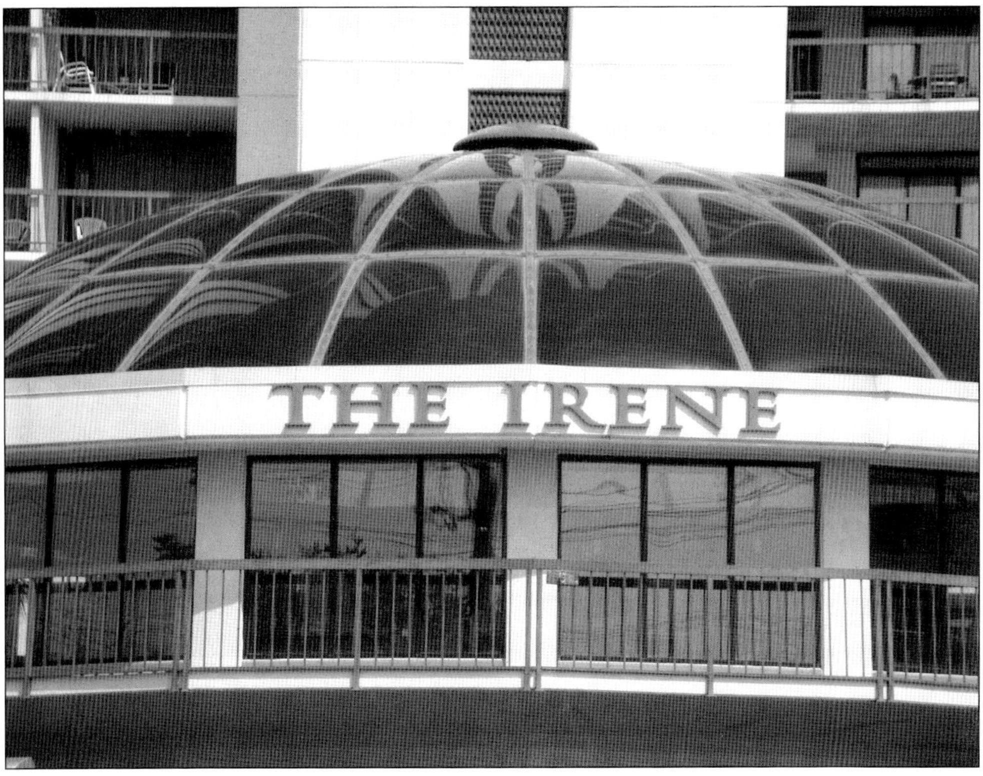

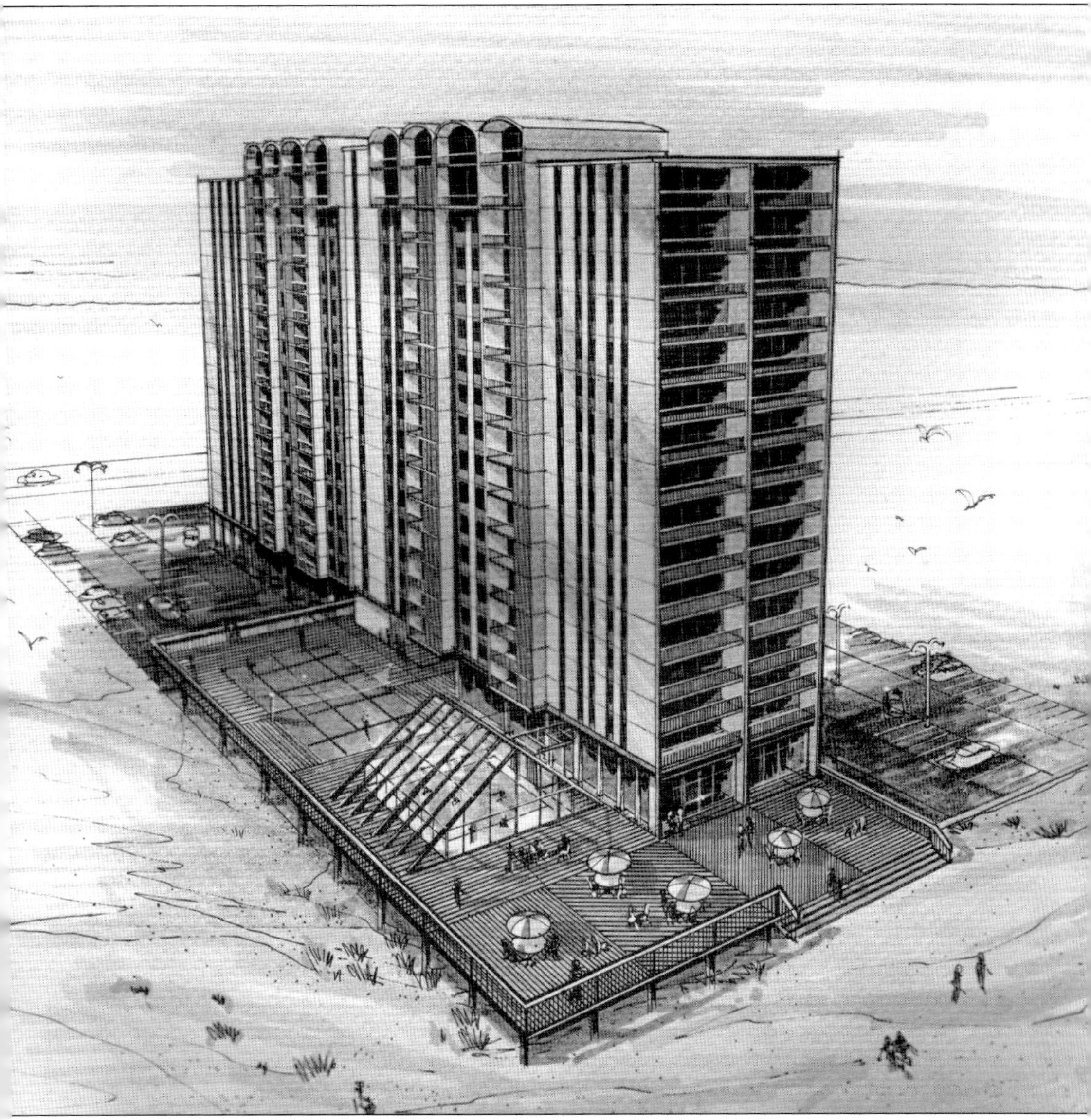

This dramatic bird's-eye rendering of The Capri, built in 1974, shows the condominium tower rising 20 stories with 222 units. Extending its thin slab from the beachfront to the Coastal Highway, The Capri presents an enormous billboard facade that blocked any panoramic view of the aligned condos along the famed Coastal Highway row. The huge building suffered from exposure to strong winds and rain from nor'easters and occasional hurricanes. By 1996, problems with moisture intrusion into the units prompted a $2.8-million retrofit of the north and south facades by DLM Architects (based in Virginia Beach), which completely reclad the building with a prefabricated wall system that utilizes the PERS (Pressure Equalized Rainshield System) concept—the first such retrofit of an existing building on the East Coast. The system was designed so that the harder the wind blows, the more watertight the building surface becomes. The design upgrades also included aesthetic changes, including new cornice work on all sides of the building slab and alterations to the rooftop parapet adjacent to the elevator tower (see page 138). (Robert M. Craig collection.)

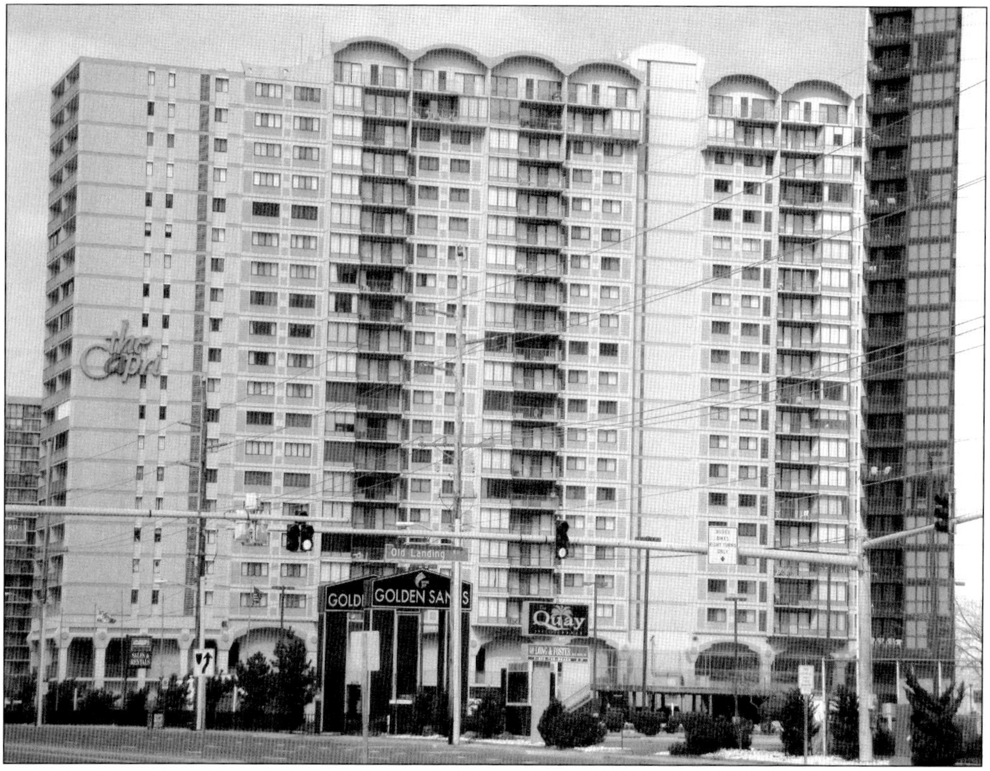

The original architect's color drawing on page 137 rendered The Capri in sepia tones that matched the timber decking at its base. As executed, the building's pink, blue, and pale green palette is stylish Postmodernism at its most saccharine. The ground-level piers with splayed capitals adorned with simple circles and the stylized rooftop arcade are New Formalist gestures that create a prettily gift-wrapped building. In the below image of surface ornament, the circle, rustication infill, upper horizontal band, and clapboarding at right are dusty pink; the shutters above the middle capital are blue, the corrugated surfaces, spandrels above and below windows and wide base below the corrugated panels are tan, and the splayed capitals (and other surfaces) are concrete grey. Altogether, this created an array of pastel surfaces too sweet for a megastructure of this scale and prominence. (Both, RMC.)

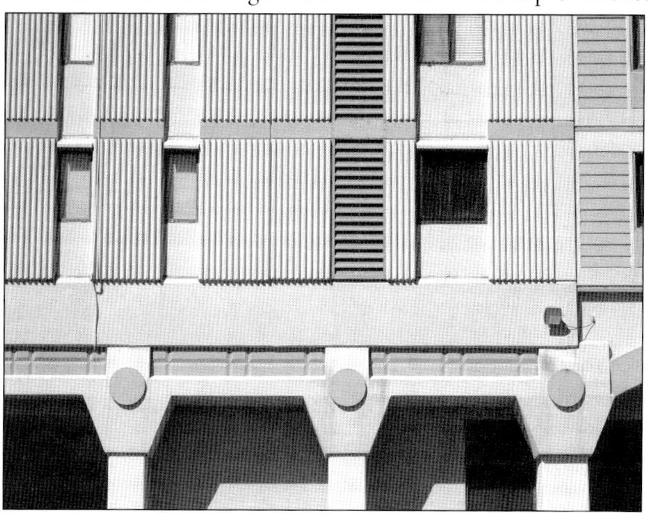

Contemporary with The Capri, and forming another thin slab orienting its narrow ends to the ocean and bay, is the 9400 Condo tower, also completed in 1974. Located at what is considered the southern entry to Condo Row, the 9400 Condo conspicuously forms a broad 22-story entry superblock at Ninety-Fourth Street. Like competing condo projects, it features a large terrace and oceanfront pool. (Robert M. Craig collection.)

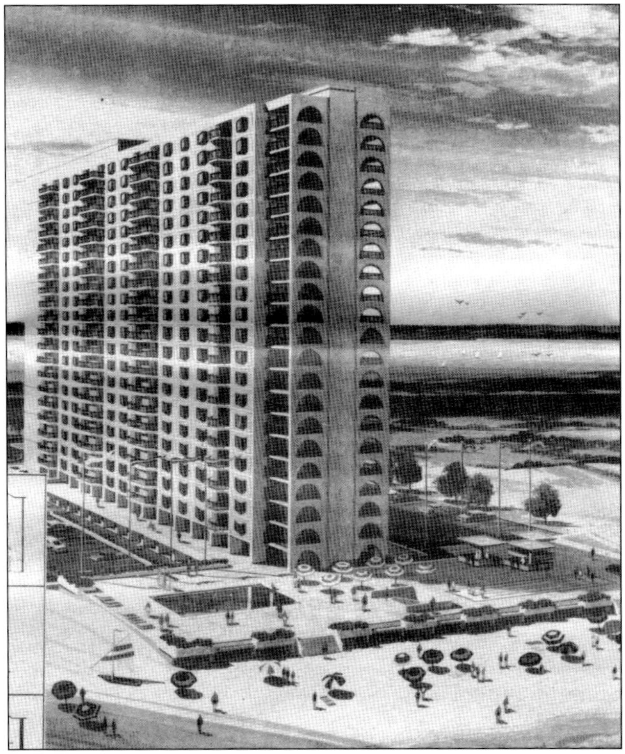

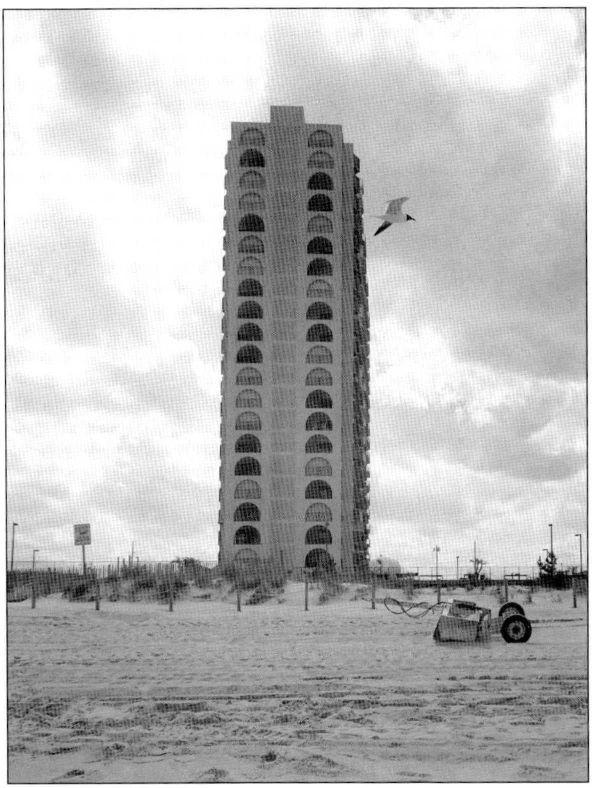

The narrow ends of the 9400 block feature half-circular openings in a single stack bayside and two stacks oceanfront, each an abstracted geometric design of reduced simplicity. In contrast, the broad expanses of the north and south elevations ripple with polygonal balconies and canted-out windows reminiscent of Marcel Breuer's Brutalist window welts installed at the Whitney Museum in New York in 1966. (RMC.)

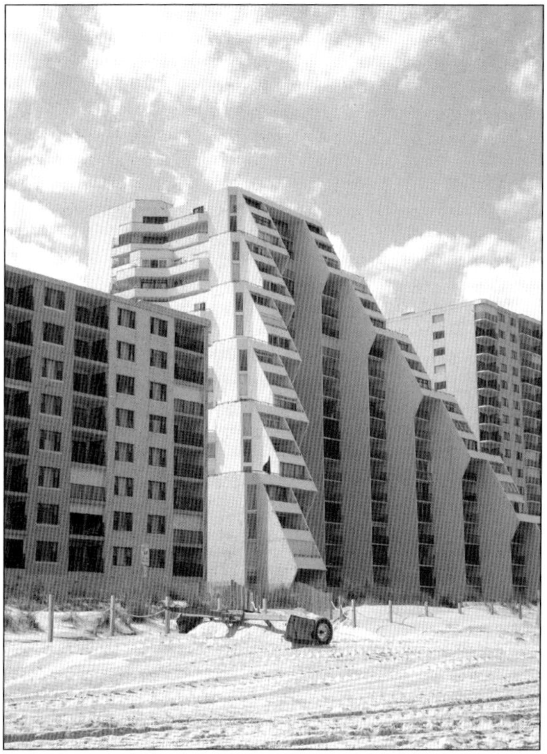

In 1975, signs of economic recovery were marked by the completion of two of the most distinguished designs on Condo Row—the iconic Pyramid and the perhaps lesser appreciated but laudable Century I tower. Pyramid–Ocean City opens cascading arms to the beach, adopting forms that recall Paul Rudolph's now-razed headquarters building constructed in 1972 for Burroughs Wellcome pharmaceutical company and considered a Brutalist landmark. Influence may well have come from the André Minaugoy pyramids in France (mentioned in the chapter introduction). In any case, the Pyramid is one of Ocean City's landmark works of architecture. (Both, RMC.)

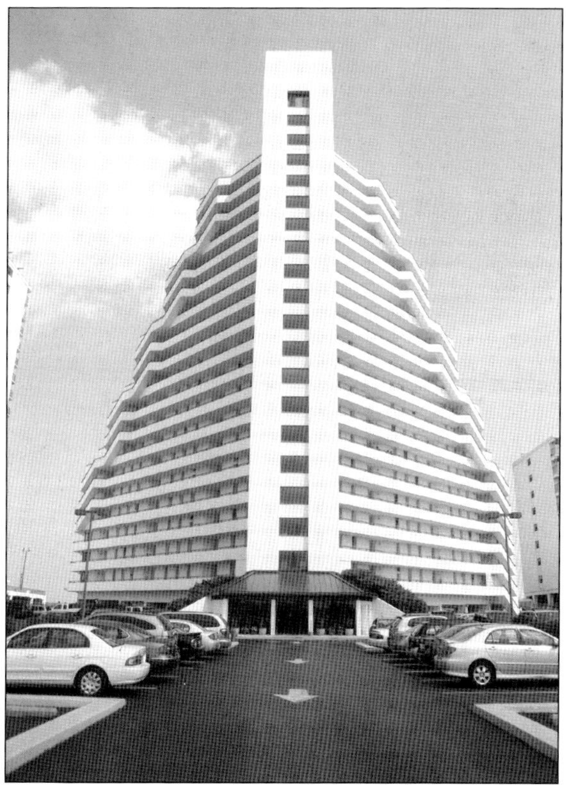

The Pyramid may be the best remembered and most photographed condo tower in Ocean City. Its stepped profile, multiple balconies, exterior corridors, and brilliant white surfaces are distinctive. The splayed oceanside arms frame an outdoor swimming pool and terrace, while the west tower spine of the building emphasizes the pyramidal shape on the bayside. (RMC.)

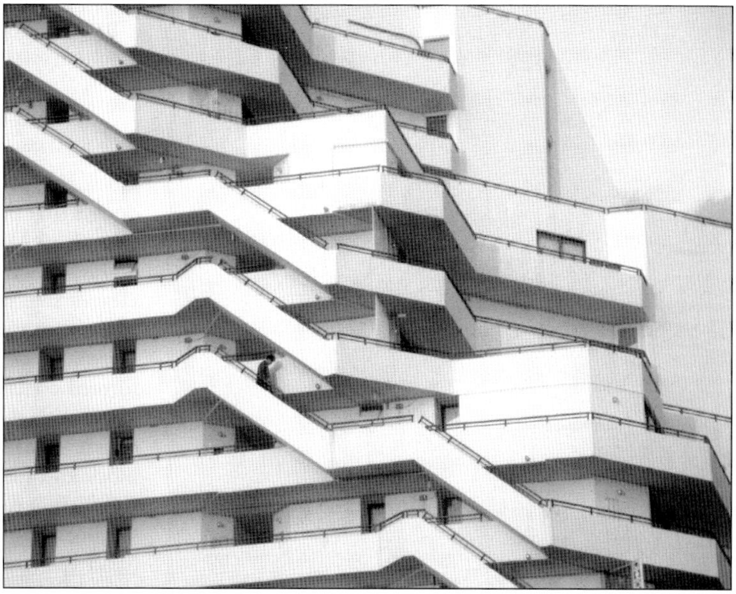

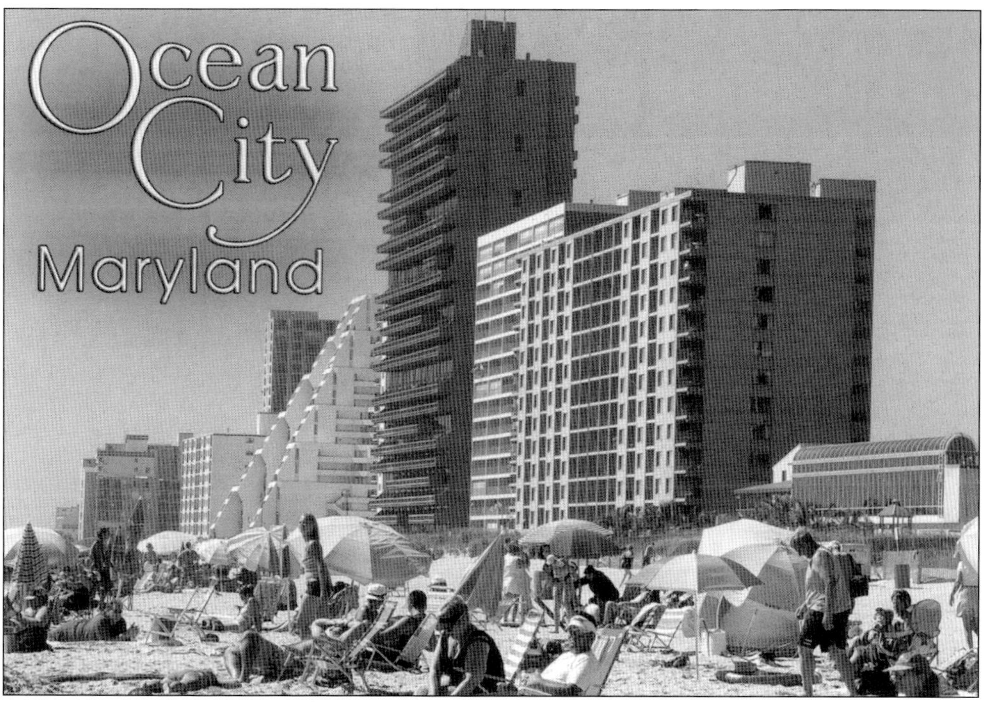

In Kevin N. Moore's postcard photograph, the Pyramid cascades its distinctive white forms down to the beach, where vacationers could relax on beach chairs and towels until the midafternoon sun fell behind the condo slabs and cast shadows across the beach. Only the Pyramid appears aware of the angles that optimally preserve direct sunshine for beachgoers. The tall, dark tower in the center of the postcard is Century I.

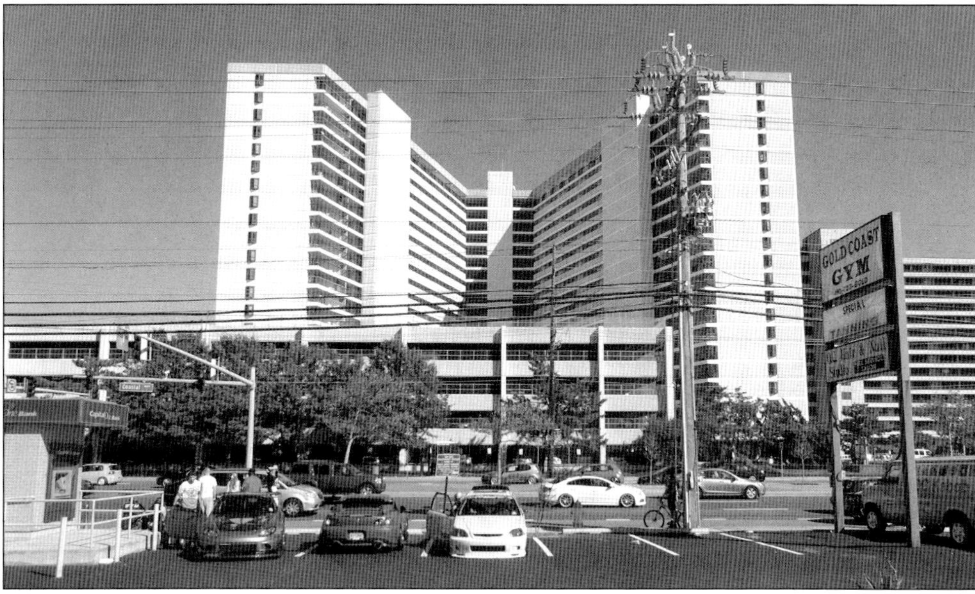

Sea Watch forms a vice of two large wings splayed out so that the continuous lines and openings of the west front's inner elevations show a strong horizontality, while balconies facing southeast and northeast are staggered, creating a textural richness and syncopated patterns of light and shadow as well as structural expression. Condo developers competed to provide designs that would attract from the exterior, maximize views, and provide a unique architectural experience. Advertised as the largest condo building in Ocean City, Sea Watch is also rich in on-site amenities, with three swimming pools, two tennis courts, a basketball court, a volleyball court, a playground, and the requisite game room, fitness facility, saunas, and even its own movie theater. These are available to keep vacationers occupied with activities when they come to the beach and then seek to avoid the beach. (Both, RMC.)

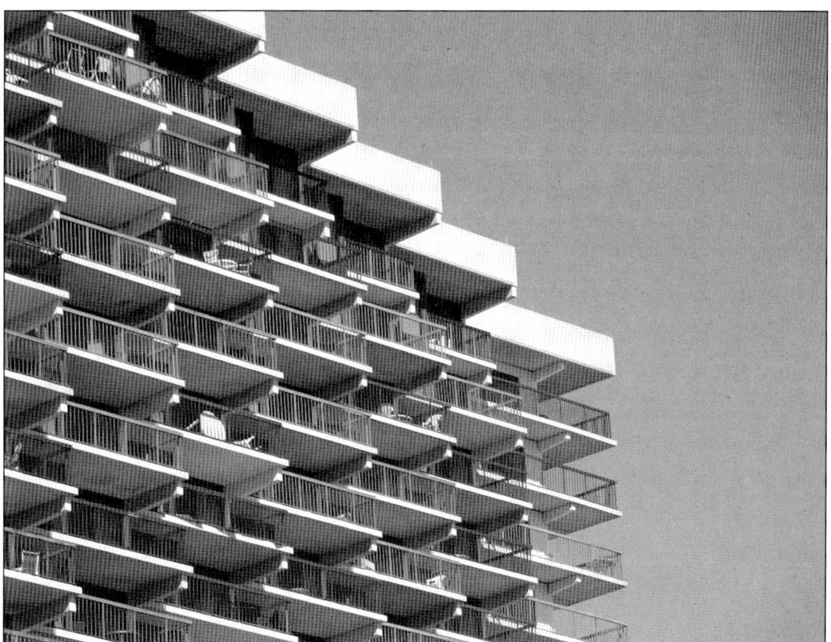

In 1975, the building of The Quay (pronounced "key"), which started in 1974, had stalled, and it was not completed until 1977. It brought the number of towers on Condo Row to 14 (or 16, counting Antiqua, built in 1976, and Sea Terrace, built in 1974, located south of Ninety-Fourth Street)—a remarkable achievement but one fraught with economic pitfalls, marketing and sales challenges, and competition. The Quay has 26 stories, 186 two- and three-bedroom units, indoor and outdoor pools, a sundeck, a tennis court, and two saunas. A quay is "a structure that is built parallel to the bank of a waterway for use as a landing place," a definition that The Quay claims to make this lodging the perfect "landing place" for vacationers. (Both, RMC.)

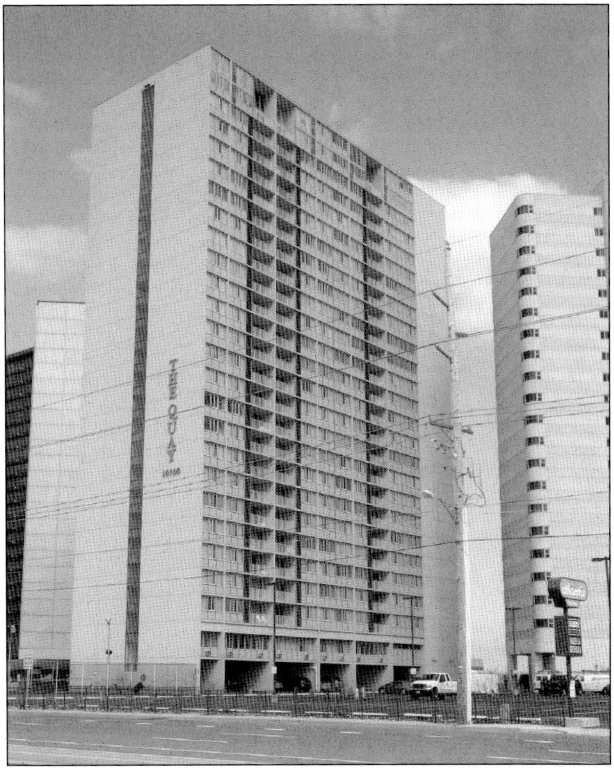

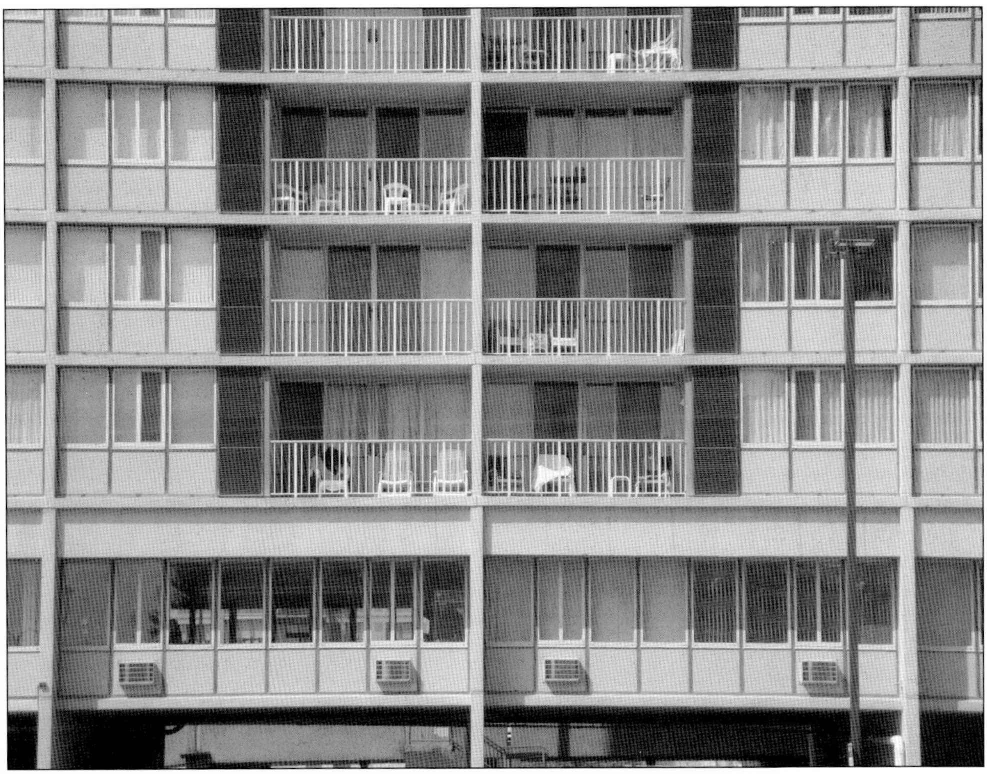

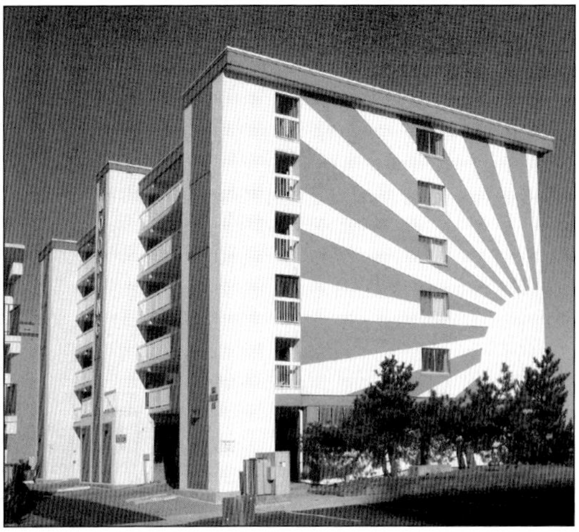 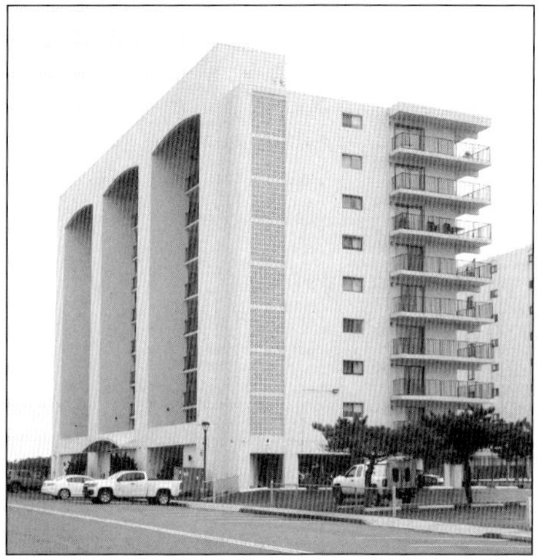

Between 1971 and 1976, new condo towers and mid-rise blocks occupied sites between Condo Row and Motel Row, as well as farther north, as property-hungry investors gobbled up any available land for development. These included Calypso (1971), three notable projects from 1973 (Camelot [above right], Braemar Towers, and Seagate [below]), and three more in 1974 (Mooring [above left], Sea Terrace, and Bluewater East). Sea Terrace and Mooring employ supergraphics on building surfaces; Sea Terrace's large-scale signage and angular four-color stripes highlight its blank west wall, while Mooring features a large mural of sunbursts and rays on its south front. The two independent blocks of Camelot evidence Formalist styling in their front elevations, displaying full-height arcades of three bays and a segmental arched entry hood. Decorative pierced concrete blocks recall 1950s tropical architecture (see pages 116, 128, and 147). (All, RMC.)

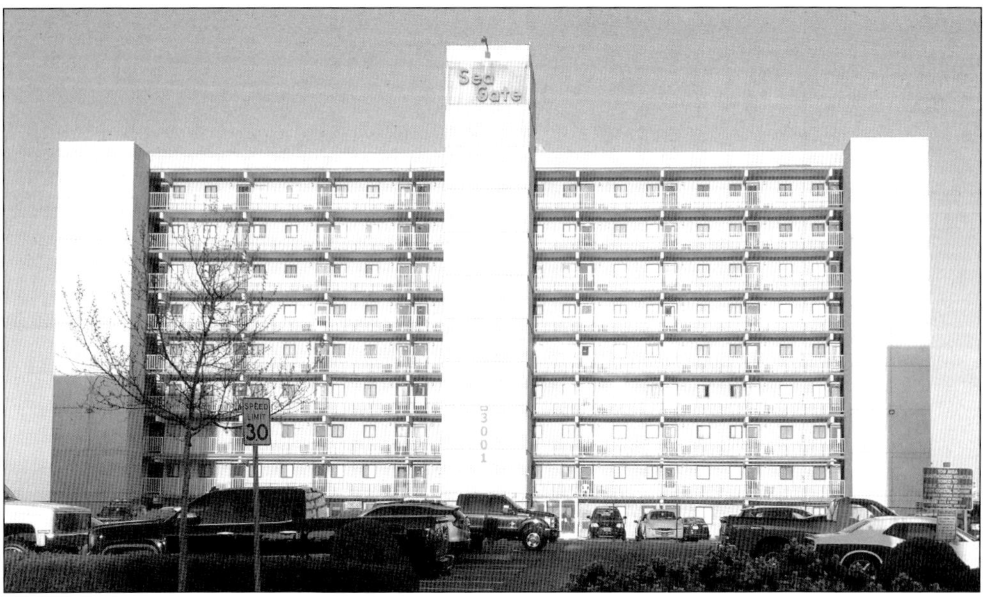

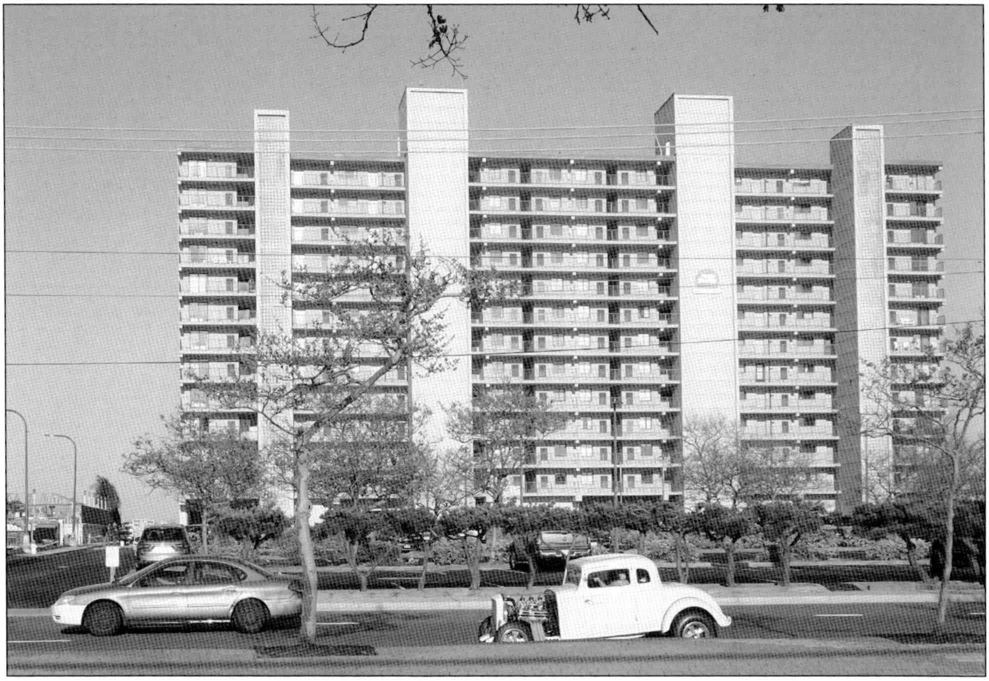

New condo towers filled the gaps of Condo Row during the early 1980s. Flying Cloud was added south of the Pyramid in 1982, Rainbow Condo was wedged into a narrow lot between The Irene and Highpoint South in 1984, and two lodgings of notable expanse, Kasa Marigot Beach (a 1984 "virtual service hotel") and the Plaza Condominiums (1985), spread along the Coastal Highway. For ornament, the Plaza, following the model of Camelot and the earlier Sun and Sea Motel (see pages 146 and 116, respectively), displays patterns of pierced concrete block. The Plaza's 17 floors offered two- and three-bedroom units and featured in-house restaurants, the oceanfront Jungle Bar, and a tiki bar and grill on the condo's half-acre sundeck. Remaining up-to-date, the Plaza now has two electric-car charging stations. (All, RMC.)

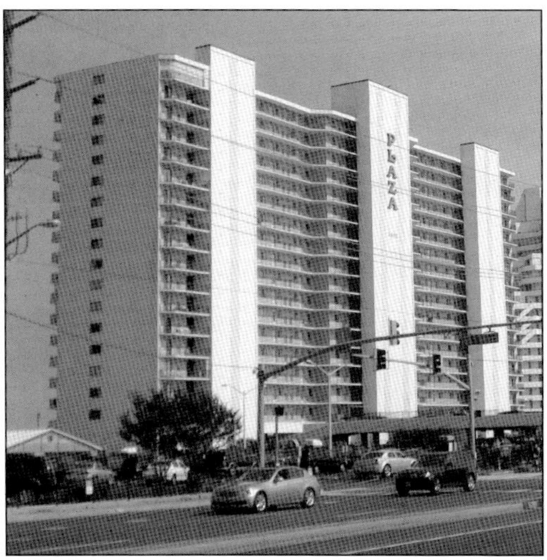

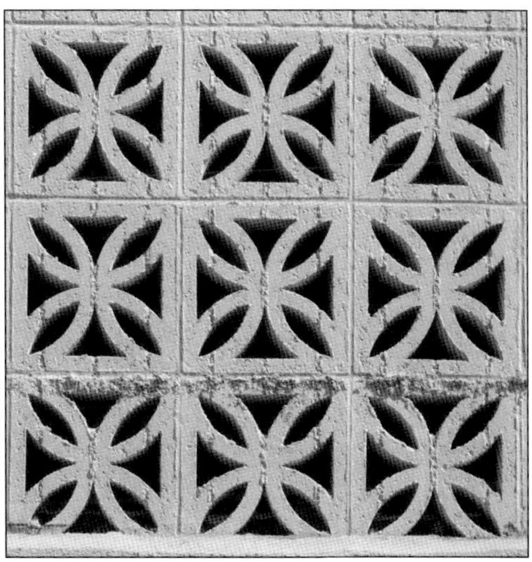

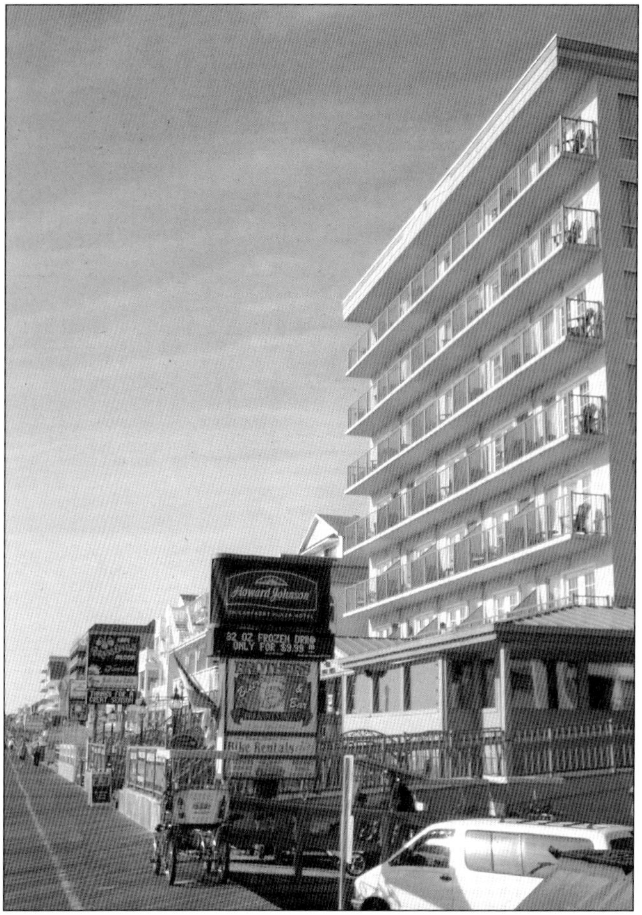

Encouraged by two decades of condo construction and out-of-date hotel lodgings on the Boardwalk, each couple of years of the late 1980s brought a new balconied box to the Boardwalk. In 1987, the shingle-clad Mayflower Hotel (c. 1927; see page 58) was taken down and replaced by the Howard Johnson Oceanfront Plaza (left). Two years later, in 1989, a cubic Postmodern Comfort Inn—with an absurdly tiny kidney-shaped swimming pool in front—was inserted in a former row of Boardwalk cottages between Fifth and Sixth Streets. In 1991, the Mirage (renamed Americana Hotel; below) replaced the 1931 George Washington Hotel (see page 66), repeating the ubiquitous formula of balconied rooms over a Boardwalk-level T-shirt shop and restaurant bar with merchandise and seating flowing out to the edge of the Boardwalk. (Both, RMC.)

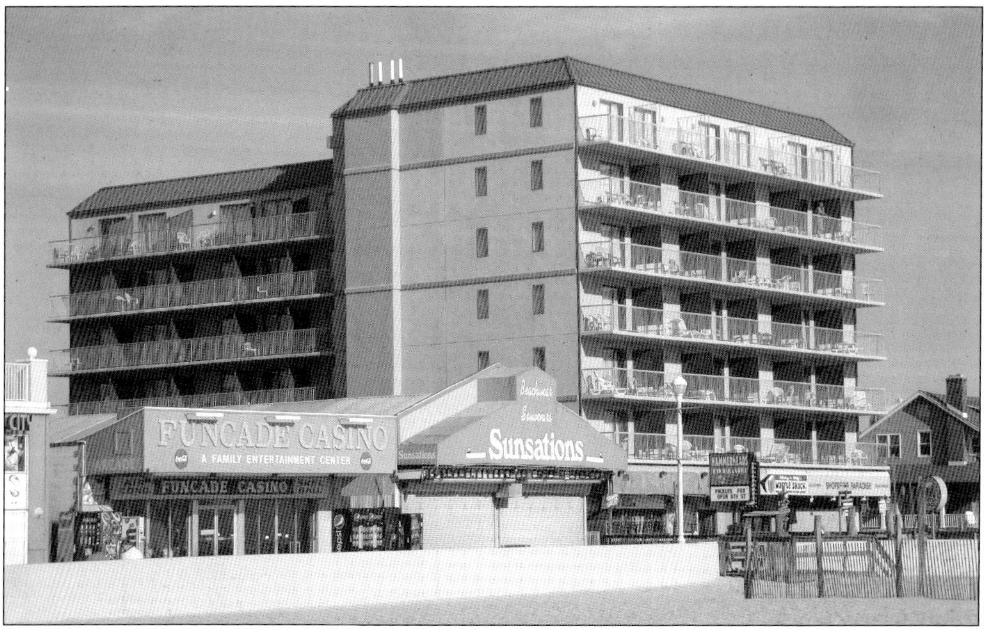

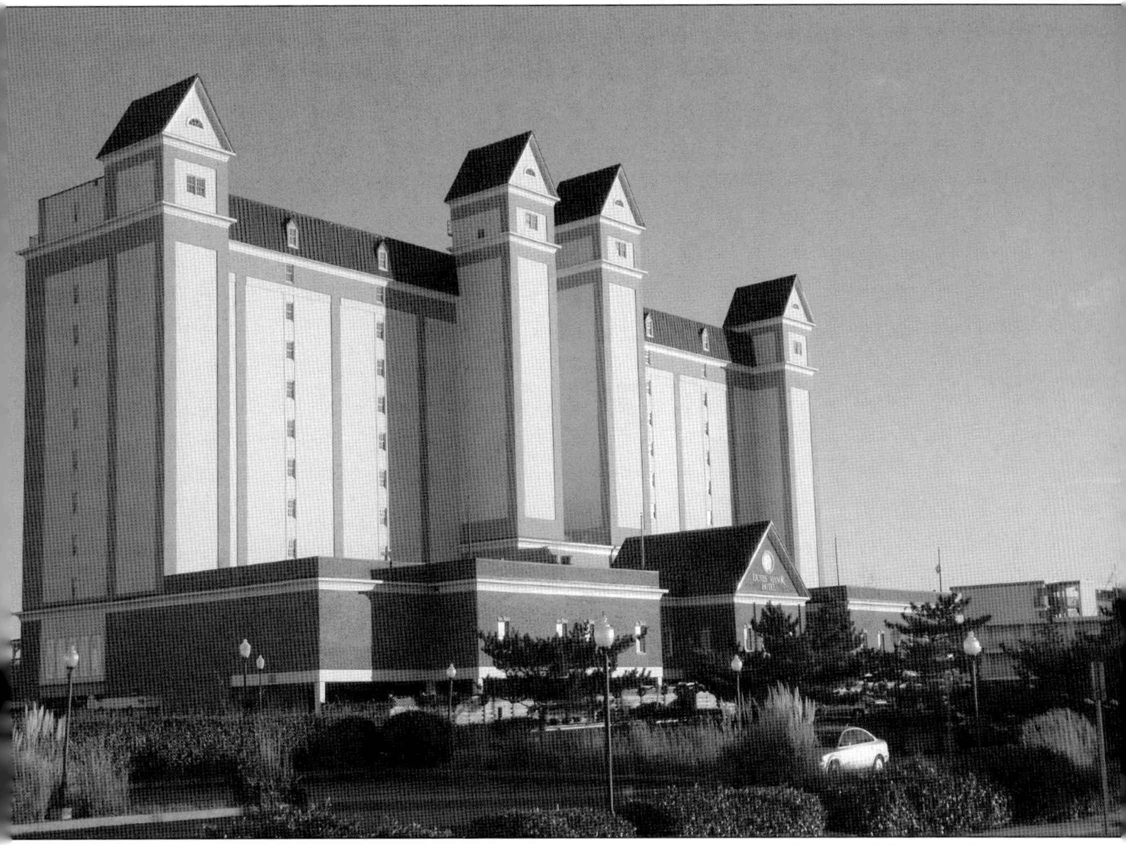

A new lodging on the scale of contemporary condo towers appeared in the heart of the Motel Row district in the late 1980s. Claiming to be a Victorian hotel (despite being built in 1987), the Dunes Manor rises 11 stories and features 160 oceanfront rooms and 10 suites. More convincingly Victorian than the hotel's architectural style, however, was proprietor Thelma Connor's practice of serving afternoon tea and cookies to guests. Her silver service, doilies, and Victorian interior furnishings matched her old-world charm as her hotel lobby became a Victorian parlor complete with a grand piano and evening sing-alongs. Even if there was nothing in the cumbersome exterior form of the hotel to suggest the enthusiastically ornate architecture built during the reign of the 19th-century queen, the Dunes Manor at least sought to continue some of the spirit of historic lodgings in old Ocean City. The brick entry with a Palladian window and flanking wings is more neo-Georgian, and the gabled towers and tiny cookie-cutter windows announce nothing Victorian but rather a giantism akin to that of chain hotel architecture and contemporary condo towers. (RMC.)

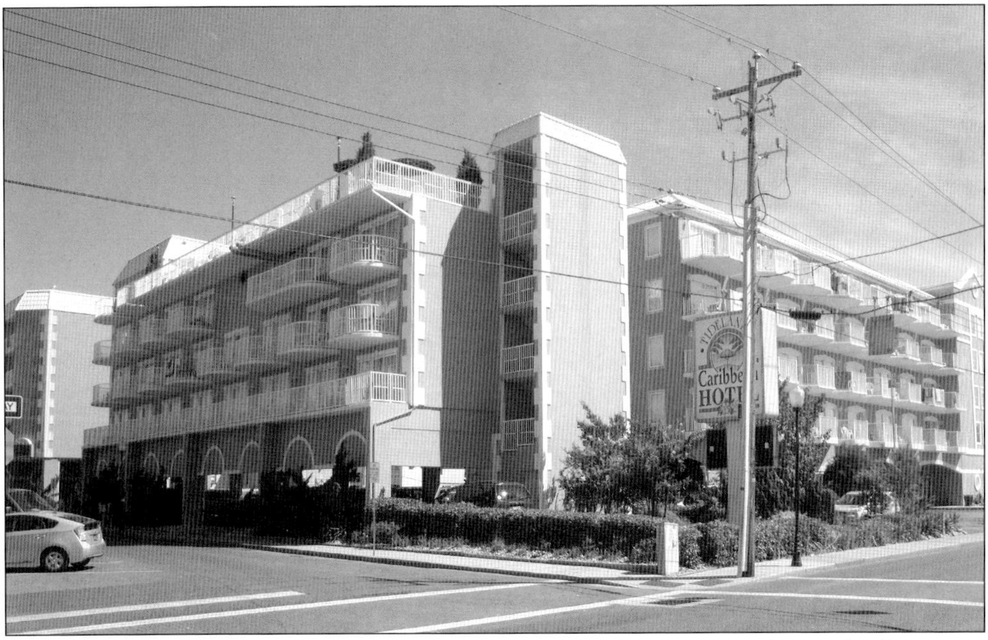

Standing out among isolated extant historic hotels and replacement condos in the downtown Boardwalk district is the Tidelands Caribbean Hotel and Suites, which was built in 1993. The Fifth Street wing reaches back the full block from the Boardwalk to Baltimore Avenue, and an additional lodging structure extends two-thirds of the block along Baltimore Avenue. The hotel's blue clapboarding with white trim is striking, but its most distinctive feature is the array of individual semicircular oceanfront balconies that create a happy rhythm across the east facade. A bridge over the alley connects sleeping units on two levels above ground-level parking with a rooftop outdoor swimming pool and sun terrace. A second elevated outdoor pool and terrace are behind the T-shaped block that fronts Baltimore Avenue. (Both, RMC.)

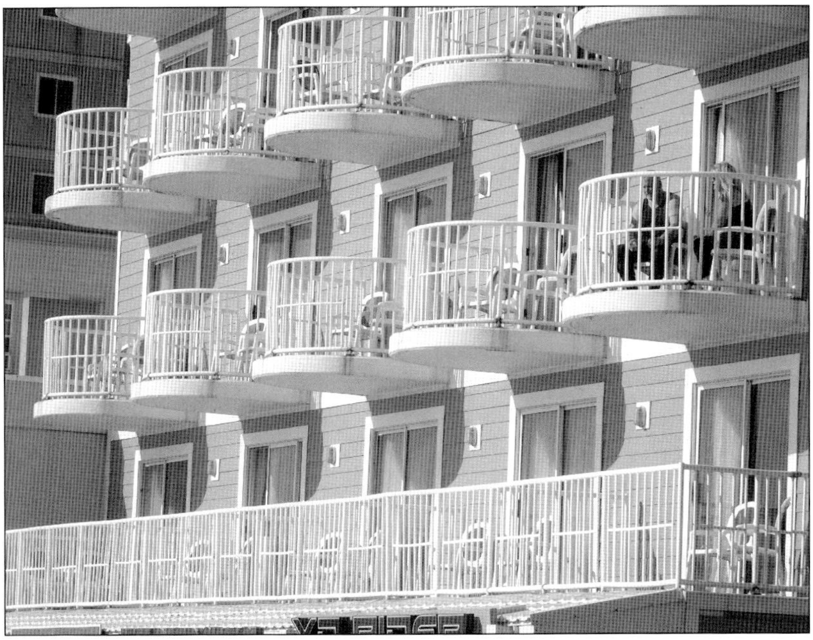

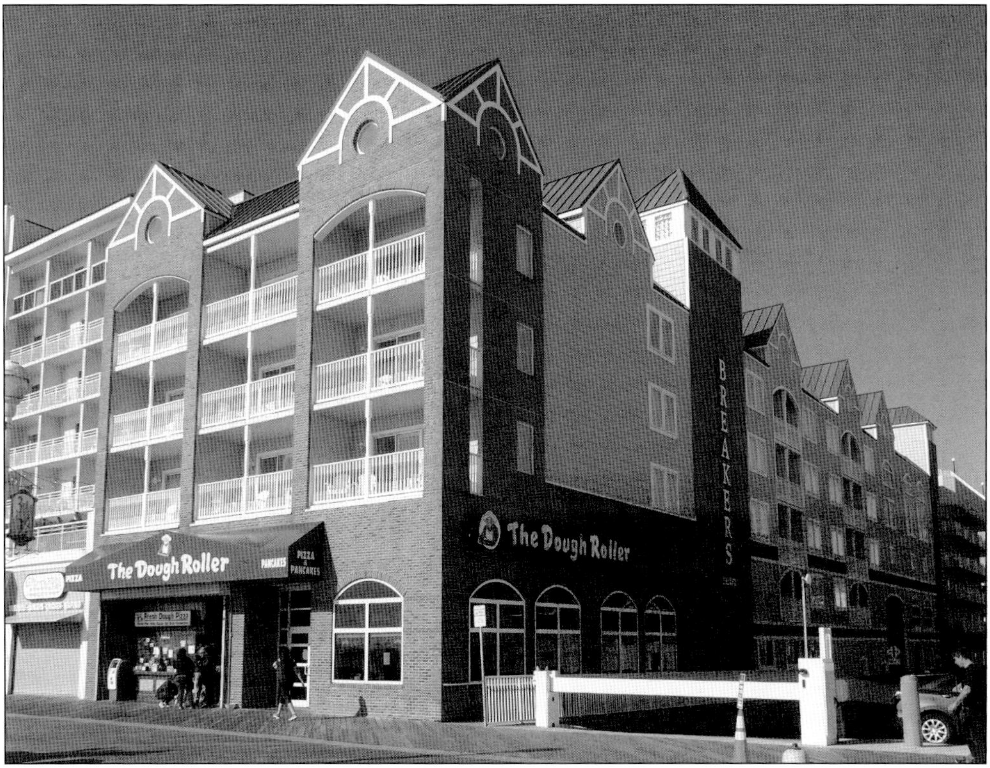

Two highly significant historic hotels were replaced during the first decade of 21st century. The Breakers Hotel (see page 40), which had stood on its Boardwalk site at Third Street for 100 years, gave way in 2004 to a rebuilt New Breakers (above). The Dough Roller restaurant had long occupied the lower floor, but in the New Breakers, historic shingle cladding was replaced by brick veneer, and topside were the all too commonplace and dead right-angled gable fronts defining side bays and implied towers. Belmont Towers (2007) went further in forcing an inappropriate scale and Postmodern pseudo-historicist forms on the historic downtown structure. Replacing the long-standing Belmont Hotel, Cottage, and Hearne complex (see pages 23–25), Belmont Towers rose awkwardly over its neighbors, although a street scale was reclaimed on its south front. (Both, RMC.)

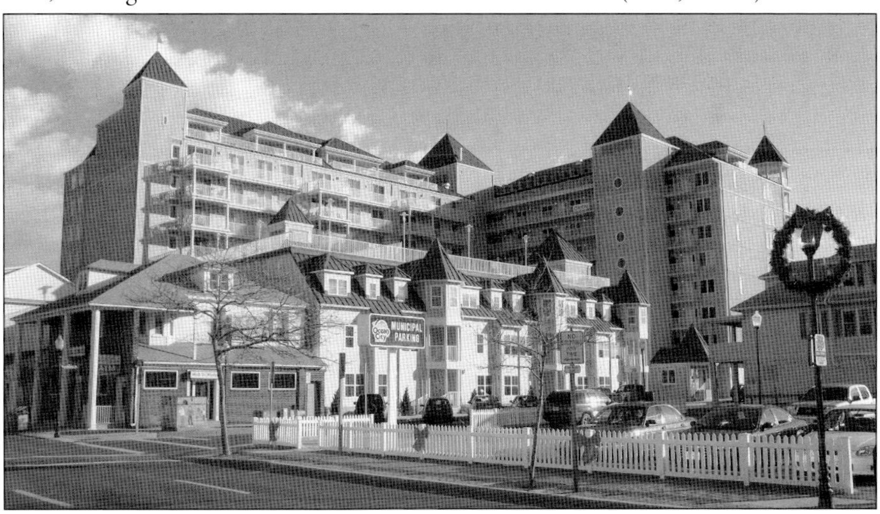

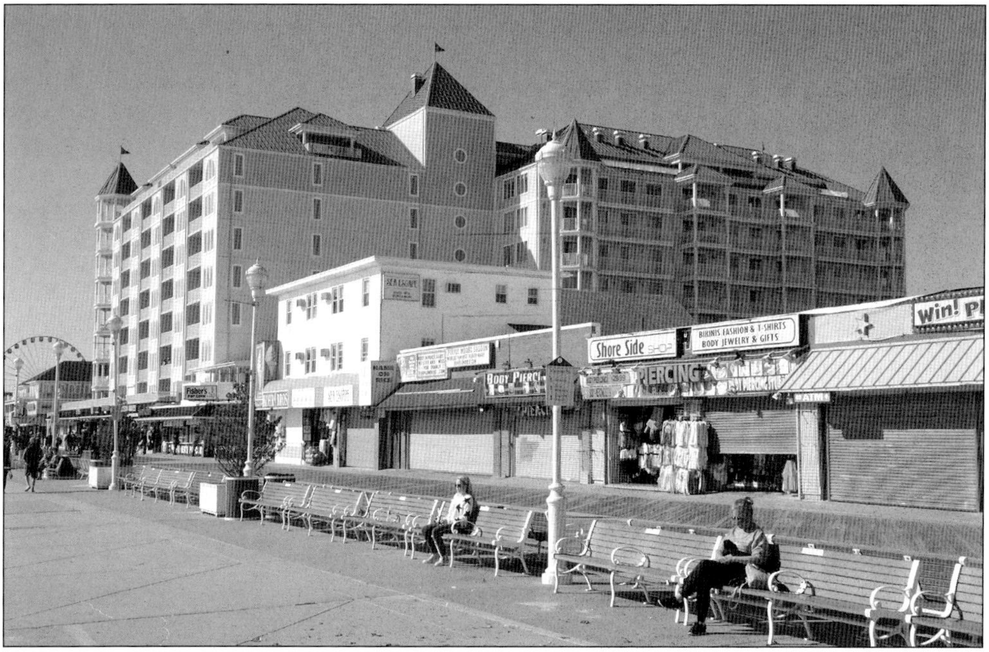

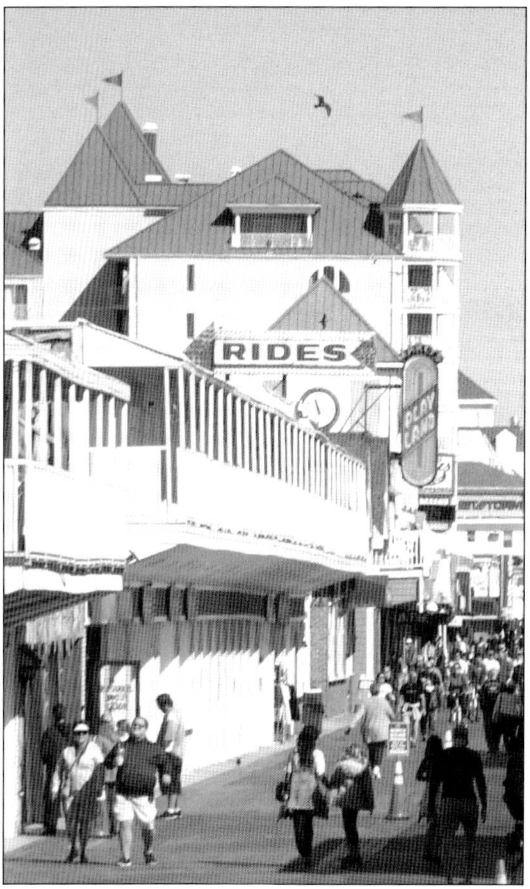

The above view of Belmont Towers from the northeast shows the condo block overpowering the pedestrian scale of the Boardwalk as it does the overall downtown skyline and historic district streetscape. Viewed from the south Boardwalk at (Windsor) Trimper's Rides (left), the blue turrets of the Belmont Towers rise above end-of-the-Boardwalk amusements, arcades, and rides, perhaps seeking to quote from the lost past of the long-disappeared Windsor Hotel, which stood at the south end of town—a simple hotel form with corner towers silhouetted against the sky (see pages 21 and 22). (Both, RMC.)

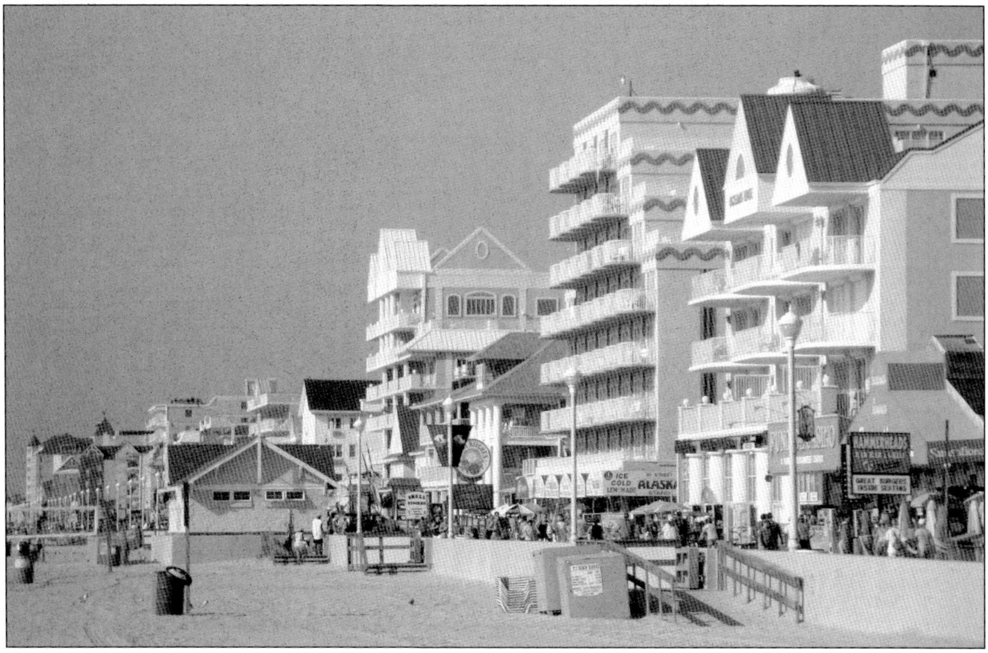

During the early 21st century, silly and unconvincing paste-ons sought to humanize megastructures with signs of home or the seaside, including projecting gables or wave motifs, as shown in these images. At South Beach Condos (2005) are three frontal gables (visible on the far side of the columned Lankford Hotel in the above image). A similar triplet group is cantilevered above balconies at Ocean's Edge (2002) (at far right in the above image). In between are the applied wave motifs at Paradise Plaza Inn, an eight-story block built in 1998 at a height that overwhelms the nearby historic Lankford Hotel and Ayresbilt Apartments to its south and adds insult to injury by rudely cramming its blank south wall against the historic Ayresbilt. (Both, RMC.)

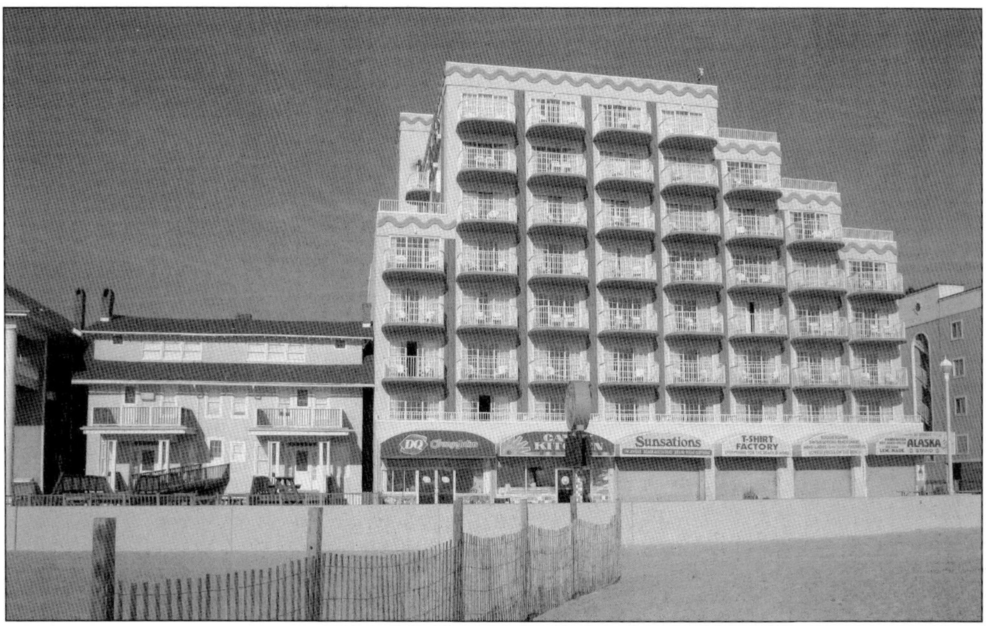

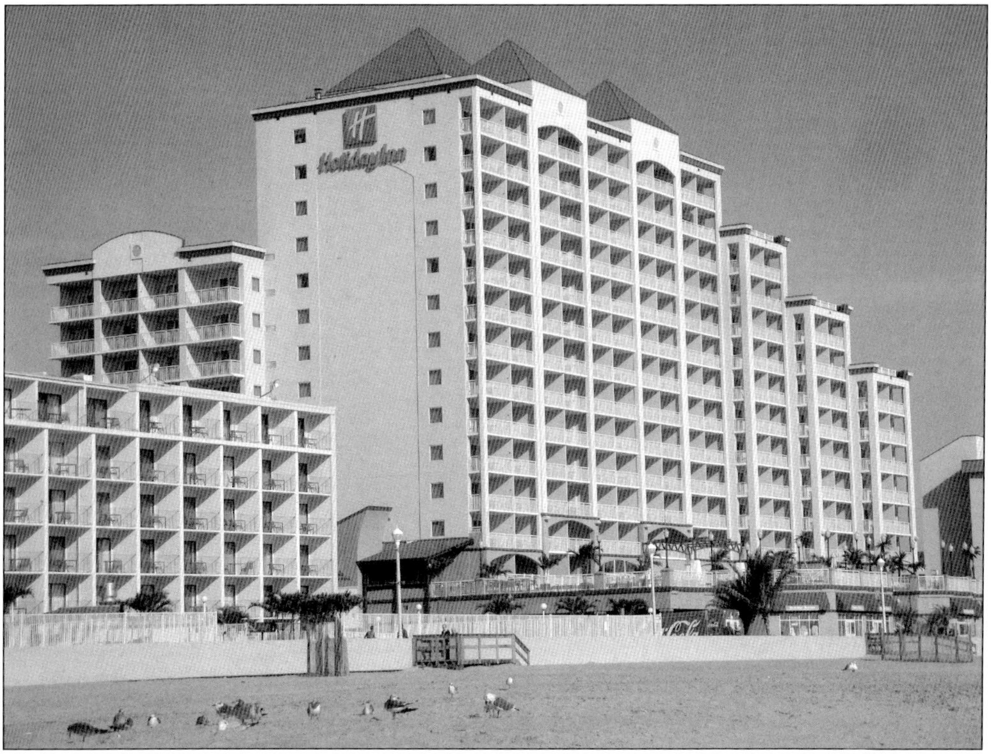

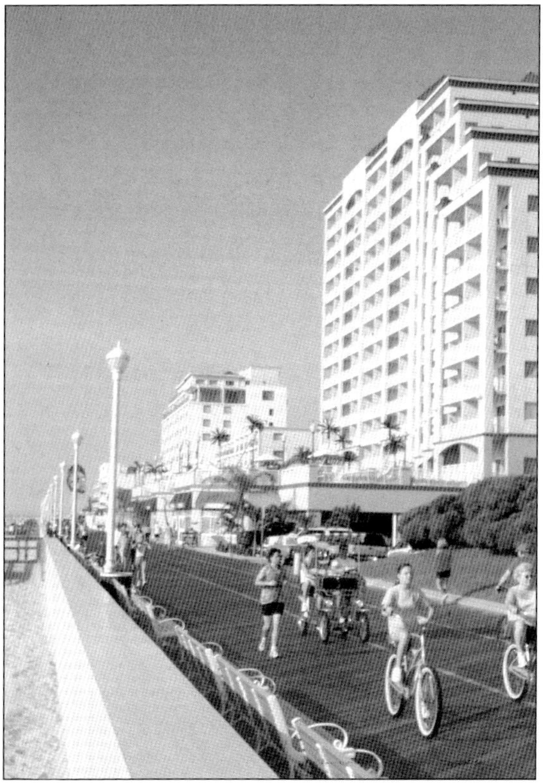

Preceded in 1974 by a Ramada Inn on Forty-Eighth Street and by the Sheraton-Fontainebleau Hotel at 101st Street, the building in 1980–1981 of Ocean City's first Holiday Inn (oceanfront at Sixty-Seventh Street), suggested that the era of mom-and-pop lodgings and motels was coming to an end, replaced by large chain hotels. The founder of the Holiday Inn chain, Kemmons Wilson, built his first Holiday Inn in 1952 in Memphis, Tennessee; by September 2018, there were 1,173 active Holiday Inn hotels across the world. Ocean City would eventually have several of these. The first, and later, the largest, were both constructed by local entrepreneurs John and Hale Harrison. Their Holiday Inn Boardwalk (located on Seventeenth Street) is a behemoth with 210 rooms, two oceanfront pools, an indoor heated pool in the atrium, and two restaurants. It was constructed from 2001 to 2003 and renovated in 2021. (Both, RMC.)

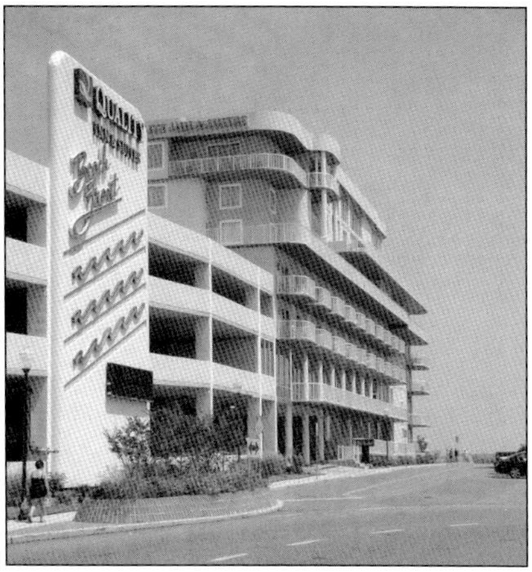

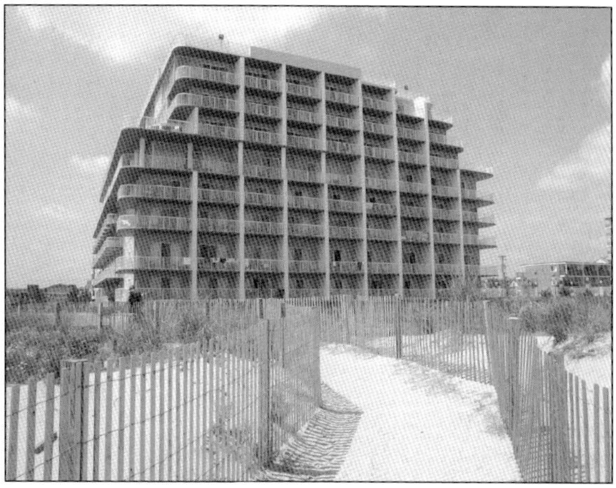

When available space permitted, lodgings expanded their earlier motels, and some changed affiliation. The 1991 Quality Inn Beachfront (above) on Thirty-Third Street was renovated and reopened in June 2018 as a DoubleTree by Hilton. The Quality Inn Beachfront features kinetic streamlined forms pulling the eye toward the beach, where the east elevation of balconies offers occupants open views across the dunes to the sea. The Quality Inn Boardwalk (below) (located on Sixteenth Street) today preserves an older motel block of units, perhaps built as early as 1968, to which a tower of additional units was added in 2015. The east front of the Quality Inn Boardwalk is a taut honeycomb of recessed balconies within a structurally expressive frame. (All, RMC.)

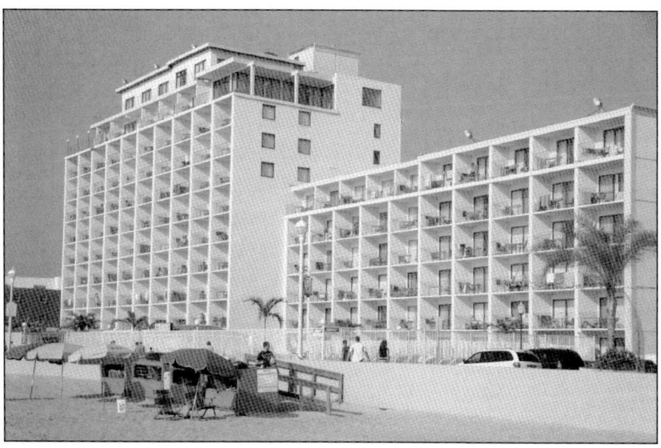

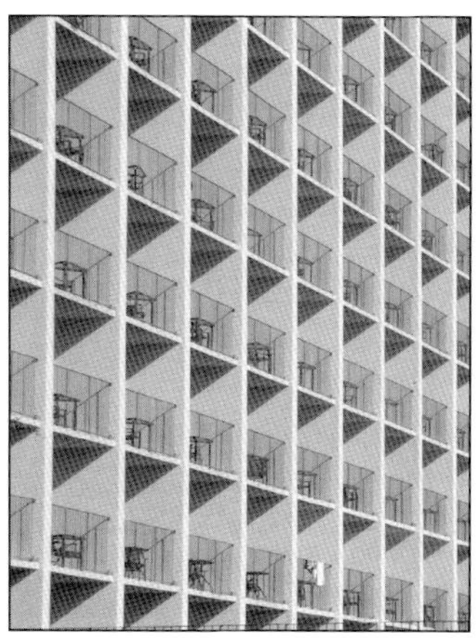

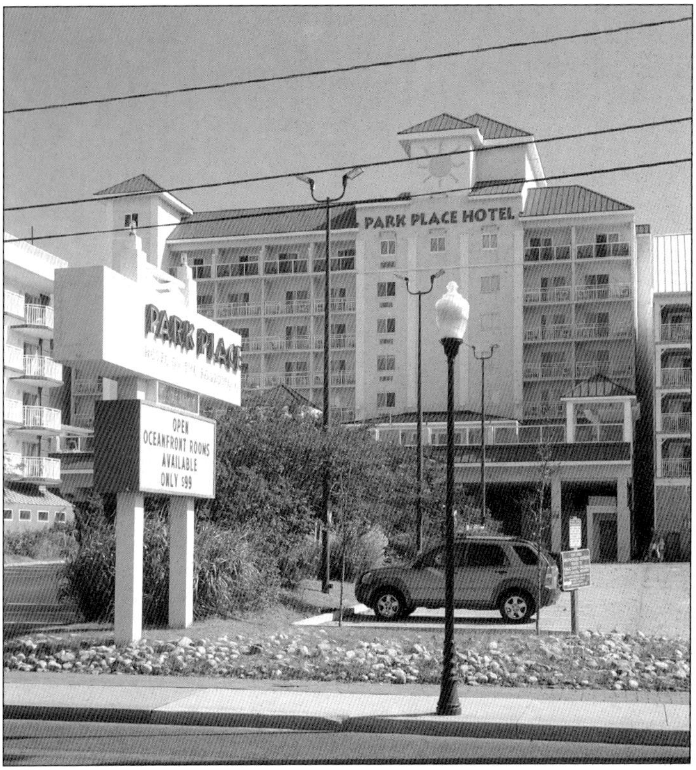

Along the length of the Boardwalk, large hotels continued to take the place of outdated shingle-clad hotels, cottages, and even the more recent motels. As early as 1975, the Hastings-Miramar Hotel group was razed, and for years, the vacant site served as a parking lot. In 2000, the Park Place Hotel (left) was built on the site and began offering 90 efficiency units with six different layouts. Park Place was renovated in 2017 to add a seventh floor. In 2006, a huge Hilton Hotel (below) appeared along the oceanfront at Thirty-Second Street, replacing the Stardust Motel (see page 108). (RMC.)

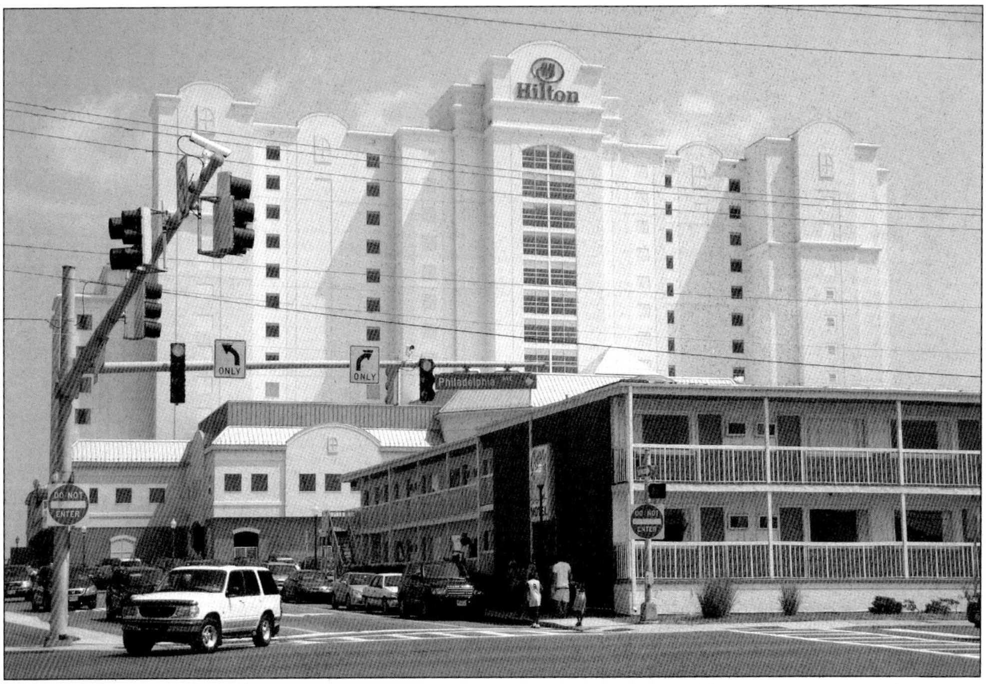

The new Hilton, another project of the Harrison Group, which would go on to own and operate 10 hotels and several restaurants in Ocean City, featured 225 one-bedroom units, two penthouses, four meeting rooms, two outdoor pools, and a heated indoor pool. (RMC.)

After the Hilton opened in 2006, hotel construction in Ocean City ground to a halt. Although an $83.8-million beach replenishment project, which began in 2005, might have been expected to attract more vacationers, necessitating increased amounts of lodging, the housing crisis of 2008 and the recession that followed resulted in a lull in hotel construction until 2014. As the economy picked up, chain hotels renewed construction; among the best designs was Fisher Architecture's at Hyatt Place (right), built in 2018 on the site of the Sea Scape Motel. (RMC.)

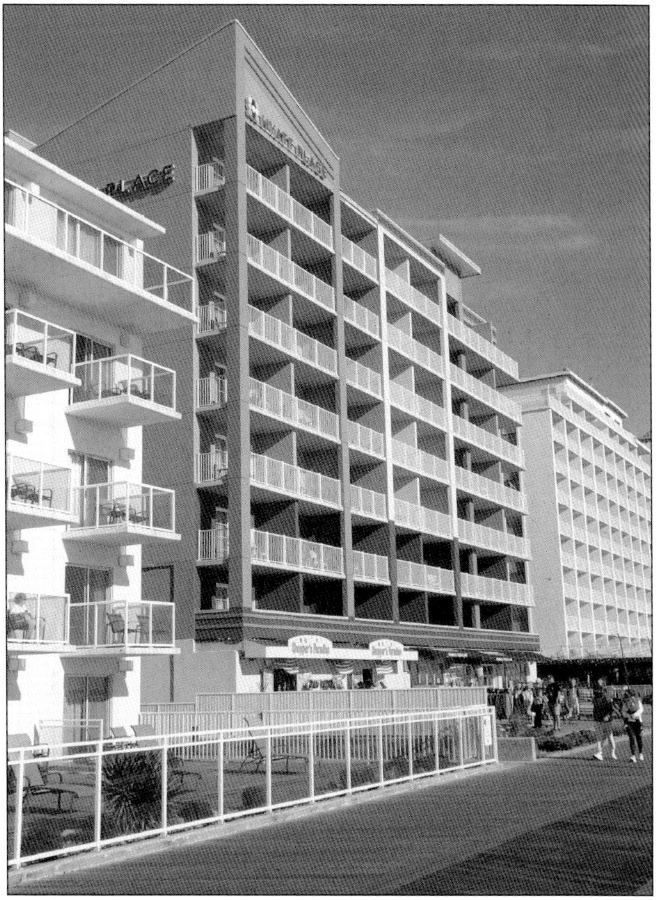

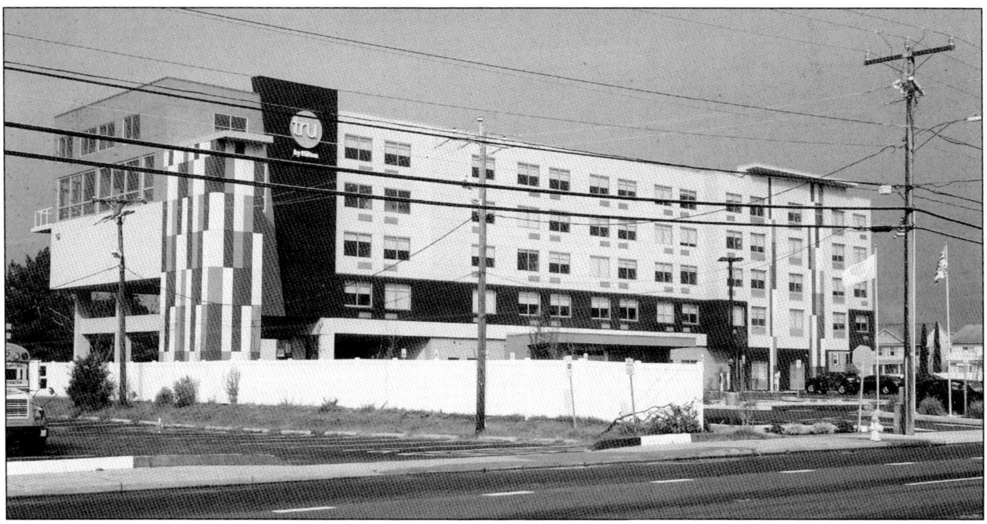

Familiar new chain motels bayside included a Hampton Inn at Forty-Fourth Street in 2014, a La Quinta Motel (displacing the Voyager Motel at Thirty-Second Street in 2014, see page 156), and a Marriott at the Route 90 bridge. Recent "design-forward" creations at Tru by Hilton (2020, above), and at Aloft by Iott A&E (2019) are noteworthy. (RMC.)

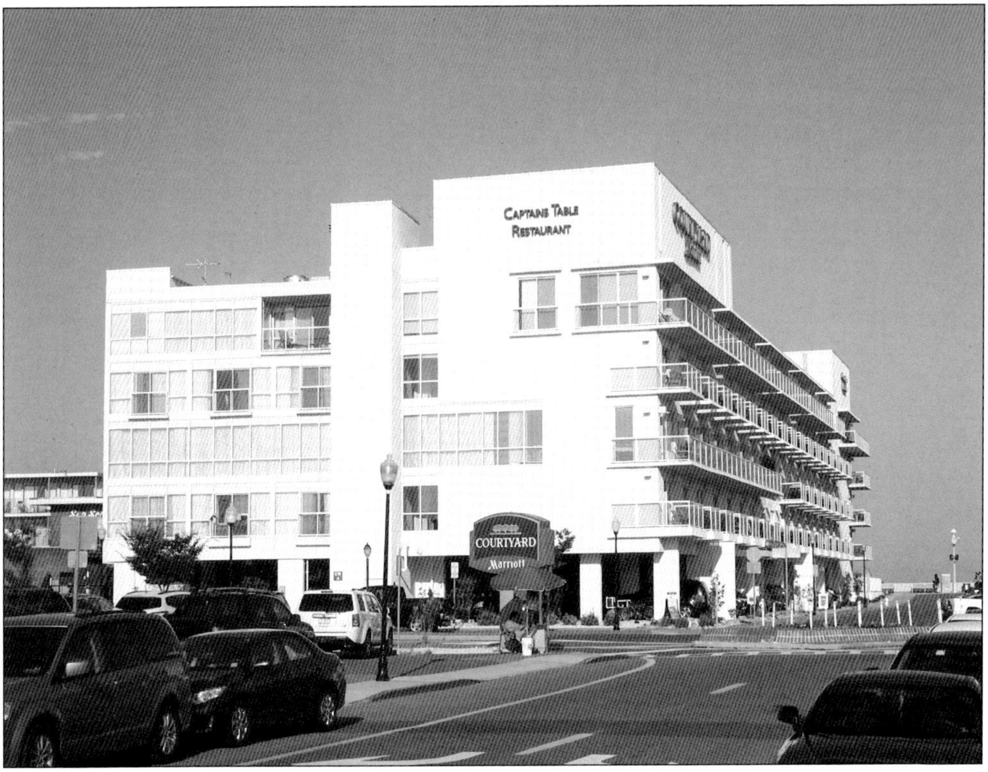

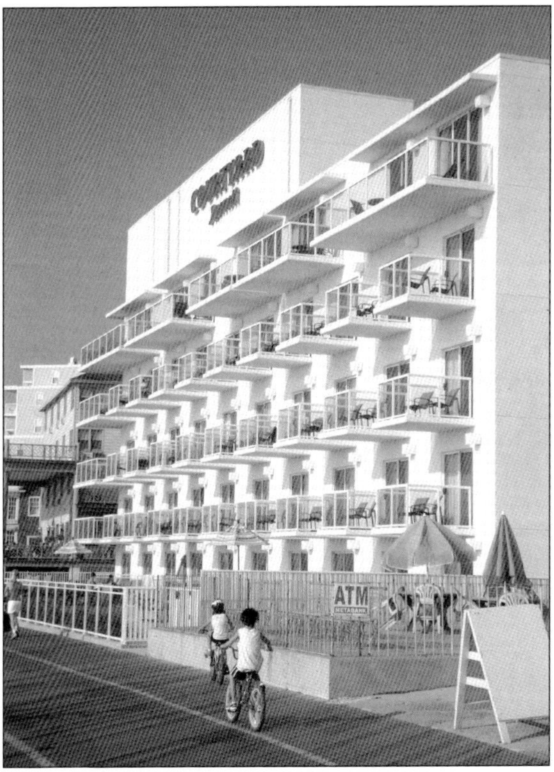

The historic Sea Scape, Ocean Park, Sandy Hill, Stardust, and other motels of Ocean City's classic Motel Row are now gone, having been displaced by chain hotels and larger lodging facilities of only occasionally better design or aesthetic interest. One of the most regrettable losses was the 1956 Santa Maria Motel (see page 105), which was razed in October 2005 and replaced in 2009 by the Courtyard Ocean City Oceanfront, now a Courtyard by Marriott. The new oceanfront recalls the evenhanded and repetitive patio/balcony spaces that once fronted the Boardwalk at a scale and rhythm exactly right for the pedestrian traffic the motel overlooked. The Captain's Table Restaurant was popular due to both its menu and its dinnertime piano-players. It has been rebranded as posh instead of folksy and is awkwardly lost in the upper reaches of an uninviting building layout. (Both, RMC.)

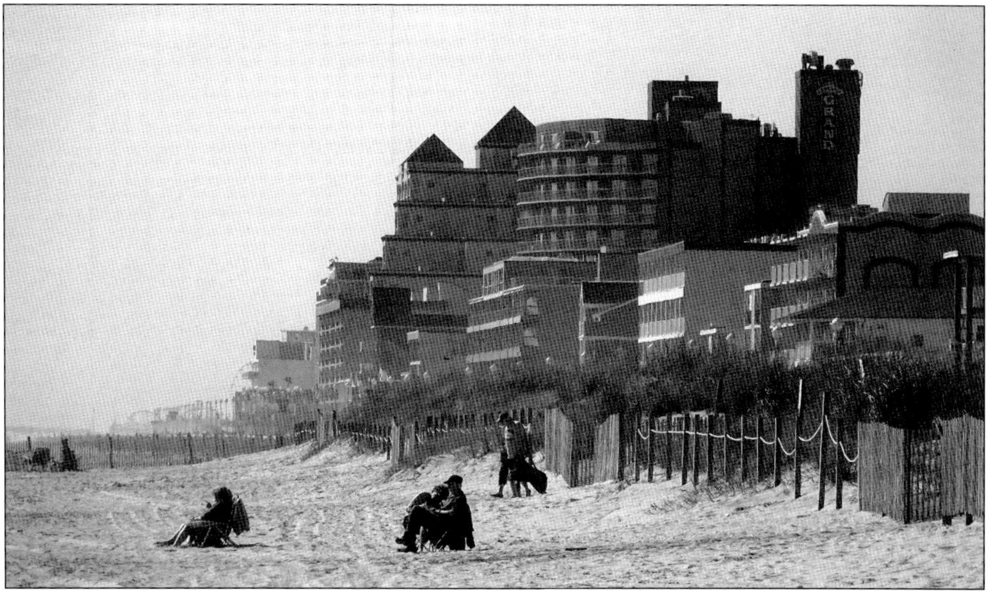

The lodgings of Ocean City are as varied as the town's many visitors. When the Stowaway Motel was built in 1956 (see page 106), it was Ocean City's largest motel. After it was razed in 1995, it was replaced in 2001 by the Grand Hotel, which now commands its Boardwalk site with a large semicircular face overlooking the beach. Perhaps as dramatic and oriented toward the waterfowl and sandbars of Sinepuxent Bay is the latest lodging facility to accent the town skyline, the Cambria Hotel, designed in 2017 by Fisher Architecture and opened in 2021. Sited at the Route 50 bridge, the Cambria's dramatic form and blinding white nighttime lights are intended, as its owner, Tauhid Islam, admits, "to be a building that, when you're driving into Ocean City, really stands out on the skyline." It does that, indeed. (Both, RMC.)

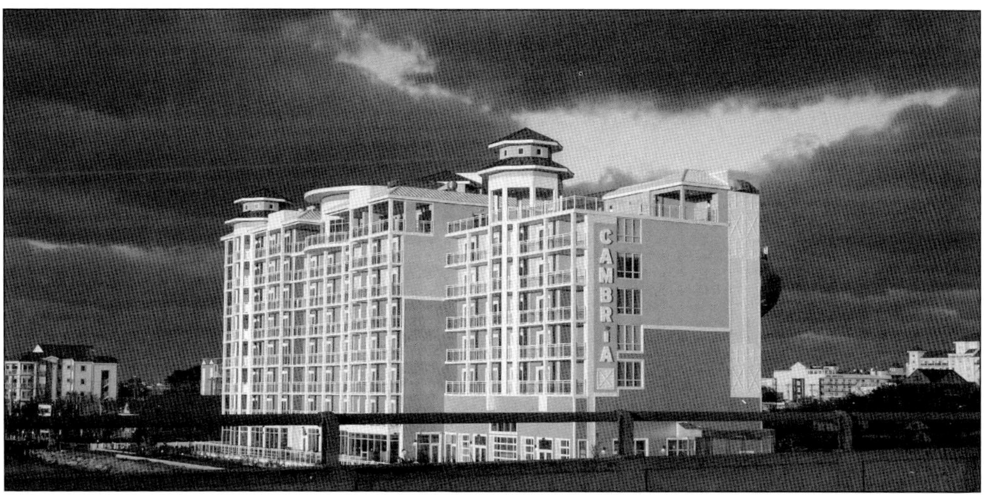

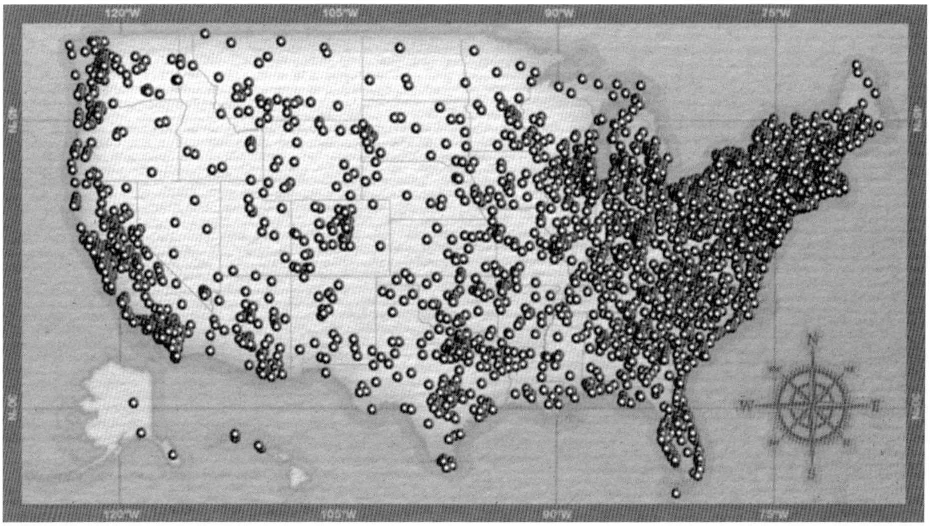

Consistent with our mission to preserve history on a local level, this book was printed in South Carolina on American-made paper and manufactured entirely in the United States. Products carrying the accredited Forest Stewardship Council (FSC) label are printed on 100 percent FSC-certified paper.

MADE IN THE USA